Greek Calendar Cookbook

A seasonal guide to cooking in Greece

Anne Yannoulis

Illustrations by Abigail Camp

Lycabettus Press

ISBN 960-7269-32-2

Typset in Greece by Fotron S.A.

Printed in Greece

Published in Greece by
Lycabettus Press
P.O. Box 17091
100 24 Athens
Greece
Tel: 363-5567

For Sofia

brought up in the tradition of Greek island cooking, but quick to learn new methods, even those in books.

Contents

Approximate Equivalent Weights and Measures

Standard 8 oz. cups are used throughout, (slightly larger than a teacup); the English "cup" holds 10 oz. One tablespoon equals 3 teaspoons and all spoons are level.

Dry Measure

25 grams = 1 oz.
50 grams = 2 oz.
100 - 125 grams = 4 oz.
225 grams = 8 oz.
250 grams = 9 oz.
450 grams = 1 lb.
500 grams = 1 lb. 2 oz.
900 grams = 2 lb.
1 kilo = 1000 grams = 2 lb. 4 oz.

Liquid Measure

	1 tsp.	=	5 ml.	
	3 tsp.	=	15 ml.	
	(1 tbsp.)			
	1 cup	=	250 ml.	
1 pint	= 2$^1/_2$ cups	=	–	= 20 fl. oz.
1$^3/_4$ pints	= 4 cups	=	1,000 ml.	= 35 fl. oz.
			(1 litre or 1 kilo)	
2 pints	= 5 cups			

Equivalent Cup Measures

Butter or Margarine,		Sugar, Rice		Cups		Flour
$^1/_4$ packet	=	50 grams	=	$^1/_4$ cup	=	25 grams
$^1/_2$ packet less 1 thin spice	=	115 grams	=	$^1/_2$ cup	=	50 grams
1 packet less					=	115 grams
1 slice	=	225 grams	=	1 cup	=	130 grams baker's flour

1 packet	=	250 grams	=	1 cup+2 tbsp.		–
–		450 grams	=	2 cups	=	225 grams
2 packets	=	500 grams	=	$2^1/_4$ cups		–
–		900 grams	=	$3^1/_2$-4 cups	=	450 grams
–		1,000 grams 1 kilo	=	4-$4^1/_2$ cups	=	500 grams $^1/_2$ kilo
		–		7 cups	=	1 kilo

Approximate Oven Temperatures

	Fahrenheit	Centigrade	Gas Regulo
Slow	300	150	1
Moderate	350	175	3
Hot	400	205	5

Acknowledgements

My grateful thanks to my neighbours Anna, Vasso, Eleni, Maria, my sister-in-law, Koula, and her convent aunt, Theofano, for instruction in their methods of preparing and cooking certain dishes.

Especial thanks go to Clare Ferguson and Diana Ladas for help and suggestions throughout the preparation of the manuscript, and to Hilde Stern Xinotroulias for reading and commenting creatively on the final text.

I am also indebted to Alan Davidson for the proper names of fish in his invaluable book, *Mediterranean Seafood* (Penguin Books).

And last but not least to Hariloas, not only for his contributions but also for his patience, usually, while I wrote and rewrote recipes, except when it got too much for him and he'd ask what we were having for supper, paper?

A.Y., Aegina, 1988

Introduction

This calendar arrangement of recipes attempts to answer the questions: What is in season now? Which fruits and vegetables are at their least expensive? How do the Greeks prepare them? As an Englishwoman learning to cook the Greek way over the last twenty years, sometimes by bitter experience, I have also introduced to my Greek family a number of foreign dishes using local ingredients - curry, chutney, and cauliflower cheese from England, red cabbage casserole from northern Europe, and squash and sweet potato recipes from America. These and others are listed as suggestions for their appropriate seasons. Tahini spread and hummus from Cyprus, where I grew up, are included although they are not truly Greek.

Recipes selected for each month are representative; many can be used for several summer months in succession, or in both spring and autumn. The introduction to each month indicates what is available in the market, and the index shows, in English and in Greek, where each recipe is to be found. Greek terms are in the index, including the names of produce and kitchen utensils. They are translated as pronounced, with the exception that the nominative masculine plural is spelt *oi* as in *xeroí karpoí* but pronounced *xereé karpeé*. Also, the letter "d," as in *keftédes*, is pronounced as the "th" in "the."

Many of the recipes are associated with the Greek church and traditional festivities, and to periods of abstinence from meat; this should appeal to vegetarians. Meat dishes are given in detail only when they have some seasonal appeal.

1

Introduction

Since I started collecting recipes by season, the availability of fresh fruit and vegetables has been extended, thanks to better refrigeration and improved agricultural methods. Many early season vegetables and more exotic fruits are now being grown, mostly in Crete, but the month's produce as given still represents the norm in a local market.

Recipes are usually given for four people, except for cakes and vegetable pies which are for a larger family and for guests. Standard cup measurements are given where possible (smaller than the English "cup") or kilos and grams where necessary. See chart of comparative weights and measures below.

Olive oil is given in most recipes, in the traditional way, but many people prefer corn oil today as being much lighter.

Greek recipe books assume a basic knowledge of methods, typically stating "the right amount of flour," or "make a syrup in the usual way." It is also impossible to check a recipe with more than one of your Greek friends as each has her own (her mother's) way, and admits no other possibility. So the following recipes can be taken as one person's practice; reverse some directions and they will still produce Greek food. In any case, this is less of a recipe book, more of a way of life. *Káli órexi*!

January

Recipes

Lentil Soup	Fakés Soúpa
Fried Cauliflower	Kounoupídi Tiganitó
Cauliflower Salad	Kounoupídi Saláta
Tripe Soup	Patsás
Casserole of Pork	Afélia
New Year Cake	Vasilópitta
Yoghurt Cake	Yaourtópitta
Fritters	Tiganítes
Chestnut Purée	Kástana pouré

See also:
   Mixed fish soup (*Kakaviá*) below and Beef and Onion Casserole in October.

Other suggestions:
   Cauliflower cheese with walnuts, spiced glazed carrots, chicken casserole with olives and lemons, orange and apricot nut loaf, mulled wine, yoghurt and apricot flan, lemon caramel bread, candied peel.

January may be the beginning of the new calendar year, but at the greengrocer's it is very much the middle of winter.

All the winter vegetables are to be found: cabbages, cauliflowers, leeks, spinach, purple brocolli, potatoes, onions, carrots, and celeriac; also sweet potatoes, pumpkins, and beetroots. Salad vegetables are available in the form of lettuce, wild greens, and radishes, as well as parsley, mint, garlic, and celery.Artichokes have just appeared and are still very expensive, and there are spring onions as well as the dry ones - *xerá*. There are virtually no tomatoes, so autumn-made chutney and tomato sauce are appreciated.

A wide variety of fish is to be found, and a mixture of small ones, bought perhaps directly from a boat, go to make a local island favourite fish soup, *kakaviá*, a sort of bouillabaisse (*see* Fish Soup in March). One of them might be the curiously-named *Christópsaro* (John Dory), with a distinctive black spot on either side where, it is said, it was picked up by Christ between finger and thumb.

Oranges and lemons are well established (oranges called *Mérlin* are the Navel variety). There are apples, pears, mandarins, local grapefruit and, now cheaper, kiwifruit (*aktinídia*); also imported coconuts and pineapples.

Pomegranates are smashed in the courtyards of houses on New Year's Day to bring good luck. They are used for very little else except in *kólyva* (*see* A Memorial Dish of Boiled Wheat in March). Grenadine is only now being produced in Greece.

The *Vasilópitta*, or New Year's Cake, is the one really January item on the menu, and the cutting of these cakes dominates the news. Those in the shops are more of a brioche, but there is a nicer version rather like madeira cake. It is necessary to have on hand recipes for using up stale cake as it has to be cut all at one go to see who has the lucky coin! There are left-overs, too, from the huge home-baked loaves of the season, which last too long even for the voracious Greek bread-eaters. A profusion of orange, lemon, and grapefruit peel over the holidays leads one to think of candying it for future use in cakes, and the end of the festivities (after 6 January) leaves time to make quantities of marmalade, preserves, and chutneys, and citrus-flavoured cognac to last till autumn, though these activities can be spread over the next three months.

Lentil Soup   Fakés Soúpa

3/4 kilo brown lentils
2 large onions, sliced
3 or 4 cloves garlic, sliced
2 bay leaves, torn
1/4 to 1/2 cup olive oil
2 tbsp. tomato paste (optional)
2 tbsp. vinegar
salt and black pepper

Lentils bought loose, from the keg, should be checked carefully for foreign bodies. Tip them out at one end of a tray and spread out a handful at a time, removing any small stones or tight little balls of earth.

Wash the lentils well in a strainer and bring to the boil in just enough water to cover. Drain and return to the pan with the onions, garlic, and oil, and about two litres of water.

Simmer till the lentils are soft, about half an hour if they are fresh. Stir the tomato paste into the vinegar, add salt and pepper, and pour it into the soup. Continue cooking gently, and taste for seasoning; add more vinegar if required.

This can be served hot as a soup or reduced to a thicker purée by longer cooking, and is equally good hot or cold.

5

Fried Cauliflower   Kounoupídi Tiganitó

Thoroughly clean a medium-sized cauliflower, breaking it up into florets, and leave to soak in salted water for a little while. Drain. Dip in seasoned flour and fry in very hot oil or cooking fat.
Serve with garlic sauce. (*See* Sauces in Basic).

Cauliflower Salad   Kounoupídi Saláta

Cut the cauliflower in quarters and clean well, as above, then boil in salted water till tender. Drain and tip into a serving dish and immediately pour over it an oil and lemon (or vinegar) dressing (*see* Sauces in Basic). Serve tepid or cold.

Tripe Soup   Patsás

When cold winds are swirling through the streets, Greeks (mostly men) are seen diving into certain tavernas known for their *Patsás*, even at 9:00 o'clock in the morning! If you like tripe and onions you might care for this thick white soup, properly made with lambs' feet, but more usually with tripe, onion, eggs, and lemon juice. The tables are equipped with a bottle of vinegar complete with a piece of garlic, but even this is inadequate to disguise the ammonia flavour of the tripe. It is a traditional cure for a hangover.

To cook *Patsás* at home, wash the tripe very well, boil briskly for ten minutes or more, and discard water. Boil in fresh water with chopped onions till soft, then stir in beaten egg and lemon juice (*see* Sauces in Basic), and season to taste.

Casserole of Pork

Afélia

Pork in red wine, from Cyprus

1 1/2 kilos stewing pork
1 1/4 cups dry red wine
salt and pepper
1 tsp. coriander seeds, crushed
2 tbsp. cooking fat

Cut the pork into small pieces and put in a deep bowl with some salt and black pepper. Add the wine and leave to marinate in a cool place for a day, or even two.

Lift the meat out, dry it, and fry it in the fat, with the coriander, until brown all over. If cooking on top of the stove, use a heavy saucepan. Then add the marinade, cover tightly, and simmer gently till the meat is tender. Stir and add a little extra liquid if necessary. Otherwise, transfer to a casserole with a lid and cook in a slow oven for 2 to 3 hours. Serve with boiled potatoes.

Store Cupboard

Red peppers, pickled, in tall jars, to be found in most shops, are invaluable for the store cupboard; slice one to brighten up a cabbage salad, cooked rice, or hors d'oeuvre, or add to goulash or stews. There are also jars of boiled beetroots. Both keep well in the fridge after being opened.

Red peppers can also be frozen. *See* Red Peppers to Freeze in September.

7

New Year Cake   Vasilópitta

4 1/2 cups self-raising flour (1/2 kilo)
1 tsp. salt
225 grams butter (1 packet less one slice)
1 1/2 cups sugar
5 eggs, beaten (at room temperature)
1 1/4 cups milk *or* 1 cup milk and 1/4 cup
    orange juice (or even all juice)
grated rind of 2 oranges *or* 1 lemon
icing sugar
one silver coin

Sift flour and salt. Cream butter and sugar, beating till light and fluffy.

Add eggs, a little at a time, beating well, adding some of the flour to prevent curdling. Beat in the rest of the flour alternately with the liquid and stir in the rind. If using only milk, add finely grated lemon rind.

Grease a round baking tin, about thirty centimeters in diameter. Pour in the batter and drop in the clean silver coin. (It can be cleaned with a mixture of lemon juice and salt, then rinsed off and dried; or it can be wrapped in foil.) This batter is much more liquid than an English one and the coin will probably sink right through. It is more reliable to insert the coin after baking, when it will stay upright and reappear in one slice only, thus preventing family squabbles.

Bake in a moderate oven for forty to fifty minutes. Cool in the tin and sieve a little icing sugar over the cake when cold. The date for the New Year, cut out of a single piece of foil can be placed on the cake before the icing sugar, and then removed carefully.

The *Vasilópitta* is cut ceremonially on New Year's Day. Each slice is named for someone: beginning with Christ, the Virgin, and *Ághios Vasílis* (St. Basil); then proceeding through the immediate family and any visitors, including

8

the house and perhaps boat, until the whole cake is cut. A matchstick identifies the first slice or can be used to write an initial in the icing sugar. The person who finds the coin in his slice will have good luck for the whole year.

As the *Vasilópitta* has to be cut up all at one time, and as each housewife is expected to bake one, there is often a lot of cake going stale during the first two weeks of January. It can be turned into a Trifle, soaked in fruit juice and spirits, covered with a layer of jam, and then a thick layer of custard, then decorated with cream and glâcé cherries; or you can slice each wedge in half and sandwich them together with an Orange Butter Cream, butter beaten together with icing sugar and orange juice and a dash of Cointreau. Another way would be to slice the pieces thinly and use them as sponge fingers for a Lemon Refrigerator Cake, or bake them to make sweet rusks.

Yoghurt Cake   Yaourtópitta

This is similar to the *Vasilópitta*, with a cup of yoghurt replacing the milk, and an extra cup of sugar (optional). The eggs can be increased to six and separated if preferred, the whites stiffly beaten and folded in at the end. Use the juice and grated rind of a lemon, bake it in a ring tin, and then dust with icing sugar.

Alternatively, the extra sugar and the lemon juice are used in a syrup and poured over the cake, which is baked in a flat baking tin (*see* Orange Semolina Cake in April).

Fritters   Tiganítes

New Year's Day is also the appropriate time to make *Tiganítes*. This name applies both to fried dough (using a piece of the dough prepared for the New Year bread) which is fried in very hot olive oil, dusted with sugar, and eaten hot by hungry children, and also to freshly made fritters, as follows.

3 heaped tbsp. self-raising flour
pinch of salt
water *or* **milk (***see* **below)**
corn *or* **olive oil**
honey and cinnamon (*or* **salt)**

Add enough water (up to a cup) to the flour and salt to make a stiffly dropping batter. Beat well and leave to stand for half an hour. For a richer batter use milk instead of water.

Drop spoonfuls into very hot oil in a frying pan and cook on both sides till golden and bubbly.

Mound on a plate and cover with warmed honey and a sprinkle of cinnamon. Eat at once before they get tough. Reserve a few on a separate plate and sprinkle with salt instead of honey for the dieter in the family.

See also Tomato Fritters in September and Fritter Batter in Basic.

Chestnut Purée (Savoury)   Kástana Pouré

1/2 kilo chestnuts
1 1/2 cups (approximately) stock or milk
3 tbsp. butter
1 medium onion, peeled and finely chopped
salt and pepper
nutmeg (optional)
4 - 6 tbsp. yoghurt (1 carton of strained) or single cream
1 tsp. cognac (optional)

Pierce the chestnuts, cover with boiling water, and simmer for about ten minutes. Drain and peel. Replace in saucepan and just cover with milk or stock (or a mixture), bring to the boil, and simmer for about twenty minutes till tender.

Melt the butter in another pan and sauté the onion till golden and remove from the heat. Mash the cooked chestnuts with remaining juice, stir into the onions and put through a food mill or sieve, or blend till puréed.

Stir in yoghurt or cream to smooth consistency, add salt and pepper to taste, and a grind of nutmeg.

Serve what's left when you've finished tasting it. Add a teaspoon of cognac, and there won't be any left to serve!

Chestnut Purée (Sweet) Kástana Pouré (Glykó)

500 grams chestnuts
1/4 cup cognac *or* rum *or* 2 tbsp. cointreau
plus 1 tsp. chosen spirit
1 - 2 tsp. sugar (depending on which spirit used)
1/2 tsp. vanilla (1/2 a packet)
1 cup double cream (*or* strained yoghurt)
1/4 cup fresh orange juice
dark chocolate *kouvertoúra or* pistachio nuts, chopped

Pierce the chestnuts and boil them for about thirty minutes, till tender. Peel at once, scooping them out of the water one at a time to keep them hot. Mash chestnut meats and add the spirit, sugar to taste, and vanilla.

Whip cream till stiff and slowly add the orange juice and a further teaspoon of spirit. Stir all but a tablespoon into the chestnut mixture and beat together.

Transfer purée to a serving bowl or individual glasses and decorate with remaining cream. Grate cooking chocolate over it, or strew with chopped nuts. Refrigerate till required.

February

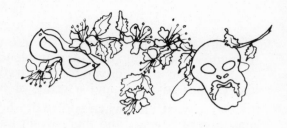

Recipes

Split-Pea Purée	*Fáva*
Spinach Pie	*Spanakópitta*
Lamb Fricassé with	*Arní Frikassé mé*
Lettuce/Endives	*Maroúli/Antídia*
Lamb Fricassé with	*Arní Frikassé me*
Artichokes	*Angináres*
White Cabbage Salad	*Láhanosaláta*
Baked Sardines or Fresh Anchovies	*Sardélles or Gávros,*
	Plakí
Boiled Chicken	*Kotópoulo Vrastó*
Egg and Lemon Soup	*Avgolémono Soúpa*
Chicken Pie	*Kotópitta*
Bitter Oranges	*Nerántzia*
Bitter Orange Peel Preserve	*Nerántzi Glykó*
Lemon Peel Preserve	*Lemóni Glykó*
Wild Herbs	*Vótana*
Teas and Tisanes	*Tsaía*
Sage Tea	*Faskómilo*

See also:
Spinach (or Leeks) with Rice in May, Quick Winter Soup in December, and Leek Pie in November.

Other suggestions:
Chicken and walnut pâté (or salted mackerel pâté), leek flan, apple and yoghurt cake, pancakes, pumpkin chutney, hot lemon pudding, coconut meringue cake, lemon mousse, bitter orange marmalade, lemon peel preserve.

One of the coldest and wettest months in Greece coincides with the almond blossom and carnival time.

All the winter vegetables are to be had: cabbages, white and red; cauliflowers, leeks, celery, carrots, potatoes, beetroots, spinach, and new artichokes. There are lettuces (and dill to go with them in salads), radishes, cucumbers,spring onions (the dry ones are beginning to sprout), and a few greenhouse tomatoes, either large and pale or red but tiny and expensive. Aubergines, courgettes, and peppers are also forced, as not properly in season yet, and therefore pricey.

There are masses of all the citrus fruits as well as apples and dried fruits, kiwifruit and imported coconuts. Pancakes for Shrove Tuesday; apple flan, and hot lemon pudding bring a north European flavour to the kitchen, while Greek preserves can be made with lemons and oranges.

Split-Pea Purée   Fáva

1/2 - 3/4 kilo yellow split peas
1 onion, roughly chopped
1/2 - 1 cup olive *or* corn oil, to taste
salt
garnish: finely chopped onions, lemon juice, olive oil

Spread the peas on a tray and check carefully for foreign bodies, especially if they were bought loose, then rinse well.

Cover generously with water in your largest saucepan and bring to the boil, skimming off the scum which froths up to the top of the pan.

When the water is quite clear add the onion and oil and simmer, uncovered or partially uncovered, till practically puréed, adding salt towards the end, after about half an hour. It may still froth up and overflow while simmering

13

with an oil and vinegar dressing or with a garlic sauce - *Skordaliá* (*See* Sauces, p. 184).

Spinach Pie   Spanakópitta

When the Greeks bake a *pítta* they do it on a grand scale in a huge baking tin and then parcel it out amongst friends and relatives. This one is also very good cold, so it is worth making a big one, especially since the commercial sheets of *fyllo* more than cover a thirty by twenty cm. tin (700 grams). Washing the rather small leaves of Greek spinach is the most troublesome part, but can be done at leisure, and the wilted (cooked or salted and squeezed) spinach can be refrigerated till required.

1 1/2 kilos spinach
4 or 5 spring onions and one dry onion, chopped
1/2 cup olive oil, cooking fat, or margarine
5 or 6 stalks of dill (*ánitho*) and the same of parsley,
    chopped fine (they will usually be added by the
    greengrocer when you buy the spinach)
salt and pepper
1/4 kilo feta cheese, or *trimáta* (already crumbled feta)
3 or 4 eggs, lightly beaten
8 to 10 sheets of *fyllo* pastry
1/2 cup olive oil and melted butter, mixed half and half

Wash the spinach in several changes of water and drain in a colander. Cut it into a bowl with kitchen scissors, sprinkle with salt, leave for at least half an hour then squeeze it out with your hands, rinse again, and drain. This removes some of the bitterness and the metallic taste, but some cooks prefer to simmer the spinach till wilted and then drain it. Cool and refrigerate if necessary until ready to assemble the pie.

Sauté the onions in the olive oil or fat, then add the spinach, dill, parsley, and salt and pepper, turning them over to combine well. Cover the pan and cook for about ten minutes. Draw off the heat and allow to cool.

Add the eggs and crumbled feta and stir well. During Lent these are often omitted and replaced by a variety of strongly-flavoured herbs from the hillsides. Half a cup of parboiled rice or dry crumbs and a handful of currants can also be added to give substance.

Line an oiled baking tin with five or six sheets of *fyllo*, oiling each one with a pastry brush. Spread the spinach over, and cover with the remaining three or four sheets, oiling each one lightly. With a sharp knife score through the last sheet in squares to serve, and sprinkle the pie with a little water. (For more details on using *fyllo*, *see* Custard Pie in May.)

Bake in a moderate oven for about forty minutes till golden and crisp. Serve warm or cold.

Note: Home-made pastry can also be used, as above, for a top and bottom crust, or to make a "snail" *pítta*, like Greek Pumpkin Pie (*see* March).

Some bechamel sauce is occasionally combined with the basic spinach mixture, and mint could replace the dill. A delicious variation served in a *pítta* bar in Athens has a cheese-covered bechamel sauce as topping instead of *fyllo*.

Lamb Fricassé with Lettuce/Endives and Egg and Lemon Sauce

Arní Frikassé me Maroúli/Antídia, Avgolémono

This is a favourite dish in the spring when green onions, Cos lettuce, and the rather bitter curly endive are abundant, but a hot dish is still welcome. Local lambs are available now before they disappear from the market till Easter, but there is always excellent New Zealand lamb. Tell the butcher you want it for *frikassé*.

2 large Cos lettuces *or* 1 kilo endives *
1 - 1 1/2 kilos shoulder of lamb
3 tbsp. olive oil *or* cooking fat
5 - 6 spring onions, chopped
2 - 3 stalks of dill, chopped
salt and pepper
egg and lemon sauce (*see* Sauces in Basic: 2 - 3 eggs,
    1 lemon, and flour for a thick sauce)

* A friend of mine prefers to reverse these quantities, using about one kilo of onions and only one lettuce.

Discard the outer leaves of the lettuces, chop off the stem, and quarter. Wash the leaves and shake dry. Cut them across in thick ribbons (having removed the tender heart for salad) and bring to the boil in a large pan of water. Boil for 2 - 3 minutes till wilted. Drain. Some people don't boil lettuce, only endive.
   Remove skin and excess fat from the lamb, cut into serving pieces, wash, and dry.
   Sauté the meat for about ten minutes and then add the onions, lettuce, and dill. Cook for another ten to fifteen minutes, then add water just to cover (liquid will come from the lettuce). Simmer for about an hour till the meat is tender and two to two and a half cups of liquid remain.
   Make an egg and lemon sauce with the hot liquid and

pour it back over the lamb over a very low heat. Rock the pan to combine the sauce with the juices and allow to thicken slightly. Serve hot.

Fricassé can, of course, be made equally well with veal, and alternatively with celery, carrots, garlic, and parsley instead of lettuce. The lemon sauce, however, is particularly successful with the rather rich lamb.

Lamb Fricasse with Artichokes   Arní Frikassé me Angináres

Prepare artichokes (*see* Stewed Artichokes in April) while the meat is cooking, as above. Add them, halved, for the last half hour or so, together with the dill and some chopped parsley, and cook till tender.

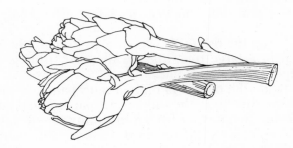

White Cabbage Salad   Láhanosaláta

Shred a small, firm, white cabbage or part of a large one. Mix in some finely chopped onion and top with grated carrot or red cabbage for colour contrast. Red cabbage is only used this way in Greece; it is never cooked or combined with meat in a main dish as in northern Europe.

When ready to serve, toss in an oil and vinegar (or lemon juice) dressing with salt and pepper.

Baked Sardines
or Fresh Anchovies

Sardélles or
Gávros, Plakí

Plakí is a universal method for almost any kind of fish, whether large ones sliced, or small ones like sardines, *frísses*, and anchovies whole, with heads and guts removed. They are plump and tasty at this season, with soft roes.

3/4 - 1 kilo fish
salt and pepper
lemon juice
2 onions, sliced
1 - 2 cloves garlic
corn *or* olive oil
1 small can tomatoes
1/2 cup white wine (optional)
parsley and dill, chopped, *or* 1 tsp. dried oregano

Clean the fish (*see* Fish, How to Prepare, in Basic), lay them in a large oiled baking tin, and sprinkle with salt, pepper, and lemon juice.

Sauté the onions in oil in a saucepan, add sliced garlic to taste, tomatoes, the white wine, parsley, and dill or dried oregano. Simmer for fifteen to twenty minutes, adding up to a cup of water, if required, to make sufficient sauce to cover the fish.

Pour sauce over the fish and bake in a moderate oven for about forty minutes or till fish is tender. Sprinkle with more chopped parsley and serve warm or cold.

Boiled Chicken

Kotópoulo Vrastó

Boiled chicken, served with the vegetables and preceded by a soup made from the broth flavoured with egg and lemon (*see* next recipe), is a very common dish in Greece. Fish is done in the same way (*see* Fish Soup in March).

1 large chicken or boiling fowl, about 2 - 2 1/2 kilos
3 - 4 potatoes, halved
2 medium onions, whole
2 carrots, scraped and sliced
salt and pepper
1 stalk of celery
2 - 3 stalks of parsley
a few whole peppercorns
1 stick of cinnamon (2 1/2 cm.)

Clean the chicken, removing some of the skin and fat. Wash the liver and heart very well.

Half cover the chicken with water in a large pan and bring to the boil. Skim surface as fat and scum rise.

Add potatoes and onions, the liver and heart, chopped carrots, salt and pepper, and the celery, parsley, and spices tied in a muslin bag. Simmer, covered, for about an hour, topping up with hot water, until the meat is tender and coming away from the bones. For a smaller chicken a pressure cooker reduces time considerably; omit black pepper and add juice of half a lemon.

Remove the chicken onto a serving dish and keep warm. Strain the contents of the pan through a colander into a clean saucepan if the soup is to be made at once, or into a deep bowl if it is rather fatty and time permits. In the latter case, cool it and refrigerate overnight, then remove the caked fat. The liquid should have become solid jelly.

Discard the bag and arrange the boiled vegetables around the chicken to serve. Most of the goodness and moisture will have gone into the soup, so a sauce of some kind will not come amiss, such as tomato or *tzatzíki*, or mayonnaise mixed with yoghurt if served cold, sprinkled with chopped parsley. *See* Sauces in Basic.

Egg and Lemon Soup   Avgolémono Soúpa

chicken stock
2 - 3 handfuls Carolina rice
2 - 4 eggs
juice of 2 or 3 lemons

Bring to the boil enough chicken stock for at least one plate of soup for each person (it is so delicious most people come back for a second helping). When boiling throw in the washed rice, cover, and simmer till rice is cooked, 10 - 15 minutes.

Meanwhile, whisk the eggs very well in a bowl and stir in the lemon juice.

Remove the soup from the heat and pour a ladleful into the bowl. Then slowly tip all the contents of the bowl back into the pan and stir it in. Taste for seasoning. Continue to cook over a very low heat to thicken the soup slightly, but do not allow to boil or it will curdle.

Defy Greek tradition and serve in hot soup plates, at once!

A "Quickie" *Avgolemono* **Soup for One Person**

Add boiling water to a chicken stock cube if no reserved fresh stock is available. Beat up an egg and add the juice of one small lemon to it. Pour on the hot stock and your nourishing meal is ready.

Chicken Pie   Kotópitta

Chicken prepared as above is stirred into a white sauce (*see* Sauces in Basic) made partly with the cooking stock and with the addition of two or three eggs, grated cheese (*kefalotýri*), chopped herbs (mint, thyme, or oregano), and some grated nutmeg. This filling is packed between sheets of *fyllo* pastry, as with Spinach Pie (*see* above).

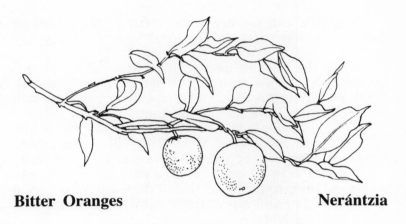

Bitter Oranges   Nerántzia

Nerántzia cannot be found at the greengrocer or even in the market, but they grow in any number of private gardens, as well as in the parks of Athens, gorgeous golden globes among the dark green leaves, but with frightfully bitter fruit. They say that it is forbidden to pick the publicly-owned ones, but you can gather them when they have fallen. The peel is usually used for a preserve (*see* below) but they also make excellent marmalade if the preliminary treatment for the preserve is followed to remove their bitterness. A couple of mandarins to a kilo of fruit makes a delicious addition. In the summer the whole small green fruits *nerantzákia* are made into a preserve.

Bitter Orange Peel Preserve   Nerántzi Glykó

1 1/4 kilos peel of bitter *nerántzi* oranges, requiring
  2 1/2 kilos whole fruit, *i.e.*, 18 - 20 large ones
1 1/2 kilos sugar
2 1/2 cups water
1 tbsp. lemon juice *or* 1/2 cup corn syrup

A 2-day process

Scrub the fruit and dry it, then grate lightly to remove some of the bitterness and the tough shiny outer layer of peel.

Score the peel in quarters (or six or eight pieces, according to the size of fruit; the narrower pieces roll up best). Pull it off carefully, and scrape away any loose pith or membranes. Throw away the fruit!

Roll each piece tightly and pierce it with a large needle and strong thread. Make necklaces of peel-rolls (about twenty on each) and tie tightly to prevent them unrolling.

Put all the necklaces in a large pan, cover with cold water and bring to the boil. Discard the water, cover again with cold water and repeat this process twice more, then drain thoroughly.

Make a syrup with the measured water and sugar, boiling it for 5 minutes. Put in the necklaces, boil fast for five minutes more. Remove from the heat and leave to soak overnight (or for twelve to fifteen hours).

Return pan to the cooker, add lemon juice or corn syrup, and boil till the syrup lightly coats the fruit. Cool, then remove the threads, lift the rolls into jars, and cover them with the syrup. If there is too much it should be reduced by further boiling (with extra lemon juice to avoid crystallization).

Half the above quantities can be used.

* I was told to remove the threads before boiling the rolls in the syrup, but they always unrolled, and I have had better success leaving them tied till the end. The threads can then be cut and pulled out with kitchen scissors.

Lemon Peel Preserve   Lemóni Glykó

1 kilo thick lemon peel
1 kilo sugar
1 1/2 cups water

Cut peel into thick strips with its white pith. It is not necessary to grate the outside. Boil as above.

Wild Herbs   Vótana

If you haven't found sage growing wild on the lower slopes of the mountains and transplanted it to your own garden or balcony, you can now buy it by the bundle at

23

greengrocers and in the markets, along with other herbs like chamomile, *hamomíli* (*see* April), and mountain tea, *tsái tou vounoú*, all of which make excellent herb teas or tisanes, beneficial for a surprising number of ailments such as coughs, sore throats, weak digestion, toothache, and high blood pressure.

All herbs should be hung in bundles, in a light, airy, dry room out of direct sunlight, and then packed into a closed container when completely dry, to preserve their aroma. The leaves can be removed from their stalks, but sage and mountain tea are usually left intact, and look attractive in tall screw-top jars. (*See* also Basil in May.)

Teas and Tisanes   Tsáia

Sage Tea   Faskómilo

Sage is very pungent so a small sprig (or one teaspoon of leaves) is enough for one cup. Put it in a small saucepan and add one cupful of cold water and bring to the boil, adding sugar, honey, or saccharin to taste. Bringing it slowly to the boil helps to release the flavour. Remove from the heat, cover, and allow to infuse for a few minutes, then strain into a cup. If you leave it too long it becomes very bitter. A slice of lemon is a pleasant addition and allays the slightly musky taste.

An 18th century English recipe combines sage and lemon-balm, a slice of lemon, sugar lumps, a glass of white wine, and boiling water. It sounds efficacious as a pick me up!

All other herb teas are made the same way, including mint (*dyósmo*), verbena or lemon-balm (*louíza*), and lime flowers (*tílion*). The Cretan mountain herb, called *díktamo* from the Dikti Mountains where it grows, has a very special flavour, and is a prized item in the store cupboards of expatriate Cretans.

March

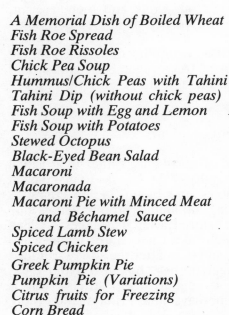

Recipes

A Memorial Dish of Boiled Wheat	*Kólyva or Stári*
Fish Roe Spread	*Táramosaláta*
Fish Roe Rissoles	*Táramokeftédes*
Chick Pea Soup	*Revíthia Soúpa*
Hummus/Chick Peas with Tahini	
Tahini Dip (without chick peas)	
Fish Soup with Egg and Lemon	*Psarósoupa Avgolémono*
Fish Soup with Potatoes	*Psarósoupa me Patátes*
Stewed Octopus	*Ktopódi Vrastó*
Black-Eyed Bean Salad	*Mavromátika Saláta*
Macaroni	*Makarónia*
Macaronada	*Makaronáda*
Macaroni Pie with Minced Meat	*Pastítsio*
and Béchamel Sauce	
Spiced Lamb Stew	*Arní Kapamás*
Spiced Chicken	*Kotópoulo Kapamás*
Greek Pumpkin Pie	*Kolokythópitta (Glyká)*
Pumpkin Pie (Variations)	
Citrus fruits for Freezing	
Corn Bread	*Bobóta or Stafidópitta*

Other suggestions:
Stuffed lambs' hearts, sautéed spinach, leek and potato soup, beetroot soup (Borscht), lemon curd, three fruit marmalade, spiced tahini biscuits.

25

This month, which may include Carnival and nearly always covers Lent, sees the same vegetables as February, with the addition of wild chicory (*radíkia*) and more prolific artichokes (*see* April for recipes). Cauliflowers are going off. Spring onions replace the dry variety, now rather scarce. Pumpkins can sometimes still be found in local shops or the market.

Oranges, lemons, and grapefruit abound, but mandarins have already disappeared. Lemons are at their cheapest and can be frozen (whole, sliced, or as juice) for the summer when they will virtually disappear from the market. Avocadoes come from Crete and there are imported coconuts. There are plenty of apples and some pears.

Lenten dishes show the versatility of Greek cooking and the excellent flavour of fresh vegetables, grains, and pulses cooked with olive oil, tomato paste, and herbs.

Lent *Sarakosti*

Lent, being a period of abstinence rather than actual fasting, stretches the ingenuity of the Greeks to make what they can of the vegetables and bloodless sea creatures available. Strictly speaking, no animal products should be eaten for these fifty days before Easter. This takes in Clean Monday; the previous weekend is Cheesefare Sunday when the last cheese is served, and thereafter the strict Orthodox will not only eat no meat or fish, but also avoid milk, butter, eggs, cheese, and yoghurt. Less strictly, this is observed only on Wednesdays and Fridays and, more generally nowadays, only during Holy Week, at least in the cities. Those who keep the rigorous fast are allowed fish on 25 March, the Annunciation of the Virgin. By giving up still more during Holy Week (when city dwellers think they are being virtuous) strict keepers of the fast are reduced to using sesame seed oil — *tahíni* — instead of olive oil, and eating *halvás*. This sweet, made of sesame seed paste, is a delight to visitors at this time, who do not imagine it to be the staple diet, with bread, olives, and boiled greens, for quite a number of the people they see around them.

But does one really need meat when the choice of dishes is so wide and tantalizing? Great dishes of green beans, broad beans fresh and tender in their skins, artichokes with them, or *a la polítá* (*see* Stewed Artichokes in April), lettuce salads with tangy dill, olives and fresh green peas.

Then there are spinach pies (which can also be made with cheese and eggs but are just as tasty with only fresh dill and green onions, *see* Spinach Pie in February); spinach with cuttlefish (*see* Cuttlefish with Spinach in October); cuttlefish stuffed with rice and pine nuts in a delicious sauce; octopus in a tomato and wine sauce (October); baked shrimps (August); lobster (crawfish); or scampi. All these are acceptable fasting food.

The pulses give us *fáva* (November) from yellow split peas and *Fakés Soúpa* from brown lentils (January), and if one adds dairy produce the choice is endless, a feast for vegetarians and fare not to be despised in these days of health foods and talk of cholesterol! (*See* recipes for chick peas and black-eyed beans below.)

Clean Monday (*Katharí Deftéra*) is traditionally a day for eating out of doors, and the weather is usually kind. Children (and their fathers) fly kites, and a typical picnic meal consists of great loaves of *lagána* bread (which contain no yeast and are covered in sesame seeds); boiled octopus in an oil and vinegar (or lemon juice) dressing and sprinkled with oregano (*see* October); fried squid (*see* August); lettuce salad with fresh dill; whole spring onions; a dish of pickled vegetables referred to as *toursí*; olives; bowls of *táramasaláta* and tahini dips; and chunks of *halvás*, plain, swirled with chocolate, or with nuts. Wine and beer are not restricted, and there is plenty of fruit; oranges, apples, and pears.

A Memorial Dish of Boiled Wheat   Kólyva or Stári

This dish is offered in church on three consecutive Saturdays (*Psychosávato*) at the beginning of Lent in memory of the dead. It consists of boiled wheat, pomegranate seeds, sultanas, sugar, and parsley; ingredients as old as Persephone. It is also served at memorial services (*Mnemósymon*) held forty days, three months, and one year after a death. It is encrusted with icing sugar and decorated with sugared almonds and silver balls. The initials of the deceased person and a cross are also inscribed on it. It is scooped into small paper bags printed with the name of the person remembered and offered to each member of the congregation.

To Make at Home
    Drop a cupful of wheat grains into three or more cups of slightly salted boiling water. Lower the heat and simmer till the wheat is soft and the water absorbed. While still warm, stir in sugar to taste. Then add crushed rusks, or flour which has been stirred in a frying pan over a low heat till it takes on a little colour; the seeds of a pomegranate; a handful of sultanas; chopped parsley leaves; and perhaps some sesame seeds.
    It must be eaten the same day as it may ferment if kept.

Fish Roe Spread   Taramosaláta

For all that it is made of imported fish roe, this is a classic fasting food for the Greek Orthodox. The roe used to be obtained from the gray mullet but now usually comes from the North Sea cod.

150 grams *taramá* **(salted cod roe)**
1 medium onion, grated or finely chopped
1 slice (5 - 6 cm. thick) stale bread *
1 boiled potato *
juice of 1 - 2 lemons
1 cup olive *or* **corn oil**

Remove crusts from the bread, soak it, and squeeze dry. Rinse *taramá* in water in a fine-meshed strainer to remove some of the salt.

Pound the onion to a pulp in a mortar (*goudí*) if you have one, then the bread and potato, then the oil and lemon juice, alternately, pounding or beating till smooth, or put it all in an electric blender. Spoon a little oil over the surface and garnish with olives.

Some roe has a richer colour than others; one can cheat and add a little beetroot juice to improve the pale variety, which in fact is of a finer quality.

* Only bread or only potatoes can be used, but the combination makes a good texture. Whole wheat bread gives a better flavour.

Fish Roe Rissoles   **Táramokeftédes**

Mix the *taramá*, as above, with mashed potato and/or soaked bread and grated onion. Then add pounded garlic with some chopped fresh herbs (mint and parsley or dill) to taste and season with pepper but no salt. The mixture should be firm enough to handle. If not, add more potato or bread. Leave to stand, then shape into rissoles, roll in flour, and fry in very hot oil. Serve hot or cold.

Chick Pea Soup   Revíthia Soúpa

The soup is classic Greek but hummus is from Cyprus

**1 kilo chick peas
1 tbsp. baking soda (optional)
2 onions, chopped
3/4 cup olive oil
1 1/2 tsp. salt
juice of 1 lemon
parsley**

The day before required, tip the peas into a deep bowl, cover with warm water, and leave to soak overnight, or at least twelve hours.

Next day, drain off the soaking water. If using soda, rub it into the peas with your hands and leave for an hour. Then roll them in a clean cloth to remove the skins. Rinse very well. Using soda is hard on your hands and not necessary when the peas are fresh. It also removes roughage! Put peas into a large saucepan, cover with fresh cold water, and bring to the boil, skimming off any scum. When clear, add the chopped onions, cover, and simmer for about two hours until tender, adding hot water as necessary to keep peas covered. Add the salt towards the end of cooking.

Take out about one-third of the peas with about six tablespoons of water and put aside for hummus (*see* below). Add the olive oil to the remaining peas in the pan and continue simmering till ready to serve the soup, with chopped parsley and lemon juice.

Hummus - Chick Peas with Tahini

**reserved chick peas (or 350 grams, boiled till soft, with salt)
3 cloves garlic, peeled and chopped finely, or crushed
6 tbsp. fresh lemon juice (2 - 3 medium lemons)**

1/4 cup olive oil
1/2 cup (approximately) tahini
salt and pepper

parsley
paprika *or* cumin

Mash the peas while still warm, or put through a food mill or food processer. Add the garlic, and then the lemon juice a little at a time, alternately with the olive oil, if using, beating continuously with a wooden spoon.

Stir up the jar of tahini to mix the paste with its oil and pour about half a cup into the purée, beating all the while. Season to taste.

Turn into a serving bowl and sprinkle with paprika or cumin and chopped parsley.

Tahini Dip (without chick peas)

Also from Cyprus, with Near Eastern origins

2 - 3 cloves garlic
salt
130 grams (half a 250 gram jar) tahini*
juice of 2 - 3 lemons, made up to 1 cup with water
2 - 3 tsp. chopped parsley
1/2 tsp. cumin or paprika

Crush the garlic with salt and stir into the tahini, then add the lemon juice and water. Add more juice or water to make a creamy mixture. (Lemon juice alone dries up the tahini, while water reduces it again to cream; vinegar can replace the lemon.) Stir in parsley and seasoning, or put sauce into serving bowl and sprinkle on top. Serve with boiled vegetables or baked fish, or alone, as a dip, with other *mezés*.

* *Tahini*, which is a sesame seed paste, resembles peanut butter, which could be used instead. The oil separates and is used by itself by serious Lenten fasters.

Fish Soup with Egg and Lemon

**Psarósoupa
Avgolémono**

2 onions, chopped
1 carrot, chopped
2 stalks of celery, chopped
3 stalks of parsley
1 bay leaf
salt and peppercorns
8 cups of water
1/2 cup olive oil
1 1/2 kilos stewing fish (*see* **Fish, How to Prepare in Basic**)
1/2 cup rice (optional)
egg and lemon sauce (*see* **Sauces in Basic**)
oil and lemon dressing and chopped parsley

Put all the vegetables into a large pan with the water, olive oil, and seasoning, and boil gently for thirty to forty minutes.

Meanwhile, clean the fish, removing the guts but leaving the heads on. Descale if necessary. Slash the sides of the larger ones, or cut in slices.

Lower fish into the stock (most easily in a chip basket or strainer which fits inside the pan), cover, and simmer for twenty minutes or more, until fish is tender.

Lift fish out onto serving dish and keep hot. Strain stock into another pan. If using rice, add it now and cook for another fifteen minutes with the lid partly on.

Add beaten egg and lemon and serve soup and fish immediately. Have chopped parsley and a fresh olive oil and lemon dressing on hand for the fish.

See July for Fish with Mayonnaise (Athenian Style).

Fish Soup with Potatoes   Psarósoupa me Patátes

Cook as above, using only large fish, cut in slices, and increase the carrots. Add five or six potatoes, quartered, together with the fish. Simmer until both are tender.

Serve up the fish on a big dish surrounded by the vegetables, strewn with fresh parsley.

Stewed Octopus   Ktopódi Vrastó

See October for various ways of cooking octopus and cuttlefish; *see* August for squid. In March the weather may be too rough for large octopus, but there is a small variety with a larger head, sometimes sold to foreigners as *kalamaroctopódi*, as it appears to be a cross with a squid (*kalamári*). Its real name is *moschoctápodo* and it is scorned by the locals. Consequently, it is half the price of octopus, but it responds to long slow cooking in a good sauce made with olive oil, wine, tomato, and onions, and earns grudging approval from said locals when they taste it.

Black-Eyed Bean Salad   Mavromátika Saláta

The beans are boiled till tender and served with an olive oil and lemon dressing, sprinkled with chopped parsley and onion. This dish goes well with stewed octopus, or canned tuna and mackerel.

Macaroni   Makarónia

Macaroni (including spaghetti) is sold in packets numbered 1 - 10, number 1 being the fattest and number 10 spaghetti.

A bewildering variety of cut pasta* is to be found, including that used for thickening soup (of which one variety masquerades as rice, *rizáki* or *manéstra*, and another as barley, *kritheráki*). Vermicelli is called *fídes* (snakes) and there are various packets of short lengths. Of these the *sélino* type, ridged like celery stalks, cooks very quickly but collapses into flat noodles if not watched. Small squares of pasta called *hilópittes*, made with eggs and milk, are usually served with chicken or roast meat. Short strips of flat macaroni, also with added milk and egg (noodles or tagliatelli) are called *lasagnáki*, also rather confusingly.

* The word *pásta* in Greek means sweet cakes and pastries.

Macaronada   Makaronáda

Boil required amount in salted water in your largest pan until soft (even softer for Greeks than the Italian *al dente*) and drain in a colander. Tip into a deap heated serving dish which has been smeared with butter and sprinkled with grated cheese. For half a kilo of macaroni melt half a cup of butter in a small saucepan until it begins to smoke, and stir it into the macaroni. Sprinkle with three-quarters cup grated cheese. Serve at once.

This is popular as one dish on the table on "Cheesefare Sunday," the last day before Lent, but is also a good serving base for thick veal stew, tomato or meat sauce (*see* Sauces in Basic), or spiced lamb or chicken *Kapamás* (*see* below), when the cheese is omitted.

Served plain as a side dish in our local taverna, it is referred to as *orphaní*, being bereft of its natural companions.

Macaroni Pie with Minced Meat   Pastítsio
and Béchamel Sauce

640 grams macaroni (number 2)

1 cup butter or cooking fat, melted and kept warm in
  a small saucepan
2 cups (250 grams) grated cheese - *kefalotýri*
3/4 kilo minced beef
1 medium onion, chopped
1 tbsp. tomato paste, diluted (in half a cup of
  red wine if liked)
salt and pepper and a pinch each of cinnamon and nutmeg
1 cup water
1/2 cup rusk crumbs (optional)
3 or 4 cups thick béchamel sauce
4 or 5 large eggs

Make up a rich meat sauce and have ready the
béchamel sauce (*see* Sauces in Basic for both). Boil the
macaroni as above, drain, and stir into half the cup of
melted butter and half a cup of the grated cheese. (You
could also add here the beaten whites of the eggs and use
only the yolks for the sauce. At least one teacher of
cookery stirs in some of the bechamel sauce.)

Butter the bottom of a baking dish and spread over it
half the macaroni.

Beat the eggs (or yolks only) and combine with the
sauce, cooled if newly made, warmed-up if already prepared, and add salt and pepper, bearing in mind the
saltiness of the cheese, and nutmeg to taste.

Stir two or three tablespoons béchamel into the meat
mixture (if you haven't put it into the macaroni) or half a
cup of crumbs, and spread it over the macaroni. Sprinkle
with half the remaining cheese, cover with the rest of the
macaroni, and press down lightly.

Cover the whole dish with the rest of the béchamel.
Pour over it the remaining melted butter, and sprinkle with
grated cheese.

Bake in a moderate oven for thirty to forty minutes till
golden and bubbling. Leave to cool slightly and cut in
squares to serve.

Spiced Lamb Stew   Arní Kapamás
A traditional dish to serve with macaroni during Carnival. It contains no onion or garlic, though for my taste they would improve it.

1 kilo lamb cut in serving pieces
150 grams butter or oil
seasoned flour
1 can tomatoes (or fresh ones in season)
1 tbsp. tomato juice diluted in 1/2 cup of white wine
1 stick cinnamon
2 or 3 cloves
1 small red pepper (tied in a muslin bag)
hot water
1 medium onion
1 - 2 cloves garlic (optional)
salt and pepper

Flour the pieces of lamb, shake off excess, and brown in the butter or oil, on all sides. Remove onto a dish and keep warm.

Add the wine, tomatoes, and tomato paste to the frying pan (first sauté some chopped onion and garlic in the fat if desired). Boil the sauce till it combines well and then return the lamb pieces to it and add the spices. Season to taste and add enough hot water to cover the meat, then simmer till tender and the sauce is thick.

Serve over macaroni, garnished with parsley.

Spiced Chicken   Kotópoulo Kapamás

Cut one kilo chicken into serving pieces and rub them over with lemon juice.

Proceed as above, and spoon the chicken in its sauce over macaroni, rice, or mashed potato. Sprinkle with grated cheese before serving.

Greek Pumpkin Pie   Kolokythópitta (Glyká)

A sweet pie usually made "snail" style

This is a more robust pie than the famed American one. It can be made with bought *fyllo* pastry, as for *Galaktoboúreko* (*see* Custard Pie in May) and in the same way , or coiled into a snail pattern. The following recipe with home-made pastry (using olive oil only) is often used during Lent for both pumpkin and spinach pies. (*See* also Pumpkin in November.)

Pie Pastry *(Zymi yia Pitta)*:

**4 1/2 cups (1/2 kilo) hard flour
1 tsp. salt
1 cup warm water (approximately)
1/4 - 1/3 cup olive oil**

Filling:

**2 - 2 1/4 kilos pumpkin
2 tsp. salt
1 - 2 cups sultanas
1 cup chopped nuts (usually walnuts, optional)
1 1/2 cups rusk crumbs
1 cup olive oil
1 cup sugar**

Syrup:

Also the same as for Custard Pie in May, and Cornbread
(*see* below):two cups sugar and one cup water, lemon juice
and peel, boiled for five minutes. (If this all seems too oily
and sweet, reduce the olive oil in the filling to half a cup but
increase the sugar to two cups and omit the final syrup.
Instead, sprinkle the top lightly with sugar.)

Cut open the pumpkin without peeling, discard seeds
and membrane, and cut flesh into fist-sized chunks. Grate
on a coarse grater (there is one sold especially for this
purpose and for quinces) and throw away the rinds.
Sprinkle with salt and leave overnight in a colander to
drain. In the morning squeeze it further with the hands and
transfer to a dry bowl.

Add the sultanas, chopped nuts, cinnamon, crumbs,
sugar, and olive oil, and mix together well.

Make the pastry, stirring the oil and half the water into
the flour and salt with a fork and finally with the fingers.
Add enough water to bind the mixture and knead it lightly
into a ball. Wrap it in greaseproof paper and refrigerate for
at least an hour.

Break off a large handful of dough and roll it out on a
floured board into an oblong, as thin as possible. It is very
elastic and will stretch a considerable way.

Lay tablespoons of the filling along one side and roll
over the dough, turning in the ends as you go. Coil it round
to make the middle of a snail and lay it in the centre of a
large oiled baking tin. Repeat with another roll, keeping it
close to the first one and leaving no gaps, increasing the
snail until it fills the tin.

Sprinkle the top with oil and bake for fifty minutes to
one hour. When it comes out of the oven, pour cooled
syrup over it.

Pumpkin Pie (Variations)

Sweet:
Snail making takes time and uses a lot of pastry to less filling. The above filling (half quantity) is also excellent in a short-crust or flan-pastry tart. Use an extra half cup of sugar mixed with a tablespoon of cornflour to thicken the juices slightly. The grated peel of an orange improves the flavour.

Line an oiled flan tin or cake tin with two-thirds of the pastry (*see* Pastry in Basic, using chilled soda water to blend it) and either bake blind or brush with beaten white of egg. Pour in the filling and cover with the rest of the pastry. Brush top with the egg yolk beaten with a little water and make two or three slits for the steam to escape. Bake in a moderate to hot oven.

Savoury:
You may still be left with grated pumpkin and a distaste for so much sweetness. I have used the basic mixture (without the cinnamon or sugar) and added it to a curry sauce, thickening it with dried crumbs or *trahanás* and then baking it in a short-crust pastry, or just packed into an earthenware dish.

Citrus Fruits for Freezing

Lemons are well worth freezing for use during August when they are rarely to be found.

To freeze as juice: Fill ice-cube trays with juice and when frozen remove and pack into small plastic bags. They take up little room in the freezer.

To freeze whole: If room permits, freeze whole lemons, wiped clean and wrapped individually. They can be grated while still frozen, but when thawed become very soft and juicy.

Oranges can be frozen in the same way, using the thin-skinned ones. They are very satisfactory for freshly grated peel for summer cakes.

Corn Bread   Bobóta or Stafidópitta

This uses olive oil instead of butter, and is suitable for Lenten fare. (It evokes mixed feelings of nostalgia in Greeks who lived through the Occupation.) Being somewhat dry and crumbly, it is better soaked in syrup, but it is delicious warm from the oven, sprinkled with sugar.

3 cups cornmeal *(kalembokálevro)*
1 cup plain flour
6 tsp. baking flour
1 tsp. salt
1/2 cup olive oil (*or* **4 tbsp. olive oil and 4 of margarine**)
1 cup orange juice (4 medium oranges)
grated rind of 2 oranges
1/4 cup brandy
1 cup (*or* **more**) **currants**
1/4 cup sugar
3/4 cup (approximately) warm water
syrup (optional) as under Pumpkin Pie (*see* **above**)

Sift the flour, baking powder, and salt into a large bowl. Heat the olive oil (or olive oil and margarine) in a small saucepan and stir it, hot, into the flour, using your fingers to mix it thoroughly.

Make a well in the middle of the flour mixture and add the orange juice and rind and beat it into the mixture, together with the brandy, sugar, and currants. Add enough warm water to make a thickish batter.

Pour it into an oiled baking tin and bake in a medium to hot oven for about 40 minutes, or until a deep chestnut colour.

Cool in the tin for a few minutes, then pour cold syrup over it.

April

Recipes

Red Eggs	*Kókkina Avgá*
Lamb Soup	*Mayerítsa*
Roast Lamb	*Arní Psitó*
Boiled Greens	*Hórta*
Chamomile	*Hamomíli*
Beetroot Salad	*Pantzária Saláta*
Stewed Fresh Broad Beans	*Koukiá Yachní*
Stewed Artichokes	*Angináres a la Políta*
Artichokes with Broad Beans	*Angináres me Koukiá*
Artichoke Salad, Boiled	*Angináres Saláta*
Artichoke Salad, Raw	*Angináres Saláta*
Butter Cookies	*Koulourákia*
Sweet Cheese Pies	*Militíni Santorínis*
Fresh Fruit as Dessert	*Froúta*
Orange Semolina Cake	*Ravaní*
Orange Liqueur	*Portokáli Likkér*

Other suggestions:
Hard-boiled eggs, various uses (*see* Eggs in Basic); beetroot coleslaw; tapenade; marinated fresh anchovies; hot cross buns; lemon refrigerator cake; orange sorbet.

Spring vegetables have come in with a rush, many of them for a short season, such as broad beans which can be cooked with their skins and also combined with artichokes to make a delicious dish, and peas (*see* Green Peas in May), which soon become large and hard. Spinach, leeks, lettuces, and carrots are still in abundance. Early tomatoes come from Crete, but as they are mostly for export we find only the very large or the very small ones on the home market. There are large spring onions and no worthwhile dry ones (unless imported) till mid-May. Parsley, mint, dill, and garlic are fresh, as is celery, distinguishable from parsley by its smell and because usually it is complete with root (though only the leaves are used). There are radishes, wild chicory, and other greens, potatoes, and cabbages, though the latter are past their prime, and the cauliflowers have mostly gone to seed. Aubergines and courgettes can be found, at a price, hot-house grown.

Oranges, lemons, and grapefruit are plentiful, as well as eating apples and huge pears. There are imported pineapples and coconuts.

Easter   Páscha

Easter usually falls during April; the Lenten vegetable dishes (*see* March) are followed by delicious Mayerítsa lamb soup, to break the fast, with red eggs symbolizing the blood of Christ, and huge loaves of home-made bread. On Easter Day we have roast lamb and sweet cake-like *tsourékia*, decorated with more red eggs.

Red Eggs   Kókkina Avgá

At this season most stores display packets of dye near the eggs, some of them with directions in English. A packet designed for fifty will colour twenty-five eggs very nicely!

Wash the eggs very well in tepid water and dry them; they will not "take" unless completely clean. Dissolve the dye in 500 grams (one and a quarter plastic bottles) of wine vinegar. Half fill a large saucepan (preferably an old one) with water and bring to the boil. Add the vinegar mixture and continue boiling for a few minutes, then skim and strain if necessary.

Lower in the eggs gently with a perforated spoon and boil for about ten minutes, making sure all are covered by the liquid. It is better to put in half the eggs first, enough to cover the bottom of the pan and, when ready, remove them onto a plate and put in the rest. Plunge the boiled eggs into cold water, then drain and dry them. The stronger the vinegar solution the better the results you will get. Scrub out the saucepan with boiling water as soon as possible.

Soak a piece of cloth in a little olive oil and rub each egg with it, to bring up the colour and add a lustre.

Place a bowl of eggs in the centre of your table from Easter Eve onwards, and offer them to any visitors who call, notwithstanding that they have their own at home, and may have brought some for you.

Good Friday   Megáli Paraskeví

Lentil soup (*see* January) is traditionally served today, boiled without oil and seasoned with vinegar. Even those who rarely go to church will avoid meat at least, and the tavernas serve a variety of fasting dishes from Thursday evening, following the Crucifixion service. On Good Friday flags fly at half-mast and church bells toll all day from the Descent from the Cross ceremony in the morning till the *Epitáfion* service and the candlelight procession of the bier round each parish in the evening.

April

Holy Saturday   Megálo Sávato

The Greek housewife will be preparing the special lamb soup today, as well as some of the other traditonal foods (*see* below) to serve on Easter Day. On returning from the midnight service of Resurrection (with white candles lit from the single altar flame and passed from person to person) the Orthodox smoke a cross on the lintels of their front doors, and relight their icon lamps for another year. Then they all sit down to a great spread; lamb soup, scarlet eggs, *feta* cheese, salad, freshly-baked bread, and wine.

Lamb Soup   Mayerítsa

heart, lungs, and intestines (optional) of the Easter lamb, and the livers if not kept for *mezes*. Extra meat (optional).*
salt and pepper
1/2 packet margarine
5 or 6 spring onions, chopped
3 or 4 stalks of fresh dill, chopped
6 or 8 outside leaves of lettuce, shredded (optional)
1/3 cup rice
egg and lemon sauce (3 eggs and 1 large lemon, *see* Sauces in Basic)

Wash the meat well, particularly the intestines if using. (They are supposed to be pulled inside out for thorough cleansing and then braided, a laborious and slippery process and hardly worth the trouble.)

Put all the meat in a saucepan, cover with water, and bring to the boil. Skim off the scum and, when clear, add salt and simmer till tender. Meanwhile, sauté the onions in the margarine till soft.

Take the meat from the stock, cut it into very small

pieces, and stir it into the onions, together with the pepper and dill and optional lettuce leaves. Allow to simmer a little, then add the stock (and extra water if needed) and the rice and continue simmering for about twenty-five minutes till the rice is soft. Reserve till required.

Have ready mixed in a bowl the beaten eggs and lemon juice.

When ready to serve, heat up the soup to boiling and remove from heat. Add a ladleful to the egg and lemon, and return the bowlful to the pan, stirring it into the soup. Reheat gently for a minute or two but do not allow to boil. Serve at once.

* In our family we buy an extra piece of lamb, which gives more flavour, and a more substantial soup.

Easter Day   Páscha

Eating on Easter Day is usually one long picnic, starting very early, as soon as the lamb has begun to turn on the spit, over glowing charcoal, where it is kept moist by basting with a mixture of olive oil, lemon juice, salt, pepper, and oregano. Everyone should take a turn at the spit, thirsty work rewarded by copious draughts of beer or retsina and tasty morsels of *mezés* (hors d'oeuvres). These are usually fried liver and spleen kept back from the *Mayerítsa* soup, cut into smallish pieces and sprinkled with lemon juice; also strips of cheese, sliced hard-boiled eggs, with a trickle of olive oil and a dusting of pepper and salt, and some tomato wedges and spring onions. A tahini (*see* March) or *tzatzíki* dip (*see* June) and some carrot "sticks" add variety, as does a dish of *saganáki*, slices of hard cheese such as *kefalotýri* dusted with flour, fried quickly, and served hot with a squeeze of lemon juice (*see* June). The Greeks prepare a delicious "sausage" of chopped liver, heart, and spleen of the lamb, wrapped in entrails and spit

45

roasted, and then sliced to serve; it is called *kokorétsi*. Fried potatoes and chunks of fresh bread are also put out, and various salads, lettuce (with dill and spring onions), boiled beetroots or courgettes, ready to serve with the first slices of lamb, hot from the spit. Fresh young broad beans are sometimes served raw, but should not be eaten together with milk, as the combination can make one ill, it is said. Sliced cucumber in a vinegary mint sauce, English style, adds sharpness to the rather fatty lamb . The Easter loaf (*Lambrópsomo*), a bowl of red eggs, and a vase of spring flowers make up the centre-piece of the table, set up in courtyard or garden near the scene of action. Passers-by and neighbours are invited in to taste the food and drink a toast. The greeting *Chrístos anéste* (Christ is risen) is answered by *Alithós anéste* (He is risen indeed), and thereafter till Ascension Day *Chrónia pollá* (many years) is the traditional greeting, as it is on name-days and New Year's, too.

Before the red eggs are eaten they are entered in a competition to see who has the most resilient one. Cupped in your closed fist you must tap your egg sharply on the exposed end of someone else's. If your egg cracks his you may go on to attack another, and so on, like "conkers" in England, till the winner is declared.

Roast Lamb   Arní Psitó

If the lamb has to be cooked in the oven, and is perhaps only a leg for a small family, it is delicious rubbed over with half a lemon and with sprigs of rosemary and halved cloves of garlic pressed into deep gashes in the sides, and sprink-led with salt, pepper, and oil before roasting, preferably in foil to start with. Open up later to brown. If not using foil, the traditional Greek way is to break dry twigs of vines to form a trellis base on which to rest the joint in the roasting pan. (A good sprinkle of powdered garlic ensures an all-over flavour, if liked.) Greek butchers will chop a leg right through the bone several times if not restrained, but in fact this helps ensure thorough cooking and allows the seasoning to penetrate the flesh. Long slow cooking is essential. The Greeks usually add quartered potatoes round the joint, sprinkled with lemon juice and a cup of water but, for the diet conscious, it is better to bake them in a separate pan with a little oil and lemon juice, salt, pepper, and oregano or some fresh sprigs of mint. Serve mint sauce or quince jelly to foreign guests.

Boiled Greens   Hórta

A favourite occupation for Greeks is to go out into the countryside in the spring, armed with a large basket and a sharp knife, to gather wild greens (*ágria hórta*) from the hillsides. Horta addicts become adept at recognizing the many varieties. Two types, *radíkia* (chicory) and *vlíta* are also grown commercially.

Wash greens very well, and shake dry. Put into boiling salted water in a large pan with the lid on to preserve the colour. Boil fast and when tender drain in a colander. Serve with oil and quartered lemons for each peson to dress his own salad. *Vlíta* is far less bitter than all other kinds, but *vroúva* (charlock or mustard) is the favourite. It is picked while still a flat rosette of leaves.

Chamomile   Hamomíli

This low-growing, starry white flower with a yellow centre is also collected this month, and dried for tisanes, eye-lotion, or mouthwash. It is not as common as might be expected, and must be selected by its distinctive smell from other similar small daisies.

Beetroot Salad   Pantzária Saláta

Beetroots are small and fresh, and are served together with some of their leaves. They are never sold ready boiled, as in England, except in jars (which, however, are a useful standby for the store cupboard).

Remove the leaves, leaving two to three inches of stalk, and wash and scrub the beets, without breaking the skin. Put on to boil with the lid on, having added salt and a little vinegar to the water. Rinse the leaves, selecting the younger and unblemished ones and add to the beets after twenty minutes, or put them in a steamer over the boiling beets. A pressure cooker is excellent for this. Leave the beets to cool in the cooking liquid — you could add the vinegar here; it helps to retain their colour — and peel when cold.

Slice, or leave whole, if tiny, and serve on the leaves, with an oil and vinegar dressing or with a garlic sauce - *Skordaliá* (*See* Sauces in Basic).

Stewed Fresh Broad Beans   Koukiá Yachní

1 1/2 kilos broad beans
2 large spring onions, chopped
3/4 cup oil
1 tsp. sugar
salt and pepper
chopped dill leaves

Wash the beans and shell them, but include any tender young pods, which have a special flavour of their own.

Sauté the onions in the oil till soft, then add the beans, sugar, seasoning, and hot water to cover.

Cover pan and cook gently till tender and the liquid has thickened into a sauce. Serve with lemon quarters and thick yoghurt. (*See* also Stewed Dried Broad Beans in October).

Stewed Artichokes Angináres a la Políta

For years I have eaten this dish with relish in tavernas, but the only time I tried to make it, I ended up with mouthfuls of spiky inedible leaves. Since then, my neighbour (who comes from the island of Tinos) has taken me in hand, mainly to show me how much to strip away, and this is her recipe, which is very satisfactory for the home; cooked in larger quantities, the artichokes are left whole, 'stood on their heads in a saucepan, and covered with a circle of greaseproof paper to fit the pan, with a hole in the middle to let the steam out.

6-8 medium artichokes
2 large lemons
1 large onion, chopped, *and* several small ones,
    peeled but left whole
2-3 carrots, peeled and cut into strips
6 or 8 small potatoes, peeled and cut in half if larger
    than about 2 inches across
3 or 4 branches of dill, leaves only, chopped fine
salt and pepper
1 cup olive oil
2 cups water
2 tsps. cornflour (or an egg, *see* recipe)

Have ready a large bowl of water and a lemon cut in half. Cut off the stalks of the artichokes, about half an inch from the globe, but keep back a further four inch piece of stalk. Pull off the hard outer leaves úntil you reach the inner ones, the lower parts of which are soft and light green. Then cut off all the dark green tops of these with a sharp stainless steel knife, not only the spikes, and shave the stalk and lower part of the globe. Cut the whole thing in half, from top to bottom, and carefully remove the "choke," leaving the base, or "heart" with its crown of leaves. Immediately rub one-half a lemon over the cut surfaces to prevent them discolouring and plunge them into the bowl of water. (When the lemon is used up for juice, throw that in, too.) Scrape off the outer layers of the reserved stalks and add the inner pieces to the bowl. Leave them to soak, held down with a plate to keep them under water while peeling the other vegetables.

Heat the oil in a wide, shallow saucepan and soften the chopped onion in it, then lay in the halved artichokes to cover the bottom of the pan, then the carrots and onions and the potatoes on top. Sprinkle in the dill, salt, and pepper (it takes quite a lot) and add the water just to cover. Cover tightly with a lid and simmer for about an hour, or until the vegetables are tender and the juice reduced to about half a cup.

Meanwhile, combine the juice of the other lemon with the cornflour in a small bowl and stir some of the hot liquid into it (as for *avgolémono* sauce; in fact, a beaten egg could be used instead of the cornflour) and pour this into the pan, rocking it to combine the juices. Bring to the boil again to thicken slightly, and then remove from the heat and leave to settle. Or, carefully remove all the vegetables onto a warm dish, then thicken the sauce and pour it over. Serve warm. (You are in Greece, remember, and food is rarely served hot.)

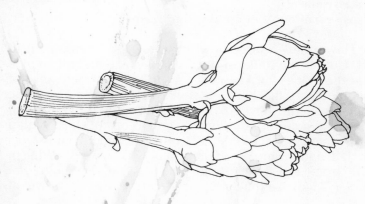

Artichokes with Broad Beans   Angináres me Koukiá

This is a delicious combination; the method is virtually the same, but the beans are put in first, with the chopped onion. A tablespoon of tomato paste can be added and, if liked, some chopped mint. Omit the potatoes and carrots. (*See* also Peas with Artichokes in May.)

Artichoke Salad, Boiled   Angináres Saláta

Again the same as the basic recipe, but omit all the other vegetables except the dill, and do not thicken the sauce. Serve cold.

Artichoke Salad, Raw   Angináres Saláta

As a *mezé* artichokes are delicious raw, as prepared in Crete, sliced thinly and sprinkled liberally with lemon juice.

Butter Cookies   Koulourákia

There are many variations of this indispensable accompaniment to the Easter fare. This recipe from Smyrna is easy and always successful. Offer to guests with red eggs. Store in an airtight tin. Double these quantities for a large family.

1 250 gram packet butter, softened
3/4 cup (175 grams) sugar
2 egg yolks
1/4 cup milk *or* orange juice (1 tbsp. brandy
   can replace some of the liquid)
4 cups hard flour and 1 tsp. baking powder, sifted together
grated rind of 1 orange and/or vanilla flavouring
another egg yolk, beaten with a little water

Cream butter and sugar, add the yolks, orange rind, and vanilla and beat well. Add the flour and then the liquid, mixing with floured hands to form a stiff dough.

Break off small pieces, roll into a rissole shape, and flatten out into an ungreased baking tin. Press lightly with the back of a fork and brush with beaten egg. If preferred, the pieces of dough can be rolled into a rope and then curled into a snail shape, or doubled back into three, or the ends joined to make an open ring. Bake in a moderate oven for about twenty minutes. (For the spare egg whites, *see* Eggs in Basic.)

Sweet Cheese Pies   Militíni Santorínis

An Easter specialty, rich in eggs and the soft white creamy cheese of springtime

Filling:

1 kilo soft *mizíthra* cheese
5 or 6 eggs
1 tsp. *mastícha*, pounded to a powder, with a little sugar
1 tsp. vanilla (or 1 packet *vanília*
1 tbsp. margarine *or* butter
1 tbsp. all-purpose flour *or* fine semolina
1/2 - 3/4 kilo sugar

Pastry:

1 kilo all-purpose flour
3/4 - 1 cup oil
water to mix

Combine the above ingredients to make the cheese filling. Make up one kilo of pastry (*see* Pastry in Basic) and roll out, not too thinly. Cut out circles, using the saucer of a teacup or coffee cup, depending on size of pies required.

Lay spoonfuls of filling in the middle of each pastry "saucer" and sprinkle with cinnamon. Fold up four corners to make a square, containing the filling but not closing in on top. Transfer pies to a greased baking tin and bake in a moderate oven till golden, about forty minutes.

Fresh Fruit as Dessert   Froúta

Puddings and desserts are rarely served in Greek homes at the end of a meal; fresh fruit is offered instead. It is nearly always prepared by the lady of the house while the dishes are being cleared away. Apples, pears, and oranges (and, later, other fruits in season) are peeled, sliced, and laid on a dish, sometimes sprinkled with a little sugar and cinnamon and spiked with toothpicks for guests to help themselves.

Orange Semolina Cake   Ravaní

1 1/2 cups plain flour
1 1/2 cups fine semolina
3 level tsp. baking powder
5 large eggs, separated
3/4 cup sugar
1 1/2 packets margarine (250 gram packets)
grated rind of 2 oranges and juice of 4 (about 1 cup)
1/2 cup blanched and halved almonds (optional)

Syrup:

2 cups sugar
1 cup water
2 tbsp. brandy
1 stick cinnamon
1 clove
grated rind of the other 2 oranges

Remove eggs from the refrigerator in good time to get
to room temperature.

Beat egg yolks, sugar, and butter in a large bowl till
light and pale and add orange rind. Sift flour, baking
powder, and salt into a medium bowl and stir in the
semolina.

Beat the flour mixture into the batter alternatively with
the orange juice. Whip the egg whites till stiff and fold in.
Turn the batter into a greased baking tin, preferably
oblong, sprinkle with nuts, and bake in a moderate oven
for forty minutes.

Boil the sugar, water, spices, and rind for three to five
minutes to make the syrup. Remove spices and add brandy;
leave it to cool. When the cake comes out of the oven cut
through in squares in the tin and slowly pour cooled syrup
all over it. Cool in the tin. (If more convenient, the cake

54

can be left to cool in the tin, and pour a hot syrup over it later.)

A similar cake made with butter is called *Halvás tis Rénas*.

Orange Liqueur   Portokáli Likkér

5 cups sugar
8 cups water
2 cups orange *or* mandarin peel
3 cups pure alcohol (*katharó inópnevma*, from chemists)
1 cup brandy
2 pieces cinnamon
5 cloves (approximately)

Wash the fruit and dry it with a cloth. Remove peel, scraping off all white pith, or carefully remove zest only with a potato peeler. Pass peel through mincer or food mill. Measure out two cupfuls and pound it a little in a mortar with a sprinkling of sugar and a tablespoon of alcohol (or chop and reduce in a blender with some sugar and alcohol).

Put peel, alcohol, and brandy in a wide-mouthed jar, cover with a thick cloth, tie down, and leave in the sun for a week, shaking occasionally.

Then boil the water, sugar, and spices for about five minutes, cool, and pour into the jar. Cover with the cloth and leave in the sun for another week. Strain the liqueur through a piece of cheesecloth or thick muslin (*toulpáni*), then through a paper filter (*hártino fíltro*), available from chemists, or through a piece of cooton-wool in a funnel. (A coffee filter would probably serve equally well.) Filtering clears the liquid like magic, producing a professional-looking liqueur; it is also very strong.

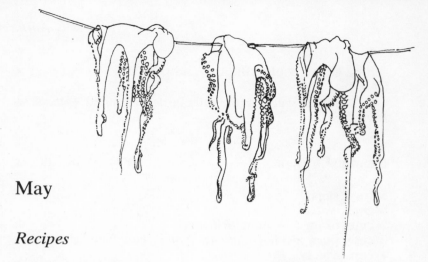

May

Recipes

Stuffed Vine Leaves	*Dolmádes Yalántzi*
Octopus in Wine Sauce	*Ktapódi Krasáto*
Lettuce Salad	*Maroúli Saláta*
Peas	*Arakás*
Peas in Oil	*Arakás Laderós*
Peas with Artichokes	*Arakás me Angináres*
Green Beans, Stewed	*Fasolákia Yachní*
Spinach with Rice	*Spanakórizo*
Leeks with Rice	*Prassórizo*
Meat Roll in Tomato Sauce	*Roló me Domáta Sáltsa*
Baked Meat Loaf	*Roló sto Foúrno*
Chicken in Tomato Sauce	*Kotópoulo Kokkinistó*
Lamb Baked in Paper	*Arní Exohikó*
Small Cheese Pies	*Tyropitákia*
Custard Pie	*Galaktoboúreko*
Jam Flan	*Pastaflóra*
Green Fig Preserve	*Frésko Sýko Glykó*
Basil	*Vasilikó*

See also:
Beef and Onion Casserole (*Stifádo Moschári*) in October and Cucumber, Garlic, and Onion Dip (*Tzatzíki*) in June.

Other suggestions:
Chilled cucumber soup, spinach paté with egg and anchovy, risotto, tongue with olives, courgette and lemon loaf, mint sauce and mint vinegar, strawberry and orange ice cream, lemon caramel bread, curd creams.

Early summer fruit is news this month. First the strawberries, and by the end of the month red cherries and probably apricots make a glowing addition to the green-grocers' stalls, and are also sold from hand-carts in the streets. Apples, pears, and lemons are still available, and also grapefruit, but oranges are past their prime, though still excellent for juice. A tasty but not too common May fruit is the easily bruised loquat (*moúsmoula*), often sold along the roadside and also found in specialty shops.

There are plenty of salad vegetables and more courgettes, tomatoes, and green beans, but aubergines and peppers are still expensive. Leeks are getting rather tough, but there are beetroots, spinach, and various kinds of greens. Artichokes are finishing and there are no cauliflowers or cabbages. New vine leaves are delectable, stuffed with rice in *dolmádes*, and there are still broad beans and peas. Mint, dill, and celery tops are at their freshest. The first dry onions re-appear at mid-month.

Several varieties of fish can be found, including mackerel (*see* Baked Mackerel in August).

Flower gardens are ablaze with all the north European summer flowers, at one burst. Scented rose petals are made into jam (It's a laxative, too!) and can be collected for potpourris, together with various sweet-scented leaves, such as scented geranium (also used in jams, *see* Quince Preserve in November) and verbena, or lemon-balm. They can also be used most attractively to strew on various desserts.

The local "popular" market, the *laikí agorá*, is a joy at any season of the year, but particularly now so when flowers in pots are also on sale (as well as empty pots and earth by the kilo). They spring up in a usually quiet street which is suddenly filled with clamour and bustle. Each district of a city has its appointed day and street, and housewives hurry along early with wheeled shopping baskets to catch the freshest fruit and vegetables, while what remains at mid-day can often be picked up even more cheaply. A pot of basil is worth buying now (*see* Basil, below) to grow on your balcony.

Stuffed Vine Leaves   Dolmádes Yalántzi

30 fresh young vine leaves
4 or 5 large leaves or some twigs from the vine
1/2 cup olive oil
3 large spring onions, sliced (the white and thick green
    parts only)
1 clove garlic, chopped fine (optional)
1/2 cup rice (Carolina or *niháki*), washed and drained
2 tbsp. parsley, finely chopped
1 tbsp. dill, finely chopped
2 tbsp. mint, finely chopped
salt and pepper
1/2 cup hot water

Rinse the leaves, snipping off any hard stalks, and blanch them in boiling water for four minutes. Drain and leave to cool.

Sauté the onions and garlic, then add the rice, stirring till transparent. Add the herbs, salt and pepper, and hot water and half-cook, till the water is absorbed. Allow to cool. (As with other rice dishes, you could parboil the rice in one cup of water, adding the oil and herbs later.)

To fill, take a leaf in the palm of your hand or lay it on a working surface, dull side up, and spoon some of the rice mixture into the widest part, turning in the bottom of the leaf and then the sides, and then rolling it up towards the tip.

Spread the large leaves or twigs on the oiled bottom of a heavy saucepan and lay the shiny little parcels, folded side down, into the pan, packing them in tightly to keep them from unwrapping, and press a plate down on top of them. Just cover with hot water and the lemon juice, cover, and simmer for about an hour.

Serve warm with thick egg and lemon sauce (*see* Sauces in Basic) or cold as *mezés*.

Vine leaves are also stuffed with minced meat, the quantity of rice reduced by half.

Note: Vine leaves are sold from barrels (and also in jars) in grocers' shops, preserved in brine. They must be rinsed well before using. They can also be frozen, so that *dolmádes* may be made fresh later in the year. Pour boiling water over fresh leaves and boil for one minute. Drain immediately and cover with cold water. When cold, drain and dry each leaf, and pack in layers between polythene sheets.

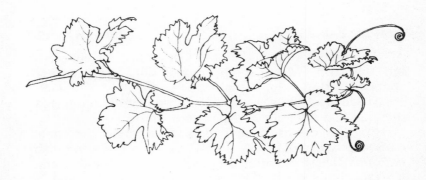

Octopus in Wine Sauce   Ktapódi Krasáto

1 large octopus (1 1/2 - 2 kilos)
1 cup olive oil
2 cloves garlic, chopped
1/2 kilo onions, chopped
pepper (no salt)
1 small bay leaf
1/2 cup red wine, semi-sweet (*imíglyko*)
3/4 kilo tomatoes *or* 2 tbsp. tomato paste in 1 cup hot water
or 1 small tin tomatoes mashed in their own juice

Wash octopus and cut into small pieces (*see* Octopus with Macaroni in October). Simmer for 10 minutes, then drain off the liquid which has gathered.Add the oil, garlic, and onions and cook over high heat for a few minutes. Add the wine and, after a few minutes, the tomatoes, pepper, and bay leaf. Reduce heat, cover, and cook very slowly until tender and the sauce is thick, about two hours.

Remove bay leaf. Serves five to six with rice, pasta, or potatoes, and a lettuce salad, or as one of the dishes for a buffet party.

Lettuce Salad   Maroúli Saláta

Thoroughly wash and drain a Cos lettuce and cut across into thin strips. Mix in some chopped dill and some finely chopped spring onions.

When ready to serve, toss in an olive oil and vinegar dressing and add salt and pepper to taste.

Cos lettuces are called *maroúli*, whereas the round ones are referred to as, simply, *saláta*, or *Amerikánika maroúlia*. These are often disappointingly limp and require a freshening spell in the fridge drawer. They should be washed in cold water, drained, and wrapped in a towel before storing, at least overnight, to become crisp.

Peas   Arakás

Green peas are a disappointment in Greece, but the recipes are realistic, as the peas so soon become large and hard. When they are fresh and small, they can be cooked with their pods (like mange tout) and nothing more than a sprig of mint and a little salt to flavour them.
Usually the following recipes are used in Greece:

Peas in Oil   Arakás Laderós

1 kilo peas
1/2 cup olive oil
1/4 - 1/2 kilo fresh tomatoes *or* **1 tbsp. tomato paste**
2 or 3 spring onions, finely chopped
1 - 2 tbsp. dill leaves, finely chopped
salt and pepper

Shell the peas. Sauté the onions in the olive oil. Add the peas, and turn them over to take on a little colour.
Add the tomatoes, peeled and chopped, or grated (or tomato paste diluted in a cup of hot water), the chopped dill, salt and pepper. Add more hot water, nearly covering the peas, and simmer, covered, until the water has evaporated, leaving the peas in a thickish oily sauce.

Peas with Artichokes   Arakás me Angináres

Peas are also cooked together with artichokes, which have been sprinkled with lemon juice. The artichokes are placed on top of the simmering peas, stalk end uppermost.
Cover the pan and cook as above. *See* also Artichokes with Broad Beans in April.

May

Green Beans, Stewed   Fasolákia Yachní

Green beans should be young enough to prepare by
topping and tailing only, and then breaking them in pieces.
The varieties called "American" and *barboúnia* respond to
this treatment, and so do the very fine ones called *ámbelo-
fásola*. Others really are string beans and need rather
laborious de-stringing and slicing. It is useful to keep some
frozen beans in your freezer compartment for emergencies,
as they defrost easily and cook equally well as fresh ones.

Prepare a basic sauce of chopped onions and garlic,
sauteed in olive oil, chopped or grated tomatoes, a tablespoon of tomato paste, and salt and pepper. Let it simmer
for a little, then stir in the beans with a good handful of
chopped parsley and a teaspoon of sugar. Add hot water to
cover. Cook till soft in a closed pan.

They are usually served cold.

Spinach with Rice   Spanakórizo

1 - 2 kilos spinach
1 onion or 2 - 3 spring onions, chopped
1 cup olive oil
1 tbsp. tomato paste
2 or 3 stalks of dill leaves, chopped (1 tbsp.)
3 cups water, approximately
salt and pepper *or* 1 whole small hot red pepper
1 cup Carolina rice

Clean the spinach very well in several changes of water,
shake dry, and chop roughly with kitchen scissors. (Some
cooks blanch it: boil for two or three minutes, without extra
water, and then drain it.)

Sauté the onion in the olive oil, add the spinach and stir
till wilted. Mix the tomato paste into a cup of warm water

and add to the pan together with the dill and seasoning. Cook for a further five or ten minutes, then add the other two cups of water, cover the pan, and bring to the boil.

Wash the rice and drain in a colander, then tip into the pan. Stir once with a fork, cover, and simmer till the rice is nearly cooked. Draw off the heat, cover with a clean cloth, replace the lid, and leave for about ten minutes till all the liquid is absorbed.

Stir once and serve warm.

If preferred, omit the tomato and squeeze half a lemon over the dish before serving.

Leeks with Rice   Prasórizo

Replace the spinach and onions with about one kilo of leeks, cleaned and cut in short lengths, using only the white and tender green parts. Sauté with half a teaspoon cinnamon, tomato paste, and optional half teaspoon sugar. Continue as above.

Meat Roll in Tomato Sauce   Roló me Domáta Sáltsa

1 kilo minced meat
3/4 cup breadcrumbs
2 tbsp. cooking fat
1 onion, grated
2 cloves garlic, crushed
1 tbsp. chopped parsley
salt and pepper
5 eggs, 2 beaten and 3 hard-boiled
flour
1 cup oil
tomato sauce (*see* Sauces in Basic)

63

Moisten the breadcrumbs, mix them with the minced meat, softened fat, grated onion, garlic, parsley, and salt and pepper, and bind together with the beaten eggs.

Gather the mixture together with floured hands and lay it in an oiled or greased baking dish which just takes it, in an oblong shape. Put the shelled eggs in a line down the middle and pull the meat mixture over them, patting the roll into shape with more flour.

Pour heated oil around the roll and cook in a medium oven till browned, turning it once.

Meanwhile, make a tomato sauce with a tin of tomatoes and juice, or diluted paste and pour it over the roll. Continue cooking gently for half an hour, basting occasionally.

Serve hot in thick slices, with mashed potatoes and green peas.

Baked Meat Loaf   Roló sto Foúrno

Make the same meat mixture (the breadcrumbs can be omitted), press it into a loaf-tin, and bake in a medium oven till cooked through.

The eggs can be replaced with a slice of cheese in the middle of the loaf, and extra flavouring is advisable: chopped mint, nutmeg, Worcestershire, or soy sauce.

To speed the cooking process, brown the mince in a saucepan till fairly dry, then turn into a greased tin and bake till done.

Serve cold with salad and a tomato sauce.

Chicken in Tomato Sauce   Kotópoulo Kokkinistó

This dish appears to be called "red" (*kókkino*) because it is cooked in tomato sauce, but older Greek recipes direct one to cook the bird over high heat in the fat till it takes on a reddish colour, and to turn it to colour on all sides. (The chicken can be cooked whole or, more easily, in quarters.)

When the juices are sealed in, add the chopped onion, parsley, and celery and sauté them for a few minutes. Then add the wine, tomato pulp, salt and pepper, and a little hot water if necessary to partially cover the chicken.

Lower the heat, cover the pan, and allow to simmer until the sauce has thickened and the chicken is tender. Stir occasionally and add a little water if the sauce starts to dry out. It is more satisfactory to transfer the chicken to an ovenproof dish and then strain the sauce over it. Cover and cook in a moderate oven for about one hour.

See also Beef in Tomato Sauce in September.

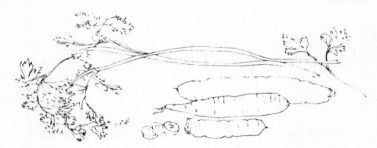

Lamb Baked in Paper   Arní Exohikó

Ask the butcher to cut a leg of lamb into about eight slices. Insert some slices of garlic, if liked, betweeen meat and bone.

In a large bowl mix three tablespoons of olive oil, one of chopped parsley, one teaspoon oregano (or one teaspoon chopped sage or rosemary leaves), salt, black pepper,

65

and the juice of one lemon. Mix well and lay the slices of lamb in the mixture to marinate for a few hours, turning them over once.

Cut squares of grease-proof paper large enough to completely enclose each piece of meat. Put a piece in each square and lay a slice of dry cheese, such as *kefalotýri*, on top of each one. Dribble the remaining marinade over them. Fold up the packets tightly and lay them in an oiled baking tin. If room in the baking tin, add some medium-sized peeled onions in foil "cups." Sprinkle a little more olive oil on top and bake in a moderate oven for about an hour. The paper should colour but not burn. Serve the lamb in the paper cases with a tossed salad and mashed potatoes.

Small Cheese Pies   Tyropitákia

Filling:

1/4 kilo feta *or* soft *mizíthra* cheese
2 eggs, well beaten
chopped parsley (and mint, optional)
salt and pepper, to taste

Pastry cases:

8 sheets of *fyllo*, cut in 3 inch strips (kept covered
    with a damp cloth)
melted butter

Mash the cheese and add the eggs, parsley (and a little mint), and pepper. Taste, and add salt if required. Brush each strip of *fyllo* with melted butter. Put a teaspoon of mixture onto one end and fold over from right hand corner over to left edge of strip to form a triangle. Continue folding to the end of the strip, enclosing all the cheese filling. Brush with more melted butter and lay in a baking tin. Bake in a moderate oven till crisp. Best served hot. These tiny cheese pies can also be fried, in very hot olive oil.

Note: this filling can also be used in a *Pítta* pastry made at home (*see* Pastry in Basic) as small turnovers. (Half this quantity would be enough to use up the cut-off strips of *fyllo* from Custard Pie, *see* following recipe.)

Custard Pie   Galaktoboúreko

Filling:

7 cups milk (1 1/2 litres *or* 3 large tins evaporated milk plus 2 1/2 tins water)
6 - 8 eggs
1 cup sugar
1 cup fine semolina
finely grated peel of 1 1/2 medium lemons (reserve the other half for the syrup)
3 tbsp. butter *or* margarine
1 tsp. vanilla *or* 2 packets (optional)

Pastry:

1/2 kilo *fyllo* pastry (10 - 12 sheets)
3/4 cup melted butter *or* olive oil (*or* a mixture)

Syrup:

2 cups sugar dissolved in 1 cup water and 2 tbsp. lemon juice
peel of 1/2 lemon
2 tbsp. brandy (optional)

Bring the milk nearly to boiling and remove from heat.

Beat the eggs till thick; add sugar and beat again. Stir in the semolina, milk, and lemon peel.

Cook on low heat, stirring continuously until mixture thickens, then remove from heat and stir in the butter and vanilla.

Grease a baking tin (about twenty-two x thirty cm.) and lay in six or seven sheets of *fyllo*, brushing each with melted butter or olive oil. Arrange them alternately, first at one end of the tin and then at the other, so that a part of each sheet hangs over the side of the tin. You must work fast to prevent *fyllo* from drying out. (Keep the sheets covered with a damp cloth throughout the process; peel off those required and quickly re-cover the rest.)

Pour in the semolina mixture and lay on the rest of the sheets (reserving two), cutting them with scissors to fit exactly and brushing each with butter or olive oil. Turn in the bottom sheets and oil again, finishing the parcel with the two remaining sheets, cut to fit. Pour over the rest of the olive oil or butter, slice through the top few sheets in squares for serving, and sprinkle with water.

Bake in a moderate oven for forty-five minutes and leave to cool.

When the pie is cold, prepare the syrup: bring all the ingredients to the boil and boil hard for five minutes. Remove from the heat and add the brandy. Cool slightly, then pour over the pie. The lemon peel will have crystallized slightly and can be left strewn over the crust; it is tasty as well as decorative.

Note: If the cut-off strips of *fyllo* are kept covered, they can be used for Small Cheese Pies (*see* previous recipe).

Jam Flan   Pastaflóra

3 cups plain flour and a pinch of salt
1 tbsp. baking powder
225 grams butter, softened (1 packet less 1 slice)
1 large egg, separated
1/3 cup sugar
2 tbsp. grated lemon peel
1 wineglass brandy
1 cup apricot or peach jam (400 - 600 grams)

Sift the flour, baking powder, and salt into a large bowl. Add the butter, yolk of the egg, sugar, lemon peel, and brandy and mix well, lastly with the fingertips, to make a soft dough. Refrigerate for thirty minutes.

Divide the dough into two pieces. Roll out one piece to the thickness of about two centimetres and lay it in a greased baking tin. Pull off about one-third of the remaining dough and form it into a long, finger-width roll to make a wall round the base dough, having first dampened the edges with water, and press firmly together. (It is much easier, however, to use a deep, straight-sided flan tin and allow the dough to come up the sides in one piece, using, of course, rather more than half of the original dough.)

Spread the jam evenly over the surface; warm it first if very stiff. Roll out the remaining dough and cut in thin strips and lay in the jam in a close lattice-work, pressing the ends firmly onto the dampened side walls.

Lightly beat the white of egg and brush it over the whole pastry surface. Bake in a medium oven for about forty minutes. Allow to cool and set the jam before cutting into squares.

Though traditionally made with apricot jam, it is just as good with whatever jam one has most of and can also be made up with chopped preserved or soaked dried fruit, moistened with lemon juice. It freezes well and makes a useful stand-by for unexpected guests.

Green Fig Preserve   Frésko Sýko Glykó

1 1/4 kilos green figs
1 tsp. green food colouring (dissolved in ten cups water)
1 1/4 kilos sugar
2 cups water
1/2 cup corn syrup *or* 2 tsp. lemon juice
3 packets vanilla *or* 2 tsp. vanilla essence
halved blanched almonds

These figs, usually found growing wild, and plump this month, are from the male tree (*askólitho*). The small green ones are used, not those apparently ripening to yellow. Copper sulphate (*galazópetro*) is traditionally used to keep the bright green colour of the figs, but it is a poison, so the fruit had to be washed thoroughly. I have replaced it with food colouring, which is perfectly satisfactory.

Wash the figs and cut off the stalks. Boil them till fairly soft, then drain.

Dissolve the food colouring in ten cups of water in the saucepan, return the figs, and bring to the boil. Remove from the heat and leave to cool, for the figs to absorb the colour, then drain.

The almonds can be pushed into the figs at this point.

Dissolve the sugar in the two cups of water in a large pan, bring to the boil, and boil for five minutes, then add the figs. Boil them for a further five minutes, then leave in their syrup overnight.

Next day, bring the panful to the boil again, skim, and add the corn syrup or lemon juice and vanilla. Continue summering till the syrup coats the fruit. Cool and pot, spooning the syrup over the fruit in the jar.

Basil   Vasilikó

The Greeks do not use basil in cooking, but they love to
have a pot on their balconies and will present visitors with a
spray of its aromatic leaves. It is said to keep flies away, but
also has a religious significance connected with St. Basil
(*Ághios Vasílis*). It is used by the priests to dip into holy
water and splash on the faithful at certain church services
and also at the "Christening" of a new house, shop, or
boat.

If you want to use the leaves for your tomato salad or
omelette you must have your own plant, as it is not sold at
the greengrocers. Buy one at the local market; the small-
leafed variety is best. Two or three small roots will grow
together to produce the perfectly round bushes one
admires later in the year.

71

June

Recipes

Courgette Salad	Kolokythákia Saláta
Courgette Flowers	Kolokythokorfádes or
	Anthí apo Kolokythákia
Stewed Courgettes	Briam or Kolokythákia Yachní
Fried Courgettes	Kolokythákia Tiganitá
Baked Courgettes with Cheese	Kolokythákia
and Tomato Sauce	sto Foúrno
Cucumber, Garlic, and Yoghurt Dip	Tzatzíki
Cracked Wheat Salad	Pligoúri Saláta
Trout	Péstrofa
Meatballs	
Fried Meatballs	Keftédes
Buffet Meatballs	Keftedákia
Meatballs with Rice in Egg	Youvarlákia
and Lemon Sauce	
Smyrna Sausages	Soutzoukákia
Baked Lamb Chops	Arní Hasápiko
Fried Cheese	Saganáki
Herbs	Vótana
Capers	Kápari
Pickled Capers	Kápari Toursí
Pickled Caper Buds	
Rice Pudding	Rizógalo
Apricot Jam	Veríkoko Marmeláda
Strawberry Preserve	Fráoula Glýko
Brandy Sour	

72

Other suggestions:
Chilled beetroot soup, sardines "a la grecque," olive tartlets, chilled chicken in lemon sauce, trout with almonds, strawberry short-cake, apricot trifle, cherry and almond dessert, lemon cordial, lemon sorbet ice, and rose geranium sorbet.

Summer is really established, with courgettes and tomatoes no longer expensive, young carrots and new potatoes, onions finally "dry" after three months of spring onions, green beans (several kinds, string beans getting rather tough but the thin varieties very tender) and still beetroots, lettuces, and cucumbers. Green peppers and aubergines are becoming cheaper and will be with us for the whole summer. For those who dislike the bitter chicory there is now *vlíta*, which is much milder.

For the first two weeks there are still strawberries, and also red cherries, plums, egg-plums, and a few small melons. Lemons, oranges, and apples are on the way out. Towards the end of the month there are the first peaches; black cherries (not *vísina*); and both sweet and water melons; several kinds of plums; and also apricots, some reasonably priced, and a very delicious variety called *diamantopoúlou*, which are extremely expensive. There are still lemons and a few oranges, becoming expensive, unripe and not very juicy, and also grapefruit.

These recipes for courgettes are mostly inter-changeable with July and August, but new young ones are best eaten "straight," as a salad, or mixed with other new vegetables in a light stew, as in *briám*, while later in the summer the larger ones are better stuffed, fried, or made into soufflé, rissoles, or casserole.

June

Courgette Salad — Kolokythákia Saláta

Choose all the same size courgettes, not necessarily small, wipe them with a damp cloth, and trim both ends. Boil in plenty of salted water until very tender, adding a few sprigs of mint for a delicate flavour not unlike asparagus. Drain well, cool, and serve with an oil and vinegar (or lemon juice) dressing. Do not keep more than a day as they go off very quickly.

Courgette Flowers — Kolokythokorfádes *or* Anthi apo Kolokythákia

Fresh young courgettes are often sold with their flowers still on, and these can be eaten too, either dipped in batter and fried in very hot oil, or stuffed, an exotic dish.

Stewed Courgettes — Briam *or* Kolokythákia Yachní

1 kilo courgettes
2 or 3 onions
1/2 kilo tomatoes (*or* 2 tbsp. tomato paste, diluted)
1 cup olive oil
1 tsp. each sugar, chopped mint, and fresh dill *or* parsley
salt and pepper
1/2 kilo new potatoes

Trim and slice courgettes thickly, and slice onions. Fry onions in oil till golden, add tomato paste or chopped skinned fresh tomatoes, and sugar and cook for ten minutes. Then add seasoning, courgettes, potatoes, and water just to cover.

Simmer until courgettes and potatoes are soft, stir once, and leave to stand until ready to serve.

74

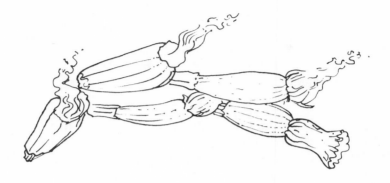

Fried Courgettes   Kolokythákia Tiganitá

Slice young courgettes very thinly, dip in seasoned flour, then shake off excess. Fry quickly in very hot oil. Serve as entree or *mezes* with garlic sauce *skordaliá. See* Sauces in Basic.

Baked Courgettes with Cheese   Kolokythákia sto
and Tomato Sauce   Foúrno

Parboil medium-sized courgettes, drain, then slice in half lengthways and lay in a flat greased oven dish. Remove some of the seeds if rather ripe, or slightly dent each half with the back of a spoon and fill the hollow with grated cheese. Heat through in the oven till the cheese has melted, and serve with tomato sauce.

June

Cucumber, Garlic, and Yoghurt Dip   Tzatzíki

1 large cucumber *or* two small ones
2 or 3 cloves garlic
salt and pepper
500 grams (3 cups) thick yoghurt - *sakkoúlas, or* "strained"
2 tbsp. oil and 1 tbsp. vinegar (optional)
mint (optional)

Wash and dry cucumber, peel it and cut in dice, or grate it coarsely, with some of the peel. Peel and crush the garlic with salt under a knife, or grate it, too, on a fine grater.

Spoon the yoghurt into a bowl, beat it well, and add the oil and vinegar mixed together, if using. Stir cucumber and garlic into the dressing. Garnish with sprigs of mint or a tablespoonful chopped fine, chill, and serve in a bowl as a dip with crusty bread and a green salad, or with fried courgettes as an entrée.

Cracked Wheat Salad   Pligoúri Saláta

This is a good time to try *pligoúri* (also called bligouri and burghul) instead of an ordinary rice salad. It is cracked wheat and has more flavour, rather like brown rice. Both are now available in Greece in the supermarkets. Pligouri had become increasingly difficult to find, except in Cyprus, where it is called *Pourgouri*. It needs less cooking in less water than rice, otherwise it quickly becomes porridge!

1 cup *pligoúri*
2 cups water
knob of butter
salt, pepper, and a bouillon cube

76

Bring the water to the boil, throw in the *pligoúri*, add butter and seasoning and simmer, covered, till the water has evaporated, stirring once or twice. Cover the pan with a cloth, replace the lid and leave on very low heat to absorb all the moisture.

Loosen the grains with a fork and serve plain with a meat stew, or as follows, in the Middle Eastern way (though there they only soak the grains in warm water till the water is absorbed, and then squeeze it dry.)

Peel and chop two or three tomatoes and an onion. Add half a cup of finely chopped parsley and mint. Make up a dressing of oil and lemon juice with salt and pepper (and garlic if liked) and toss the salad in it.

Fold this into the cooled *pligoúri*. Serve chilled.

Trout   Péstrofa

Fresh trout is increasingly readily available and not expensive. Fish farms have been established in many places in northern Greece and the Peloponnese where there is fresh running water.

Usually grilled and served with oil and lemon juice, it is delicious,individually wrapped and cooked and served in foil. This is also a boon for entertaining in a small flat to avoid any fishy smells.

Clean the fish, remove heads, tails, and guts, and place each on a piece of foil, large enough to fold round it. Dab small pieces of butter on top of each fish, sprinkle with salt and pepper, fresh chopped parsley, thyme, or other herbs, and fold up the sides of the foil.

Before closing the top, pour in a teaspoon of white wine or lemon juice. Seal and lay on a greased baking tin, and bake in a hot oven for about twenty minutes.

Serve each fish in its foil to retain the juices.

June

Meatballs

Three kinds, fried, stewed, and spiced, are made in Greece, not tied to any particular season. *Keftédes* are useful at this time to prepare in advance for parties or picnics.

Fried Meatballs   Keftédes

**1 kilo lean minced beef
1 medium onion, very finely grated
2 cloves garlic, crushed
2 slices bread, soaked in water and wrung out
2 eggs, beaten
1 tbsp. finely chopped parsley
1 tsp. finely chopped mint
1 tsp. oregano
salt and pepper
1 tbsp. vinegar and a little oil
oil for frying**

Combine the mince, onion, garlic, and soaked bread in a bowl. Add the eggs and herbs and mix well with your hands, adding vinegar and enough oil to smooth the mixture. Season to taste and leave in a cool place, covered, for about one hour.

With floured hands, break off pieces and shape into balls, roll in seasoned flour, shake off excess, and fry in very hot oil until brown. Drain and serve hot with a rich tomato sauce (*see* Sauces in Basic) and mashed potatoes.

They can also be heated through in the tomato sauce till ready to serve.

Buffet Meatballs   Keftedákia

Tiny meat balls, the size of a pigeon's egg, are a useful dish
for buffet parties or picnics, but they need more seasoning
if served cold: double the mint and oregano, add some dry
mustard, a shake of cumin, or a tablespoon of ouzo for
moistening. The smaller the balls the finer must be the
grating of onion and herbs, and in a hurry powdered onion
and garlic are perfectly adequate.

Meatballs with Rice   Youvarlákia
in Egg and Lemon Sauce

Meatballs:

1/2 kilo minced beef
1 onion, grated, or finely chopped
1 tsp. salt
pinch of black pepper
1 - 2 cloves garlic, crushed (optional)
2 tbsp. chopped parsley
1 tbsp. chopped fresh mint or dill *or* 1 tbsp. dried
    mint or oregano
1/4 cup Carolina rice
flour

Stock:

5 cups stock
1 tbsp. margarine
1 tsp. salt, if required

Sauce:

2 eggs
juice of one lemon

Mix together all ingredients for the meat balls, kneading to combine well. Roll into walnut-sized balls with floured hands. Makes about twenty-five.

Bring stock to the boil in a wide shallow pan, lower meat balls into it, cover, and simmer for half an hour.

Beat the eggs thoroughly in a bowl with a little water and stir in the lemon juice. Ladle some of the broth from the pan into the bowl, stir, and pour back over the meat balls.

Return pan to very low heat, rocking it to cover the meat balls with sauce and combine with the juices, but do not allow to boil. Serve hot or warm.

Smyrna Sausages   Soutzoukákia

Another variety of meat balls which are highly spiced are these small sausage-shaped ones made, like *keftédes*, with minced meat, onion, breadcrumbs, and an egg, but flavoured with cumin and garlic. They are fried in oil and then simmered in a rich tomato sauce. They can also be baked instead of fried, their sauce added when they have browned.

See also Meat Patties (*Biftékia*) in July, which are like hamburgers, made of all meat and usually grilled.

Fried Cheese   Saganáki

Saganáki is really the name of the small, two-handled frying pan in which this dish is usually made, and very likely served as well. It is a national speciality in Cyprus, made with the distinctive *haloúmi* cheese, and is even served for breakfast.

hard cheese, such as *kefalotýri*, **in thick slices**
flour
olive oil or margarine
lemon juice
oregano

Heat a little olive oil or margarine in the pan. Dip the cheese slices in water, shake, then dust them with flour and fry on both sides till golden and sizzling.

Serve immediately with a squeeze of lemon juice and a sprinkle of oregano if desired.

Herbs   Vótana

Collect thyme for drying while flowers are still in bud; also oregano, to pick *in flower*. Capers are picked in bud from the end of May and into July (*see* Capers below). Mint is cut back before the flowers come.

June

Capers   Kápari

Caper bushes are coming into flower now on roadsides and
rocky walls and should be picked in bud for pickling. This
recipe is an old English country method for nasturtium
seeds as a substitute for real capers!

When the Greeks pickle capers they put in whole
stalks, leaves and all. *See* below.

Pickled Caper Buds

Wash the buds in cold water and soak overnight in cold
salted water. Drain.

Make up spiced vinegar as follows: To one litre (one
kilo) of vinegar add two tablespoons salt, twelve peppercorns, two cloves, and one bay leaf. Bring to the boil and
simmer for three minutes. Cool and strain.

Put the caper buds in a jar and cover with the vinegar.
Seal and store for a year before using.

Pickled Capers   Kápari Toursí

Pick short branches from a caper bush, wash well, lay
in a bowl, and cover with boiling salted water (fifty grams
of salt to one kilo of branches). Leave in the sun for three
or four days, changing the (cold) water every day.

Strain and put into a jar; cover with vinegar and a
handful of salt. They are ready to eat in a few days, drained
and served with anchovies in an oil dressing.

Baked Lamb Chops   Arní Hasápiko

1 kilo lamb chops (*païdákia*)
3 fresh tomatoes *or* 3 cups canned tomatoes with juice

June

3/4 cup olive oil
salt and pepper
garlic
parsley (*and/or* **rosemary**)
potatoes

Remove excess fat from chops, wash and dry them, and lay them in an oiled baking tin.

Spread over them the chopped tomatoes, sprinkle with oil, salt and pepper, and, if liked, sliced garlic and chopped parsley and a little rosemary. Some potatoes cut fairly small can be pushed between the chops, but more liquid may then be required. Bake, uncovered, in a moderate oven till the meat is tender.

Note: Veal chops can be cooked in exactly the same way. Strew with oregano instead of rosemary.

Rice Pudding   Rizógalo

A surprising number of visitors appreciate the Greek rice pudding, perhaps because it fills the long gap between lunch and the late evening meal. They can be bought from *kafeneía* or dairy shops, which also sell yoghurt and *kréma*, a cornflour mould.

4 tbsp. glâcé rice
3 cups evaporated milk
3 cups water
vanilla *or* **grated lemon rind**
sugar to taste

Wash and drain the rice. Mix the milk and water in a saucepan and bring to the boil. Add the rice, flavouring, and sugar, and simmer till thick. Pour into individual bowls and sprinkle with cinnamon to serve.

Apricot Jam   Verýkoko Marmeláda

The most satisfactory jam to make as it sets so easily.

3 kilos apricots
1 1/2 cups water
Juice of 1 small lemon
2 1/2 kilos sugar
1/2 cup split almonds *or* apricot kernels
1 tsp. almond essence (optional)

Wash the fruit, halve or quarter it, and remove the stones. Do not skin.

Butter the bottom of a large pan and put in the fruit with the water and lemon juice. Simmer uncovered for about half an hour till mushy and skins are soft. Add the sugar and almonds (and optional almond essence) and continue simmering till sugar has dissolved completely. Then raise the heat till jam boils and is bubbling vigourously. Boil fast for up to twenty minutes, stirring frequently, but start testing for setting point after ten minutes (*see* Jams, Jellies, and Preserves in Basic).

Run a little butter over the surface to disperse scum. Cool jam slightly and then pour into warmed jars. Seal when cold.

Strawberry Preserve   Fráoula Glykó

1 kilo firm strawberries
1/2 cup lemon juice
1 cup water
1 tsp. lemon juice

Clean the fruit and lay it in a dish. Sprinkle with the lemon juice and leave for three or four hours.

Put the sugar and water into a saucepan, stirring as the sugar dissolves over low heat. Bring to the boil and boil for a few minutes till it becomes syrupy.

Strain the strawberries and put into the syrup, and allow to boil for six to eight minutes over medium heat.

Remove pan from the heat and carefully lift out the strawberries with a slotted spoon onto a dish.

Bring the syrup to the boil again and boil till thick. Return the strawberries to the pan, add a teaspoon of lemon juice, and boil till they are covered by the syrup.

Cool and spoon into jars, covering with the syrup. Seal when cold.

Brandy Sour

This most refreshing drink is a Cyprus speciality.

Into a tall glass sprinkle Angostura bitters (now available in supermarkets) and then add a measure of brandy and the same amount of fresh lemon juice.

Add several ice cubes or some cracked ice, fill up with soda water, and press a thin slice of lemon upright over the rim of the glass to serve.

July

Recipes

Tomato Salad	Domátosaláta
Village Salad	Horiátiki Saláta
Aubergine Purée	Melitzánosaláta
Aubergine "Shoes"	Melitzánes Papoutsákia
Courgette "Boats"	Kolokythákia Papoutsákia
Cheese and Onion Stuffing	Yémisma me Tyrí
	kai Kremmýdia
Aubergine Fritters	Melitzánes Tiganítes
Fried Sliced Aubergines	Melitzánes Tiganités
Fish with Mayonnaise	Psári Vrastó Mayonéza
(Athenian Style)	(Athinaikó)
Barbecue	Kréas Skáras
Barbecued Lamb Chops	Arníssia Païdákia Skáras
Barbecued Lamb Kebabs	Souvlákia
(Cyprus Style)	
Meat Patties	Biftékia
Swordfish Kebabs	Xifías Souvlákia
Compôte of Fruit	Kompósta
Cucumber as "Fruit" Dessert	Angoúri
Chocolate and Biscuit Refrigerator Cake	Mosaíko Glykó
Sour Cherry Preserve	Vísino Glykó
Cherry Cordial	Visináda
Cherry Brandy	Tsérri Bránti

86

Other suggestions:

Tomato aspic and fish mousse, garlic bread, barbecue sauce, courgette rissoles, green beans with parsley, liver pâté, potted cheese, peach flan, plum juice dessert (kissel), peaches poached in brandy, melon fruit salad bowl, apricot and yoghurt ice cream, tomato chutney.

The heat has set in for the next two months and we try to plan meals which can be cooked fairly quickly or prepared and even cooked out of doors in the comparative cool of early morning or late in the evening, ready for serving the next day. Gelatine is a boon for a whole range of dishes such as chicken in aspic, salmon mousse, or fruit jelly, and it can now be bought in packets, in crystal form, labelled *agní zelatíni skóni*. Previously, and still in older stores, it could only be found in sheets, where each sheet equalled one teaspoon of powder. Three teaspoons set one pint of liquid, or two "glasses" (use only two Greek cups in hot weather). The ubiquitous fruit flavoured packet jelly crystals are handy as a standby, but are very sweet and are best made up with part lemon juice or the juice of some stewed fruit in place of some of the water.

Aubergines and courgettes are the staple vegetables for cooking this month, frequently stuffed whole or with the stuffing piled into halves, as in *papoutsákia*, although the easiest way with courgettes is still one of the best, boiled whole and served cold with a vinaigrette (*see* Courgette Salad in June). Huge firm red tomatoes are also very welcome stuffed (*see* Stuffed Tomatoes in August), together with green peppers, or they make the easiest Greek salads, *domátosaláta* or *horiátiki saláta* (*see* below).

New this month in the market is okra (*bámies*), also called ladies' fingers, which is delicious when properly prepared (*see* Okra in August). *Vlíta* and chicory are also served cold as a cooked greens salad. Carrots are young enough for grating for salad, and parsley, celery tops, and dill are to hand for garnishing and flavour. There are several kinds of green beans. Newly-dried sage and oregano, fresh basil, and rosemary add piquancy to barbecue meals, either in marinades or chopped and strewn on chops and steaks, the stalks also adding their aroma when thrown onto the charcoal fire.

There are several varieties of small fish now in season, delicious fried, or baked with sliced tomatoes, onions and chopped parsley (*see* Fish in Basic and Baked Sardines in February): fresh anchovies (*gávros*) are the tastiest, but the much cheaper sardines (*sardélles*) are not to be despised, and young red mullet (*barboúnia*) are much cheaper than when fully grown, and just as good. Slightly larger fish called *gópes* (a kind of small sea bream) are also excellent fried or grilled (*see* Fish in Basic). Groupers (*sfyrída*) and tunney (*tónnos*) are usually cooked as steaks. Sea bream (*lithríni* and *synagrída*) are also served as steaks, or poached, then coated with mayonnaise and served cold, "Athenian style" (*see* below).

Peaches are being sold on every street corner, and small open-backed trucks tour the streets, piled high with watermelons, their approach heralded by loudspeaker: *karpoúzi,karpoúzi*. Mounds of these dark geeen or striped fruit suddenly appear on vacant lots in the city, or along the roadsides, often attended only by a small boy, sheltered from the sun by a makeshift tent. One or two melons are cut open to show their tempting, juicy, dark rose flesh. Two kinds of sweet melon (*pepóni*) are on sale, the oval ones being the cheapest; the small round ones are the most aromatic, hailing from the island of Zakynthos.

There are black cherries, dark red plums (*vaníllias*), and small green pears, which are unexpectedly ripe. For a few weeks the tiny egg plums (*korómila*) put in an appearance, and they are very good for stewing and juice. Later the sour cherries (*vísina*) may be found for a brief period. They are made commercially into syrup called *visináda* and are gorgeous for cherry brandy; they are also popular for a "spoon sweet" (*see* below).

Lemons are going off, or are green and unripe (except in restaurants!). At the end of the month we get the first grapes and figs. There are no apples to be had, and only a few Valencia oranges; Greek orange juice in tins or cartons, however, is excellent. Apricots are rather battered in the markets, but perfect for stewing or for jam.

Tomato Salad   Domátosaláta

   This simplest of salads is always greeted with cries of delight by sun-starved northern visitors, and the bowl is never big enough. The tomatoes are cut in quarters (or smaller pieces from very big tomatoes, but never sliced) and the dark stalk end is cut out. Oregano should be crumbled over the salad, which is tossed in oil and seasoned with salt and pepper. Chunks of onion and cucumber can be added. In tavernas it is cheaper to order this salad and a separate slice of *feta* cheese rather than the following, which frequently comes to the same thing.

Village Salad   Horiátiki Saláta

   To the basic tomato salad (above) with onion and cucumber, the addition of some sliced green peppers, huge black olives, capers, and squares of *feta* cheese make of this salad a complete meal, with fresh crusty bread and chilled wine. (If the wine itself is not chilled, add ice or soda water for a more refreshing drink - according to the old Greek proverb - *Sto mína pou den échi "ro," vále sto krasí neró*: "When the month has no ' r, ' put water in your wine.")

July

Aubergine Purée   Melitzánosaláta

2 or 3 round aubergines
2 cloves of garlic, grated or mashed
1 onion, grated
lemon juice *or* vinegar to taste
1/2 cup olive oil

Wipe two or three aubergines, pierce them with a fork, and bake them whole in the oven or under the grill, till they are soft or even charred. If the skins burn, so much the better; the slightly smoky flavour is an improvement, and more authentic as they used to be cooked over a wood fire or buried in hot ash. They can also be held over a gas flame on a long fork and twirled around till cooked.

Hold each one by the stalk under a cold tap and peel off the skin, upwards towards the stalk, with a silver or stainless steel knife. Discard stalk and skin, halve the aubergines into a bowl, and remove any excessive amount of seeds.

Chop and then pound the flesh in a mortar, with some finely chopped garlic, grated onion, and salt and pepper. Add lemon juice or vinegar and olive oil, and keep pounding till smooth and light. You can also whisk the mixture in a blender, but this tends to neutralize the flavours and give it the consistency of baby food.

Variations:

1) Instead of the olive oil and vinegar, mix in a tablespoonful of mayonnaise, which gives a smoother mixture. Some people also add tomato pulp, others add finely chopped walnuts.

2) A milder version is mixed only with a little milk and butter as soon as it has been mashed and seasoned.

3) An Eastern variation uses the finely chopped onion and salt and pepper, and then adds fresh chopped mint, powdered cumin, and "strained" yoghurt.

90

Aubergine "Shoes"   Melitzánes Papoutsákia

These stuffed aubergines are attractive and convenient to serve. Use the longer shiny dark aubergines, of medium size. With their stalks on they somewhat resemble the old Greek shoes with turned-up toes.

8 - 10 medium aubergines
olive oil for frying
1/2 cup chopped onions
350 grams minced beef
500 grams (2 large) ripe tomatoes, peeled and chopped, or grated
salt and pepper
chopped parsley
1 - 2 cups white sauce, fairly stiff (*see* Sauces in Basic)
1 egg
1/2 cup grated cheese
1/2 cup crushed rusk (optional)
1/2 cup melted butter

Wipe the aubergines, cut off their stalks and "petals," and cut them in half lengthways. Sprinkle with salt and leave to drain for half an hour or so, then dry on kitchen paper. Fry in hot olive oil until wilted, and lay in a baking dish, cut sides up, pressing down the inside to form the "shoes."

Sauté the onions lightly, add the mince and salt and pepper and stir till browned, then add the tomato pulp and parsley and cook till firm, when the tomato juice has been absorbed or driven off. Spoon the mixture into the shoes and cover each with white sauce, into which an egg has been beaten. Sprinkle this with the cheese (and then with the rusk if using) and dribble melted butter over each one.

Bake in a medium oven for half an hour or under the grill until browned.

Courgette "Boats" Kolokythákia Papoutsákia

10 - 12 large courgettes
filling and white sauce as for Aubergine "Shoes" above

Top and tail the courgettes, scrape them lightly, and boil in salted water for about eight minutes. Take out and split in half lengthways, and leave upside down to drain.

Scoop out most of the centres with a teaspoon, leaving the two ends intact. Add the courgette pulp to the cooking meat mixture.

Fill the shells, cover with white sauce and grated cheese, and bake as for Aubergine "Shoes."

See also Stuffed Courgettes, a simpler version without white sauce, in August.

Cheese and Onion Stuffing Yémisma me Tyrí kai Kremmýdia

Use for either Aubergine "Shoes" or Courgette "Boats." Instead of mince, add three-quarters cup grated hard cheese, *kefalotýri* or *regátto*, to the softened onion and omit the tomato. Use plenty of parlsey and pepper, and thicken with dry breadcrumbs. Cover with a mixture of crumbs and melted butter and bake in a greased pan to which a little hot water has been added until golden brown.

Aubergine Fritters Melitzánes Tiganités

3 - 4 round "flask" aubergines
fritter batter
olive oil for frying

Wash and dry the aubergines, top and tail them, partly peel in stripes if skins are tough, and slice fairly thinly. Leave to drain, sprinkled with salt, for half an hour. Pat dry on kitchen paper.

Prepare a rather stiff batter* and leave in the fridge for one or two hours. Fold in the stiffly-beaten egg white just before use.

Dip slices in the batter, flick off excess, and fry in very hot oil for about three minutes on each side, till brown and crisp. Drain and serve hot with garlic sauce (*see* Sauces in Basic) and a salad.

* Batter: 1 cup plain flour, a pinch of salt, up to 1/2 cup tepid water, egg white (*see* Fritter Batter in Basic).

Fried Sliced Aubergines   Melitzánes Tiganités

Prepare aubergines (either kind) as above and then dip in seasoned flour (powdered garlic enhances the flavour) before frying. They can also be fried without any coating, but, uncoated, they devour the olive oil and are thus much richer and more fattening. Serve hot, at once, with a sprinkle of lemon juice and chopped parsley. They lose their crispness if kept waiting.

Fish with Mayonnaise   Psári Vrastó Mayonéza
(Athenian Style)   (Athenaïkó)

Use a large whole fish, usually a sea bream (*synagrída* or *lithríni*), or grouper (*sfyrída*). Poach gently till tender, but not falling apart. (*See* Fish Soup in March and Fish in Basic.)

Lift out carefully onto a large dish. Remove the head and tail (reserve) and the skin and bones (discard), but keep the rest of the fish whole in two fillets. Allow to cool.

Assemble the fish on a serving dish and mask entirely with mayonnaise, preferably home-made (*see* Sauces in Basic), adding the head and tail again for effect. Decorate with cut-up carrot (which, with a little ingenuity, can be made to resemble fish scales), parsley, capers, sliced hard-boiled egg, beetroot or pickled peppers, and olives. Chill before serving.

Barbecue   Kréas Skáras

Strew the coals in your barbecue with branches of rosemary for a delicious aroma, or beg some sawdust (*prionídia*) from a sawmill or builder's yard for a smoky flavour.

Beef chops are *brizóles moskarísies* and pork chops are *brizóles hirinés*.

Barbecued Lamb Chops   Arnísia Païdákia Skáras

Marinade for 1 kilo chops:

juice of 1 lemon
1/3 cup olive oil
1 tsp. oregano

Mix together and pour over trimmed chops in a shallow dish. Turn them over periodically for three or four hours.

Grill the chops on both sides, basting with the marinade.

Sprinkle with salt, pepper, and lemon juice.

See also Yoghurt Marinade (Dairy Products)in Basic.

Barbecued Lamb Kebabs (Cyprus Style)   Souvlákia

1 kilo lean lamb, cut in cubes
1/2 kilo liver, sliced
1/2 kilo peppers, green and red
2 medium onions
fresh bay leaves *or* oregano

Marinate the lamb and put the liver to soak in milk, both overnight.

When ready to assemble the kebabs, drain liver, dry, and cut it into squares, clean peppers and cut into chunks of the same size, cut onions into quarters and use the thickest pieces. Pierce peices of meat onto long skewers alternating with the vegetables and a half bay leaf near each piece of lamb. (If no bay leaves are available, scatter oregano over the whole skewer.) Sprinkle with salt and black pepper and baste with olive oil, lemon juice, and oregano while on the spit.

Meat Patties   Biftékia

These are often cooked over hot coals. Don't be taken in by the Greek name. They are made of minced meat, and should properly be called *biftékia me kimá*. They resemble meat balls (*keftédes*) but have no bread in them, only salt and pepper and an egg to bind.

Swordfish Kebabs   Xifías Souvlákia

Steaks of swordfish are excellent for grilling on skewers, cut in chunks and interspersed with slices of peppers, tomatoes, onions, mushrooms, and bay leaves.

Serve with an olive oil and lemon dressing.

Compôte of Fruit   Kompósta

Peaches, pears, apricots, plums, and egg-plums; all these fruits are now to be found. When slightly battered, they are considerably cheaper, and suitable for stewing, either separately or combined.

Prepare the fruit, cutting out the damaged parts, halve or quarter as necessary, and remove stones. Sweeten with sugar, honey, or some syrup from jars of "spoon sweets," and simmer till softened, with a piece of cinnamon. Add a little liqueur or brandy or sprinkle with rose water.

Chill and serve with vanilla ice cream or yoghurt, and sponge fingers.

Cucumber as "Fruit" Dessert   Angoúri

Dessert is unusual in a Greek taverna (except a few which make a specialty of yoghurt with walnuts and honey) but fresh fruit may be served, peeled and sliced (*see* Fresh Fruit as Dessert in April). In hot weather someone may call for chilled cucumber sliced in lengths, which is most refreshing at the end of the meal. A round variety called *xilágouro* has a mild flavour and is crunchy when chilled.

Chocolate and Biscuit   Mosaïkó Glykó
Refrigerator Cake

2 packets "Petit Beurre" biscuits
packet (250 grams) margarine
100 grams (3/4 cup) sieved icing sugar
2 tbsp. cocoa powder (unsweetened)
1 or 2 eggs, beaten
2 tbsp. brandy, *or* orange juice

Melt the margarine in a medium saucepan over low heat (or leave out in the July sun for ten minutes) and stir in the cocoa. Take the pan off the heat, add the brandy, egg, and sugar, and stir thoroughly.

Break each biscuit into four or five pieces and stir them into the chocolate sauce, ensuring that each is covered.

Line a loaf tin with greaseproof paper or foil (or even the biscuit paper if it comes off in one piece), leaving some hanging over the side. Spoon half the mixture in, press it down well, then the rest. Fold the paper over and press down firmly with the palm of your hand.

Refrigerate for several hours and keep in fridge till ready to serve. Peel off the paper and turn cake out onto a plate. Slice thinly to serve; it's quite rich.

Sour Cherry Preserve   Vísino Glykó

1 kilo sour cherries (*vísina*)
1 kilo sugar
2 cups water
1 tbsp. lemon juice

Wash the cherries and extract the stones carefully so as to leave them whole; it's rather tricky, but there's a small gadget on the market for this purpose.

Boil them with the sugar and water for about twenty minutes, skimming off the scum. Leave overnight in their syrup. Next day add the lemon juice and boil till thick. (*See* Jams, Jellies, and Preserves, Tests for Setting, in Basic.)

Cherry Cordial   Visináda

This can be made at the same time as the preserve, by increasing the sugar to one and a half kilos and the water to

three and a half cups. Pour off the extra syrup before
boiling, to set the preserve, and bottle.

To serve, pour into glasses, as for bottled concentrated
lemonade — *dío dáktila*, two (horizontal) fingers deep, in
the expressive Greek phrase — fill up with iced water, and
stir.

Cherry Brandy   Tsérri Bránti

This is not to be confused with sherry; to the Greeks
the pronunciation is identical. Quantities of brandy or rum
can be varied according to taste. As youngsters have a
passion for it, complete with cherry, it can be made with
the smaller amount of low grade brandy. This can be
bought "loose" from shops (*inopoleía*) selling from the
barrel.

1 kilo sour or morello cherries
750 grams sugar
500 grams - 1 kilo brandy *or* rum
2 cinnamon sticks, each about 5 cm. long
3 cloves

Wash the cherries and remove the stalks. Leave the
stones, which add flavour. Drop the cherries into a wide-
mouthed jar, pour in the sugar, cover the jar lightly, and
leave in the sun for about a month. Shake the jar every few
days to distribute the sugar.

After a month, add the spices and brandy and leave for
a further two weeks.

Strain into a bottle if desired, and serve neat, or with a
cherry in each glass. If it is strained, the cherries should be
transferred to a smaller jar and covered with enough of the
liqueur to preserve them. They are useful for adding to a
fruit salad or to any other drink in place of a maraschino
cherry. With the stones removed they are excellent in
Christmas cake.

August

Recipes

Stuffed Tomatoes with Rice	Domátes Yemistés me Rízi
Stuffed Tomatoes with Mince	Domátes Yemistés me Kimá
Stuffed Peppers (with Rice or Mince)	Piperiés Yemistés
Tomato Scrambled Egg	Strapatsáda
Fried Squid	Kalamarákia Tiganitá
Stuffed Courgettes with Mince	Kolokythákia Yemistá me Kimá
Stuffed Courgettes (without meat)	Kolokythákia Yemistá
Baked Shrimps in Tomato Sauce with Cheese	Garídes me Feta Youvétsi
Okra (Ladies' Fingers)	Bámies
Okra with Tomatoes	Bámies Yachní
Aubergine and Cheese Casserole	Melitzánes me Tyrí
Cheese-Stuffed Aubergines	"Bourékia" me Melitzánes
Baked Mackerel	Koliós sto Foúrno
Peach Jam	Rodákino Marmeláda
Fig Jam	Sýka Marmeláda
Fig Preserve	Sýko Glykó

Other suggestions:
Rice salad with green dressing, tomato and onion tart, chicken stuffed with juniper, gazpacho soup, melon ice cream, fresh figs with ouzo, fruit cup.

High summer heat continues unremittingly for most of the month and the cities are almost empty, while the islands are overflowing. Many restaurants and some greengrocers' shops in Athens close their doors for the whole month, but those which are open are full of inviting fruit and vegetables: aubergines, courgettes, green beans, tomatoes bursting with ripeness (also small plum tomatoes), cucumbers, carrots, and *vlíta*; okra and peppers are at their best. Peaches are at their cheapest, as are watermelons. Several kinds of sweet melon are to be had, and juicy golden pears. New, and for about a month only, are nectarines (*nektarínia*; sometimes called "apple peaches," *mílo-rodákina*) and, of course, figs, and both black and white grapes. Apples return at the end of the month.

The first fortnight is a fasting period for the strict Orthodox, but this is not much of a hardship with such a choice of fruit and vegetables. All the bloodless sea creatures are also acceptable fasting foods, so the choice for sea-side holiday-makers remains wide, including octopus (*see* Octopus in Wine Sauce in May and Octopus with Macaroni and Pickled Octopus in October), squid, shrimps, shell-fish, crabs, and even spiny lobsters or crawfish. Quite a delicacy is the sea urchin (*achinós*), eaten raw with lemon juice, the coral spooned out of the half shell (*see* Old Wives' Remedies, below).

The fifteenth of the month sees the big celebration of the Assumption, or rather Dormition, of the Virgin Mary (*Panayía*), after which the townspeople begin to trickle back home, wishing one another, rather startlingly, a good winter (*kaló himóna*), leaving the beaches comparatively deserted for another month or so of excellent swimming. Fresh fish is in short supply during the period of the full moon, but wine still flows freely from the barrels of outdoor tavernas and at the wine festivals.

Short thunderstorms often attend the *Panayía*, but they clear the air and the nerves and freshen up dust-laden trees. The raging *meltémi* wind should also drop by the end of the month.

Stuffed Tomatoes with Rice

Domátes Yemistés me Rízi

These are without meat, and very popular with observing members of the Orthodox Church who are fasting. Half quantities can be used, but this amount fills a normal (30 cm.) baking tin and, if taken to the local baker's oven (*foúrnos*), gains a little extra flavour.

12 large, ripe, but firm tomatoes
1/2 kilo onions
1 cup olive oil
1 tsp. tomato paste
1 tbsp. chopped parsley
2 tsp. chopped mint
1/2 cup currants
1 cup rice (Carolina *or* niháki)
salt and pepper
1 tbsp. sugar
1/2 tsp. powdered cinnamon
dry breadcrumbs *or* crushed rusks

Stand the tomatoes on their stalk ends and cut a lid from the top of each. Scoop out the pulp into a bowl and leave tomatoes upside down to drain. Strain the pulp and reserve juice.

Sauté the onion in the oil till soft, then add the mint, parsley, rice, tomato pulp and paste, seasoning, and currants. Stir together and cook for a further five minutes, adding a little of the tomato juice if necessary. Leave to cool.

Up-end the tomatoes, arrange them in a roasting pan, and sprinkle a little sugar inside each one. Spoon the stuffing into them loosely, leaving room for the rice to swell. Replace the lids and sprinkle with breadcrumbs. Pour the remaining tomato juice into the pan, dribble some olive oil over each tomato, and bake in a medium oven

101

until the tops are crisp. Some potatoes, cut into small pieces and salted, can be popped in between the tomatoes to soak up the juice.

Stuffed peppers are often included in this dish (*see* below).

Stuffed Tomatoes with Mince   Domátes Yemistés me Kimá

Proceed as above, but use half a kilo minced meat, half a cup rice, and only one large onion. Omit the currants. Add the mince to the onions when lightly sautéed, and stir for a few minutes till browned before adding rice, parsley, seasoning, and tomato pulp.

Stuffed Peppers (with Rice or Mince)   Piperiés Yemistés

Cut round the stalk end and remove a "lid" to be replaced later. Discard all the seeds. Rinse well. Parboil in boiling salted water for five minutes. Drain.

Stuff and cook as above, either with the tomatoes or alone.

Tomato Scrambled Eggs Strapatsáda

A light supper dish, quickly prepared from enormous juicy tomatoes

8 large tomatoes
olive oil
salt and pepper
2 sprigs of basil, finely chopped, *or* **some crumbled thyme**
4 - 6 large eggs, lightly beaten
    Peel and chop the tomatoes, or grate them on the large holes of a cheese grater, throwing away the skins.
    Barely cover the bottom of a large frying pan with olive oil and, when hot, tip in the tomato pulp and juice. Add salt and pepper, and herbs, and cook till the liquid has just evaporated, stirring from time to time. Turn down the heat and stir in the eggs to mix lightly with the tomato. Check seasoning. Continue to cook gently till eggs have set.
    Serve at once with fresh bread and chilled wine. Follow with cheese and fruit.
    See Courgette Omelette in September.

Fried Squid Kalamarákia Tiganitá

    Wash squid very well, separating the head from the lower part and removing the ink sac and soft "innards." Cut in pieces if rather large. Dry thoroughly. Dip in seasoned flour, shake, and fry in very hot olive oil. They spatter terribly, so be dressed for the occasion.
    Drain and serve with a salad.
    See Cuttlefish in Tomato Sauce in October for a richer dish.

Stuffed Courgettes with Mince

Kolokythákia Yemistá me Kimá

2 kilos courgettes
1/2 kilo minced meat
1 onion, chopped or grated
1 clove garlic (optional)
1/2 cup Carolina rice, washed and drained
chopped parsley
2 cups stock
salt and pepper

Wash courgettes, scrape lightly, and cut off stalk ends. Remove soft centres with an apple corer or potato peeler, being careful not to pierce the skins.

Mix minced meat, onion, garlic, rice, and parsley, and season with salt and pepper. Fill the courgettes loosely, so that the rice can swell during cooking. Then pack them into a wide shallow pan, cover with hot stock and a knob of margarine, and simmer, covered, for about one hour, or bake in a covered dish in the oven.

Serve with a thickened egg and lemon sauce, made with the juices from the pan (*see* Sauces in Basic).

Stuffed Courgettes (without meat) Kolokythákia Yemistá

For a meatless stuffing, use the same mixture as for Stuffed Tomatoes, above, omitting currants and using a chopped fresh tomato and some of the pulp from the courgetttes instead of tomato paste.

Sauté the rice in a little olive oil, then add the rest of the ingredients and mix together with a little water to moisten. Cook gently for a few minutes, then stuff the courgettes and continue as above.

Baked Shrimps in Tomato Sauce with Cheese

Garídes me Féta Youvétsi

A classic Greek dish, a favourite at the harbour-side tavernas of Mikrolimano, Piraeus

home-made tomato sauce (*see* Sauces in Basic), made with 3/4 kilo tomatoes, 2 medium onions, 2 cloves garlic, salt, pepper, and olive oil
3/4 kilo large shrimps, shelled and deveined
1/4 kilo feta cheese (or *trimáta*, already crumbled)
chopped parsley

Make the sauce while shelling the shrimps. Combine them and distribute among six small ovenware dishes.

Break up the cheese with a fork, or use *trimáta*, and sprinkle on the top of each dish. Bake in a very hot oven for ten to fifteen minutes and serve hot, sprinkled with chopped parsley.

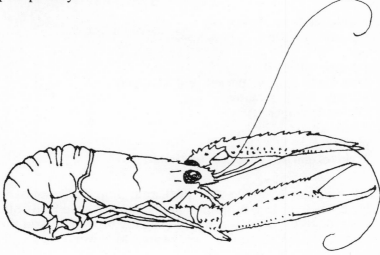

Okra (Ladies' Fingers)   Bámies

To prepare: Wash the okra well, cut off the stalks, and shave the rim of the cone-like tops without cutting them open, allowing the juices to escape. Lay in a dish, sprinkle liberally with salt, half a cup of vinegar to a kilo of okra, and leave for half to one hour, or even longer, if possible in the sun. Then rinse them, drain, and pat dry with a cloth. If using frozen okra, which is indistinguishable and sometimes cheaper than fresh, drop contents of a kilo packet into boiling water to defrost. When separated, drain well and put into a bowl; pour over half a cup of vinegar but leave for fifteen minutes only. Wash in hot water and drain.

Canned okra is also possible as a substitute for fresh, and no cone trimming is necessary. Some vinegar adds piquancy, but can be omitted; just drain and add to the onions and tomatoes. Canned tomatoes could be used if necessary.

Stewed Okra   Bámies Yachní

1 kilo fresh *or* frozen okra
1/2 cup vinegar
salt
1/2 cup olive oil
2 medium onions, peeled and chopped
1/2 kilo fresh tomatoes
salt and pepper
1 tsp. sugar
parsley
2 cloves garlic, chopped (optional)

Prepare as above and peel and chop the tomatoes. Heat olive oil in a large pan and sauté the onion till soft. Add the okra, turning gently till slightly browned. Add the tomatoes and seasoning, and water to cover.

August

Cover the pan and simmer very gently for about forty-five minutes, till most of the water has been absorbed. Shake the pan but do not stir, to avoid splitting the okra. Alternatively , transfer them to an ovenproof dish and allow to cook slowly in the oven for about forty minutes. The use of a pressure cooker helps to keep the òkra whole, and they are done in five minutes. Serve warm or cold.

Aubergine and Cheese Casserole Melitzánes me Týri

1 1/2 kilos fat shiny aubergines
3 - 4 cups tomato sauce (*see* Sauces in Basic)
300 grams mild cheese, sliced (Fontina, Gouda, *Killínis*)
4 level tbsp. grated hard cheese (*kefalotýri*)

Peel aubergines with a potato peeler, or leave only a little skin, in stripes. Slice in thick rounds (about 4 cm. thick) and leave to drain, salted, for half an hour. Pat dry.

Fry quickly in very hot olive oil for a few minutes each side, take out with a slotted spoon, and lay in a baking tin or wide, shallow, ovenproof dish.

When all the slices are fried and arranged in the dish, lay slices of mild cheese on top of each, pour over tomato sauce, and sprinkle with the grated cheese.

Bake for thirty minutes in a medium oven. Sprinkle with parsley. Without an oven this can all be cooked in a frying pan on top of a stove, transferred to a baking dish and put under a grill to sizzle the cheese.

August

Cheese-Stuffed Aubergines   "Bourékia" me Melitzánes

1 kilo small, round aubergines (about 6 or 7)
1 1/2 cups olive oil
2 cups mashed feta, *or* other cheese, grated
1 tsp. black pepper
1 small onion, finely chopped, or grated
1/2 cup parsley, chopped
2 cups breadcrumbs
3 eggs, well beaten

Peel the aubergines and remove stalks; cut a slit in each and shake a little salt inside. Leave to drain for twenty minutes, slit side down. Dry, and fry lightly in one cup of the olive oil.

Mix together the cheese, pepper, onion, and parsley (and salt to taste if the cheese is mild) and push the mixture into the slits.

Roll the aubergines in one cup of the breadcrumbs and dip into the beaten egg. Roll again in the rest of the crumbs and fry until golden brown in the remaining olive oil. Serve hot or cold.

If any of the breadcrumbs, egg, or cheese, is left over, *see* Courgettes au Gratin, below.

Note: *Bourékia* are really small pies. These get their name from the crust when they have been fried.

Baked Mackerel   Koliós sto Foúrno

"Each to its own season, and mackerel in August" - old saying

108

This is about the best season for big catches of mackerel, complete with roes, and the simplest way of cooking them is the tastiest.

Clean the fish, removing heads and guts, and lay them in an oiled baking tin which takes them fairly tightly. Cut 2 or 3 slashes in the top side of each, and press slivers of garlic into them.

Cover with chopped or grated tomatoes and thinly sliced onion, and strew with oregano or chopped parsley. Season with salt and pepper. Some potatoes cut in quarters can go into the spaces between the fish.

Pour over a cup (or more) of tomato juice or water, and up to half a cup of oil, and bake, uncovered, in a moderate oven for about an hour, basting occasionally.

Serve warm or cold.

Peach Jam   Rodákino Marmeláda

2 kilos of peaches, firm and not over-ripe, yielding
**   just over 1 1/2 kilos when cleaned and de-stoned**
1 1/4 kilos sugar
1 1/2 cups water
juice of 1 lemon
3 tbsp. chopped almonds

Pour some boiling water over the peaches, turn them over in it for about thirty seconds, and replace with cold. Skin them, remove the stones and dark membranes surrounding them, and chop into quarters or eighths. Butter a large, heavy-bottomed pan to prevent burning and simmer the fruit for twenty to thirty minutes with the water. Mash the fruit with a potato masher or the back of a wooden spoon, but if some of the pieces stay intact they make a pleasant fruity jam compared with peach butter, which is sieved to produce an intended smooth texture. When soft, add the sugar and lemon juice, stir to dissolve, and bring to a fast boil. Boil for fifteen to twenty minutes, stirring occasionally, wearing oven gloves as it spits horribly. Test after fifteen minutes (*see*Jams and Jellies, Tests for Setting, in Basic). Stir in the almonds and cool slightly before spooning into warm jars.

Note: If no scales are available, use seven cups of chopped fruit (packed in) to four and a half cups (1 kilo) sugar and one cup water.

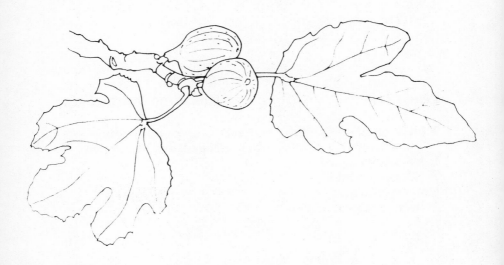

Fig Jam   **Sýko Marmeláda**

Black figs, which have tough skins, make excellent jam. Skin and halve them, simmer till soft with a little water (as above) and add *half* their weight in sugar and plenty of lemon juice. Continue as for Peach Jam, above.

Fig Preserve   Sýko Glykó

This recipe was adapted from one for Strawberry Preserve, so it is only a "Greek-type" spoon sweet. *See* Fresh Fig Preserve in May for the usual Greek recipe.

1 kilo figs, green /yellow variety, small, whole, and not over-ripe
1/2 kilo sugar
1 cup water
1 tbsp. lemon juice
1 cinnamon stick (5 cm.)
2 - 3 cloves

Snip off stems of the figs and lightly scrape off any blemishes, otherwise leave skin intact. Put the sugar into a fairly large pan, add the water and lemon juice, and stir over low heat till quite dissolved. Bring the syrup to a rapid boil and boil till "soft ball" stage is reached (235° approximately, *see* Jams and Jellies and Preserves in Basic).

Add the figs, turning them over gently to coat with syrup. Cover the pan, remove from heat, and leave to cool for at least twenty minutes. Return the pan to the stove and add the spices. Bring the syrup to the boil, uncovered, until it rises and covers the figs, then remove from the heat again and allow to subside. Skim the surface and repeat boiling process twice more. Lift out the figs with a slotted spoon into a bowl and tip any extra syrup back into the pan. Boil syrup rapidly till setting stage is reached (tested on a chilled saucer). Then return the figs to the pan, bring to the boil again, and boil for eight minutes. Remove spices, cool slightly, and pour into warmed jars with wide mouths, distributing the figs evenly. If it sets too thickly or begins to crystalize (even with only half weight of sugar to fruit), stir in another teaspoon of lemon juice.

To serve as a "spoon sweet" (*glykó tou koutalioú*), scoop out a whole fig onto a small saucer together with a spoonful of the syrup. Offer with a glass of cold water.

September

Recipes

Tomato Fritters — *Domatokeftédes Santorínis*
Vegetable Fritters — *Pseftokeftédes*
Stuffed Aubergines — *Imám Bayaldí*
Snails — *Salingária*
Red Pepper Salad — *Piperiés Saláta*
Red Peppers to Freeze — *Kókkines Piperiés yia to Katapsíkti*
Fried Peppers — *Piperiés Tiganités*
Courgette Omelette — *Kolokythákia me Avgá*
Beef in Tomato Sauce with Aubergines — *Moschári Kokkinistó me Melitzánes*
Moussaka — *Moussaká*
False Moussaka — *Pseftomoussakás*
Nutty Semolina Mould — *Halvás tou Monasterioú*
Grapes in Syrup — *Soultanína Glykó*
Brandied Grape Jam — *Stafýli Marmeláda*
Pickled Onions — *Kremmydákia Toursí*

Tempestuous rains often break the scorching summer heat, usually in the first few days of the month (if not at the very end of August), and spirits as well as plants and trees are revived. Thereafter the sun returns, to ripen apples, pears, grapes, pumpkins, and all the nuts: almonds, walnuts, hazelnuts, pistachios.

112

Peppers are the dominant theme this month, in every shape and size, the new ones being long, red, and carrot shaped (from Florina in northern Greece), or pale green and curled like a horn, hence their name, the Greek word for horn, *kérata*. The big round green ones are ripening to a glossy scarlet or are still parti-coloured. Cabbages are new in mid-month and so is spinach. Beetroots are back after only a short break. There are still green beans and some kinds have ripened to give pink beans in a dried-up skin. The long aubergines have shown no sign of giving up, but the round ones have shrivelled, to return at the end of the month, when small courgettes also make a come-back, together with the large, marrow-like ones. Cucumbers are large and have rather a lot of seeds, but are fine for *tzatzíki*, and parsley is plentiful, as are tomatoes, celery, carrots, and onions. Towards the end of the month the tiny onions appear, and the first cauliflowers. Okra is still to be had, as are chicory and *vlíta* for boiled salads.

Tiny *marídes* (often called smelts or whitebait, but, officially, pickerel) should be in the market at the end of the month (it is illegal to catch them earlier), and there are long thin garfish (*zargánes*), with vicious looking noses and green bones, nevertheless delicious fried. The first hake arrives, local and fresh, later to be overtaken by imported cod which goes by the same name, *bakaliáros*. After heavy rain there are some live snails (*salingária*) in the market. The Greeks keep them for some days after purchase, feeding them on branches of thyme, or flour, to cleanse and sweeten them.

There are plenty of watermelons, but fewer honeydew melons, which are replaced by round yellow ones striped' with black. These have little flavour but are good chilled, and useful for mixed fruit salad basket. The best grapes are the muscat and the small seedless white variety, *soultanínes*, nice for preserves. Grape juice (*moústo*) also becomes available (*see* Must in October). Peaches are going off, to be replaced by eating apples, and there are still big golden pears. Figs are usually expensive or are being given away, as they do not keep. Eaten fresh, they are also delicious sprinkled with ouzo. They are being dried this month and packed away between bay leaves, or sprinkled with sesame seeds or crumbled thyme. Prickly pears (called French or Arabian figs, *Frangósyka* or *Aravósyka*) are sprouting ripe fruit round the edges of their large fleshy leaves. Their spines are poisonous, so the fruit should not be picked without thick gloves. They are said to be good for kidney complaints. Green lemons are offered, and a few may have ripened by the end of the month. Fresh walnuts and almonds are moist, their shells easy to crack. There are no currants till next month when the small black grapes have dried. Many have grown in the Corinth area, which accounts for their English name, currants.

Pistachio nuts are being harvested from the end of August, many on the island of Aegina, which gives them their Greek name, *Fistíkia Aigínis*, but also around the shores of the Saronic Gulf. Whole families are involved in the picking, shelling, and drying. The nuts in their hard shells are removed from their sticky, resinous outer skins and washed in salty water, or rolled in the sea in sacks, when the waves do both jobs. After drying slowly in the oven, they are sprinkled with salt and citric or tartaric acid (*xinó* or *kitrikó oxí*), which enhances the characteristic pink and green colour of the nuts. They are also good to eat now, unsalted, fresh, and moist.

Corn (*kalambóki*) on the cob is being sold on the streets, roasted over braziers. It is, however, not sweet corn but another kind of maize. Corn for popcorn is called just that and can be found in shops selling dried fruit and nuts.

Tomato Fritters   Domatokeftédes Santorínis

Add water or milk and water to about four tablespoons of self-raising flour in a bowl to make a fairly thick batter. Season with salt, pepper, and oregano. Add drained, skinned tomatoes cut into very small pieces and finely chopped parsley. Alternatively, use the juice of the tomatoes instead of the milk and water. In Santorini they also stir in some of the local speciality, puréed split peas (*fáva, see* Split Pea Purée in February), and chopped fresh basil.

Drop tablespoonfuls into very hot fat or olive oil and fry quickly on both sides. Serve hot.

See Fritter Batter in Basic for a richer batter mixture with egg.

Vegetable Fritters   Pseftokeftédes

Another version adds grated courgette, chopped mint, and garlic, if liked, to the above.

Stuffed Aubergine   Imám Bayaldí

Many recipes in English describe halved (or even sliced) round aubergines for *Imám*, but the Greek consensus is with the whole long variety, slit once or twice, stuffed with an onion, parsley, and tomato mixture and baked in the oven or simmered in a saucepan on top of the cooker. (For the other way, *see* Aubergine "Shoes" in July.)

1 kilo long aubergines (but not so long they won't fit
  in the frying pan, whole)
1 1/2 cups olive oil
4 - 6 very ripe tomatoes
2 - 3 onions, peeled and chopped
4 cloves of garlic, sliced
1 tbsp. chopped parsley
salt and pepper
1 tsp. sugar

Wash and dry the aubergines, remove stalks and green caps. Make one or two slits in them on top as they lie flat, nearly from end to end. Prize them open a little, salt inside, and leave upside down in the sun to drain for at least thirty minutes to remove the bitter green liquid, or soak in warm salted water and then drain well.

Meanwhile, prepare the filling. Grate the tomatoes into a bowl, holding the stalk end and starting to rub where they have burst with ripeness. If they are not so ripe, peel and chop them. Saute the onions and garlic in half a cup of the oil, add the tomatoes, parsley, salt, pepper, and sugar. Cook the mixture till most of the moisture has evaporated. Put aside to cool.

Rinse the aubergines and pat dry on kitchen paper, wiping inside as well, and fry gently on both sides in the other cup of oil. When limp, lift them into a flat baking dish for the oven, slit side up, or into a wide-based saucepan to cook on top of the stove (a fish kettle is excellent). Either way, it is convenient to use a pan that can be brought to the table, so as not to disturb the prepared dish. Spoon the mixture into each aubergine and pour the remaining oil from the pan over them. If cooking on top of the stove, add some tomato juice or one cup of water and a teaspoon of tomato concentrate (a wineglass of red wine is also a distinct improvement). Let simmer for thirty minutes to one hour.

This dish is satisfactorily done in a saucepan, especially

if both aubergine and stuffing have been well cooked first, so that a shorter time is required and there is less chance of burning. Rock the pan to swill the sauce all around as it thickens.

Serve warm or cold, with something plain to mop up the oil; country bread, boiled potatoes, or rice. Alternatively, a large potato, cut into small pieces, can be used to fill in the spaces between the aubergines.

Snails   Salingáriá

Sprinkle the snails with plenty of salt, turning them over so they are all salted, then thoroughly wash them in several changes of water. Drain and parboil them (six minutes) and drain again, then simmer in a seasoned onion and tomato sauce till tender, approximately forty-five minutes. Serve with chopped parsley.

Red Pepper Salad   Piperiés Saláta

The long red peppers in the shops now are a delight to the eye. They are easily prepared as a delight to the palate, as either an hors d'oeuvres or a side salad with a herb omelette.

Wipe peppers and cut a ring round the stalk, removing it like a cork, seeds and all. You may also slit them in half and remove the seeds more easily. Grease a baking tin and lay them in it, not touching one another. Bake in a hot oven for about half an hour or put them under the grill, turning them over before they char. Leave to cool.

Peel off the skin, dribble a little olive oil over them, and sprinkle with salt before serving. They are delicious served with anchovies or sliced thin with julienne strips of *graviéra* cheese and a vinaigrette dressing. *See* Sauces in Basic.

117

Red Peppers
to Freeze

Kókkines Piperiés
yia to Katapsíkti

Wash pepper, slice in half, and remove stalk and seeds.
Blanch in boiling water for four minutes. Drain, and
plunge into cold water. Drain again and dry. Wrap in
polythene to freeze.

Fried Peppers

Piperiés Tiganités

My friend Hilde Stern Xinotroulias told me of this
method of preparing peppers to serve as a salad. She
suggests the ordinary green, or bell, peppers or the long,
yellowish wax variety.

1/2 kilo peppers
1 - 2 cloves garlic
olive oil
vinegar
salt

Prepare peppers as above and heat olive oil in a heavy
pan. Fry peppers and garlic for about five minutes (cover
the pan), then turn them over to wilt the other sides.
Discard the garlic and continue cooking in uncovered pan
till peppers are soft. Sprinkle them with salt.
Remove to a serving dish with a little of the olive oil
and add vinegar to taste.
Serve warm or cold. They will keep a week in the
refrigerator, but they are so good that this rarely occurs.

Courgette Omelette

Kolokythákia me Avgá

1 kilo courgettes (large size)
1/2 cup olive oil and margarine, mixed half and half
parsley, chopped
salt and pepper
1 - 2 cloves garlic, crushed (optional)
5 - 6 eggs, lightly beaten
3 - 4 tbsp. grated cheese (optional)

Wash and scrape the courgettes, cut them in half lengthways, and remove the seeds. Cut in thick slices.

Heat the olive oil and margarine in a large frying pan and cook the courgettes and seasoning in it, covered, till soft, about half an hour.

Stir in the eggs gently (and cheese, if liked) and cook for a further few minutes, covered, over low heat. Serve at once.

(*See* also Tomato Scrambled Eggs in August.)

119

Beef in Tomato Sauce   Moschári Kokkinistó

1 - 1 1/2 kilos stewing beef, cut into serving pieces
3 - 4 tbsp. vegetable cooking fat *or* half fat and half oil
2 onions, chopped
2 cloves garlic, chopped
1/2 kilo fresh tomatoes, grated
3 - 4 tbsp. tomato paste
2 cups chopped celery, carrot, and parsley
1/2 cup dry white wine
pinch of cinnamon
salt and pepper

Heat the fat and fry the meat on all sides. Add the onions and garlic and sauté them lightly. Stir in the tomato pulp, chopped vegetables, and wine. Season and stir, adding water if necessary to cover the meat. Lower the heat and simmer for about an hour, till the meat is tender.

Transfer the meat to a serving dish and keep hot. Strain the liquid into another pan, add a little water, bring up to a boil again, and pour over the meat.

Serve with boiled potatoes or macaroni.

Beef in Tomato Sauce   Moschári Kokkinistó
with Aubergines   me Melitzánes

Braise beef as above. Chop some long aubergines in half (the thin ones are the best) and leave them in salted water for about half an hour. Drain and dry them, and fry before adding to the stewing beef for the last twenty minutes or so. If not fried, they must be added soon after the meat. They should not be disturbed or they will break up. It is more satisfactory to finish the cooking in a casserole in the oven, or in a pressure cooker.

See also Chicken in Tomato Sauce in May and Stewed Beef with Quinces in November.

Moussaka   Moussaká

The dish which seems to spell Greece for so many visitors is this one, usually made with aubergines but sometimes with courgetttes or, later in the year, potatoes, which alters its character completely. It can also be made with all three, with a base of potatoes, then aubergines and, lastly, courgettes, inter-layered with minced meat and topped with béchamel sauce.   .

Its main advantage is perhaps that it can be partly prepared overnight and assembled in the morning, as it is rather time consuming.

meat sauce, double quantity (*see* Sauces in Basic)
2 kilos aubergines, preferably the long ones
3 - 4 cups béchamel sauce, double quantity (*see*Sauces in Basic)
1/2 cup dried breadcrumbs *or* crumbled rusks
1 - 1 1/2 cups grated cheese

Make up a meat sauce in one saucepan and a bechamel sauce in another. (Keep covered till ready to use.) Fry the sliced aubergines quickly, without flour (*see* Fried Aubergines in July) or, for a lighter, less oily dish, grill or roast them in the oven, lightly oiled, till soft. They are better freshly prepared, but can also be done the evening before if time is short.   .

To assemble: Lightly grease a baking tin, usually oblong, and sprinkle with breadcrumbs or crumbled rusks. Lay in half the fried aubergines to cover the bottom completely and spread the thick meat sauce over them. Then lay on the rest of the aubergines and cover with bechamel sauce. The cheese can be sprinkled over each layer or some of it can be mixed into the sauce but, either way, some cheese should be sprinkled on top.

Bake for forty-five minutes, till crusty brown on top, or take your dish to the communal oven at your local bakery and relax while it cooks and your own kitchen stays cool. It costs only a few drachmas. Serve warm or cold.

False Moussaka   Pseftomoussakás

A family dish which uses up vegetables in the store cupboard

Fry some aubergine and courgette slices and reserve. Chop and fry onions and garlic. Slice tomatoes and potatoes. Boil potato slices for five minutes, or lightly fry these as well. Drain. Chop parsley and slice a couple of sweet peppers.

Dribble oil over base of oven dish or *tapsí*. Lay in a layer of aubergines, then potatoes, then onion and garlic, then courgetttes, parsley, peppers, and, lastly, tomatoes, seasoning between each layer with pepper and salt. Press down firmly and cover with a mixture of four eggs beaten into one cup of milk. Top with grated cheese and bake in a moderate oven for forty-five minutes.

Nutty Semolina Mould   Halvás tou Monasterioú

This recipe is from a convent and the cake is cooked on top of the stove. It requires a steady hand as it involves pouring hot syrup into boiling oil. It is called the 1, 2, 3, 4 method, but three cups of sugar is rather sweet, and 4 becomes four and one-half cups of water.

122

1 cup olive oil
2 cups coarse *or* fine semolina, as preferred
2 - 3 cups sugar
4 1/2 cups water
chopped nuts (almond or pistachio)
1 stick of cinnamon (5 cm.)
lemon peel, grated (one lemon)
2 - 3 cloves
powdered cinnamon

Make a syrup with the sugar, water, grated lemon peel, and spices in one saucepan, boiling it for four minutes. Meanwhile, bring the oil to the boil in another, larger saucepan. Keep the syrup on the side of the stove.

Throw semolina and nuts into the corn oil, quickly stirring till absorbed. Continue cooking slowly for a further ten minutes, stirring to prevent sticking. Pour the syrup (having removed the spices) into it — stand back! — and stir till the mixture thickens and comes away from the sides of the pan.

Allow to cool slightly and press into dampened jelly moulds or breakfast cups. Double the above quantity fills a two pint ring mould. Tip out after a few minutes onto a dish and dust with cinnamon. Decorate with a few more nuts. If the lemon peel is pared thinly in strips it becomes crystalized in the syrup and can be used as decoration.

See also Orange Semolina Cake in April.

Note: This has no connection with the *Halvás* from Macedonia which you can buy in slabs during Lent, made of sesame seed oil and either honey or a sugar syrup.

Grapes in Syrup   Soultanína Glykó

1 kilo seedless white grapes (*soultanínes*)
3/4 kilo sugar
3/4 cup water
2 - 4 tsp. lemon juice
1/2 tsp. vanilla *or* 1 tbsp. brandy

Choose firm, plump grapes. Remove them from their stalks, wash well, and drain in a colander.

Put the sugar, water, and two teaspoons lemon juice into a pan and bring to the boil, stirring to prevent sticking. Boil till syrupy (thread stage). Remove from the heat and add the grapes. Bring to the boil again, and boil rapidly (rapid boiling helps to maintain the colour of the fruit), removing from the heat two or three times to allow froth to subside, until the syrup coats the fruit, about ten to fifteen minutes.

Remove pan from the heat and stir in vanilla or brandy (and the rest of the lemon juice to counter crystalization) and leave to cool a little. Pour into jars and cover when cold. As it is a "spoon sweet," the syrup will be a little runny. For a jam, *see* the next recipe. *Fraoúles*, the red "strawberry" grapes, are done the same way, but the pips must be removed first.

Brandied Grape Jam   Stafýli Marmeláda

Use the same quantities of fruit, sugar, and lemon juice, but omit the water and increase the brandy to six tablespoons (half a cup). Put all into the pan together and boil till set.

Pickled Onions   Kremmydákia Toursí

2 kilos baby (pickling) onions (*kremmydákia or kokkári*)
salted water to cover
8 cups white wine vinegar
1 hot red pepper
1 whole piece of ginger root,* crushed, *or* powdered ginger
1 torn bay leaf
2 tsp. peppercorns, crushed

* Available in specialist spice stores (*piperórizo*).

Peel the onions. This is done most easily by putting them into a colander or chip basket which will sit inside a large saucepan. Half fill the saucepan with water and bring to the boil. Lower the colander into the water and leave for thirty seconds only. Transfer to a bowl of very cold water. The skins then slip off easily.

Leave the onions in cold salted water for forty-eight hours, then drain.

Bring the vinegar to the boil and skim off the froth. Boil the onions in the vinegar for five minutes. Spoon them into heated jars and fill up with vinegar.

Into each jar put a small piece of hot red pepper, a piece or a pinch of ginger, a torn bay leaf, and a few crushed peppercorns. Close the jars when cold, using a plastic lid.

October

Recipes

Octopus with Macaroni	*Ktapódi me Macaronáki*
Octopus as an Hors d'oeuvre	*Ktapódi Mezé*
Pickled Octopus	*Ktapódi Toursí*
Cuttlefish in Tomato Sauce	*Soupiá me Sáltsa*
Cuttlefish with Spinach	*Soupiá me Spanáki*
Mushrooms	*Manitária*
Stewed Dried Broad Beans	*Koukiá (Xerá) Yachní*
Dried Ful Medames Beans	*Foúlia*
Beef and Onion Casserole	*Stifádo Moschári*
Walnut Cake with Syrup	*Karydópitta*
Baked Quinces	*Kydónia sto Foúrno*
Home-Made Wine	*Spitikó Krasí*
Must	*Moústos*
Grape Mould	*Moustalevriá*
Grape Syrup	*Petimézi*

See also:
Beetroot Salad (April), Cabbage Salad (February), Green Beans (July), Spinach Pie (February), Spinach with Rice (April).

Other suggestions:
Potatoes dauphinois, chicken with walnut sauce, pork chops with herbs and wine, curd creams, cheesecake, tomato ketchup.

October in Greece is still early autumn, with plenty of sunny days. Summer salads are still possible, with lettuces and small plum tomatoes, as well as ordinary tomatoes. Also available are cabbages, both red and white; beetroots; carrots, potatoes, aubergines, courgettes, chicory, and green beans. Spinach and cauliflowers are back, and there are masses of peppers of all sizes. There are huge onions and also tiny ones, for *stifádo* (*see* below) and for pickling (*see* Pickled Onions in September). Pumpkins and sweet potatoes can be found in some greengrocers' shops.

For fish, *marídes* are still small, and delicious fried. Shrimps (*garídes*) and scampi (*karavídes*) can be simmered in lightly salted water, peeled, and eaten unadorned, or served with an oil and lemon dressing (*see* Sauces in Basic). Octopus, squid, and cuttlefish are plentiful this month as the weather is usually fine for the fishermen.

There may be catches of small tunny fish (*tónnos* or *tonnáki*), which make marvelous rich, tasty steaks, grilled or baked in the oven with a wine or tomato sauce. (*See* Fish in Basic.) A similar rich fish, the *palamída*, a bonito, is also excellent for steaks. In the old days they were often baked in the communal oven in a curved roof-tile *keramída*, hence *palamída keramída*. The larger bonita are preserved in salt for the winter and appear in the greengrocers' shops as *lakérda*, thick slices in oil, without bones, alongside imported salted herrings, *rénga*.

Grapes, apples, and pears continue from September, along with a few figs, and in mid-month we get quinces and pomegranates, and the green lemons are juicy though not yet ripened. Grapes are also being harvested for wine, great baskets overflowing with sticky fruit and in the towns and villages huge barrels are lined up outside each taverna to be cleaned out in anticipation of the new grape must which is delivered by huge tankers.Dried fruits from this summer are ready: currants and sultanas and the larger raisins; prunes; figs; peaches; cherries; apricots, the latter mostly imported.

October

There are walnuts, hazelnuts, fresh pistachios, almonds, and, by mid-month, chestnuts.

There are few melons to be had, except the rather insipid winter type, and oranges have not yet ripened.

The soft cheeses are to be found again this month, fresh *mizíthra*, *anthótyro*, and *manoúri*, which make excellent desserts such as curd creams, cheesecake, and Sweet Cheese Pies (*see* April).

Loukoumádes are to be found bubbling in oil at corner shops and some *kafeneía*. Resembling ring doughnuts, they are served hot, with a topping of honey syrup and cinnamon.

Octopus with Macaroni   Ktapódi me Makaronáki

To serve as a main dish

1 large octopus or 2 small ones (1 1/2 - 2 kilos)
1/4 cup wine vinegar
1/4 cup olive oil
1 medium onion and/or 2 cloves garlic, chopped
1/2 kilo tomatoes, peeled and chopped *or* 1 tbsp. tomato
  paste dissolved in 1/2 cup hot water
pepper (no salt)
2 cups macaroni (short lengths)
parsley, chopped

If you have caught your own octopus it must be rubbed and slapped on a rough rock for about 1/2 hour to tenderize it. Wash it in plenty of fresh water and cut it into chunks with kitchen scissors or a sharp knife. Cut out the hard centre core, or beak. You can also simmer the whole octopus first, drain and cool it, and then cut it in pieces, removing some of the skin if preferred and discarding the beak.

Put the octopus into a saucepan, without water, cover,

and simmer it for fifteen minutes (liquid will seep out of it), then add the vinegar and continue simmering for another fifteen to twenty minutes. Add the oil and onions (and garlic), tomato, and pepper, cover, and continue cooking over low heat for about two hours. Liquid accumuulates in this dish, rather than drying out.

Boil the macaroni in salted water for twenty minutes, drain, and either stir into the sauucepan or put into a casserole, preferably earthenware. Add the octopus and sauce and cook in a medium oven until both octopus and macaroni are tender.

Sprinkle with chopped parsley before serving.

Octopus as an Hors d'oeuvre   Ktapódi Mezé

Wash octopus and chop up into small pieces. Either simmer till tender as above or boil in about four cups water over moderate heat. Drain and put into a dish, pour over some olive oil, and sprinkle with vinegar and oregano. Alternatively, make a dressing of three-quarters cup olive oil, one-quarter cup lemon juice, three to four crushed cloves of garlic, pepper, and oregano or chopped parsley, pour over the octopus, cover, and leave to marinate overnight in the fridge.

See Octopus in Wine Sauce in May.

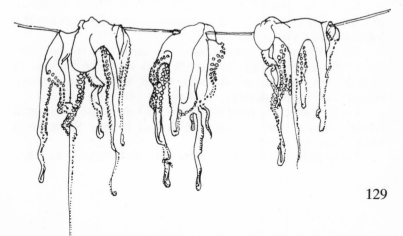

Pickled Octopus   Ktapódi Toursí

    An octopus, prepared as above and marinated in an oil and vineger dressing, will keep in the fridge for three to four days, and the flavour improves with keeping. To keep for even longer, add more vinegar to make Pickled Octopus and keep in the fridge in a screwtop jar for up to a month. (Keep for a week before opening.) We put the cooked octopus pieces into a large jar, add the marinade, top up with more vinegar and oregano, screw down firmly, and take it by air to England where it is greeted with cries of delight. It is also quite a topic for discussion at the Customs!

Cuttlefish in Tomato Sauce   Soupiá me Sáltsa

1 1/4 kilos cuttlefish
1 cup olive *or* sunflower oil
2 large onions, chopped
1 clove garlic, chopped
1 cup white wine vinegar
1/2 kilo fresh *or* 1 can tomatoes
salt and pepper
parsley, chopped

    Clean the cuttlefish very well, washing them in plenty of water. Discard the eyes and beak. Carefully remove the ink sacs and put aside.

    Heat the oil in a saucepan and saute the onions and garlic till soft. Cut the cuttlefish into strips and allow to brown with the onions. Add the wine, tomatoes, salt and pepper, chopped parsley, and about one cup of water.

    Cover and cook over very low heat or in the oven until tender, about one to one and a half hours. Serve with boiled rice or noodles.

    For a richer dish, some of the ink can be added with the

wine. The ink can also be fried in a little oil and used as a dip.

Squid (*kalamarákia*) can be cooked in the same way, but the rice is usually added to the simmering squid to cook till it absorbs the liquid. *See* Fried Squid in August for cleaning squid.

Cuttlefish with Spinach   Soupiá me Spanáki

A delicious dish for weight-watchers

Replace the wine in the above recipe with the juice of one lemon and omit the tomatoes. Reduce the amount of oil in the cooking. Add about one and a half kilos spinach, washed, chopped, and drained, when the onions and cuttlefish have browned. Season, and stir in the parsley. Cook as above, adding water if required when the spinach has wilted. It must all be reabsorbed by the end of cooking.

Mushrooms   Manitária

Greek recipe books totally ignore mushrooms, and the word is associated in the popular mind with the occasional case of poisoning. Fresh, cultivated mushrooms are now available in the larger greengrocers. The following recipe appears in foreign recipe books as Mushrooms à la Grecque.

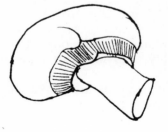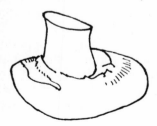

1/4 kilo fresh mushrooms
3 tbsp. olive oil
1 tbsp. water
salt and pepper
juice of 1 medium lemon
1 - 2 cloves garlic, crushed
3 tbsp. parsley, finely chopped

Wipe the mushrooms and cut larger ones in half.

Pour the olive oil and water into a frying pan. Stir in the remaining ingredients except the mushrooms, and bring to the boil. Add the mushrooms and simmer for about ten minutes or till tender.

Cool and check seasoning to serve cold.

Stewed Dried Broad Beans   Koukiá (Xerá) Yachní

1/2 kilo dried broad beans
1/2 kilo tomatoes
2 large onions
1/2 cup olive oil
salt and pepper
1 tsp. sugar
1 tbsp. parsley, chopped
pinch dried mint

In this in-between season when the summer vegetables have begun to pall, dried beans are a great standby. They must be soaked overnight like pulses, drained, and the the black "key" to the sprouting end of each is usually cut out.

Boil beans rapidly for ten minutes in water to cover, then simmer with chopped tomatoes and onions, olive oil, salt and pepper, sugar, parsley, and mint, or bake in a casserole in the oven.

They cook very successfully in a pressure cooker. Their rather strong flavour earns them the title "poor man's meat."

See Stewed Fresh Broad Beans in April.

Dried Ful Medames Beans   Foúlia

These Egyptian dried beans are to be found in the
market. They look and taste like small broad beans, though
darker, and the skins are tougher (they are also sold
without skins).

They can be cooked in the same way as broad beans
(above) but in Egypt they are boiled in water only, drained,
and then served with chopped garlic, hard boiled eggs,
chopped parsley, olive oil, lemon juice, and salt and
pepper.

Beef and Onion Casserole   Stifádo Moschári

Also made with hare, rabbit, or tongue. The onions are in
equal proportion to the meat and the sauce is highly spiced,
a rich and warming meal for the first cold days.

1 - 1 1/4 kilos stewing beef
1 - 1 1/4 kilos baby onions
1/2 cup oil
1 tsp. tomato paste stirred into
    1/2 cup red wine and
    2 tbsp. red wine vinegar
1 large bay leaf
3 - 4 cloves garlic
1 small stick cinnamon
pinch of cumin
sprig of rosemary

Cut the meat into cubes and brown them all over in the
oil. Barely cover with hot water, add the tomato paste and
wine, and simmer for about one hour in a heavy-bottomed

133

pan or, preferably, bake in an earthenware casserole in a medium oven.

Peel the onions and lightly criss-cross the base of each with a small sharp knife to keep them whole.

Stir the spices and herbs into the stewing meat and add the onions on top. They could be browned in oil beforehand. If cooking in a pan, a little more hot water may be required.

Simmer gently for a further hour, or more, without stirring to avoid breaking up the onions.

The flavour is improved if this dish is cooked the day before required and heated through slowly but thoroughly before serving.

Walnut Cake with Syrup   Karydópitta

A rich cake without flour

**115 grams butter (1/2 packet less 1 thin slice), softened
4 eggs, separated
1/2 cup sugar
2 cups finely chopped walnuts
1 wineglass brandy
2 cups crushed rusks (about 3/4 packet of *friganiés*)
1 1/2 tsp. baking powder
1 tsp. ground cinnamon
1 tsp. grated orange peel
1/2 cup orange juice (optional, *see* below)**

Syrup:

**2 cups water
1 1/2 cups sugar
lemon peel
1 short cinnamon stick**

Beat the margarine well with the yolks and sugar till light and fluffy. Add the walnuts and brandy.

Stir together the rusks, baking powder, cinnamon, and orange peel. Whip the egg whites till stiff, then add each alternately to the batter and fold in lightly. Add half a cup orange juice if the mixture seems too dry. Turn into an oiled baking tin and bake in a medium oven for about forty minutes.

Prepare the syrup, boiling it for five to six minutes, and then leave to cool.

When the cake comes out of the oven, leave to stand for a few minutes, prick with a fork, then douse with the cooled syrup. When cold, cut in squares or diamond shapes.

Baked Quinces   Kydónia sto Foúrno

Bake quinces, whole, for about forty-five minutes, after scrubbing and buttering them lightly. Cool a little, then scoop out cores and discard. Fill hollows with sultanas, chopped nuts, sugar, and cinnamon. Pour over half a cup warm water. Continue baking till tender, basting occasionally.

If you are in a hurry and they are too hot to handle, they are also very nice with the cores left in, with sugar, or honey, and cinnamon and two tablespoons of water sprinkled over them.

Serve with cream or ice cream.

See Baked Spiced Pears in November.

Home-Made Wine   Spitikó Krasí

It is not difficult to make your own wine if you invest in a barrel and find out from a local taverna when the wine-tanker comes to your neighbourhood.

The barrel must first be rinsed out with lime-water (four or five pieces of lime (*asvésti*) from a local builder's yard to a bucket of water for a 200 kilo barrel) to clean a new one or remove wine stains from a used one. Then it has to be washed out again. The day before the must (*moústos*) is due, half fill the barrel with hot water to expand the wood, add a branch of lemon or pine leaves, and leave to soak overnight.

You can also obtain a lump of resin if you want to make *retsína*; tell your supplier the size of the barrel for the right amount.

After emptying the barrel, fill it nearly to the top with must, plug lightly with a branch of pine or cover with a cheesecloth and leave to ferment, or "boil" (*vrázi*) for a week. Then the alcohol content has to be checked, and there are wine chemists who will do this for you if you take them a sample. The gravity should be 12 1/2 degrees. If it is more you will be advised to add so much water, and if less so much sugar. They may also give you some preservative (*fármako*) to add (tannin and citric acid, removed in the pressing), but it is not always necessary for *retsína* as the must is usually already treated with metasulphate. A second check is taken after a further two or three weeks.

Leave the wine to bubble gently for a month or six weeks and, when it is quiet, plug with a cork and seal with plaster of Paris (*gýpso*).

"How soon can we start drinking it?" prompts the surprising answer, "When the north wind blows." In other words, a cold snap is necessary to bring the wine to maturity. This should be in December.

Old Greek Saying

In old tavernas which still have barrels of wine lining the walls, one may not be served vinegar (*xýdi*) with one's salad, only lemon juice. Vinegar should not even be mentioned in case the wine in the barrels takes fright and turns sour! There is even a special word coined to disguise any reference to vinegar; you should ask for *glykádi*, meaning sweetness, so as not to cause offence!

Must   Moústos

Must is obtainable now the grapes are being pressed for wine (*see* above). To make your own, use sweet white grapes which yield half their volume in juice, so you will need three or four kilos for a reasonable quantity of must, i. e. a litre. Wash the grapes, strip them from their stalks, and boil for twenty minutes or so, with a cup of water, pressing the fruit with a potato masher to extract all the juice. Pour the panful into a cloth bag (as for a jelly) hanging over a bowl and allow to drip all night. Squeeze out the last drops of juice and discard the pulp. *See* Grape Mould, below.

137

October

Grape Mould   Moustalevriá

Half fill your largest pan with grape must. Boil for
about forty minutes, till reduced by half, then remove from
the heat and sprinkle with one tablespoon wood ash
(*stáchti*) or a special pinky-white earth (*hóma*) to clear the
liquid. It will froth up. Stir, skim, and leave to stand. (If
preferred, tie the earth in a cloth bag and drop into the
boiling must and discard later. If ash or earth are hard to
come by, a piece of firm dry bread will have nearly the
same effect.) After a couple of hours, strain through a
piece of cloth into another pan or bowl (stainless) and leave
to stand overnight. The next day, pour off the juice
carefully and discard any remaining deposit.

Now measure the must: For seven cups use one cup of
fine semolina (*semigdáli psiló*), mixing it with two cups of
the must. Bring the rest to the boil and add the semolina
mixture over low heat. (*Alévri* in the name *moustalevriá*
means flour, but semolina is usually used. Cornflour is used
in the quick version, below.) Simmer, stirring, till it
thickens (ten to twenty minutes) and bubbles form on top.

Pour into shallow bowls ready to serve and sprinkle
with cinnamon and finely-chopped nuts or sesame seeds.
Leave to cool and set. If turned out onto plates the moulds
have a lovely shiny surface.

It can also be poured into a baking tin to a depth of one
and a half to two centimetres, sprinkled with cinnamon,
and cut into squares when cold. If these are turned out onto
a large tray and left in the sun for several days to dry out (or
in a very slow oven for a few hours if the sun is unobliging)
they become chewy candies which can be stored in tins.
Flour or cornflower can be used in the same proportions as
semolina, but flour requires rather long cooking. A spoon
drawn through the boiling mixture should reveal the base
of the pan momentarily. Cornflour produces a jelly-like
consistency (and one can use a jelly or ring mould to good

138

effect), while flour gives a soft toffee-type candy. The process is similar to that for Quince Paste (*see* November).

Quick Version

**3 tsp. sugar
3 tbsp. cornflour
2 cups must (can be canned grape juice)
nuts
cinnamon**

Mix sugar and cornflour together in a bowl. Add juice slowly and stir till smooth.

Bring to the boil and simmer for five minutes, stirring all the time. Pour into individual bowls and sprinkle with chopped nuts or sesame seeds and cinnamon. Leave to cool.

Grape Syrup   Petimézi

You can prepare Grape Syrup for storage by boiling the strained must steadily till it becomes syrupy (large thread stage). Bottle when cool.

November

Recipes

Bean Stew	*Fasólia Yachní*
	or Fasoláda
Baked Beans	*Gígantes Plakí*
Pork with Celery	*Hirinó me Sélino*
Pork with Celeriac	*Hirinó me Selinórizo*
Green Pepper and Onion Salad	*Piperiés kai Kremmýdi*
	Saláta
Stewed Beef with Quinces	*Moschári me Kydónia*
Stewed Pork with Quinces	*Hirinó me Kydónia*
Shark	*Galéos*
Leek Pie	*Prasópitta*
Pumpkin	*Kolokýtha (Aravikí or Kókkini)*
Sautéed Pumpkin	*Kolokýthia Pouré*
Pumpkin Seed "Nibbles"	*Pasatémpo*
Marrons Glacés	*Kástana Glassé*
Aubergines	*Melitzánes*
Pickled Aubergines	*Melitzánes Toursí*
Aubergine Preserve	*Melitzanáki Glykó*
Olives	*Éliés*
Throumbes	
Fruit	*Froúta*
Baked Spiced Pears	*Ahládi Kompósta sto Foúrno*
Quince Preserve (English)	*Kydóni Glykó*
Quince Preserve (Greek)	*Kydóni Glykó*
Quince Jelly	*Kydóni Beldé*
Quince Paste	*Kydonópasto*
Dates in Syrup	*Hourmádes Glykó*

Other suggestions:
Leeks in yoghurt sauce, marinated raw fish, goulash, fig sauce, mincemeat, apple cake, orange and date chutney, mint and apple jelly.

The winter vegetable season is in full swing now: cabbages (red and white), leeks, onions, celery, cauliflower, beetroots, spinach, carrots, and potatoes. There are still peppers, aubergines, courgettes, cucumbers and lettuces, but red tomatoes are going off. Sweet potatoes and pumpkins can be found, and several methods of cooking the latter are given which can be used at any time till spring (*see* Pumpkin Pie in March). Olives are at last being harvested, and the new season's pulses are ready: lentils, split peas, haricot beans, and chick peas.

As well as the fish mentioned in October there are also small sharks (*galéos*) full of roe, and delicious fried, accompanied by a garlic sauce (*see* below).

Quinces are at their best and cheapest, asking to be made into preserves and jelly; they are also cooked with meat in Greece, rather surprisingly since the Greeks say they dislike the western use of sweet with savoury food. There are quantities of eating apples and pears, and also cooking apples *xynómila*. Lemons are ripe at last, but oranges are still rather sour. Clementines (*Klementínes*) have been introduced recently, and are now ripe, before the mandarins. Kiwifruit (*aktinídia*) are another fruit now produced abundantly in Greece. All dried fruits are to be had, as well as pomegranates, chestnuts, walnuts, and pistachios. Chestnuts are being roasted on charcoal braziers at the corners of city streets and sold in small bags. Some figs are still to be found in the smarter shops and grapes are abundant till the end of the month. Wine grapes have been pressed by now and the remaining pulp (*tsípouro*) is the basis for the rather fierce spirit of the same name (also called *rakí* or *tsikoudiá* in Crete where it is the regional drink). It is also used for making ouzo, when it is flavoured with anise.

Anglo-Saxons start thinking of traditional Christmas cakes and mincemeat, though the Greeks are horrified at the thought of making a cake a month in advance (let alone a pudding a year ahead). Mincemeat can be made with margarine, as suet is not a normal Greek product, unless one takes considerable care with the raw fat. We can, however, prepare Marrons Glâcés very easily, and walnuts appear in several delectable Middle Eastern and Russian dishes.

Bean Stew   Fasólia Yachní
                                 or Fasoláda

1/2 kilo haricot (navy) beans
1 large onion
1 - 2 cloves garlic
1 carrot
1 - 2 stalks of celery (leaves only)
2 - 3 stalks of parsley (leaves only)
2 fresh ripe tomatoes *or* a small can with some juice and/*or*
**   1 tbsp. tomato paste, diluted in hot water (for *Yachní*)**
1/2 cup olive oil, or more
red pepper (1 tsp. *or* a whole tiny pod)
salt
1 bay leaf

Check the beans carefully for small stones or other foreign bodies. Beans in packets are usually cleaned.

Soak the beans overnight in a large bowl with twice their depth of water. The next day boil for about ten minutes, then drain and throw away the water. (If time is short, you can bring the beans to the boil without soaking and then leave them stand for an hour or so before draining.)

Cover the beans again with hot water and boil for

about forty-five minutes, till the water has nearly evaporated.

Meanwhile, prepare the vegetables: peel and chop the onions, garlic and carrot; clean the celery and chop small; chop the parsley and tomatoes if using fresh ones. For *Fasoláda*, add them to the beans with the olive oil and water to cover, and cook till soft. (Twenty minutes in a pressure cooker with salt added afterwards and the recommended amount of water also achieves good results.)

For *Fasólia Yachní* proceed as follows: Sauté the onions and garlic lightly and add the other vegetables and the tomato paste. Simmer for six to eight minutes, then add the beans and turn them in the sauce together with the bay leaf and red pepper. Add more hot water and boil gently for a further hour till soft. Cover the pan and keep the liquid topped up. Add salt to taste towards the end of cooking. This can also be completed in a closed earthenware casserole in an oven, which preserves the flavour better and won't need topping up with water. Remove bay leaf and, especially, the whole pepper before serving.

This is a meal in itself, with bread, salad, and feta cheese, but on the islands it is often served together with fried fish.

Baked Beans   **Gígantes Plakí**

Large butter beans are usually baked in the oven, till all the liquid is absorbed into a thick tomato sauce. Sprinkle with chopped parsley to serve.

This is a popular entrée dish in tavernas, as a little goes a long way.

Pork with Celery   Hirinó me Sélino

1 kilo shoulder of pork (*or* tell the butcher what it is for)
1/2 cup cooking fat *or* oil
2 onions, chopped
salt and pepper
1 kilo celery
1 carrot, sliced (optional)
egg and lemon sauce (*see* Sauces in Basic): 2 eggs and
    1 large lemon

Wash the meat, remove excess fat, and cut into conveniently sized pieces (or chops).

Melt the fat in a pan, put in the meat, and cook for a few minutes on each side to seal. Add the onion and, after a few minutes, three or four cups of water and the seasoning. Cook for forty-five minutes to one hour.

Meanwhile, wash the celery, pulling off any stringy pieces, and cut it into short lengths, reserving some of the leaves. Scrape the root and cut in quarters. Boil it all in a separate saucepan for four or five minutes, to remove bitterness, and then drain. Add to the pork to complete cooking.

When ready to serve, make an egg and lemon sauce, adding a ladleful of the hot stock. Return it to the pan to combine with the juices and thicken slightly, and remove from the heat.

Sprinkle with the remaining leaves, chopped, and serve hot.

Pork with Celeriac   Hirinó me Selinórizo

The celery can be replaced by celeriac which is now available in the cities.

It is peeled, cut in thick slices, and parboiled, as above, before being added to the meat. The egg and lemon sauce can be the thick variety.

Green Pepper and Onion Salad

Piperiés kai Kremmýdi Saláta

3 *or* 4 large green (*or* red) peppers
boiling salted water
4 tbsp. vinegar
2 tbsp. water
2 tsp. sugar
1/2 large onion, grated

Wash peppers, cut off tops, and remove the seeds.

Slice them in fairly thin rings, place in a bowl, and tip boiling salted water over them. Allow to cool in this water before draining.

Make a dressing with the rest of the ingredients and stir the pepper slices into it.

Stewed Beef with Quinces

Moschári me Kydónia

1 kilo stewing beef
1 large onion, chopped
100 grams cooking fat
1 cup hot water *or* stock
2 tbsp. tomato paste *or* a small tin of tomatoes and 1 tbsp. paste
3/4 kilo quinces, peeled, cored, and quartered
    (1 1/2 kilos bought weight)
salt and pepper

Sauté the onions in the fat and add the beef, cut in pieces. Allow to brown, then add the tomato paste stirred into the stock, salt, and pepper.

Simmer for a while, then add the quinces. Cover, and continue cooking gently for about an hour, till the meat is tender. Add more liquid if required, but the resulting sauce should be thick.

Stewed Pork with Quinces   Hirinó me Kydónia

Cook as for beef above, but add one tablespoon sugar and a shake of cinnamon. Replace half a cup water with white wine.
See Beef in Tomato Sauce in September.

Shark   Galéos

Galéos is a small shark (also charmingly called smooth hound), a near relation to the dogfish (*skylópsaro* or *skyláki*). (The Greek name for another variety of dogfish, the well-known English huss, is cat, *gátos*, just to confuse you.)

Remove the head and guts, wash well, and sprinkle with salt and lemon juice. The roes in them at this season are good to eat, too, also fried.

Shark is usually sliced, fried (floured, or in a light batter), and served with a thick garlic sauce (*skordaliá*) made with potatoes (*see* Sauces in Basic). Alternatively, it can be simmered in lemon juice and olive oil, and seasoned with salt, pepper, and oregano. This way it can be served with sauce tartare.

Leek Pie   Prasópitta

A speciality from northern Greece

1 1/2 kilos leeks
300 grams feta, crumbled *or* 1 cup grated cheese
3/4 cup *trahanás* (crushed wheat and milk cereal) *or* a white sauce
3 - 4 eggs (optional)
salt and pepper
1 small bunch of dill

1/2 - 3/4 cup vegetable fat *or* **olive oil and butter mixed**
1/2 kilo *fýllo* **pastry (***see* **Pastry in Basic)**

Cut leeks in quarters, wash thoroughly, and then chop small. Leave to drain in a colander. Some finely chopped dill enhances the flavour.

Melt the vegetable fat or olive oil and butter in a frying pan, but reserve one quarter cup and keep it warm. Saute the leeks gently in the rest till they give up and then re-absorb their liquid. Put aside to cool. (If preferred, the leeks can be used raw, in which case melt only enough vegetable oil or olive oil and butter to oil the pastry sheets, one quarter cup.)

Mix the cheese, *trahanás*, and eggs in a bowl and season with salt and pepper to taste. Stir in the leeks.

Lay five or six *fýllo* sheets in a baking tin, oiling each one lightly (*see* Spinach Pie in February), and then either spread all the filling and cover with the remaining sheets, or spread half, then two or three sheets of *fýllo*, then the rest of the filling, finishing with the remaining sheets.

Cook in a moderate oven for about an hour.

Pumpkin   Kolokýtha (Aravikí or Kókkini)

Pumpkins can be cooked in a variety of ways, which is probably just as well as they come in such enormous sizes, though you can often buy pieces of them by the kilo. North Americans think first of pumpkin pie, especially this month for Thanksgiving Day; the Greeks have a totally different version (*see* Pumpkin Pie in March). But it is excellent cooked as a purée with herbs (*see* Sautéed Pumpkin, below), boiled and mashed as with potatoes or, again in place of potatoes, baked in chunks with roast meat or chicken. A chicken casserole with diced pumpkin and a teaspoonful of turmeric makes a very colourful dish. It can also be steamed, or baked in the oven, before peeling, just cut in large pieces and roasted in a greased pan in the oven on low heat till tender, then scraped out of its shell, far easier and more flavoursome. (This, though, I owe to my American cousins.)

To prepare, cut pumpkin in quarters with a sharp knife, starting near the stalk. Remove seeds and membrane and cut again into manageable pieces. Peel with a potato peeler, then chop into dice. A kilo (bought weight) of pumpkin yields about two and a half cups purée.

See also grating method for Pumpkin Pie in March.

Sautéed Pumpkin   Kolokýtha Pouré

Turn diced pumpkin in margarine melted over low heat, add salt and pepper, and a good tablespoon of oregano or two tablespoons of thyme. Try not to add water, as enough liquid will seep out of the pumpkin during cooking.

Pumpkins can also be used in scone making (using sixty grams mashed pumpkin to seventy-five grams flour), and also soup, chutney, marmelade or as a preserve, though these, of course, are not Greek.

Last, but not least, reserve the seeds for "nibbles":

Pumpkin Seed "Nibbles"   Pasatémpo

To "pass the time" on a journey, at the cinema, or
around the family hearth, Greeks consume quantities of
salted seeds, whether of pumpkin, melon, or sunflower.
They are sold on street corners or in dried fruit stores, but
can easily be prepared at home.

Clean seeds, washing them free from the fibre. Drain
and dry. When enough are collected, cover with water in a
saucepan, adding one teaspoon of salt for each cup of
water. Simmer for up to two hours. Drain and dry in the
sun. (If there is no sun, roast them in a low oven with a
little oil and salt.)

Marrons Glâcés   Kástana Glassé

A three to four day exercise

1 kilo chestnuts

Syrup:

1 kilo sugar and 1 tsp. lemon juice *or*
   **1/2 kilo sugar and 300 grams (4 tbsp.) corn syrup
   (*glykósi*)**
2 cups water
1 tsp. vanilla essence (*or* 1 packet)

First day: Nick the skins of the chestnuts on each flat
side and cook, a few at a time, in a small saucepan of
boiling water for about five minutes. While still hot,
remove shells and skins, taking care not to break the nuts.
This is the hardest part, but half nuts will "take" just as
well.

Put the peeled chestnuts in a pan of cold water and

bring to the boil. Simmer gently for about thirty minutes, till tender, then drain.

Make a syrup with the sugar and water, and corn syrup or lemon juice, bringing it to the boil, uncovered, and boiling fast for five minutes. Add the chestnuts, bring up to the boil again, remove from the heat, and leave in the pan overnight.

Second day: Bring syrup and chestnuts to the boil again and leave for another night. (If the syrup is much reduced, go on to the third stage.)

Third day: Add vanilla to the syrup, bring to the boil, and leave to cool. Lift the nuts out with a slotted spoon and put to drain in a sieve or on a wire rack, with a dish underneath to catch the syrup. Drain overnight. Store between sheets of waxed paper, or wrap in wax paper and foil.

Any smaller pieces can be served as an unusual sweet with a spoonful of the syrup. The remaining syrup can be used as a glaze for other dishes; it is delicious with carrots.

Aubergines   Melitzánes

In the autumn one can sometimes come by long baby aubergines which failed to swell and ripen. They make a delicious preserve (*see* below). They are also excellent pickled, using slightly larger ones of the round variety.

Pickled Aubergines   Melitzánes Toursí

Cut the aubergines in half lengthways, scoop out the soft centres and discard. Boil in salted water for two to three minutes. Drain and stuff with a mixture of chopped carrots, garlic, and minced hot red pepper.

Fit the halves together again, and bind round with the stringy part of celery stalks. Put into large, wide mouthed jars and cover with wine vinegar. Seal with a layer of olive oil.

Cover and store for a week or two, but do not keep too long before using.

Aubergine Preserve   Melitzanáki Glykó

1 1/2 kilos tiny aubergines (the size of a gherkin, about 5 cm. long)

Syrup:

1 1/2 kilos sugar
2 cups water
1 tbsp. lemon juice
1 piece of cinnamon, about 3 cm. long
1 - 2 cloves
blanched almonds (optional)

Remove the stems from the aubergines and cut a slit in the side of each. Put them on to boil till tender, but not soft enough to disintegrate. Drain and cover again with cold water and leave to cool. Drain thoroughly and lay on a cloth to remove all moisture. Push a half almond into each slit (optional).

Make up the syrup and boil till it begins to thicken. Add the aubergines and bring to the boil again. Remove from the heat and leave to cool. Then remove them with a slotted spoon and boil the syrup till thick. Add the aubergines again, bring once more to the boil, and take off the heat. Pot when cool.

November

Olives   Eliés

Slit each olive down one side and put them to soak in cold water, preferably in a glass or pottery jar. Change the water every day for approximately twenty days until the bitterness has gone, which you can verify by tasting. Then soak them for a week in a salt solution strong enough to float a fresh egg.

Rinse well and then soak in vinegar for twelve hours. Drain off the vinegar (keep it for other uses) and place the olives in glass or earthenware jars, covered with olive oil. If you like, you can add flavourings, which can include garlic slivers, lemon slices and leaves, thyme, oregano, or even orange peel.

Throúmbes

These are olives which have ripened on the trees and may have fallen. Huge sheets or nylon netting are spread under the trees to facilitate gathering. They can be preserved in coarse salt but may be good eaten as they are, fruity and soft.

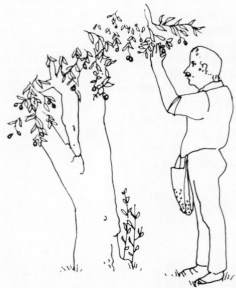

Fruit

There are a number of delicious ways of presenting this month's fruit, apples, pears, and quinces, in spiced syrup, some for storing. The first recipe given here is for pears, but it can be followed also for the other fruit.

Baked Spiced Pears   Ahládi Kompósta sto Foúrno

4 ripe pears
1/2 cup sugar
1 cup fresh orange juice
1 tbsp. fresh lemon juice
1 short cinnamon stick
4 whole cloves
pinch of salt
grated nutmeg

Peel, quarter, and core fruit and place in a casserole. Mix the rest of the ingredients in a saucepan, bring to the boil, and pour over the fruit.

Cover and bake in a moderate oven for thirty minutes. Remove lid and leave a further ten minutes or till fruit is tender.

Quince Preserve (English)   Kydóni Glykó

This 19th century English recipe, adapted slightly, results in a "spoon sweet" suitable for serving to guests in the Greek style (*see* Jams, Jellies, and Preserves in Basic). *See* also the Greek version, below. Both are fruit in a thick syrup, not quite set, but which, if cooked too long, will set into a clear red jelly.

6 large ripe quinces (1 1/2 - 2 kilos)
2 - 2 1/2 cups water
1 - 1 1/2 kilos sugar
lemon juice (from one small lemon or 1/2 a large one)
2 cinnamon sticks (5 cm.)
4 - 5 leaves of scented geranium, *arbaróriza*

Choose ripe, unblemished fruit. Wash, scrub, and dry them. Pare the quinces, cut in quarters, remove cores, and cut again into eighths or, as the cores are frightfully hard, cut the flesh off in chunks and discard cores. Put fruit into a large saucepan and cover with the water. Cover tightly and simmer till tender but not soft, and turning slightly pink. Remove from heat and leave till cold. Then strain off juice, measure, and make up to two and a half cups, adding water if necessary.

Make a syrup with the sugar and measured juice, adding lemon juice, cinnamon sticks, and geranium leaves. Bring to the boil, and boil for only three minutes. Skim well, put in the quinces, and leave to stand for up to three hours. Then remove sticks and leaves, cover pan, and simmer gently till syrup thickens and has turned a deep red and the quinces have become clear. This may take nearly an hour, but the longer time spent in a covered pan improves the colour of the preserve.

Pour into glass jars while still warm, allowing the syrup to cover the fruit completely.

Quince Preserve (Greek) Kydóni Glykó

The Greek version of the above, but it is more like a jam.

Use the same quantities, but the unpeeled fruit is first grated on a very coarse grater (which is sold in Greece for this purpose). Or it can be cut off the core in chunks which can then be put through a mill or food processor, or chopped to produce fat matchsticks, as for French fried potatoes.

Simmer the fruit in the water gently in a covered pan till tender and turning pink. Add the sugar, lemon juice, geranium leaves or cinnamon or one teaspoon vanilla, and continue to simmer till syrup thickens and takes on a good colour.

Stir to distribute fruit and pot while warm.

Quince Jelly   Kydóni Beldé

1 kilo quinces
5 cups water
2 - 3 leaves scented geranium
sugar (*see* below)
2 tsp. lemon juice

Peel and core the quinces. Cut up the flesh and boil gently in the water in a covered pan with two or three leaves of scented geranium till soft, adding the peel and cores tied in a muslin bag. Squeeze bag of cores slightly and discard. Strain the fruit into a bowl overnight, preferably through a jelly-bag.

Measure the juice and add an equal quantity of sugar and lemon juice. Simmer till dissolved, then boil fast till set lightly (*see* Jams and Jellies, Tests for Setting, in Basic). Cool and pot.

This makes a good substitute for red currant jelly for expatriates, served with roast lamb.

The remaining pulp can be used for the following recipe for quince paste, but, inevitably, some of the flavour has been lost. It can also be boiled up again, with added sugar, lemon juice, and cinnamon to make a jam useful for tarts.

Quince Paste Kydonópasta

The Greek version of Quince "Cheese"

2 kilos quinces
1 3/4 kilos sugar
1 scant tsp. ground cinnamon
1 tsp. lemon juice
1/2 cup blanched almonds
a little melted butter *or* corn oil
brandy
bay leaves

Scrub the quinces and dry with a cloth. Bake till tender. Then peel, cut in quarters, and discard cores. If you do not have an oven, cut up the fruit, discarding peel and cores, and boil gently in water to cover till soft.

Boil with the sugar, lemon juice, and cinnamon in a thick-bottomed pan, previously greased. Stir continuously with a wooden spoon, on low heat, till the paste comes away from the sides and wraps around the spoon.

Some of the almonds can be chopped and stirred in, the rest kept for decoration.

Cut a piece of greaseproof paper to fit a baking tin and line the bottom. Spread the mixture onto it to a depth of about three centimetres. Arrange half almonds at regular intervals, pressing them in. The paste should now be left in the sun to dry out for a week, but failing a week's sunshine in November, not to mention dust (the sunshine is a possibility in Greece, the dust a probability), put into a cool oven and leave till quite dry.

Turn onto a large sheet of oiled greaseproof paper (*ladóharto*), remove the original paper, brush that surface of the paste with a little brandy, and sprinkle with sugar. Turn back onto the first piece of paper, brush again with brandy, cut in squares or diamonds, and sprinkle with sugar.

If it is to be stored, layer between greaseproof paper in a biscuit tin and, if you have them, put fresh bay leaves between the layers.

This preserve is eaten like a sweet and can be bought as such, wrapped in cellophane, at counters selling dried fruit, Turkish Delight (*loukoúmia*), and sesame seed toffee (*pastéli*).

Dates in Syrup   Hourmádes Glykó

Sometimes one may come across fresh dates and, ripe or unripe, they make a delicious preserve. They can also be kept in the refrigerator for a month or more to use in cakes.

1 kilo fresh dates (large with stones *or* small without)
1 kilo sugar (*or* weight of fruit without stones)
juice of one lemon
3 - 4 cloves *or* vanilla flavouring

Peel large ripe dates and soak for an hour or two. Small ones don't need peeling; unripe ones must be boiled till soft, about an hour. Drain them but keep the water. Remove any stones.

Measure the boiling or soaking water and make up to five cups (one kilo) with cold water. Add sugar and simmer till melted, then bring to the boil, adding lemon juice and flavouring. Lower heat, put in the dates, and simmer for about twenty minutes.

Strain the syrup into another saucepan and remove the cloves. Boil the syrup fast till it reaches setting point (*see* Test for the syrup of preserves, p. 181)); then return the dates and stir them into the syrup over low heat. Pot while still warm.

December

Recipes

Quick Winter Soup	*Trahanósoupa*
Fried Trahanas	*Trahanás*
Salt Cod	*Bakaliáros (or Bakaláos) Pastós*
Stewed Salt Cod	*Bakaliáros Vrastós*
Stuffed Cabbage Leaves	*Láhanodolmádes*
Stuffed Turkey	*Galopoúla Yemistá*
Sweet Potatoes	*Glykopatátes*
Red Cabbage	*Kókkino Láhano*
Honey Cakes	*Melomakárona*
Christmas Shortbread	*Kourabiédes*
Dried Fruit Salad	*Kompósta Anámikta*
Prunes with Fresh Pears	*Kompósta Damáskina kai Ahládi*
Christmas Bread	*Christópsomo*

See also:
  Lentil Soup (January), Split Pea Purée (February), Bean Stew (November), Chick Pea Soup (March).

Other suggestions:
  Baked onions; hot pea soup; kedgeree; red cabbage casserole; curried apricot, orange, and nut stuffing; osso buco; turkey pate; grapefruit poached in brandy; cheese fondue; candied yams; brandy butter; bread sauce; fruit cake; date and sultana loaf; muesli; grenadine.

Vegetables in the market are the same as in November. Tomatoes are hot-house grown, pale and uninteresting, and are better bought in tins; aubergines are also forced. Pulses (lentils, split peas) are a good buy, as are chick peas and many kinds of dried beans: large and small haricot beans, broad beans, and black-eyed beans (*mavromátika*).

Quinces, kiwifruit, mandarins, and clemantines are the most interesting fruit this season, and all the other citrus fruits are in good supply. Pomegranates and pineapple are more for eye appeal, and coconuts and persimmons also appear. Apples, including green cooking apples, and pears are still to be had. There is a wide range of dried fruit, including peaches, cherries, dates, and figs; apricots more rarely as, until recently, they were imported. Chestnuts are at their best, ready for Christmas, and all other nuts are fresh.

Fruit on sale in jars, preserved in syrup: Bitter orange peel and whole green ones, cherries, bergamot, green figs, grapes, pears, strawberries, quinces, pistachios, and baby aubergines.

Candied fruits: chestnuts (marrons glâcés), bitter orange peel, green figs, apricots, pears; and cherries, the latter not so easy to find.

On a drive into the countryside one can buy oranges, eggs, and pumpkins by the roadside. One might also see a whole roasted pig (*gourounópoulo psitó*) for sale in portions.

The traditional sweets offered to visitors at Christmas and New Year are honey cakes and almond shortbread, the latter heavily dusted with icing sugar (*see* below).

Quick Winter Soup   Trahanósoupa

This nourishing soup is made from *trahanás*, crushed
wheat mixed with fresh milk (sweet, *glykós*) or milk that
has gone sour (*xynós*), not necessarily yoghurt, and then
dried in the sun. The best is home-made, using sheep's
milk, and it is often pressed into small cakes which must be
crumbled to use. A real home-made or *spitikós trahanás*
from Crete is sold commercially and is worth searching for.
It is rather more lumpy than the factory product.

This is how I learnt to make it from my husband, a
basic from seafaring days:

1 1/2 cups *trahanás*
1/2 cup olive oil
6 cups water *or* water and tomato juice
salt and pepper

Bring the water and olive oil to the boil and scatter in
the *trahanás*. Season with salt and pepper and simmer till
soft, about twenty minutes. Serve as thick or medium soup
as preferred, by adjusting the amount of water.

Fried Trahanas   ·   Trahanás

A more filling and stronger flavoured dish is made by
frying the *trahanás* first in a mixture of olive oil and butter,
then adding the water and boiling till it is all absorbed (like
preparing fried rice). Small cubes of hard cheese are stirred
in just before serving, by itself, or with a meat or vegetable
dish.

Salt Cod   Bakaliáros (*or* Bakaláos) Pastós

Although this is an imported fish it has become very much a Greek speciality, usually fried in batter (*bakaliáros tiganitós*) and served with a garlic sauce (*skordaliá, see* Sauces in Basic).

It is lighter when stewed and served as follows, and is delicious made into rissoles with mashed potato (*bakaliáros keftédes*).

Stewed Salt Cod   Bakaliáros Vrastós

1 kilo salt cod
juice of one lemon
1 torn bay leaf

Optional extras, as for fish soup:

1 medium onion
1 - 2 carrots
1 stalk of celery
1/2 cup olive oil
pepper

For serving:

oil and lemon dressing *or* mayonnaise
chopped parsley
black olives

Soak the cod for twenty-four hours, changing the water several times. Drain. Cut it into serving portions and remove the skin and bones.

Cover with water in a large saucepan and add the rest
of the ingredients. Simmer for about thirty minutes or until
soft. Drain, reserving the cooking liquid, remove any
remaining bones, and arrange on a serving dish.

Serve with chosen dressing and decorate with chopped
parsley and black olives (and the sliced carrots, if used).
Some of the cooking water could be used to make *skordaliá*.

Stuffed Cabbage Leaves   Láhanodolmádes

The already curved leaves of the white cabbage are a
useful substitute for vine leaves for stuffing at this time of
year.

Blanch the inside leaves in boiling water (six minutes),
drain, and leave to cool. Remove hard stems and use half
leaves. Stuff and cook as for Stuffed Vine Leaves in May.
Cover with a thick egg and lemon sauce (*see* Sauces in
Basic).

Stuffed Turkey   Galopoúla Yemistá

A Greek island recipe, with some additions

1 4 - 5 kilo turkey
2 tbsp. melted fat
1 cup dry white wine
2 cups stock
vinegar
salt and pepper
1 tbsp. flour (optional)

Stock:

Giblets (neck, wing ends, liver, heart, of turkey)
1 onion, chopped
2 stalks of parsley
1 stalk of celery
1 tbsp. salt
1/2 tsp. black pepper
1/2 tsp. ground allspice
4 cups water

Stuffing:

1/2 cup margarine
2 small onions, chopped
giblets, chopped and cooked, from stock (some extra
    cooked liver, chopped small, adds flavour)
2 cups toasted crumbs *or* parboiled (five minutes) rice
1/2 kilo chestnuts, roasted whole, peeled, and chopped
1 cup walnut meats, chopped
1/2 - 3/4 cup currants soaked in 1/4 cup dry white wine
1/2 tsp. grated nutmeg
2 stalks celery, chopped fine
1 tsp. salt
1 cup stock
2 tbsp. tomato paste

Wash the turkey and hang it up over the sink to drain.
Pour some vinegar through it for thorough cleansing. Prepare stock and boil till meat is soft. Strain and reserve liver,
heart, and meat from neck for stuffing. Prepare stuffing:
Sauté onions, add other ingredients, and simmer for ten
minutes. Add extra liquid if required, as the crumbs or rice
will swell further during roasting. Taste and season as
required. Cool.

   To stuff bird: Tie the legs together and partially sew up
the cavity with a large sewing needle and coarse black

163

thread (so that it is easy to see when removing). Spoon the stuffing into the remaining hole and complete sewing. Lay the turkey into the baking tin with the fat and pour over the cup of wine and salt and pepper. Cover with foil and roast in a moderate oven for four hours.

Heat remaining stock (about two cups) and pour over turkey towards the end of cooking. Continue roasting, uncovered, to brown well, basting when necessary.

People with no oven, or too small a one, surround the bird with quartered potatoes, add pieces of chopped margarine (one-quarter packet), salt and pepper, sprinkle it liberally with lemon juice, and take it to the local bakery; they are then free till lunch time.

Sweet Potatoes   Glykopatátes

These are baked, parboiled and then baked, or just boiled, and then split open or peeled and eaten with butter and salt. They can be peeled and then fried like chip potatoes. Otherwise, the Greeks don't seem to use them in sweet dishes as in America.

Red Cabbage   Kókkino Láhano

Though in reasonably plentiful supply, these are only used in Greece grated over White Cabbage Salad (*see* February) or in mixed vegetable salads.

Honey Cakes   Melomakárona

A very old sweetmeat, said to have been introduced by the Phoenicians. The old style cakes were made with semolina and olive oil, but most new recipes give only flour and butter. This is a combination of the old and the new.

225 grams butter (1 packet less 1 slice)
1/2 cup sugar
1 cup olive oil
1/2 cup orange juice and grated rind (about 2 oranges)
1/2 cup brandy *or* retsina *or* white wine,*or* even beer
3 cups fine semolina (a 500 gram packet)
4 1/2 cups plain flour (soft, *malakó*,or all-purpose)
3 tsp. baking powder
1 tsp. powdered cinnamon
1/2 tsp. powdered cloves
1/2 tsp. powdered nutmeg

Syrup:

2 cups honey
1 cup sugar
1 cup water
2 tsp. lemon juice

Decoration:

chopped nuts
cinnamon

Beat the butter or margarine with the sugar and add the oil, orange juice, and brandy in a big bowl. Sift the flour and baking powder into a smaller bowl with the grated rind and spices. Add the semolina to the oil mixture, and then add the flour, stirring constantly to mix thoroughly, adding more flour if necessary, to make a fairly stiff dough. Knead well with the hands.

Pinch off pieces about the size of an egg, form them into ovals, and flatten slightly into a baking tin, pressing them with the back of a fork. Bake in a moderate oven for about thirty minutes, till brown.

When the honey cakes have cooled slightly, boil the syrup for about five minutes until it is frothy and pour over them in the baking tin. Leave till well soaked but not disintegrating, about fifteen minutes, and then lift them out with a spatula onto a serving dish. Alternatively, lower them into the hot syrup with a slotted spoon, or in a chip basket in batches, and leave to soak for about five minutes, keeping the syrup simmering till all have been soaked. Sprinkle with cinnamon and finely chopped nuts.

Note: Do not store in a tin; they go mouldy in no time. Leave them in the serving dish or a party bowl (covered with a cloth) to offer visitors over the Christmas and New Year holidays.

Christmas Shortbread   Kourabiédes

225 grams unsalted butter (1 packet less 1 slice)
1/2 cup sugar
1 egg yolk
1 - 2 tbsp. brandy *or* masticha
vanilla
2 1/2 - 3 cups soft *or* all purpose flour
1/2 tsp. baking powder
1/2 cup almonds, blanched and finely chopped (optional)
rose water (optional)
1 - 2 cups icing sugar

Beat the butter well till white and light ("forty-five minutes with the hand"). While continuing beating, add the sugar, egg yolk, brandy, and vanilla. Stir in the sieved flour and baking powder and, if using, the almonds. Knead well.

Break off egg sized pieces and shape into rounds, ovals, or crescents. Lay in a lightly greased baking tin, flatten slightly, and bake in a moderate oven for fifteen to twenty minutes. Do not allow to brown.

Remove cookies onto a big dish, sprinkle them with rose water, and sieve the icing sugar over and around them so that they are completely covered. Pile high on a serving dish and sieve on more icing sugar to make a snowy mound. When the festive season is over, those remaining can be stored in an air-tight tin.

Dried Fruit Salad   Kompósta Anámikta

A delicious winter fruit salad can be made with the minimum of effort by combining dried prunes, apricots, peaches, figs, and cherries (or any two varieties) with some sultanas and nuts (blanched almonds and or unsalted pistachio nuts, pine nuts, or hazel nuts) in any proportion you fancy. (Very sweet prunes or figs go well with the rather tart apricots or peaches.) Pour over freshly made, strained, tea, to cover. Bring slowly to the boil and simmer gently until all the fruit is soft, sweeten to taste if necessary, and sprinkle with orange blossom water (*anthónero*). This imparts a strange and very exotic flavour to the fruit. If not using apricots, a curl of lemon peel or the grated rind of half a lemon gives a tang to the other over-sweet fruits, and extra flavour can be given by adding a stick of cinnamon. An orange liqueur or a few drops of angustura bitters can be used instead of the orange blossom water. Leave overnight to steep in the juice.

Another way is to leave the fruit to soak overnight in hot tea (or plain boiling water) and bring it to the boil in the morning when the fruit has had time to swell.

Serve chilled with strained yoghurt, evaporated milk, or thick whipped cream decorated with fresh pomegranate seeds for an attractive effect. Or serve with raw rolled oats soaked in milk as a kind of muesli for a quick breakfast dish.

Prunes with Fresh Pears   Kompósta Damáskina me Ahládi

Prunes alone are, of course, often cooked in the same way, as in the previous recipe. Try also soaking and cooking about one-quarter kilo of prunes in a cup of sweet red wine, mixed with water. Add lemon peel and a cinnamon stick or cloves. Pears combine well with this, quartered and simmered long enough to become tender, but very hard pears should be stewed separately and then added to the prunes.

Christmas Bread   Christópsomo

6 - 7 dried figs, chopped roughly
    and soaked in water to cover overnight
1 cup warm water
30 grams fresh yeast (*see* Yeast, under Bread, in Basic)
3/4 cup sugar
1 kilo plain hard flour *or* use half wholemeal (*starénio*)
1 1/2 tsp. mastic (*mastícha*)*
1 tsp. salt
1 cup warm milk
3 - 4 eggs, lightly beaten
115 grams melted butter (1/2 packet less 1 thin slice)
1/2 cup walnuts, chopped roughly
3/4 cup sultanas

Glaze:

                          or:

1/4 cup corn syrup
1/4 cup honey .   **1 beaten egg white**
2 tbsp. orange juice   **1 tbsp. sugar**
blanched almonds   **1/4 cup crystalized fruit**

Mastícha is the resin tear-drop from the slashed trunk of the *mastícha* tree grown mainly on Chios. It is excellent raw, as a chewing gum, and is also made into a strong cordial like ouzo. It can be found on the spice shelves of supermarkets.

Dissolve the yeast with one teaspoon of sugar in the cup of warm water and leave to stand in a large mug, covered, in a warm place, until foamy.

Pound the mastic with another teaspoon of sugar and add to the sifted flour and salt, together with the sugar, in a large warmed bowl.

Make a well in the flour, add the rest of the ingredients (including the figs in their liquid), and mix all together, working with the hands to form a soft dough. Knead well, until elastic.

Put to rise in a greased bowl in a warm place, cover with a clean cloth or cling-foil, and leave till doubled in size (about one and a half hours). Punch down the risen dough and divide into two pieces. Knead both again well, shape into loaves and put into greased tins (twenty-two centimetres). Cover and leave to rise again for a further two hours.

Bake loaves in a fairly hot oven for about fifteen minutes, then take out and spread on the glaze. Lower the oven to medium and continue baking for about forty minutes, till the tops are brown and the bottoms sound hollow when tapped. Cool on wire racks.

My sister-in-law, who makes excellent bread, crumbles the yeast into a third of the flour, mixes it with some of the warm water, and leaves it overnight in a warm place (usually a spare bed, under a blanket!) to rise before setting about baking in the morning. She doesn't use fruit or a glaze in the Christmas bread, but shapes a cross from the last piece of dough and lays it on top, pressing walnuts into the ends and sprinkling it all with water and sesame seeds.

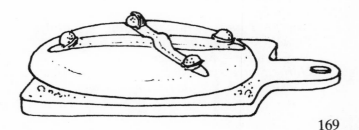

Basic Recipes and Shopping Hints

Bread   *Psomí*
 To buy
 Uses for stale bread
 Yeast - Mayiá
Coffee   *Kafé*
Dairy Products
 Milk - Gála
 Cream - Afrógala, Santiyí
 Cheese - Tyrí
 Butter - Voútyro
 Yoghurt - Yaoúrti
  Sweet, Savoury, Marinade
Eggs   *Avgá*
 Separated, uses for
 Hard boiled, some ways of serving
Fish   *Psári*
 To prepare for grilling, baking, frying, poaching, or soup
Fritter Batter   *Kourkoúti*
Jams, Jellies, and Preserves Marmaládes, Glyká, and Beldé
 Tests for setting jam and jelly
 Test for the syrup of preserves and spoon sweets
 To prevent syrup from becoming sugary
Oil   *Ládi*
Pastry   *Zými*
 Home made pastry for pitta - Zými yia pítta, spitikó
Rice   *Rízi, Piláfi*
Sauces   *Sáltses*
 Egg and Lemon Sauce - Avgolémono
 Thick Sauce
 Olive Oil and Lemon Dressing - Ladolémono
 French Dressing or Sauce Vinaigrette
 Mayonnaise - Mayonéza
 Garlic Sauce - Skordaliá for Tzatzíki (see Cucumber,
  Garlic, and Yoghurt Dip in June)

170

White Sauce (Béchamel) - Sáltsa Bésamel
Béchamel for Moussaká
Cheese Sauce
Onion Sauce
Egg Sauce
Parsley or Caper Sauce
White Sauce in quantity
Meat Sauce - Sáltsa me Kimá
Tomatoes   *Domátes*
    Tomato Sauce - Domáto Sáltsa
    Greek Country Tomato Paste - Domáto Beldé
    Tomato Juice - Domáto Hymós
    Dried Tomatoes - Domátes Xerés
Tea   *Tsái*
Wine   *Krasí*
    House wine - Heema
    Home-made - Spitikó (see October)

Bread   Psomí

To buy:
A baker's shop which bakes its own bread is called an
artopieíon or simply *foúrnos* (oven), while a shop selling
bread is *artopoleíon*. A long loaf is a *frantzóla* and a round
loaf is a *karvéli*.

Kinds of bread:
Brown (*mávro*)
Country (*horiátiko*) Lenten (*lagána*)
New Year (*Vasilópitta*)
Rye (*sýkeli*)
Special for church (*prosforá* and *ártos*)
Sweet, with eggs (*tsouréki*)
White (*lefkó*)
Extra white (*politelías*)
Wheatmeal (*starénio*)

171

These shops also sell baked sliced bread or rusks (*friganiés*), white or wholemeal, and thicker slices called *paximádia*, usually wholemeal, sometimes containing some olive oil. Then there may be small cakes for dipping in your morning milk (*kouloúria* and *voutýmata*), and other biscuits covered with sesame seeds.

Uses for Stale Bread:
The Greeks like to buy their bread fresh, so they also have several ways of using the less fresh loaf. More often than not it is sliced and baked in the oven for later use as rusks (*paximádia*), or it is crumbled for Fish Roe Spread (*see* March), Garlic Sauce (*see* Sauces, below), meatballs, and au gratin dishes. There are also, of course, apple charlotte, brown bread ice cream, stuffings for poultry, "Swedish" apple cake, chocolate cake, and rissoles. My family enjoys fried bread, introduced from England, as, surprisingly, it is not known in Greece.

In snack bars everywhere what is known as *tost* has almost overtaken pizzas and hamburgers. This is taken to mean a toasted sandwich, usually with a ham or cheese filling; if you want plain toast you have to order *psomí psiméno*.

Fresh Yeast - *Mayiá*:
Fresh yeast can be bought from any baker with his own oven for a few drachmas for a sixty gram slice; it keeps in the fridge for three or four weeks.

To use fresh yeast when a recipe specifies dried, double the quantity, stir it into part of the measured warm liquid and stand it in a warm place to froth up. Then add to the flour and salt and the rest of the liquid. (Dried yeast is now available in supermarkets, but fresh is much nicer.)

To use dried yeast when fresh is indicated, use half given quantity. Dissolve one level teaspoon sugar in one cup of water, rather hotter than that used for fresh yeast. Sprinkle yeast over the water and leave in a warm place for about ten minutes till frothy. Stir and use as for fresh yeast.

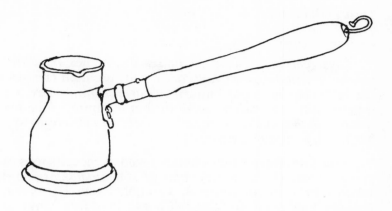

Coffee   Kafé

Turkish (or, rather, Greek, to be patriotic) coffee is very finely ground. A heaped teaspoonful is brought to the boil with a coffee cupful of cold water in a tiny saucepan called a *bríki* in four strengths: plain (*skéto*), one teaspoon coffee to one sugar (*métrio*), one teaspoon coffee to two sugar (*varí glykó*), the same but allowed to boil (*glykí vrastó*). Normally, the *bríki* is whipped off the heat when the coffee rises and should be returned twice to rise again before being poured into the cup. If two or more cupfuls are made together, the froth (*kaïmáki*) is distributed between the cups.

First-time drinkers are disturbed to find the grounds sitting heavily in the bottom of the small cup; those who know sprinkle a few drops of cold water into the cup before drinking to make the grounds stay at the bottom. A glass of cold water is invariably served with these "thimblefuls" of coffee.

Most other coffee served in *kafeneíons* is instant, called "Nes", though some may serve "frappé." Grocers sell other varieties.

173

Dairy Products

Cheese - Tyrí:

Curd cheeses. These go under the names *mizíthra*, *manoúromizíthra*, or *anthótyro*, all soft, unsalted cheeses, the latter having more butterfat than *mizíthra*. They are usually stiff and rarely need further draining. *Malakiá* means soft and *análata* without salt. *Mizíthra* also dries to a hard, salty, grating cheese.

Feta. This sheep's milk cheese is sold at cheese shops or counters straight from the barrel, soft (*malakiá*), hard (*sklirí*), or medium (*métrio*). Crumbled feta is *trimáta*, cheaper and ready for Small Cheese Pies (*see* May) or Baked Shrimps in Tomato Sauce with Cheese (*see* August).

Grating. Usually *kefalotýri*, or ask for cheese for grating (*tyrí yia trípsimo*). It is also sold ready grated in packets, as is parmesan, usually more expensive. *See mizíthra,* below.

Milk - *Gála*:

Milk is sold fresh in dairies (*galaktopoleía*) and also in supermarkets, as are cartons of "long life" milk and packets of powdered milk (*skóni gála*). Also available is milk in cans: evaporated (*evaporé*) or sweetened condensed (*zacharoúcho*).

Cream - *Afrógala, Santiyí*:

Apart from canned concoctions, one can buy real cream (often whipped with white of egg when sold in confectionary shops and called *santiyí*), but untreated cream for whipping (*afrógala* or *anthógala*) can also be bought from dairies. Take your own container. A scalded version is called *kaïmáki*, which word, however, also refers to a creamy ice cream as well as the froth on top of coffee. Recently, fresh cream has become available in cartons at supermarkets.

Other cheeses. *Kaséri*, the most common, is a cheddar type; most Greek *kapnistó*, meaning smoked, is from Metsovo; *graviéra* is a gruyère type from several areas. A number of foreign cheeses are available by weight: Dutch (Edam and Gouda), German, Austrian smoked, and Danish blue (called *rokfór* with gay abandon), but the selection is not large. A wider variety, in packets, is to be found in the luxury supermarkets.

Butter - *Voútyro*:

This word is used loosely for all cooking fats in Greek recipes, including an oily product of sheep's milk (*voútyro gálaktos*) which is clarified butter, sold in jars. Then there are various kinds of shortening (vegetable oil solids) and margarine (*see* Oil above). Consequently, "real" butter is called "fresh," or "sweet" butter. Fresh Greek butter is white and strongly flavoured if it is made from sheep's milk, when it is called *Kerkýras*. When it is made from cows' milk it is called *Alpíno*.

All these products are avaliable in various packets and cartons, but *Alpíno* is also available in small packets for individual servings.

Butter and margarine from other European countries are available. Dutch butter is also sold loose, by weight, at cheese counters.

Yoghurt - *Yaoúrti*:

Yoghurt is made either from sheep's milk (*próveio*) or cows' milk (*ayeládino*), of which the latter is less rich. The best yoghurt is sold in pottery containers, but it is also available in plastic cartons, from full-cream to fat-less. Thick yoghurt, called *Yaoúrti Sakoúlas*, is best bought "loose" from a cheese shop (take your own container), but it is more generally available in cartons labeled "strained" (*strangisméno*). Apart from eating it plain with sugar or stirring it into curries, stews, or cucumber soup, it is used in Greece in Cucumber, Garlic, and Yoghurt Dip (*see* June) and in Yoghurt Cake (*see* January).

Fresh local sheep's milk yoghurt is ambrosia served with honey and walnuts. Try it also thinned down as follows (again, these are not Greek):

Sweet. Thin *yaoúrti sakoúlas* with evaporated milk and/or fruit syrup whipped in and with chopped fresh fruit added. Chill before serving in small bowls.

Savoury. Mix a carton of yoghurt with two tablespoons rich tomato sauce (*see* Tomato Sauce, below) and two of vinaigrette. Add a few chopped capers and finely chopped fresh dill or parsley for a seafood dressing, or with chopped basil or crumbled oregano or thyme to serve with meatballs or grilled chops.

Yoghurt Marinade. Beat two cups of yoghurt till smooth, then add one small grated onion, the juice of half a lemon, and salt and pepper and marinate meat in it overnight.

Eggs   Avgá

Separated eggs:
While separated eggs are often used in the same recipe, it might be helpful to be reminded of other uses for left-overs of either half. Most of these are *not* Greek.

Yolks:
Cream ices, confectioners' custard, cream mousses (sweet or savoury), sauces (*see* Sauces, below), cheese biscuits, butter cookies (*see* April), in pastry bases for flan, or brushed on top of pies or bread.

Whites:
Meringues, meringue topping for pies, Pavlova flan, soft fritter batter, souffles, lemon or orange water ice, royal cake icing, cream cheese dessert, "lining" for pastry not baked blind.

176

Hard boiled eggs - some ways of serving:
1. Stuffed eggs, the yolks mashed with mayonnaise, replaced in halved whites, and garnished with capers, dill, anchovies, etc.
2. Halved and served cold, covered in mayonnaise thinned with olive oil and yoghurt, garnished as above.
3. Halved and served hot in white sauce, flavoured with capers, cheese, onion, or parsley, or any two of these, topped with cheese and breadcrumbs (au gratin).
4. "Scotch" eggs, whole eggs, rolled in thick minced meat, coated in breadcrumbs, and fried in deep fat.
5. Kedgeree, a mixture of rice and salted fish with curry powder or paprika, buttered and served hot.
6. Sauce tartare.
7. Meat loaf (*see* Baked Meat Loaf in May).
8. Yolks chopped fine for "eggs mimosa."
9. Chopped fine, mixed with melted butter (and anchovies) for sandwich fillings.
10. Chopped fine and mixed with mayonnaise, curry powder, and chopped green onion to spread on rye bread.

Fish   Psári

For grilling (*schára*):
Tunny, bream (*tsipoúra or lithríni*), red mullet, mackerel:

1. Wash fish in a bowl of cold water.
2. Descale.
3. Slit up the belly, remove gills, and pull out guts. Wash again and salt inside and out.
4. Lay on grill, sprinkle with olive oil, cook till tender.
5. Prepare a bowl of three parts olive oil to one part lemon juice, whisking it with a fork, to serve separately.

Basic

For baking (*plakí*):
  Tunny, bream (*tsipoúra, lithríni, synagrída, fagrí*)
bogue (*gópes*), mackerel, sardines, fresh anchovies
(*gávros*):

1. Wash fish in a bowl of cold water.
2. Descale.
3. Slit up the belly, remove gills, and pull out guts.
Wash again and salt inside and out. Remove heads
from fresh anchovies.
4. For large fish such as tunny or bream, cut into
steaks, or make three or four slashes in the side
and insert slivers of garlic. Lay in oiled
baking tin. Bake alone or as recipe.
For smaller fish, strew with sliced onions, tomato,
herbs, and garlic, and sprinkle with oil.

For frying (*tiganitó*):
  Red mullet, "whitebait" (*marídes*), mackerel, bogue
(*gópes*), and other small fish, also sole (*glóssa*):

1. Wash fish in a bowl of cold water.
2. Slit up the belly and remove guts, but leave head on.
Rinse well. Small whitebait (*marídes*)
can be left whole. Drain well, pat dry on kitchen
paper.
3. Roll fish in seasoned flour (soft, *malakó*, is best).
Shake off excess flour and lay in very hot olive
oil, filling the pan. Shake the pan occasionally,
tipping the oil around the edges. Fry till brown
on one side.
4. Turn fish over carefully with a fish slice and a fork,
or lay a large plate over the pan and turn the whole
thing over onto the plate, trickling the oil into a
second frying pan. Then slide all the fish back in
one piece, into the first pan, and dribble the olive
oil over them again.
5. Transfer to serving dish. Keep hot.

6. If not cooking fish immediately, sprinkle with salt, olive oil, and lemon juice, and refrigerate.

For poaching and boiling for soup:
White fish, groupers (*stíra* and *sfyrída*), bream (*lithríni* and *synagrída*) and other small fish:
1. Clean fish, removing guts, but leaving on the heads which help to thicken the stock and are also enjoyed by most Greeks for the tasty cheeks. Scrape off scales towards the head.
2. Cut very large fish in slices. Medium ones can be slashed once or twice, and small ones left whole.
3. Prepare cooking liquid (*see* Fish Soup in March) and lower fish into it to poach till cooked.
4. Serve broth plain with lemon juice, or with egg and lemon (*see* Sauces, below) and fish with olive oil and lemon dressing or, for *synagrída*, *lithríni*, or *sfyrída* with mayonnaise (*see* Fish with Mayonnaise [Athenian Style], p. 93.

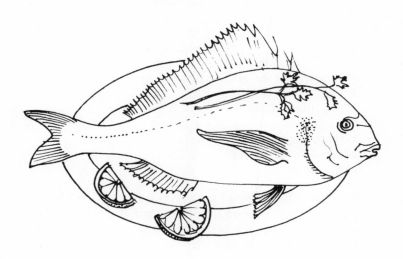

Fritter Batter   Kourkoúti

For vegetables and fish; aubergines, courgettes, cauliflower
florets, salt cod:

1 1/3 cups plain flour
1 tsp. salt
a pinch of pepper
2 eggs, separated *or* **whites only**
3/4 cup water *or* **flat beer** *or* **white wine**

Put the flour and salt into a bowl and mix in the egg
yolk (if using). Make a well in the middle and slowly add
the liquid, stirring all the time till well blended.

Leave to rest in the fridge covered for at least two
hours, or even overnight, for a lighter batter as a result of
fermentation. Whites of eggs only can be used for a very
crisp coating, but the yolks will prevent an excess of olive
oil being soaked up during frying. When ready to use, add
the two stiffly beaten egg whites, coat the vegetables, and
fry in deep olive oil.

See Tomato Fritters in September for a lighter batter.

For fruit:

2 eggs, separated
2/3 cup milk *or* **fruit juice**
1 tbsp. melted butter
1 cup plain flour
1/4 tsp. salt
1 tbsp. sugar
oil *or* **fat for frying**
icing sugar

Beat together the egg yolks, milk or juice, and butter.
Sift flour and salt into a large bowl and add the sugar. Stir
in the liquid. Allow to rest, then beat again till smooth.
Fold in the egg whites, stiffly beaten.

Dry the fruit, dip in the batter, and deep fry. Drain and dust with icing sugar.

Jams, Jellies, and Preserves   Marmeládes, Beldé, and Glyká

In Greece all jam or jelly is *marmeláda*, not only that made with citrus fruit. Whole fruit in syrup is *glykó tou koutalioú*, to be served in individual dishes and eaten with a spoon, *koutáli*. It is always accompanied by a glass of water and is a traditional gesture of hospitality to guests when they come to the house. Sadly, this habit is degenerating in an effort to be more "European," and bought pastries or chocolates, or even the more chic whiskey, *éna wiskáki*, served neat, are offered instead.

Tests for setting jam and jelly:
1. Take up a spoonful of boiling juice and let it drip back into the pan. It is done if the last drop clings to the spoon.
2. Spoon a little boiling syrup onto a cold saucer. Stand it in the fridge for two or three minutes. If it then coagulates, wrinkling when pushed with your little finger, it is ready.
3. Use a jam thermometer.

Test for the syrup of preserves and spoon sweets:
To test for "soft ball stage" (235°), spoon a little syrup into a glass of iced water. If it disperses, the preserve needs more boiling, but if it can be collected and rolled into a ball between finger and thumb, it is ready.

To prevent syrup from becoming sugary:
To every kilo of sugar add two teaspoons lemon juice or two tablespoons corn syrup, *glykósi*.

181

Basic

Oil   Ládi

Olive oil (*elaiólado*) is sold in bottles or large tins like those for petrol, usually decorated with an olive branch. Corn oil (*kalambokélaio* or *aravositélaio*) and sunflower oil (*iliélaio*) are similarly decorated with a picture of the plant of origin, but oil from cottonseed (*vambakélaio*) is often disguised as "from selected seeds" (*éklekto sporéllaio*). The same names apply to margarines and shortenings in packets and cartons (*see* Dairy Products, above).

Pastry   Zými

Greek pastry for pittas (sweet or savoury)

Píttas are any kind of pie, covered top and bottom with pastry, or rolled round a filling and curled into a baking tin in a snail pattern (*see* Pumpkin Pie in March).

Home made pastry (*zými yia pítta, spitikó*) can be made as in the following recipe, or with the addition of chopped pieces of butter, as in puff pastry, when it is called *zými sfoliátas*.

Leaf pastry (*fýllo*) is the paper thin pastry made commercially and used for spinach, cheese, and custard pies and *baklavás*. Buy half a kilo or sheets as indicated in the recipes, freshly made from special shops or frozen from supermarkets.

Kataífi pastry, the one that resembles shredded wheat, is also sold in the special *fýllo* shops.

Home made pastry for pittas - *Zými yia pítta, spitikó*

Pítta pastry is very different from a shortcrust, which is kept cool and barely touched by hand. Using olive oil and water, it is kneaded hard and long, like bread, and then, either immediately, as my sister-in-law does, or after a spell in the refrigerator, which I prefer, it is rolled out to a thin elastic sheet, which is very easy to use.

4 1/2 cups plain flour (1/2 kilo)
1 tsp. salt
1 - 1 1/4 cups water *or* soda water
1 tbsp. vinegar
1/2 cup olive oil

Sift the flour and salt into a bowl and stir in the water and vinegar till smooth. Add the olive oil slowly, working it in with the hands. Knead well, stretching the dough till it is malleable and elastic. Use at once or after an hour or more refrigeration. Roll out thinly and use according to recipe.

Rice   Rízi, Piláfi

2 cups long grain rice
5 cups water *or* stock
salt and pepper
2 tbsp. butter *or* margarine

Wash the rice well, drain, and then either sauté it in the butter till transparent and then add hot water and seasoning, or bring the water to the boil with butter and seasoning and throw in the rice.

Cover the pan and simmer till tender and the water is nearly all absorbed. Cover the pan with a clean cloth, replace the lid, and leave on very low heat till all moisture has evaporated. Fluff up the rice with a fork before serving.For *piláfi* stir in another two tablespoons melted butter, press the rice into a mould (or individual cups for separate portions), and turn out onto a platter or plates to serve, covered with a tomato sauce.

For rice salad, add chopped red peppers, peas, or button mushrooms to the rice.

Sauces   Sáltses

Egg and Lemon Sauce - *Avgolémono*

Thin Sauce or Soup (*see* Tripe Soup, p 6; Lamb Fricassé with Lettuce/Endives and Egg and Lemon Sauce, p. 16; Lamb Soup, p. 44; and Pork with Celery, p. 144):

2 - 3 eggs *or* yolks only and 2 tbsp. cold water
juice of 1 large *or* 2 small lemons
1 cup stock from the dish being cooked

Beat eggs and water in a bowl and add the lemon juice. Take the boiling stock straight from the heat and pour some of it slowly into the bowl, stirring all the time. Pour the bowlful back into the pan of soup or stew and remove from the heat, or lower heat enough to cook sauce to thicken slightly. If allowed to boil it will curdle.

Thick Sauce (*see* Stuffed Vine Leaves, p. 58; Stuffed Courgettes with Meat, p. 104; and Pork with Celeriac, p. 144):

2 tbsp. butter *or* margarine
2 tbsp. flour
2 cups boiling stock
3 eggs *or* yolks only
juice of 1 *or* 2 lemons
2 tbsp. cold water

Melt butter in a saucepan and stir in the flour. When smooth, add the stock and keep stirring till it boils. Lower heat. Beat the eggs, lemon juice, and water together in a bowl. Add some of the hot stock slowly to the egg and lemon, a ladleful at a time, and then return it all to the pan, stirring vigorously till combined and heated through, but without allowing it to boil. A double boiler is an advantage.

Olive Oil and Lemon Dressing - *Ladolémono*

1 cup olive oil
1 1/2 - 2 tbsp. lemon juice
salt and pepper

Mix together in a bowl, beating with a fork. Serve with fish.

French Dressing *or* Sauce Vinaigrette

The standard proportions are three or four parts olive oil to one part lemon juice or vinegar, plus salt and pepper and sometimes dry mustard and one teaspoon sugar. Put all the ingredients in a bowl and whisk thoroughly, adding any chosen extras, such as herbs and garlic. Whisk again before serving, or pour into a screwtop bottle and shake before dressing the salad. If making in quantity, remove herbs and garlic before storing. Other additional flavourings could be finely minced onion, capers, parsley, or chives.

Mayonnaise - *Mayonéza*

2 egg yolks
1/2 tsp. salt
1/2 tsp. pepper
2 tbsp. vinegar *or* lemon juice
1/4 tsp. sugar
6 tbsp. oil

Break the eggs carefully, putting the yolks into a bowl and reserving the whites for some other use (*see* Eggs, above). Add seasoning and stir together. Then add the oil drop by drop, stirring all the time, adding increasing quantities of oil as the mayonnaise thickens. Add the vinegar towards the end, and then the rest of the oil.

Basic

If it curdles, break another yolk into a clean bowl and add the spoiled mayonnaise slowly.

It is much quicker to use a blender, having all the ingredients at room temperature. Put all except the oil in the goblet and blend for a few seconds at high speed. Remove the small cap and drip in the oil while blending at low speed, until the mayonnaise is the right consistency. Store in the refrigerator.

Cucumber, Garlic, and Yoghurt Dip - *Tzatzíki* (*see* June)

Garlic Sauce - *Skordaliá*
This is usually made with fresh breadcrumbs, but mashed potatoes are often used, or even a thick white sauce; anything as a base for quantities of garlic.

6 - 10 cloves garlic
1 tsp. salt
2 cups breadcrumbs, soaked and squeezed out
  ***or* 2 cups mashed potato**
1/2 - 3/4 cup olive oil
1/3 cup vinegar *or* juice of 1/2 lemon

Crush the garlic with the salt and pound to a paste. Stir in the breadcrumbs or potato. (Some people use half of each.) While beating vigorously, add half a cup of olive oil very slowly alternately with the vinegar or lemon juice. More oil and garlic would be appreciated by most Greeks. Add a little water if too thick. Leave to stand to improve flavour.

Serve with Beetroot Salad (*see* April); fish, especially Stewed Salt Cod (*see* December); or Shark (*see* November).

186

White Sauce (Béchamel) - *Sáltsa Besamél*

2 1/2 - 3 cups milk
4 tbsp. butter (1/4 packet)
1/2 cup flour
salt and pepper

Optional, for "real" bechamel:

1 medium onion
1 bay leaf
1 clove
1 stalk celery
6 peppercorns

Heat the milk to nearly boiling in a small pan with the spices. Remove from the heat, cover, and leave to infuse for at least ten minutes. Strain when ready to use.

Melt the butter in a larger pan, remove from the heat, and stir in the flour. Cook for a minute or two, then remove from the heat again and add a little more of the warm milk, stirring vigourously to blend, using a whisk for best effect. Stir in the rest of the milk, a little at a time. Season with salt and pepper.

Bring the sauce to the boil, stirring continuously, and simmer for two or three minutes. Add more liquid if a thinner sauce is required.

Put aside to cool a little before using, especially before adding eggs.

Bechamel for Moussaká(see September) and Macaroni Pie (see March):
Beat two eggs and a grate of nutmeg into the basic sauce (or four into a double quantity).

Cheese sauce:
Add half to three-quarters of a cup of grated cheese and half a teaspoon mustard to basic sauce.

Onion sauce:
Slice one medium onion, sauté it gently in a little butter, and stir into sauce. Taste and add extra seasoning.

Two other sauces which, however, are not Greek:

Egg sauce:
Add two or three hard boiled eggs roughly chopped and flavour sauce with finely chopped anchovies or ketchup.

Parsley or Caper sauce:
Add two tablespoons of freshly chopped parsley or pickled capers (*see* Capers, p. 82) to basic sauce, and half to one teaspoon lemon juice for fish dishes.

To keep sauce hot while preparing rest of the dish:

Reserve the last two or three tablespoons of milk till the end and pour them over the completed sauce. Cover and leave in a warm place. When ready to use, stir milk into sauce.

White sauce made in quantity:

1/2 cup butter *or* margarine (1/2 packet)
3/4 cup plain flour
2 cups milk

Prepare as above, stirring well as it thickens. Pour into a bowl with a close fitting lid and cover lightly to let cool. Close tightly when cold and refrigerate.
When ready to use, turn into a saucepan, heat gently, and add further liquid as required.

Meat Sauce - *Sáltsa me Kimá*

A basic mixture for pouring over rice or macaroni or, slightly thickened, as a filling for Aubergine "Shoes" (*see* July), tomatoes, peppers (*see* Stuffed Tomatoes and Peppers in August), or the meat layer in macaroni pie (*see* Macaroni Pie with Minced Meat in March). (Stress the correct syllable when buying minced meat, *kimá*. When the stress is on the first syllable it means a wave.)

2 medium onions, chopped fine
3 - 4 tbsp. oil *or* butter
1/2 kilo minced meat
1 - 2 cloves garlic, finely sliced
1 can tomatoes (about 400 grams) mashed with their juice *or*
    1/2 kilo fresh ripe tomatoes, grated, *or* peeled and chopped
1 bay leaf
salt and pepper
1/2 tsp. sugar (if wine is medium sweet, omit sugar)
1/2 tsp. cinnamon
a pinch of cloves *or* nutmeg
2 tbsp. tomato paste
1/2 cup red wine

Sauté the onion in the oil or butter in a thick bottomed pan. Add the minced meat, breaking it up and stirring till browned all over. Add the garlic and the tomatoes, mix well, and simmer for five or ten minutes. Add the herbs, spices, and the tomato paste diluted in the red wine.

Stir well, lower heat , cover, and simmer gently for half an hour or more. Use as required, either further diluted, or thickened by longer cooking without lid (or by adding crumbs, white sauce, or rice).

Tomatoes   **Domátes**

Tomato Sauce - *Domáta Sáltsa*

2 tbsp. olive oil
1 onion, chopped
1 - 2 cloves garlic (optional)
1 kilo fresh tomatoes, grated or peeled, and chopped *or*
   a can of tomatoes with half their juice
2 tbsp. tomato paste if using fresh tomatoes *or*
   1 tbsp. tomato paste if using canned tomatoes
2 - 3 tbsp. red wine (optional), sweet *or* dry
salt and black pepper
1/4 tsp. red pepper
a pinch of cinnamon
1 tsp. oregano *or* thyme *or* basil
1/4 tsp. sugar if using dry wine

Sauté the onion in the olive oil in a medium saucepan.
Add the rest of the ingredients and simmer, uncovered, for
about forty minutes or until thick. If not thick enough, mix
one teaspoon cornflour with a little water, stir into the
sauce, and continue cooking. Remove the bay leaf and use
as required.

Tomato Paste, Greek Country Style - *Domáto Beldé*

Chop up several kilos of tomatoes and cook with a
handful of salt until reduced to a pulp. Sieve and return to
the pan to continue cooking uncovered, over low heat until
most of the liquid has been driven off. Ladle into a baking
tin and leave in the sun until quite dried out. Store in
pottery bowls, sealed in with olive oil.

Tomato Juice - *Domáto Hymós*

Tomato ketchup seems not to be made by the housewife in Greece, but they may boil superfluous ripe tomatoes to a pulp and then strain off the juice, flavoured only with salt, and bottle it, topping up with olive oil to keep out the air. Without any sugar or vinegar it doesn't keep very long.

Dried Tomatoes - *Domátes Xerés*

On the island of Tinos tomatoes are preserved for the winter by being sliced in half and left in the sun to dry. When required, the tomatoes are soaked to regain their plumpness and are ready for cooking.

Tea   Tsái

Tea is usually offered in Greece if someone is feeling off colour, and can mean "European" tea or a herb tisane, usually sage (*faskómilo*), "mountain tea" (*tsái tou vounoú*), or *díktamo* from the Dikti Mountains in Crete (*see* Teas and Tisanes in February). If one is really ill, chamomile (*hamomíli*) is prescribed (*see* April).

Well known brands of packeted tea can be found in the better supermarkets, as well as tea bags. The latter are on sale in every small grocer in opened boxes, allowing any flavour they may have had to escape. It is possible, however, to find in the Athens market area of Athinas Street excellent Orange Pekoe tea from Sri Lanka, sold packeted or loose but full-flavoured.

Wine   Krasí

House Wine - *heéma:*
To buy unbottled "house wine" from tavernas with their own barrels, take your own bottle.

Bottled Wine:
Bottled wine, of course, is also available from wine and spirits merchants, as it is from supermarkets and grocers.

Dry white (sec) *sék*
Dry red *broúsko*
Medium dry red *kokkinélli*
Resinated *retsína*
Rosé *rozé*
Semi-sweet *imíglyko*
Sweet (douce) *glykó*
Unresinated *aretsínato*
White *lefkó*

Home-made - *Spitikó* (*see* October)

INDEX

Achinós - Sea urchin, 100
Afélia - Pork in red wine, 7
Agorá - Market
Ahládia - *see* Pears
Ahní záhari - Icing sugar
Aktinídia - Kiwi fruit, 4, 141
Aláti - Salt
Allspice - *Bahári*
Almonds - *Amýgdala,* 114
Anchovies
  canned or salted - *Antsoúyia*
  fresh - *Gávroi,* 18, 88, 178
Angináres, see Artichokes
Angoúri, see Cucumber
Anise seed (aniseed) - *Glykániso*
  (a flat, pungent seed used in
  bread and for flavouring ouzo)
Ánitho - Dill weed
Ánthi apo kolokythákia - Courget-
  te flowers, 74
Anthónero (flower water) -
  Orange blossom or rose water,
  obtainable from chemists
  - in fruit salads, 167
Anthótyro - Curd cheese, 128, 174
Antídia - *see* Endives
Antsoúyia - Anchovies, canned or
  salted
Appetizers, *see* Hors d'oeuvres
Apples - *Míla* (cooking a. - *xýna*
  or *xynómila*)
  - as dessert, 53
  - baked in syrup, spiced, *see*
  Baked spiced pears, 153
Apricots - *Verýkoka*
  - fresh, for jam, 84; for com-
  pôte, 96
  - dried, as in fruit salad, 167
Arakás - Peas, 61
Aravósyka - Prickly pears, 114
Aravósito - Maize, Indian corn,
  114
Arbaróriza, see Scented geranium
  leaves

Arní, see Lamb
Aroma, see Spices
Artichokes - *Angináres*
  - salad - *a. saláta,* 51
  - stewed - *a. a la políta,* 49
  - with broad beans - *a. me
  koukiá,* 51
  - with peas - *a. me arakás,* 61
  - with fricassé of lamb - *arní
  frikassé me a.,* 17
Astakós - Lobster, Crawfish, 27,
  100
"Athenian style" fish - *Psári vrastó, Athinaïkó,* 88, 93
Aubergines - *Melitzánes* (round -
  fláskes, long - *makróstenes*)
  - casserole with cheese and
  tomato sauce, 107
  - fried or frittered - *m. tiganités,*
  92, 93
  - *moussakás,* 121
  - pickled - *m. toursí,* 150
  - preserve - *m. glykó,* 151 -
  purée - *melitzanosaláta,* 90
  - stuffed whole - *Imám Bayaldí,*
  115
  - stuffed whole with cheese -
  "bourékia me m.", 108
  - stuffed halves ("shoes") - *m.
  papoutsákia,* 91
  - stuffed halves (with cheese
  and onion) - *m. papoutsákia,*
  92 - with beef - *moschári kokkinistó me m.,* 120
Avgá, see Eggs
Avgolémono - see Egg and lemon
  sauce/soup
Avocadoes, 26

Bahári - Allspice
Bahariká - Spices in general
Bakaliáros or *bakaláos* - Salted
  cod, 161 (also fresh hake, or
  whiting, 113)

193

Index

Index

- cooking - *kouvertoúra*, for cake icing
Chops - *Brizóles*
- beef - *b. moscharísies*
- pork - *b. hirinés*
  see also Barbecue, 94; and lamb chops - *païdákia (arní hasápiko)*, 82
Christmas bread - *Christópsomo*, 168
Christmas shortbread -*Kourabiédes*, 166
Christópsaro - John Dory fish, 4
Christópsomo - Christmas bread, 168
Cinnamon - *Kanélla*
Citric acid - *xinó kitrikó* or *kitrikó oxí* (on some jars translated as "sour")
- for pistachio nuts, 114
Citrus fruits for freezing, 139
Clemantines - *Klemantínes*, 141
Cloves - *Garýfala*, which also means carnations, so via clove carnations or pinks, sometimes labelled "pink!"
Cocoa - *Kakáo*
Coconut - *Karýda indién* or *indikí karýda* or even *kókonat*, 4, 26, 159
Cod - roe - *Taramás* (spread - *táramosaláta*), 28, rissoles - *táramokeftédes*, 29
- salted - *bakaliáros* (or *bakaláos*), 161
Coffee - *Kafés*, 173
Cognac - *Koniák*, *see* Brandy
Compôte of fruit - *Kompósta*, 96, 153, 167
Conserves, *see* Preserves - *Glyká tou koutalioú* and Jam - *Marmeláda*
Cookies
- for Christmas - *kourabiédes*, 166
- for Easter - *koulourákia*, 51
Coriander - *Kolíandros*

Corn
- barley - *krithári*
- bread, *see* Cornmeal bread, 40
- maize (sweetcorn, Indian corn) - *kalambóki, aravósito*, 114
- oats - *vrómi* (and *kwáiker!*)
- wheat - *stári, sitári, see* under Wheat
Corn oil - *Kalambokélaio*, 182
Corn starch - *Kornfláour* or *ánthos aravosítou*
Corn syrup - *Glykózi* (Glucose), 22, 70, 149, 181
Cornflour, *see* Corn starch
Cornmeal - *Kalambokálevro*
- c. bread - *bobóta* or *stafidópitta*, 40; syrup for, 38
Courgette flowers - *Kolokythokorfádes*, 74
Courgettes (baby marrows, zucchini, summer squash) - *Kolokýthia, kolokythákia*
- baked, with cheese and tomato sauce, 75
- boiled, as salad - *k. saláta*, 74
- fried - *k. tiganitá*, 75
- omelette - *k. me avgá*, 119
- stewed, with potatoes - *briám, k. yachní*, 74
- stuffed halves ("boats") with mince - *papoutsákia*, 92
- stuffed halves with cheese and onion, 92
- stuffed halves with rice and tomato, 104
- stuffed whole - *k. yemistá*, 104,
Crabs - *Kavoúria*, 100
Cracked wheat - *Pligoúri, pourgoúri*
- salad with tomatoes and mint, 76
  see also *Trahanás*
Crawfish, or Spiny lobster - *Astakós*, 27, 100
Crayfish, or Scampi - *Karavídes*, 127

196

Index

198

199

Index

Index

202

Index

Persimmons - *Lotoús*, 159
Péstrofa - Trout, 77
Petimézi - Grape juice syrup, 139
Phýllo, see Fýllo (Pastry), 182
Picarel - *Marídes*, 113, 178
Pickles - *Toursí*
- aubergines - *melitzánes t.*, 150
- capers - *kápari t.*, 82
- mixed vegetables - *toursá*, 27
- octopus - *ktapódi t.*, 130
- onions - *kremmydákia t.*, 125
Pie - *Pítta*, pastry for, 182
- cheese, savoury - *tyropittákia*, 66
- cheese, sweet - *militíni*, 52
- chicken - *kotópitta*, 21
- custard - *galaktoboúreko*, 67
- leek - *prasópitta*, 146
- macaroni - *pastítsio*, 34
- pumpkin - *kolokythópitta*, 37
- spinach - *spanakópitta*, 14
see also Cakes, Pastry
Pig, sucking - *Gourounópoulo*, 159
see also Pork
Piláfi, see Rice, 183
Pineapple - *Ananás*, 4, 159
Pipéri - Pepper
Piperiés, see Peppers, sweet
Piperórizo - Ginger, 125
Pistachio nuts - *Fistíkia Aigínis*, 114
Pítta, see Pie
Plakí - thick tomato and onion sauce for baked fish or beans, *q.v.*
Pligoúri, pourgoúri - Cracked wheat, 76
Plums - *Damáskiná*; varieties - *vanílies, koromila*, 88
- in compôte - *kompósta*, 96
see Prunes, also called *Damáskina*
Pomegranates - *Ródia*, 4, 159
- in *Kólyva*, 28
Pork - *Hirinó*

- casserole, with red wine - *Afélia*, 7
- chops - *hirinés brizóles*, 94
- with celeriac - *h. me selinórizo*, 144
- with celery - *h. me sélino*, 144
- with quinces - *h. me kydónia*, 141, 146
see also Pig, sucking - *gourounópoulo*, 159
Portokália, see Oranges
Potatoes - *Patátes*
- crisps - *tsips*
- fried - *p. tiganités*
- mashed - *p. pouré*
see also Sweet potatoes
Pouré, see Purée
Prása, see Leeks
Prawns, *see* Shrimps
Preserves - *Glyká tou koutalioú, Glykó*
- aubergine - *melitzanáki g.*, 151
- bitter orange peel - *nerántzi g.*, 22
- fig - *sýko g.*, 70, 111
- grape - *soultanína g.*, 124
- lemon peel - *lemóni g.*, 23
- quince - *kydóni g.*, 153, 154
- sour cherry - *vísino g.*, 97
- strawberry - *fráoula g.*, 85
- test for syrup, 181
see also Jams and jellies
Prickly pears - *Frangósyka* or *Aravósyka*, 114
Prunes - *Damáskina* (same word as for plums); with fresh pears, and in dried fruit salad, 167
Psarádika - Fish market
Psári, see Fish
Psarósoupa - Fish soup, 32
Pseftomoussakás - False moussaka (without meat), 122
Pséftokeftédes - Vegetable fritters, 115
Psitó - baked or roasted

204

Index

greens, boiled - *hórta*, 47
- lettuce, with onion and dill - *maroúli s.*, 60
- red pepper - *piperiés s.*, 117
- tomato - *domáta s.*, 89
- village - *horiátiki s.*, 89
see also Dips, spreads and purées
Salad dressings, 185
Saláta, see Salad (also refers to round lettuces and to dips and some purées, q.v.)
Salingária - Snails, 113, 117
Salt - *Aláti*
Sáltsés - Sauces, 184-189
Santiyí - Whipped cream, 174
Sarakostí - Lent (church season, fasting), 26
Sardélles, see Sardines
Sardines - *Sardélles*, 18, 88, 178
Sauces - *Sáltses*, 184-189
see also Dips, spreads and purées
Scallions, *see* Onions, spring
Scampi (crayfish) - *Karavídes*, 127
Scented geranium leaves - *Arbaróriza*, 57
- in quince preserve and jelly, 154, 155
Scháras - a grill, hence grilled (broiled), *see* Barbecue, 94
Sea bream, *see* Bream
Sea urchin - *Achinós*, 100
Sélino - Celery, with pork - *hirinó me. s.*, 144
Selinórizo - Celeriac, with pork - *hirinó me s.*, 144
Semolina - *Simigdáli*
- dessert - *halvás tou Monasterioú*, 122
- cake - *ravaní* (or *halvás tis Rénas*), 54
- in custard pie - *galaktoboúreko*, 67
Sesame seeds - *Sousámi*, 27, 114
Sesame seed oil and paste - Tahini, 26
- as a dip, 31

- with chick peas - hummus, 30
Sfyrída, see Grouper (white fish)
Shark - *Galéos*, 141, 146
Shortbread - *Kourabiédes*, 166
Shrimps - *Garídes*, 100, 127
- baked in tomato sauce with feta cheese, 105
Simigdáli, see Semolina
Sitári, see Wheat
Skórda, see Garlic
Skordaliá - Garlic sauce or dip, 186
Skoumbrí, see Mackerel
Skylópsaro, skyláki - Dogfish, 146
Smyrna sausages - *Soutsoukákia*, 80
Snails - *Salingária*, 113, 117
Sole - *Glóssa*, 178
Soultanínes - seedless white grapes, 113, 124
Soup - *Soúpa*
- chick pea - *revíthia s.*, 30
- chicken, with egg and lemon - *avgolémono s.*, 20
- fish - *psarósoupa*, 4, 32, 179
- lamb - *mayerítsa*, 44
- lentil - *fakés s.*, 5
- tripe - *patsás*, 6
- wheat and milk - *trahanás* or *trahanósoupa*, 160
Soupiá - Cuttlefish, 130, 131
Sour - *Xynó*
Sour cherries - *Vísina, see* Cherries
Sousámi - Sesame seeds
Soutzoukákia - Smyrna sausages, 80
Soúvla - a spit, hence meat cooked on it
Souvlákia - Kebabs, 95
Spanáki, see Spinach
Spices - *Bahariká* or *Arómata*
Spinach - *Spanáki*
- pie - *spanakópitta*, 14
- with cuttlefish - *soupiá me s.*, 131
- with rice - *spanakórizo*, 62

206

Index

- juice, 191
- salad - *d. saláta* and in *horiátiki s.*, 89
- stuffed - *d. yemistés*, 101, 102
- with baked fish - *psári plakí*, 178
- with cuttlefish - *soupiá me sáltsa*, 130
- with lamb chops - *arní hasápiko*, 82
- with scrambled eggs - *strapatsáda*, 103
- with stewed okra - *bámies yachní*, 106

Tomatopoltós - Tomato paste
Tongue, beef - *Glóssa vodinoú* or *moscharísia*
- for *stifádo*, 133
Tónnos or *tonnáki, see* Tunny
Tost, see Toast, 172
Toursí, see Pickles
Toúrta - Gateau, cream cake
Trahanás - Crushed wheat and dried sheep's milk
- sweet - *t. glykós* or sour - *t. xynós* (also called *hondrós*)
- *t. soúpa*, 160
see also Leek pie, 146
Trífti - grater, hence *triméno* - grated
Trimáta - crumbled feta cheese, 174
Tripe soup - *Patsás*, 6
Trout - *Péstrofa*, 77
Tsái - Tea, 191; herb teas, tisanes, 24
Tsipoúra - Gilt-head bream or daurade, *see* Bream
Tsípouro - wine must pulp and spirit made from it, 141
Tsips - Potato crisps, not chips!
Tsouréki - Easter bread (sweet), 42
Tsoutzoukákia, see Soutzoukákia, 80

Tunny or bluefin tuna- *Tónnos, tonnáki*, 88, 127, 177
Turkey - *Galopoúla* or *gálos*, 162
Tyrí, see Cheese
Tyropittákia - small cheese pies, 52, 66
Tzatzíki - Yoghurt dip with garlic and cucumber, 45, 76

Vanilla - *vaníllia* (sold as a white powder)
Vaníllias - dark red plums, 88
Varélli - Barrel; tavernas may serve wine from it - *ápo to varélli*
Vasilikó - Basil, 71
Vasilópitta - New Year Cake, 4, 8
Veal - *Moschári, see* Beef
Vegetables - *Lahaniká*
- fritters - *pseftokeftédes*, 115
- moussaka - *pseftomoussakás*, 112
see also under each kind, tomatoes, etc.
Verýkoka - Apricots; jam - *v. marmeláda*, 84
Village salad - *Horiátiki saláta*, 89
Vine leaves, stuffed - *Dolmádes Yalántzi*, 58
Vinegar - *Xýdi*, also *glykádi*, 137
Visina, see Cherries, sour
Visináda - Cherry cordial, 97
Vlíta - Salad greens (white goose foot), 47
Vótana - Wild herbs, 23
Voútyro - Butter, 175
Vrastó - boiled
Vroúva - Charlock (mustard) for boiled salad greens, 47

Walnuts - *Karýdia*, 114, 128
- cake - *Karydópitta*, 134
- in Christmas bread, 168
Water - *neró*
Watermelon - *Karpoúzi*, 88
Wheat - *Stári* or *sitári*
- boiled - *kólyva*, 28

208

Other Lycabettus Press Publications

Athens-Auschwitz, by Errikos Sevillias
Christians in the Arab East, by Robert B. Betts
Cookbook of the Jews of Greece, by Nicholas Stavroulakis
Delphi, by Alan Walker
Doorway to Greece, by Mary Winterer-Papatassos
Epidaurus (Greek), by Nikolaos Faraklas
Excuse Me, Miss, Have You Seen the Acropolis?
    by S. Joseph and D. White
Greek Dances, by Ted Petrides
Hydra, by Catherine Vanderpool
Kos, by Chris and Christa Mee
Lefkadia (English and German editions),
    by J. Touratzoglou
Mythistorima and Gymnopaidia, by George Seferis
    (poetry) translated by Mary Cooper Walton
Nauplion, by Timothy E. Gregory
Naxos, by John Freely
Paros (German), by Jeffrey Carson and James Clark
Paros, Roads, Trails, and Beaches,
    by Jeffrey Carson and James Clark
Patmos (English and German editions), by Tom Stone
Poros, by Niki Stavrolakes
Spetsai, by Andrew Thomas
*St. John of Patmos and the Seven Churches
    of the Apocalypse*, by Otto F. A. Meinardus
St. Paul in Ephesus and the Cities of Galatia and Cyprus,
    by Otto F. A. Meinardus
St. Paul in Greece (English, French, and German
    editions), by Otto F. A. Meinardus
Tom Stone's Greek Handbook, by Tom Stone
Tom Stone's Greek Food and Drink Book, by Tom Stone
Vergina (English and Greek editions), by M. Andronicos

CAT IN A VEGAS
GOLD VENDETTA

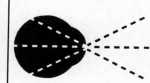

This Large Print Book carries the
Seal of Approval of N.A.V.H.

A MIDNIGHT LOUIE MYSTERY

CAT IN A VEGAS GOLD VENDETTA

CAROLE NELSON DOUGLAS

THORNDIKE PRESS
A part of Gale, Cengage Learning

GALE
CENGAGE Learning®

Detroit • New York • San Francisco • New Haven, Conn • Waterville, Maine • London

GALE
CENGAGE Learning®

Copyright © 2011 by Carole Nelson Douglas.
Thorndike Press, a part of Gale, Cengage Learning.

LIBRARY OF CONGRESS CATALOGING-IN-PUBLICATION DATA

Douglas, Carole Nelson.
    Cat in a Vegas gold vendetta : a midnight Louie mystery / by Carole Nelson Douglas.
        p. cm. — (Thorndike Press large print mystery)
    ISBN-13: 978-1-4104-4399-1 (hardcover)
    ISBN-10: 1-4104-4399-X (hardcover)
    1. Midnight Louie (Fictitious character)—Fiction. 2. Barr, Temple (Fictitious character)—Fiction. 3. Women private investigators—Fiction. 4. Women cat owners—Fiction. 5. Cats—Fiction. 6. Las Vegas (Nev.)—Fiction. 7. Large type books. I. Title.
PS3554.O8237C27699 2012
813'.54—dc23   2011037974

Published in 2012 by arrangement with Tom Doherty Associates, LLC.

Printed in the United States of America
1 2 3 4 5 6 7 16 15 14 13 12

For all the warm-hearted, caring people who take in homeless cats and work tirelessly in animal rescue

CONTENTS

PREVIOUSLY IN MIDNIGHT LOUIE'S LIVES AND TIMES . . .

Las Vegas is my beat.

And take it from me: now that the economy is down, the heat is up. I am not just talking about the Strip when the temperature hits the low hundreds.

Even the biggest names in this rambling, gambling entertainment capital are no longer feeling the love as they used to. Still, visitors can get some great deals in Vegas nowadays, and not just at the casino tables.

The lights, the security and tourist cameras, the action remain as bright and frenetic as always. The landmark hotel-casinos and allied institutions are still puttin' on the glitz.

Me, I have always kept a low profile for a Las Vegas institution.

You do not hear about me on the nightly news. That is how I like it. That is the way any primo PI would like it. The name is Louie — Midnight Louie. I am a noir kind of guy, inside and out. I like my nightlife shaken, not stirred.

11

Being short, dark, and handsome — really short — gets me overlooked and underestimated, which is what the savvy operative wants anyway. I am your perfect undercover guy. I also like to hunker down under the covers with my little doll.

Miss Temple Barr and I make perfect roomies. She tolerates my wandering ways. I look after her without getting in her way. Call me Muscle in Midnight Black. We share a well-honed sense of justice and long, sharp fingernails and have cracked some cases too tough for the local fuzz. She is, after all, a freelance public-relations specialist, and Las Vegas is full of public and private relations of all stripes and legalities.

I must admit that our last crime-busting outing took us a step beyond the beyond to a conspiracy of magicians and a collision with the mean streets of international terrorism and counterterrorism, which left us both breathless.

Let me just say that everything it seemed you could bet on is now up for grabs, and my Miss Temple may be in the lose-lose situation of her life and times.

So, on the current situation of where we are all at:

None can deny that the Las Vegas crime scene is big-time, and I have been treading these mean neon streets for twenty-three books now. I am an "alphacat." Since I debuted in *Catnap* and *Pussyfoot,* I commenced to a title sequence that is as sweet and simple as B to Z.

My alphabet begins with the B in *Cat on a Blue Monday.* After that, the title's most colorful word or phrase is in alphabetical order up to the — *ahem* — current volume, *Cat in a Vegas Gold Vendetta.*

Since Las Vegas is littered with guidebooks as well as bodies, I wish to provide a rundown of the local landmarks on my particular map of the world. A cast of characters, so to speak:

To wit, my petite roommate and high-heels devotee, Miss Nancy Drew on killer spikes, freelance PR ace Miss Temple Barr, who had reunited once before — and now reconnected again — with her elusive love . . .

. . . the once and future missing-in-action magician Mr. Max Kinsella, who has good reason for invisibility. After his cousin Sean died in a bomb attack during a post–high-school jaunt to Ireland, he joined the man who became his mentor, Gandolph the Great, in undercover counterterrorism work.

Meanwhile, Mr. Max has been sought on suspicion of murder by another dame, Las Vegas homicide detective Lieutenant C. R. Molina, single mother of teenage Mariah.

13

Mama Molina is also the good friend of Miss Temple's freshly minted fiancé, Mr. Matt Devine, a radio talk-show shrink and former Roman Catholic priest who came to Vegas to track down his abusive stepfather and ended up becoming a syndicated radio celebrity.

Speaking of unhappy pasts, Miss Lieutenant Carmen Regina Molina is not thrilled that her former flame, Mr. Rafi Nadir, now living and working in Las Vegas after blowing his career at the LAPD, and for years the unsuspecting father of Mariah, now knows what is what and who is whose.

Meanwhile, Mr. Matt drew a stalker, the local lass that Max and his cousin Sean boyishly competed for in that long-ago Ireland, . . .

. . . one Miss Kathleen O'Connor, deservedly christened Kitty the Cutter by Miss Temple. Finding Mr. Max as impossible to trace as Lieutenant Molina did, Kitty the C settled for harassing with tooth and claw the nearest innocent bystander, Mr. Matt Devine, and came to a spectacular end in a motorcycle crash.

Now that Miss Kathleen O'Connor's sad and later sadistic history indicates she might not be dead and buried like all rotten elements, things are shaking up again at the Circle Ritz. Mr. Max Kinsella is no longer MIA and feared dead, though I saw him hit the wall of the

14

Neon Nightmare club with lethal impact while in the guise of a bungee-jumping magician, the Phantom Mage.

That this miraculous resurrection coincided with my ever-lovin' roommate having gone over to the Light Side (our handsome, blond upstairs neighbor, Mr. Matt Devine) in her romantic life only adds to the angst and confusion.

However, things are seldom what they seem, and almost never that in Las Vegas. A magician can have as many lives as a cat, in my humble estimation, and events now bear me out. Meanwhile, Miss Lieutenant C. R. Molina's domestic issues past and present are on a collision course as she deals with two circling mystery men of her own — Mr. Rafi Nadir and Mr. Dirty Larry Podesta, an undercover narc who has wormed his way into her personal and professional crusades.

Such surprising developments do not surprise me. Everything is always up for grabs in Las Vegas 24/7 — guilt, innocence, money, power, love, loss, death, and significant others.

All this human sex and violence makes me glad that I have a simpler social life, such as just trying to get along with my unacknowledged daughter, . . .

. . . Miss Midnight Louise, who insinuated

herself into my cases until I was forced to set up shop with her as Midnight Investigations, Inc. . . . .

. . . and needing to unearth more about the Synth, a cabal of magicians that may be responsible for a lot of murderous cold cases in town, now the object of growing international interest, but as MIA as Mr. Max had been lately.

So, there you have it, the usual human stew — folks good, bad, and hardly indifferent — totally mixed up and at odds with one another and within themselves. Obviously, it is up to me to solve all their mysteries and nail some crooks along the way.

Like Las Vegas, the City That Never Sleeps, Midnight Louie, private eye, also has a sobriquet: the Kitty That Never Sleeps.

With this crew, who could?

CHAPTER 1
TEMPLE BARR, PI

Temple's fingers were doing the flamenco across her laptop keyboard, writing an e-mail press release, with Midnight Louie, her twenty-pound black cat, playing his usual role of paperweight beside her, when her phone rang.

She jumped.

Midnight Louie growled in alarm and rose up on his forelegs.

Temple wasn't the skittish type. You had to have nerves of steel to deal with the emergencies and sudden zigs and zags that a freelance public-relations person had to control, particularly in Vegas, and particularly in these Internet character-assassination days.

She had a right to be jumpy after that international phone call twelve hours ago from the late great Max Kinsella, missing magician and ex–significant other, back from the presumed dead. He was even now flying back to Vegas on her say-so, after he'd encountered danger, death, and memory-melting head trauma in Northern Ireland. She was picking him up at the airport later today.

So this phone call could be full of woe.

Or, since her new and true love and official fiancé, radio counselor Matt Devine, was flying back from Chicago in two days and had family there, he could be calling to report snags, feuds, or winning the Power Ball lottery.

Either way, she was now a nervous Nellie about the simple act of answering the phone.

No caller name popped up on the phone screen. Normally, a blank screen meant new business, but just right now Temple was a little shaky on dealing with voices from the Blank Nowhere.

She picked up the phone and said, "Hello." Cautiously.

"Temple Barr?"

Relief. A woman was calling. The ghost from her recent past wasn't calling back. Yet.

"Right," Temple said.

"Do you mean this is the right Temple Barr?"

"Yes."

"*The* Temple Barr?"

"I like to think so."

By now Louie's softly growled warnings were a musical accompaniment. He knew when she was tense or worried.

"I didn't reach that eatery out on Temple Bar at Lake Mead somehow?" the voice persisted. "It sounds like a kid is whining in the background."

"No, you've reached me, the Temple Barr with two *r*s."

The voice, both breathy and chesty, was beginning to sound awfully familiar. "Awful" in the deeply serious sense of the word.

"May I ask who's calling, please?" Temple said. Her normal voice had a slightly hoarse edge, and it was getting raspy with impatience and . . . dawning horror.

"This is Savannah Ashleigh." Pause for effect. "The screen star."

The second sentence was highly debatable. The first was . . . all too true.

Temple had crossed paths and swords with the ditsy, glitzy C-movie queen several times. The worst was the occasion when Midnight Louie had been cast in cat food commercials with Ashleigh's Persian beauty, Yvette. When Yvette proved to be with kittens, Savannah had accused Louie of illegal littering and had actually tried to do him

19

bodily harm.

Fortunately, twenty pounds of ex–alley cat Louie can handle any scheming human from murderer to media minx. He came out of the incident proved innocent, in tact, and on top, as usual.

Temple, however, was terminally disgusted with Savannah Ashleigh and all her works.

"What can I do for you, Miss Ashleigh?" Temple asked in a businesslike monotone, polite and oh-so-wishing the connection would break. Cell phone reception was extremely iffy in Las Vegas, especially near the Strip. Connections could be hard to hold. This one wasn't. Alas.

Temple sat and listened and nodded, not inclined to take the woman seriously. Finally, she got a sentence in.

"Murders happen every day in Las Vegas and surrounding suburbs, Miss Ashleigh. . . . No, not in your neighborhood, I'm sure. . . . Oh. Never, you say?"

Temple couldn't quite believe that any Vegas neighborhood hadn't hosted murder old or new.

"Um, you want to *hire* me to investigate a murder? And where do I see *clients?*" she echoed her caller.

Temple thought hard. She was now too curious to indulge her dislike. Although she had a knack for solving murders, no one had ever wanted to hire her to do it. And the "case" would take her mind off . . . impending men.

She did not want the memory of Savannah Ashleigh polluting her living quarters. Not that the woman was bad — besides at acting; she was just a Ditz Queen who usually traveled with a purse pet of some kind. Midnight Louie would never get over his turf being so invaded after what Savannah had done.

She glanced again at Louie, getting an idea. He'd once favored hanging out near a canna-lily stand and koi pond, like Sam Spade keeping office hours behind the . . .

"Of course," she told Savannah Ashleigh. "We could meet at the Crystal Phoenix Hotel."

"Yes," she repeated her caller's reaction, "it *is* 'always gracious to do business over a good belt.' I'll meet you at the Crystal Court Bar. One P.M."

Temple shut off the connection.

Louie was regarding her, enormous green eyes reducing his pupils to their most condemnatory slits. Temple made excuses, fast.

"It *is* Savannah Ashleigh, as you heard. Maybe she meant 'belt' in the sense of . . . a

21

solid Austrian crystal Judith Leiber designer belt — yum — or conchos or shells or even a black belt."

Louie gave his opinion of this meeting by swiping the last printed-out pages off her desk. Now that was a "good belt."

"You can come along and visit Midnight Louise," she coaxed him. "Wouldn't that be nice?"

Midnight Louise was a black stray who'd taken Louie's position of house cat at the Phoenix after he'd moved in with Temple at the Circle Ritz condominium and apartment building.

Nice? Louie had no comment but chewing the hairs between his toes.

"Besides," Temple mused. "I'm wondering why Savannah Ashleigh wants to see me about a murder. Aren't you even curious?"

That comment propelled him off the desk to the floor.

Temple checked her watch. Eleven A.M. It must be five o'clock somewhere, and she could use a "belt" or two as well. Matt wasn't coming home from a career-changing personal appearance on *The Amanda Show* in Chicago for three days, but what was left of Max was flying in from Northern Ireland late this afternoon.

Temple guessed she could use a time-wasting rendezvous with a has-been, B-minus movie actress to keep her mind off the forthcoming personal apocalypse.

CHAPTER 2
A VERY FERAL FELLOW

I am not accustomed to rolling up to the Crystal Phoenix's elegant front entrance in style. Usually, I must slink in the side or back of the fabled Las Vegas hotel-casino like a common stray.

Frankly, I prefer it that way. No PI in the business wants to announce his or her particular sources and haunts.

However, I feel obligated to escort my esteemed roommate on this difficult day. I am doing all I can to distract her from the impending reunion with her former roommate, Mr. Max Kinsella. If I must throw a few papers around, or a tantrum, I will.

I will even show my mug on the front passenger seat of Miss Temple's red Miata. Usually I hitch a ride on the dark carpeting of backseats, unseen and inhaling a lot of foot odor and the scent of all the ugly things a human shoe can stomp on. Unlike we of the superior breed, humans *never* clean their soles but reuse them unwashed again and again.

On the bright side, this filthy habit does make the human kind much easier to track.

"Why, Louie," Miss Temple says as I slip in the open driver's side door and hop onto the passenger seat. "You want to ride shotgun?"

After an exasperated look and a check of the large dial of her wristwatch, she caves. "If this were an airport run, I'd kick you off the leather seat, but it's only the Crystal Phoenix, and I suppose you want to arrive at your old place in style. Remember. Velvet paws. No claws on the leather upholstery, not even if I have to brake suddenly. The floor carpeting is all right, though."

I do like the way my Miss Temple acts as if I am totally conversation-worthy, although I would never deign to talk back to humans.

I blink my agreement to her terms and prepare to enjoy what some of the commonest dogs do — a spin in the car.

Las Vegas is offering a warm spring day, so my Miss Temple has donned lots of lightly scented sunscreen that helps ban any offensive human odors. She is a red-cream kind of kitten with sun-sensitive face and body leather.

Of course, my glistening black coat shines like wet tar in the sunshine and even under the Crystal Phoenix's front canopy of mirror and tiny crystal lights when we shortly arrive there, sans sudden braking.

I jump out when the doorman opens my side and wait politely for Miss Temple to precede me within while tourists gawk. They do not know my long history here as hotel cat and unofficial house detective before I linked up with Miss Temple and the Circle Ritz bunch.

Before we can enter I am upstaged, however.

Out of the row of brass and glass doors rushes one Fontana brother.

Just one. What a disappointment! There are ten in all, and Nicky, the youngest, owns the Crystal Phoenix. Out comes Aldo, the eldest. The fickle tourist cameras turn toward his five-star looks and high-style, pale-mango Italian suit and the petite redhead on his arm who embraces my Miss Temple and does kissy-cheeks.

Those of my breed do not deign to do kissy-cheeks. It would disarrange our magnificent, delicate vibrissae, aka whiskers. We do sniffy noses. Wait! That is not as off-putting as it sounds.

"Temple," the former Miss Kit Carlson, her maternal aunt, says. "We are just back from abroad and were heading to the Circle Ritz to see you."

26

I stare rebukingly at the new Mrs. Aldo Fontana until the searing burn of my regard forces her to look down.

"To see you *and* Midnight Louie, of course," she corrects herself.

By now, Aldo is doing the kissy-cheek thing with Miss Temple. Continental, I am told, but it strikes me as unsanitary.

"How was Italy?" Miss Temple inquires, it being impolite to baldly ask how these post-wedding flings called "honeymoons" went, which is, of course, what everyone really wants to know.

"Divine," Miss Kit replies.

I do not abide by human conventions. I do not care if Miss Kit Carlson is married; she is still a Miss Kit to me. *Missus* is such a dé-classé word.

"How are things going here with you?" Miss Kit adds with an amiable smile.

"You would not believe," my Miss Temple answers. "Meanwhile, I'm late; I'm late for a very insignificant date. May we catch up later, please?"

"Of course," Miss Kit says. She is a thirty-year-older version of Miss Temple, and her prime state of preservation for an old dame should cheer up my now-distracted roomie.

I am not about to miss a word that these two exchange about the Current Crises, for they are more gal-pals than aunt and niece. Since Miss Temple has only older brothers in Minnesota, it is fortunate she has a hip, ex-Manhattanite aunt on the scene to help me provide aid and comfort in the coming end of days.

We bustle inside. That is, my Miss Temple bustles, slinging greetings to bellmen and other passing hotel staff. I follow her in slink mode so she will not have to answer awkward questions about my ability to heel like a dog if I so choose.

My breed is not expected to trot docilely along, and Bast forbid that I should let my breed down. Besides, I know that Miss Temple is headed for the Crystal Court, so I race to install myself discreetly before her arrival. She will think that I have headed to the rear pool area to drool over the nearby koi pond.

Soon my baby greens are peering through the indoor greenery to the cocktail table for two where Miss Savannah Ashleigh has arranged herself.

Being five-foot-nothing, Miss Temple favors high heels, but they are usually the classy three-inch designer kind. Miss Savannah goes for what are called "hooker shoes," high-rises of four or even five inches. She also wears inflated blond hair (extensions) and inflated lip and chest parts (collagen).

I can understand the human urge to supplement their scanty hair, but not to emphasize bare skin devoid of fur.

I examine the bulky purse thankfully concealing the Ashleigh footwear at the moment. A pair of small shiny black eyes peeks out. Or is that "Pekes" out? I know the fickle actress has forsaken her Persian cat beauties for mere pip-squeak canines these days. Recalling my recent undercover gig as a "purse pussy," I am in sudden sympathy with the pathetic pooch. The front paws and full head are now visible, and it is too small for even the tiniest Chihuahua.

I pad over to inspect and sniff. Dear Predatory, Bountiful Bast! It is vermin of some kind! Barely have I realized its, ah, composition, than it slithers out of the designer bag, runs out of sight behind me, and hitches a ride on my terminal member.

Spinning, I discover it is clinging there with all four tiny paws, like a quartet of staplers. I cannot whip around fast enough to dislodge the furry little imp, and I am soon dizzy and in danger of making an exhibition of myself, which is the last thing an undercover operative wants to do.

On my final spin I lose the unwanted "tail" and spot its face once again peeking out from the side pocket of the blasted bag. Surely such a savage little thing is not housebroken. The mind boggles at what it must be doing in Miss Savannah Ashleigh's purse all day.

Behind me I hear the crisp approach of Miss Temple's Stuart Weitzman petite-platform ankle-strap shoes. *Rats!* I need to dive back under cover. Rats? Why would Miss Savannah Ashleigh have a pet rat? One that is not even an attractive laboratory-white but plain dumpster-brown?

I had been planning to make a sentimental journey back to my old PI office near the poolside canna lilies out back — back by Chef Song's koi pond. Now, I must guard Miss Temple platform-and-ankle-strap from some street vermin playing footsie with her.

I settle onto my haunches for a long eavesdropping session, when a low hiss at my rear tells me we are not alone.

"I thought I smelled a rat," says Miss Midnight Louise, all narrowed gold irises and fluffed black fur, nosing her obnoxious way alongside me so close you could not slip a piece of onionskin paper between us, "but it is just you."

"Most amusing. If you will keep an eye on Miss Savannah Ashleigh's bag, you will spot a real rat."

"No! Has purse poochery come down to this? At least, the underground link to Gangsters has been certified rat-free by the health department, and the Neon Nightmare access has been cemented shut."

"That case and the secret tunnel may be closed, but more crime in the making is brewing somewhere. Just keep watching and listening."

Something more than mere vermin is afoot, and it has peroxided hair and mighty high arches.

CHAPTER 3
VIOLETS ARE BLUE

"I want to hire you," Savannah Ashleigh told Temple, after their ordered drinks had arrived.

"I'm strictly Las Vegas–based," Temple said, although that might shortly become Chicago if Matt's career break materialized. "You . . . work out of L.A., I would think."

"You would think wrong. I've relocated to Las Vegas because my precious Captain Jack is not allowed to be maintained in the style to which he is accustomed in California."

"Your 'precious Coco,' isn't it? I saw during the Red Hat Sisterhood convention that you'd retired your Persians, Yvette and Solitaire —"

"Please. Solange."

"— and Solange, in favor of a small dog."

"Coco is a papillon, but he too is retired. Too much piddling."

"So Captain Jack would be — ?"

Savannah reached down to probe her

designer bag, which carried enough clanking brass straps and buckles to outfit an ancient Roman soldier. She lifted out something lean, long, brown, and crew-cut furry that resembled no minidog or -cat Temple had ever seen.

A small face masked like a raccoon's peered over Savannah's thin, veined hands.

Words like *weasel, mink,* and *wolverine* — wait! *chinchilla* or *sable* — darted through Temple's mind, but they were hardly domesticated. She decided to find out.

"Well, Captain Jack seems to have the eyeliner concession down for the role. Is that a baby raccoon?"

"Of course not. A raccoon is a wild animal. Captain Jack is just wildly darling."

Savannah reached a dagger-nailed hand into the side pocket and pulled out a long supple creature that reminded Temple of an animated blond mink from the bad old days when women flounced around with a posse of full animal skins flagellating their shoulders.

Captain Jack ably escaped his mistress's clutches to circle her neck, run down and along the boosted ledge of her bodice, and cradle himself on her forearm.

Temple studied the close-set, bearlike ears, the ratlike pink nose, and clawed toes.

She now saw the rhinestoned harness fastened around the lean and furry body. A pet that some states might allow and others ban would be a . . .

"He's a ferret?"

"Not just any ferret," Savannah cooed. "He is his mumsy's adorable little mischief maker."

Watching Savannah's seriously over-collagened lips making kissy-face with a ferret had to be high on anyone's Ick List. The actress chattered on.

"Captain Jack is a daring and brilliant rascal. Did you know, Temple, that ferrets are the third most popular pet in the country and members of the cat family?"

"Nope." Temple, dumbstruck, doubted Savannah's extravagant claims but forgot them when she felt a feathery agitation at her bare ankles. She gazed down at a creeping carpet of glossy-leaved indoor groundcover to spot two bewhiskered black furry faces with narrowed eyes of green and gold.

"What are the predators for this sort of creature?" Temple asked, worried.

"Coyotes, great horned owls, golden eagles, prairie falcons, badgers, foxes, and bobcats," Savannah answered proudly from some guidebook, probably *Ferrets for Dum-*

34

mies. "But that's in the wild. We're in Las Vegas."

"I've known plenty of coyotes, badgers, foxes, and bobcats in Vegas," Temple said. "Birds of prey, not so much."

"Whatever, nobody is going to get Mama's little *oochum-moochum.* Really, Temple. May I call you that?" When Temple nodded, she rushed on. "You must consider dumping that misbehaving alley cat of yours for one of these darlings. They can even be vasectomized, as I so kindly — if accidentally — provided that service for your Twilight Toby, or whomever. So they have the cutest fuzzy little —"

"Ouch!" The agitation at Temple's ankles had developed claw tips.

"Oh, my dear," Savannah said, "you mustn't personalize 'fixing' our little boys. The surgery really doesn't hurt. Don't be so . . . tenderhearted."

"I'm more tender-ankled at the moment," Temple said. "And my cat's name is Louie, Midnight Louie."

"Don't be grumpy either. It can't be good for your business to contradict clients."

"You're not my client yet."

"I will be."

Temple sincerely doubted that, but sipped her wine spritzer, giving Savannah time to

35

take a huge gulp of her mint julep before continuing.

"You see, Temple, you do remember Yvette and Solange. Who could forget my silver and golden Persian beauties? My apartment in L.A. was too crowded for them when I got Captain Jack, and I travel so much, so . . . I left them with my aunt Violet here in Vegas."

Temple noticed the groundcover at her feet shifting as if a huge, hungry boa constrictor were slithering beneath it. She guessed that Midnight Louise was restraining Midnight Louie from going for Savannah's ankles for real.

He had performed in TV cat food commercials with Yvette, and Solange was no stranger to him, either. Hearing they'd been dumped for a dog, for a purse pooch at that, and dumped so near to his own doorstep and he'd never known, would not soothe the savage feline soul.

"I don't understand," Temple said, glancing at her watch.

The half-wine, half-sparkling-water drink was not settling the butterflies in her stomach, and she had a lot of driving to do this afternoon and tonight. Granted, distances around the Las Vegas Strip were short, but they were traffic jammed too.

"You want me to dream up another commercial gig using the ferret?" Temple asked.

"Captain Jack is not an ordinary ferret, but this isn't about him or your Midnight Moocher. It's about my aunt Violet's yardman being found dead in some kind of . . . sinkhole at the back of her property. I find the incident most suspicious. Violet lives alone and has collected a lot of nice things. She's been harassed by phone calls and e-mails. She's reported some of her suspicions about neighbors to the police, but they brushed her off like a case of dandruff, so Violet doesn't want to involve the cops any more than they have to be after the death she is certain was meant for her. I need a PI to look into things."

"Not a PR?" Temple asked, joking. That was on her business card: TEMPLE BARR, PR, with the words PUBLIC-RELATIONS SPECIALIST below.

"Why would I want a Puerto Rican?" Savannah wondered aloud. "My cousin lives near a Mexican neighborhood."

Temple shook her head, knowing Savannah was too ditsy to grasp the concept of political correctness, much less the name of the cat she had once falsely accused of fathering Yvette's first and only litter.

On the other hand, Temple was a teensy

37

bit flattered. This was a legitimate offer to investigate.

"Why me?" she asked.

"Oh, you are always around when bad things happen in this town, and I figure you wouldn't want anything fatal to befall Yvette and Solange, since your Chewie or Chewbacca or whomever is sweet on them. My aunt Violet is a pretty smart ginger cookie, but she does have her little ways. She won't give me the cats back, and I'm afraid if her yardman was murdered, like I think, the evil will seep into the house pretty soon."

Temple nodded. "I have some business that will take up the rest of today, but I could look into this tomorrow. Where does your aunt live?"

Savannah passed over a letter the aunt had sent her in L.A. before she'd moved. The return address was one of those small printed rectangles that comes on an adhesive sheet from places where you've once donated money; and your name and address aren't forgotten until the Apocalypse.

VIOLET, was all it read, in capital letters flanked with violet bouquets, and then the street address. Touches of gold foil decorated the tiny label.

"How long has your aunt lived in Vegas?" Temple asked.

"Oh, years. I take the gigs here that I do so I can look in on her. Not that she doesn't resent that. She's quite set in her own way, always was. We haven't been in touch that much through the years, but now . . ."

"Now what?"

"She has terminal cancer, and her only daughter died six years ago, so . . ."

"Violet's daughter died? How?"

"Drugs," Savannah intoned dramatically. "It was very sudden and shocking."

"She must have been . . . young."

"A late-in-life only child. Just twenty-something. Violet was shattered."

"The young woman's father — ?"

"Long gone, along with husbands one through three. Who even knew who the *father* was?" Savannah rolled her eyes.

"What kind of cancer does Violet have?"

"Something deeply personal people do not discuss."

That set Temple's speculations running amok. Enlightened people weren't reticent talking about even terminal AIDS anymore. But then, they weren't dealing with Savannah Ashleigh.

"I'm so sorry about Violet's diagnosis," Temple said. "And you say she's at home? Alone, and frightened?"

"She's had a daily woman come in for

years. Doesn't believe in doctors. Crystals are more her treatment of choice."

"As her niece, can't you — ?"

"All she wants from me is for someone to look into Pedro's murder. He'd worked for her for years and was in her will. She's made it clear that no relative will inherit any of her money or belongings. This might sound strange, Temple, since you seem to be the family-dependent type, and if you don't have any around you find them, but Violet was my youngest aunt and she ran away from our home and family. I finally did, too, and found her when I came out to L.A. We did . . . cling together a bit in our younger days for security's sake, but after Violet had Alexandra, I couldn't believe how she'd doted on that ugly infant. She left the world of glamour in which I was making my way to have no greater ambition than be a single mother and a successful real estate agent. She once was gorgeous, of course. She could have had it all, too. After Alex died in Tucson, Violet moved her daughter's cats to her home here and then started taking in more stray cats to dote on. As you can see, I've moved on."

Captain Jack said *Aye, aye,* by climbing her shoulder, his little clawed "hand" presenting a tiny diamond ear stud he'd found loose in the depths of her bag.

Temple had to admit that the clever ferret and his not-so-clever mistress had certainly distracted her from impending doom, or at least high anxiety. In honor of these unpleasant states, she checked her wristwatch and noted that time had flown.

"Oh! I must be running along. I've got an important pickup at the airport."

They agreed to meet at Violet's house on Aloe Vera Drive the next day. In the *late* morning, Savannah stressed. Violet would be feeling better then and Captain Jack would have had his walk and playtime.

Temple skittered through the Crystal Phoenix crowds, Louie's claws scratching marble underfoot behind her, letting Savannah and her poor aunt fade into the mist of must-dos on her schedule. She could easily get to the airport, but she needed time to dress appropriately to face the most mixed-feeling moment of her life.

Welcoming Max back from the dead.

CHAPTER 4
DEAD LAST

Midnight Louie lay curled atop the bed-
spread like the dark center of a daisy. Making the colorful petals scattered around him
were half the items in Temple's entire
wardrobe, it seemed.

He still looked miffed from overhearing
Savannah Ashleigh play fast and loose with
his unique, entrancing street name. Or
maybe, Temple thought, he remained in a
state of high dudgeon over the cavalier way
Yvette and Solange had been passed from
flaky niece to possibly delusional and seriously ill aunt.

Temple drove the afternoon's distractions
from her mind.

Normally, she wasted no angst on what to
wear. She enjoyed being a girl, as the petite
female usually can. Being a freelance public-
relations professional required more business suits and heels than the average Sunbelt wardrobe, but "business" in Vegas could

be flashier than the whole navy-blue Elsewhere beyond it.

No, she was agonizing over remembering what Max Kinsella had seen or might remember seeing her wear or not, and whether she should try to jog or confuse his missing memory of her when she picked him up at McCarran Airport in . . . her wristwatch's inescapably bold dial told her, seventy-five minutes. A PR person is on perpetual deadline; she can't always be digging out a cell-phone face for the time.

"Louie," she exhorted in a blend of aggravation and plea, "must you exercise squatter's rights on my bed every day? If you're going to lie there like a lump, pick something for me to meet Max in, then."

He slit open his blasé green eyes, yawned to show much tongue and teeth, and stretched a lazy foreleg to a chartreuse polished-cotton suit.

"He'll sure spot me in a crowd if I wear that," Temple admitted, "and it matches the lighter streaks in your eyes — not that you're going with me this time."

With the outfit determined by a clawing instead of drawing lots, Temple next had to confront a deeper problem. To wear her Miracle Bra or not, as she usually did with that figure-flattening suit.

No. She should dress as if retrieving a maiden aunt . . . although her aunt Kit Carlson, now Mrs. Aldo Fontana, was much too chic for the role. A Miracle Bra would be . . . calculating . . . could be misinterpreted. In no way would it be actually inciting, despite her foolish hopes when buying it.

Red patent high-heeled sandals and matching tote bag lifted her spirits if not her bustline. She surveyed herself in the mirror. A petite woman can wear just about everything that is not voluminous or large-patterned. At least her longer, dark strawberry-copper hair color softened the red-and-lime-green, escaped-from-a-jelly-bean-jar look.

Max was not the jelly-bean type. He could spot her easily and then go, *Ick, I could never have slept with that woman, even in my right mind.* And it was true; they'd made an odd couple — the tall, dark, mysterious master magician and the short, firecracker-red-haired PR hotshot.

You're supposed to know me.

Those were among the first words she'd heard on her cell phone only moments after she'd finished talking to Matt just last night. She hadn't instantly recognized the voice, but the call was from Northern Ireland, and

44

the caller admitted he'd been drinking.

Temple was not used to hearing from melancholy, drunk ex-boyfriends. She didn't have that many, for one thing. For another, Max had been far more than a boyfriend.

She glanced at the glittering Art Deco ring on her left hand. Matt had bought it where the movie stars shopped (and borrowed for the Red Carpet), Fred Leighton's Vegas vintage-rocks store. Matt had gone from a vow of poverty to making enough money to needing an agent. He'd rather give it away and knew she cherished vintage things, but sometimes she didn't wear the valuable ring going out alone, for security reasons.

To wear or not to wear. Rubies matched her red shoes and tote bag. Diamonds matched everything. Wear. Max had always been a realist.

So. She'd do her duty, shepherd him back into town, and then get as far away from him as fast as possible . . . except duty, she knew, had a way of slopping over established borders of behavior. If only Aunt Kit had returned from her honeymoon a day earlier than she had to advise her! She was sure Kit would be there to lap up the gory details afterward, though.

Temple marched out of her condo to follow the circular hallway to the single elevator, not reveling in its 1950s touches of burled wood and chrome, as she usually did. The fifties-era round building had an eccentric array of differently laid-out units. It was only five stories at the penthouse level, and the small lobby was usually deserted at midday.

"Well, don't you look spiffy, kiddo!"

Oops. Today of all days, Electra Lark, landlady, would happen to be waiting for the elevator. Or just lurking to make trouble for Temple.

"Um, thanks," Temple said. "You don't think this outfit is too . . . garish?"

"Since when did 'garish' bother you or me or Vegas, Temple honey?"

Electra's halo of white hair was zebra-striped today, with black glitter. Her capacious muumuu was leopard print, and her lipstick was orangutan orange. She was a zoo gone amok.

"Silly of me to worry," Temple said. "I've got to run."

"Oh?" Nosy landlady was a cliché Electra took pride in living up to.

"I've got a quick pickup at McCarran. Kit's back," she semi-lied. "Can't wait. I'm late, I'm late."

And she clattered out the door, her spike heels echoing in the high, empty space.

46

The sun-softened parking lot asphalt forced her to dig in those heels at a sober pace and don her sunglasses before she reached her red Miata. She decided to leave the top up. Some vague notion about not messing her hairdo, or maybe about not being seen going to pick up Max.

You're supposed to know me.

The voice repeated pitch-perfect in her mind. Every word of that one-way "conversation" was etched on her memory. No amnesia on this end, unfortunately.

You're supposed to know me.

That works two ways, dude, Temple thought, starting the Miata. If he didn't recognize her, that might be the best solution.

Forty minutes later she was in Terminal D, wandering among the famous desert-wildlife cast-concrete sculptures crouched on the shiny terrazzo floor. All five sand-colored critters were larger-than-life enough to dwarf kids and most adults. Temple couldn't decide which one to station herself beside.

The sluggish bulk of the desert tortoise really wasn't her speed. The black-tailed jackrabbit hunched into his awesomely long rear legs was the only furry one and reminded Temple that she presently felt like

47

Alice plunging down a dark and mysterious hole.

The scorpion's upraised stone stinger looked too hostile, as did the low, long Mojave rattlesnake.

The horny toad was spined and spiked like a punk rocker, so ugly it was cute, but had an unfortunate name under the circumstances. Luckily, there were no nameplates on the critters, and the horny toad's foreleg was just the right size for Tiny Alice to sit upon, so Temple did.

Her watch told her she was twenty minutes early for the first passengers exiting Max's flight to get through the security checkpoints for arrivals from foreign countries. She began scanning the people pouring from the terminals toward the baggage-claim area anyway, mentally phrasing how she'd explain this to Matt, in person, when *he* arrived on his flight from Chicago in three days.

He was stranded in Ireland without a memory, but with the IRA after him again. Or somebody. His traveling companion was dead. No, I don't know "Why me?" Someone must have told him about me. I couldn't just . . . leave him out there. Christian charity.

"Only redhead sitting on a toadstool. You must be Temple," said a voice behind her.

48

She jumped up and spun around at the same time. "How'd you get through so fast, and past me?"

"I'm told I *was* a magician."

They stared at each other, strangers.

"You look . . ." she began.

"Ghastly?"

She almost retorted, *Ghostly.*

His skin was washed out, not just pale, despite the deliberate smudge of a three-day beard. His expensive wrinkle-shedding clothes weren't the invariable black, but a designer shade of ultradark moss green. He seemed even taller, maybe because he was even thinner. A huge duffel bag crouched like a giant desert lizard at his feet, and he was leaning on a cane like Dr. House of *House,* the TV show.

"You look . . . not like yourself," Temple finally answered.

"Good," he said.

Max wore sunglasses, so she couldn't see his blue eyes, but she sensed him looking her up and down, too. Someone needed to say something next; it might as well be her.

"I, ah, wanted to make sure you couldn't fail to spot me."

"Your eye-catching ensemble does remind me of a Christmas ornament that's gone terribly wrong . . . but this is the first time

I've smiled in four days. Your hair color alone would have done the recognition job, Red."

"You never called me that."

"What did I call you?"

Your paprika girl.

"Temple. Doesn't allow for nicknames. And you've never seen my hair this color."

"What color was it?"

"The natural, really red."

"You needed a new look?"

"I needed a disguise. Long story."

"At least you have one. What are you going to do with me?"

Good question. Luckily, she had an answer. "I thought you'd want to see if the Strip rang any bells, and at least eat something other than travel food."

He nodded as they joined the crowds flowing around them. Temple was used to keeping up with taller people, but she found herself slowing her pace.

I've got two recently broken legs that will ache in this blasted damp weather for the rest of my life if I stay in the damned country. . . .

"I'm in the parking lot," Temple said, "but I drive a . . . Miata."

She saw the fine lines at the outer edges of his eyes wince.

"You own a Maxima," she reassured him.

He winced again. "Am I that egotistical, or do I just have a corny sense of humor?"

"A bit of both." She smiled. "The car is black, like what you always wear."

"I had a feeling I was drawn to the color too much for my own safety."

"I'm . . . taking you to dinner. An orientation exercise."

"I suppose I owe you whatever explanation I can remember. Will that restaurant have a bar? This could be a 'bumpy night.' "

She smiled again, this time at the famous Bette Davis line. He remembered some things just fine.

"You've had a long flight," she said. "I planned on stopping for an early dinner so you can stretch your legs. Or would that be too much right now?"

"I've been alone for four days. I could use some apparently familiar company."

"Aside from the awkwardness," Temple confessed, "I'm dying of curiosity."

"Me too," Max said.

"Why are you doing this, curiosity aside?" Max asked ten minutes later. He'd folded himself like an origami napkin into the Miata's front seat after jamming his crushable duffel bag into what passed as a trunk.

51

"I'm supposed to know you." Temple paused in unfastening the convertible top.

He didn't recognize the near-quote as his. She got out of the car to fold down the top. As she'd anticipated, not enough headroom for Max. He'd never ridden in her Miata, although she'd been a frequent passenger in his cars.

His head turned to follow her around the small car. "You're 'supposed to know me,' but now you don't, I see. *I* don't even know 'me.' "

"Do you . . . remember . . . know . . . *me* at all?"

He shook his head. "Oh, wait."

Temple's breath caught in her chest as she stood still.

"I know you're a generous woman to do this," he said.

Letdown.

"Girl Scout," she agreed.

They were back to banalities, which was a relief, Temple thought, as she returned to the driver's seat.

McCarran Airport was on Wayne Newton Boulevard, and you could see the multinational panorama of the major Strip hotels on the flat desert landscape. Temple drove up the Strip, passing the landmarks: the Luxor, the MGM Grand, the Goliath, the

Crystal Phoenix, Caesars Palace, the Bellagio, the Paris, the Wynn, and the Venetian. She turned around and cruised down the Strip's other side. Max's sunglasses gazed at the exotic views on both sides, but his mind seemed a continent away.

"I made dinner reservations at a steak house," Temple said at last. "I know it was an ungodly long flight. I can cancel."

Her words seem to jolt Max out of his spell. "Yes, but no. Long flight, don't cancel. A prime, rare American steak is just the medicine I need."

"We'll be the first seating, so the place will be quiet at this hour. It's white-tablecloth expensive but four-star. And I reserved a banquette table for four, so you can sit on cushy leather and stretch your legs out under the empty seat kitty-corner."

"And I let you get away?"

Temple didn't answer. She couldn't. He *had* let her get away, probably for her own safety, judging from what had happened to him.

"That was too . . . too flip," he said. "Sorry."

"Wait'll you see this place and the menu, then you'll *really* be sorry," Temple said, her usual composure back and sassy. "I need to . . . orient you to some things. We can

53

answer each other's burning questions over dinner while you get a break from riding in my pip-squeak car."

"Thoughtful, but don't let this cane mislead you. I stopped using one, then I . . . reinjured myself a little recently, and then came the endless flights. You're right that explaining myself and your explaining me to me should be on neutral ground."

"Gosh, you're way more agreeable than you used to be."

He grinned for the first time. "I was hoping to learn I was a cantankerous bastard."

She just smiled and concentrated on her driving.

He read the giant "ph" sign as she turned off the Strip into an entrance driveway. "Isn't that something to do with skin care?"

"Planet Hollywood." She nodded at the building's top that spelled out the words in uncapitalized white neon, understated for Vegas.

"It's an entire hotel now," he asked, "not just a restaurant?"

It had been for four years, and Max had only been gone a couple months. She felt a sharp interior wrench to realize how much personal history he'd lost in such a short time.

"Yup," Temple said. "I find this the classiest interior on the Strip, aside from the Crystal Phoenix. We're a bit early because you came through faster than I anticipated, so we can have a cocktail at the Living Room bar."

"Sounds cozy," Max said, struggling to take off the Miata while the doorman held out a hand for his cane. The parking valet saw Temple out.

"Do you remember *any* Vegas hotels?" she asked as they entered and were instantly immersed in a gigantic, dim, cool space where even the gaudy slot machines looked primped for a Red Carpet stroll.

"The Crystal Phoenix rang a bell," Max said. "Lots of high-end crystal."

"A client of mine," she said.

"This place too?"

"Not. I'm a one-woman operation. I just like the ambiance here."

"Aha. That'll betray a lot about you."

"Not hard. I'm wearing a fifties-vintage suit and this place is understated Art Deco, unless it's overstated Art Deco."

"Vintage is your thing, really?"

He had to study the damn suit, of course. Temple felt an unreasonable pang for her missing Miracle Bra.

"Chartreuse was hot in the nineteen-fifties," she said, "and classic suits are classic suits."

"Chartreuse is hot in twenty-somethings, too."

No comment. Temple bustled across the busy patterned carpeting all casinos demanded for maintenance to a pair of escalators set between towering, color-changing rectangular lights.

"I forgot. Can you do escalators?" she asked, looking back. "Where's your cane?"

"Sure. Saves steps." He patted the side pocket of his long, European-styled blazer. "The cane is collapsible."

They glided up, surveying the subdued casino below, nearing the solid ceiling blocks of marquee-shaped neon lighting that kept shifting colors.

"I commend subtle," Max said.

"I'm not," Temple said.

"I like honesty better."

"You must be drawing on memory to venture opinions."

"I know what I like," he said. "I just don't remember why or who or when or where. Or what." He slipped his sunglasses into his inside breast pocket.

Even in the muted lighting, she could see his features' new gauntness and a healing forehead gash the frames had obscured. And a haunted look of loss in his eyes.

Or what with whom. Temple diverted herself back to the tour-guide role. "Come into my fave parlor on the Strip."

They turned left and they were there. Venetian glass-framed mirrors seemed to float on hanging walls of red velvet curtains. The Living Room was furnished with low bronze leather sofas and tiny bronze metal–sculpted cocktail tables. A spectacularly gilt-rimmed dome hosted a glittering chandelier that reflected in the metal and glass bar.

Thankfully, Max was impressed. She was more Hollywood than he. "Gloriously decadent. Something from an Anne Rice vampire novel."

Max had read Rice? She'd never known that before.

Only a few customers impeded the view. When the sleek cocktail waitress offered a small padded menu of signature drinks from the polished black altar of the towering bar, something quickly caught Temple's eye.

"An Albino Vampire?" Max asked, following her gaze. "Like a Chocolatini, the menu says, but with white chocolate and Chambord."

"White chocolate and raspberry." Temple needed to loosen her tension, and this sounded like dessert. "What about it, Rice reader?"

"A little girly, but you're driving, after a long dinner."

"It's got surprising kick," the waitress told Max.

"A Vegas motto," he said. After she left, he noted, "I hope you can stake me for a couple days."

"I was planning on it. Do you have access to any operating funds here at all?"

"Since I'm told I was pulled out of some local nightclub dressed as a bungee-jumping maniac advertising himself as the 'Phantom Mage,' I had no ID, no credit cards, nothing. But I did have —"

Max stopped. "I need a drink before I go any further. What about you?" He glanced at the vintage ruby-and-diamond ring on her third finger, left hand. "What did you know about my sudden . . . absence?"

"Next to nothing. You'd been . . . withdrawing. You'd never told me about your Phantom Mage escapade. There were reports a nameless performer had crashed into the polished black walls of the Neon Nightmare club when a bungee cord broke. Rumors said he'd died and had been taken away by an emergency crew. Yet no one matching those circumstances had ended up at a local hospital. So was it you, or some other masked magician? I didn't like to

58

think you'd leave without telling me if you could, but you'd been acting strange lately."

"In what way?"

"In pretty much encouraging me to encourage a friend into turning more than." She fanned the fingers on her left hand.

"Another magic trick. I was told about Matt Devine, yeah."

"You remember him?"

"Only from the radio station Web site I saw in Europe. I saw yours, too, so you really didn't need to don the jelly-bean colors."

"How? Where?"

"It's called the World Wide Web for a reason."

He paused while the martini glasses and their white contents with a setting sun of red in the bottom's V were set before them. Temple raised a right forefinger for the bill. They had a dinner reservation to get to.

"We'd better sip some booze before I go on," Max suggested. "It'll get a little heavy from here on."

She lifted the glass. "I'm sorry, but 'Cheers' anyway."

"Cheers," he replied in the hasty, absent, British way.

Their glass rims *tinged* together. After a couple sips, Max asked, "What's in these things?"

"Vodka and white Crème de Cacao, besides the other liqueurs."

"All booze," he said. "Great. Are we there yet? Because I'm afraid I need to report a resurrection and death."

Temple was struck by the phrase's reversal of the religious "death and resurrection." She was wishing Matt was here; this was starting to sound like a confession.

"Did you know," Max asked, "a man named Garry Randolph?"

"I'll do like you and say the name sounds vaguely familiar for some reason, but I can't attach any memories to it."

"Maybe because you never knew him, except in disguise."

She shook her head and sipped her drink. She could feel the tension draining down her neck and arms.

"And shortly after, dead, at that," Max added.

"Are you talking about the recently dead Synth magician from the Neon Nightmare? I thought his name was known."

"No. That place is really knocking off magicians, isn't it?"

"Apparently. Back to Garry Randolph. It's not an exactly memorable name."

"Gandolph make it easier?"

"Gandolph!" Temple sat up and put her drink down. "The Great. The magician and your mentor and partner in counter-terrorism. He died last Halloween at the crazy Haunted House attraction, where a bunch of psychics were trying to bring back Harry Houdini. He was disguised and was rather scarily convincing, as a flaky, over-ripe female psychic."

Max's lips quirked on the glass rim as he drank more Albino Vampire.

"Oh, Garry could carry off anything. No, Temple, if I may call you that, he didn't die. Like a lot of magicians, he was accustomed to using doubles in his act, and did so there, which was a subtle tribute to Houdini, because Harry'd done that too."

"How did . . . Garry get away with it?" Temple asked. "He must have put his ID on the dead double and allowed him to be buried in his place." She glanced hard at Max. "Like you, it was convenient to vanish completely from the hounds of your earlier counterterrorism work on the Continent and in the British Isles."

"Brava," Max toasted her, shutting his eyes as he swallowed.

Temple had to continue speculating aloud. "You said . . . 'resurrection and death.' You don't mean . . . Gandolph?"

61

The man who was my only family for half my life is dead, as good as assassinated, and I suppose I'm next on the list.

Temple wanted to be sure she understood. "Garry . . . Gandolph, your old mentor and former partner in magic and espionage. He's really dead now?"

"Really dead. Not a double in sight, would God there had been. Irony incarnate. I'd made him fasten his seat belt as we were fleeing both illegal surviving wings of the IRA. Never had time to fasten mine. I was driving."

"Despite your mending legs and mussed-up mind? Oh, Max! You hit your head on the windshield, didn't you? And your legs and body must have been brutally jolted."

"Yeah. Absolutely accurate deductions. You *are* good. Can you deduce what happened when our car got caught in the cross-fire?"

She shook her head.

"I had to brake fast then spurt away to get our pursuers shooting at each other instead of us. Braking so hard thrust me forward just as the bullet meant for my head passed behind me and —"

"— and into Gandolph held upright by his seat belt. Max. That's beyond awful.

I'm . . . so sorry."

"Got this gash" — he touched it — "from the windshield, not the bullet. Garry died instantly, but I couldn't leave him."

"You had to."

Max nodded. "That's what he said."

Temple didn't have a reaction to that solemn belief. She didn't doubt Max had "heard" his mentor's voice between the daze of his head blow and realizing the older man was dead.

Max set down an empty martini glass with a few watery drops of red at the bottom. Her glass was still half full. Or half empty, like Max's eyes.

"I couldn't even make arrangements for the body. I had to drop him and the car off near some of the Irish contacts he'd made. He had colleagues over there from years ago. I trust they had the decency to bury him with some ceremony. He had no . . . other family."

The man who was my only family for half my life is dead. . . .

"Speaking of family," Temple said, "you must not remember, even know, how to contact your own here in the U.S. now."

"Apparently, we've been estranged for almost twenty years, since my cousin Sean died in that IRA bombing in Ulster. I would imagine the Kellys and the Kinsellas had trouble dealing with one son lost, one son saved."

"That's true," Temple said. "You told me that pulling away from both families was your choice. Survivor's guilt infected your immediate family as well as you."

Max rubbed the back of his neck as if reliving the fatal impact. "I have a double dose of that now, for sure."

"So maybe you should just concentrate on the surviving part for a while."

He looked up at Temple. Her tone had been matter-of-fact.

"I can't argue." He sounded surprised.

"And we need to move downstairs for dinner."

"Garry was right about you."

"In what way?"

"You're easy to underestimate, but hard to beat."

I've been told by the only man I ever trusted you're a pretty smart and gutsy girl. . . .

Temple handed him her glass. "Finish my Vampire. It was fifteen bucks. Then we'll go downstairs to get you a decent dinner and you can continue your traveler's tale."

"Yes, ma'am," he said, draining the glass.

He sat back then heaved himself up from

64

the low couch without needing Temple's support, although she'd come around to stand by him.

"If I leaned on you," he commented, "you'd snap like a toothpick."

"Try me."

But he didn't have to. He moved slowly but certainly out of the Living Room to the escalators. Temple let him lead, watching his steps. Gandolph still alive all those months . . . Max must have known that. He had been living in "dead" Gandolph's house, had "inherited" it. Which now was absolute truth.

She would have given them both hell for the secrecy, and Max for leaving her in the dark so long, but who could lay recriminations on an injured, mourning man?

Not Temple.

Not until Max was well and himself and then . . . she might not be Irish but she had temperamental fire to match her natural hair color.

CHAPTER 5
HOUSE WARMING

Six P.M. was an unfashionably early dining hour in Las Vegas. The mostly empty Strip House restaurant produced the promised red leather banquette and dim lighting, but the crimson walls were lined with black-and-white pinup photos of Hollywood starlets.

Temple had never eaten here before — who could cover every restaurant in Las Vegas? — and had taken the "Strip" in the name as a tribute to its easy access from Las Vegas Boulevard and for, uh, strip steak.

Once more Midwestern naïveté had reared its innocent head. Instead, the restaurant walls showcased plenty of naked female flanks, loins, and ribs.

"Oops," Temple said. "I've never been here before. The Web site didn't show all the wall cheesecake, just the dessert on the menu."

"That's okay," Max said, "I'm sitting with

66

my back to the wall, so I'll have to leer long-distance, anyway. Your fiancé would frown on the decor?"

"How do you know so much — ?"

"Garry was trying to give me a trip down memory lane via his laptop computer in between following the trail of Kathleen O'Connor back to her beginnings."

"Kathleen O'Connor? Beginnings?" Before Temple could catch her breath and ask for more, the waiter came to take their drink orders.

"Double single-malt whisky. No ice," Max said.

Temple had planned to skip another drink but changed her mind. She wasn't going to let Max out of this place until he'd revealed every shock in the Book of Life.

"I'll have a" — *What was a long-sipping drink?* — "house Margarita, no ice, no salt."

By then the busboy was bringing goblets and bottled water, so the barriers to instantly shaking the news about Kathleen O'Connor out of Max remained.

" 'Kitty the Cutter,' " he said when they were alone again. "You'd be interested to know that nickname may have been appropriate even in her early teens."

"Why on earth? Where on earth?"

He immediately understood what she was

asking. "Apparently, I'd instructed Gandolph to, ah, track down her background, if he could, if he survived me. He considered my almost fatal brush with mortality enough reason to do just that. *Where* is that drink?"

She'd never heard Max impatient before. She'd never seen him visibly hurting both physically and psychically before.

The waiter skated back with a tray and set down the drinks. Max's was low and deep amber colored, Temple's was high, wide, and the color of diluted snot, if you thought about it.

"That cocktail is bigger than you are," he noted.

She shrugged and stirred it with her straw. "Do you mean that Kathleen may have been a cutter as a teen? Self-abuse? Or assault even then? She had a police record?"

"She had a history that might have started her off mutilating herself rather than other people. Look, Temple, it's not a pretty story."

"What have you got to tell me that is?"

"Good point." He took what detective novels call a "slug" of the expensive whisky.

Her credit card company might be calling to check up on a sudden increase in her spending. No problem.

"Tell me a little about me," he said,

"before I go into my dark-and-stormy-night-of-the-soul routine."

"I'm sorry, Max."

"I know. That's why you let me come back. I don't quite remember all of that call."

She did.

Yes, I've been drinking; that's what we Irish do at wakes, even private ones.

"Gandolph must have told you," she said after a halfhearted sip of her Margarita, "about your long and unhappy relationship with Ireland and the IRA, about your counterterrorism work with him."

"Yes."

"How much," she asked, "did he know about what Kitty the Cutter did here?"

"More than he should have, come to think of it. He was always a master spy as well as a spymaster. I don't suppose too many people know that she slashed . . . your current fiancé," Max said.

"No! I would have said three, four people, tops, including you. That's impossible."

"Nothing was impossible with Garry." Max said with a sigh. "Except a surprise resurrection, like in the book."

"The book? Oh, you mean the *books. The Lord of the Rings* trilogy. That's right, Gandalf the wizard plunged to his apparent

69

death in the Moria abyss, fighting the Balrog, but then came back."

"Garry isn't coming back." Max sipped his drink and paused to master his grief before speaking again. "Maybe taking the stage name of Gandolph the Great wasn't just chutzpah. He *could* be a wizard. He spent all that time under cover here in Vegas — from his purported death at the Halloween séance to two months ago when he spirited me from the Neon Nightmare to a Swiss clinic in the Alps — looking into the Synth and, in the past two months, Kathleen O'Connor abroad."

"She was a broad, all right," Temple said, surprised to hear a bitter note in her voice. "After you, trying to track you down, maybe for the same obsessive reason you wanted to uncover her past, even after your own 'death.' "

"I'm not leaving this planet without knowing why she manipulated a couple Irish-American teenaged boys to betray each other over her."

"And did you find out?"

"Gandolph . . . Garry . . . did. Maybe. But we're back to the insoluble, inhuman tragedy. What about the immediate present? What was I like when I lived here? Was I happy?"

"Were we happy? Yes."

"Why'd I blow it?"

"Someone was always on your trail. Kinda hard to keep up a normal life." Temple sipped just as the waiter returned with padded leather menus big enough to give her carpal tunnel syndrome.

Max reached across the table to take and shut hers. "Let me order for you. Keep talking."

It was good he kept his eyes on the menu while she recited the highs and lows of their interrupted two-year relationship.

"You swept me off my feet, literally, at the Guthrie Theater in Minneapolis, and distressed my over-fond family of pushy brothers and protective parents by whisking me away to your year-long gig at the Goliath Hotel here in Vegas. Then you disappeared on the closing night of your magic show, the very night a dead man was found in the spy area above the gaming tables. A local homicide detective was on your trail for that, but I knew nothing and said nothing. A year later you came back, but you didn't dare occupy the condo we'd bought together at the Circle Ritz building, so you lived in a house that I now realize had been Gandolph's. You and I were trying to trace a weird magical cult called the Synth for

71

masterminding several unsolved Vegas murders. Then you must have gone under cover at the Neon Nightmare, which has now been revealed to me as the Synth headquarters. You fell or were sabotaged and disappeared once more. And, *voila!* Here you are again."

So was the waiter. Max ordered quickly to regain their privacy.

"All right?" he asked of his double order as the waiter vanished.

"It has to be. It's a Max Kinsella Production."

"So," he said, nodding at the ring on her finger, "where did the fiancé come in?"

"His name is Matt. You can say it."

"I know. . . . I was shown that online."

"Just that radio station Web site?"

He nodded.

"It's all hype."

"Of course."

"His name is Matt Devine, as you know. You may not know he and you actually kinda got along. When Lieutenant Molina would go into her usual rants about you, Matt defended you. Even to me."

"Lieutenant Molina?"

"Homicide. She was sure you'd offed the guy in the Goliath ceiling."

"So this hard-case lieutenant gave you a

rough time about me and my whereabouts?"

"Of course."

"And you didn't crack?"

"Of course not."

"Did we always talk like a Humphrey Bogart movie?"

"No. Just when we were trying to pretend everything was okay, like now."

Their salads arrived, forcing them to lean back and away from their opposite sides of the table. Max ordered another double. Temple had barely lowered her drink below the unsalted rim level. She was driving. He wasn't.

"Thank you," Max said in the pause after the food had arrived and the waiter had left.

She understood why. "You're welcome."

Pinning parts of their salad with the fork tines was a good way to not look at each other and carry on an abbreviated conversation.

"Matt sounds like a solid guy," he said.

"He is."

"He must have a hell of a backstory."

"So did you, it turns out," she said.

"He knows . . . what . . . about me?"

"Pretty much everything."

Silence. "It's a bit numbing that my replacement knows more about me than I do."

"Nobody could replace you, Max," Temple

73

said wryly.

"Now eat your salad and listen," she continued. "You were gone the first time for almost an entire year with no word. Matt is the most . . . genuine guy in the world. Way too nice for his own good, but I've brought him around to reality some." She couldn't help smiling. "You're a hard act to follow, but he can do it. I love him. We're working on getting married in a way that will satisfy two geographically and culturally different families. I loved you, but even you finally made me see we couldn't live with all the kickback from your secret life. I'm not going to let you flail around alone, not knowing anyone now, here or anywhere, who knows anything about you but enemies."

His fork had been poised over the salad for a long time, and now he put it down for a hit of the second double whisky. She'd quoted his phone-call words almost exactly, but she could see he couldn't quite place them.

I don't know anyone now, here or anywhere, who knows anything about me but enemies. They tell me my name is Michael Aloysius Xavier Kinsella. . . .

"So, Michael Aloysius Xavier Kinsella," she went on, "since you've still got enemies and I've still got unanswered questions that affect me and mine, including Matt, and there are still unsolved Synth-related deaths out there and signs that some IRA rogues are aiming their sights on Las Vegas, and since Lieutenant C. R. Molina is still suspicious of you and me and the Circle Ritz palm tree, it's to my advantage to shake the cobwebs out of your head and get you on the road to your real future life, without me."

He just stared at her for a few moments. "That sounds like it would be a damn shame."

"And no flirting, no Irish charm, no inveigling, seducing, or magic tricks."

He shrugged. "I don't feel in the mood for any of those things. It's funny. I felt better, more in control, when I was on my own, almost, running for my life, in Europe, anyway. Ireland got . . . out of control. Yet here in Vegas, where I loved, lived, and almost died, I seem to feel lost, out of steam."

And Temple could, and would, use that.

I've got a case of amnesia where all I'm remembering is a bit about the IRA, a dead woman named Rebecca or a possibly live one named Kathleen. . . .

"What's this about a 'possibly live . . . Kathleen'?" she asked.

75

"Did I say that? On the phone?"

"Yes."

"Maybe something like that."

"That. Exactly. You think I'm going to forget any words from a 'possibly dead' man?"

"You'd given up on me. What a bummer to have me show up again."

"I was never really sure you were dead, Max. Maybe years from now, I'd believe it. You don't die easy." Temple grinned. "Oh, how I wish I could tell Molina."

"Not good to tell anyone, but I suppose you can't keep things like me from the fiancé."

"No."

"Where is he?"

"Out of town for a couple more days."

"I always have this good timing?"

"Yup. Your timing is annoyingly impeccable. Years of being a magician, I guess."

The appearance of the attentive waiter struck Temple with a fresh little jolt each time tonight. Overhearing must be avoided. She eyed the surrounding diners and met Max's eyes returning from the same mission.

Their massive steak platters were still sizzling before them, accompanied by huge-handled steak knives.

"Nice of the staff to arm us," Max said. "I could have used these last week. If the sight of blood disturbs you, I warn you this will be really rare."

She thought the sight of blood would disturb *him,* but Max had obviously put the raw details of the shoot-out in Ulster behind him. Maybe he felt in limbo because he was busy burying the recent past and trying to grasp the present. As for any future, forget it.

Steak required a lot of attention to eat, and that's what they did. Temple's side of black truffle–creamed spinach made the vegetable almost like dessert, and Max had both the Potatoes Romanoff and baked. He'd always been steel-spring lean, but now he ate like a starving vampire drank.

"So," he asked, after the waiter had removed their empty platters, plates, and drink glasses. "Where are you planning to park me, or should I just get a room at the . . . Goliath, was it? See if anybody there remembers me?"

"Negative," Temple answered with emphasis. "Remember, you have a house here. Seeing it might jog your memory. No reason you can't move right in. I planned to take you on a tour of the place after dinner."

No reason not to move in, she thought —

except it might be haunted . . . by an unidentified stalker who'd shredded Max's wardrobe and also speared an illegally present Molina, or maybe by Garry Randolph's real ghost this time. There was nowhere else to park Max for tonight, though.

"Are we having dessert, or what?" she asked, hoping for more pleasant topics.

"How about Baileys Irish Cream and coffee while I tell you about Kitty the Cutter?"

"My favorite after-dinner combo," Temple said, with a lemon twist in her voice. "Depressants, stimulants, and psychopaths."

Max laughed for the first time and signaled the waiter. When they were ensconced behind small crystal liqueur glasses and full cups of coffee, he began.

"The long and short of the matter is that Kathleen was always a rabid IRA agent, even after the peace. She raised gun money from wealthy men who sympathized for the cause from Europe to North and South America."

"Whoring for the homeland? We'd figured that out before you left."

"Not why. She'd had a . . . rough upbringing. Ireland was always poverty-stricken with few natural resources and no competitive living wage until the very recent technological revolution. The wrongs against the

Irish are long and many and bitter."

"Then you and your naive cousin were just practice, early in her career?"

"Something like that." Max downed the dainty liqueur glass of Baileys in one gulp then concentrated on the coffee.

"What's this 'dead woman named Rebecca' have to do with Kathleen?" Temple said.

"I said that in the phone call? Or, more improbably, you remembered that?"

"I tend to remember every damn word from a ghost. It's my job to know about everything and remix it into something else. Rebecca?"

"A literary reference."

"Oh. *That* Rebecca, the literal femme fatale from the Daphne du Maurier novel of the same name. I devoured that book in eighth grade. I wanted to rekill that lying, manipulative, unfaithful Rebecca and marry Maxim de Winter."

He stared at her. Maybe it was her rerun of childish but uncharacteristic venom or . . . oh, right. Wrong! *Max* de Winter. Temple had just confessed that her preadolescent self wanted to marry a tall, dark, mysterious but tormented man named Max.

"That was just an old, outdated book," Temple explained in unseemly haste, although she considered *Rebecca* a timeless classic. "A lot of forties mystery novels featured murderous, manipulative women from hell. Probably a ploy to get women back out of the workforce after World War Two."

He laughed again and shook his head, hiding his weary eyes behind a forked hand. "Your mind jumps around like a knight on a chess board. So one minute you're a murderous romantic, and the next you're a feminist?"

"Makes perfect sense to me. What does the name *Rebecca* have to do with Kitty the Cutter?"

"It was the name given her at the Irish orphanage where she was . . . reared. She obviously identified with Du Maurier's book, too, but in a very different way. She may have been using the name *Rebecca* as an alias these last several years of détente on the Irish question, which means that the Kitty the Cutter who visited Las Vegas may still be alive and well and elsewhere."

"You saw her dead," Temple said. "Then again, I saw Gandolph the Great 'dead' at that Halloween séance, and it was just a magician's trick."

"It was a *master* magician's trick," Max said, his expression hardening with grief.

80

Then he doffed the mood with a shake of his head. "I've . . . glimpsed that motorcycle accident in recent dreams. I saw myself checking her carotid artery for a pulse. That woman was dead — really dead."

"You believe in dreams and visions now?"

"That's where the jigsaw pieces of my memory are reassembling. I've got to believe in something."

Temple didn't know what to answer; it was so sad to imagine living on shards of yourself.

I have a decision to make as to where I'll live and die or if there's any point to the years in between those states.

She thought some more while Max finished his coffee. Sipping the sweet liqueur with the bitterness of all that tragic past lingering in her mouth was like drinking a shot of scouring aquavit.

"Then," she suggested finally, "maybe the woman who was pursuing your car by motorcycle *wasn't* Kitty, aka Rebecca. Maybe the real Kitty has been in hiding here all these months." Temple finished her Baileys almost as fast as Max had his. "Think about it. Meanwhile, time to visit Gandolph's former house and your crash pad."

Temple paused to deal with the waiting

81

credit card and receipt, gathering up her tote bag. "Are you telling me everything, Max? I get a feeling of . . . missing chapters."

"I'm telling you everything I can handle at the moment," he said. "You say I can claim a roof and a bed under it in Las Vegas? Let's go."

Some bed, Temple thought, remembering the elaborate opium bed in that house, even if Max didn't.

Yet.

"Timed it right," Temple said, a half hour later as the Miata pulled up, top raised, to 1200 Mojave Way.

The sun had set behind the western mountains, leaving residential streets dark, dramatically lit, and quiet. Like all Sunbelt homes, this one had few visible windows and a well-shaded front entry, the better to fend off the grueling sunlight.

Max sighed deeply after the car's engine stopped, then he untangled his legs from the passenger seat to stand and gaze at the question mark of a one-story house.

"Think I can get in?" he asked.

"Lieutenant 'Nosy' Molina did. You believe a homicide dick can beat you at breaking and entering into your own place?"

"You're kidding. A cop did a B and E?

That would be —"

"— Against the law and police conduct rules. Yeah, she did. She confessed to me just a couple weeks ago. I told you she was obsessed."

"What is it about me?" he asked wryly. "Kitty the Cutter, this Molina woman?"

"They just can't let you get away," Temple said. "Not my problem, apparently."

"Smart. I'm obviously trouble."

The continuing silence indicated he was thinking about Gandolph. Garry Randolph. Clever merging of a pop-culture name with his real one to create a memorable stage name, Temple thought. She knew *about* Gandolph, although she'd never knowingly met the man himself in his own offstage guise, Garry Randolph. He'd been Max's father figure from a vulnerable age and time until he'd died several time zones away, either two or three days ago. How do you compute the distance from such a bitter loss?

"Let's see," Max said, shambling up the walk, "if the Magic Fingers can still do their thing."

"Magic Fingers?"

"That's how I survived on the escape run from the Swiss clinic, which might have been a haven for assassins. I lifted tourist

83

credit cards."

"Oh."

"Don't worry about those ripped-off tourists losing faith in their fellow man. If they were regular Joes, I used their cards only once before destroying them. If they were rich bastards, I enjoyed myself. No ruined trips of a lifetime for the ordinary blokes."

"Robin Hood." Temple gave the name a sarcastic twist.

By then Max was using a Swiss Army knife to jimmy the front door lock. How had he gotten that through security? Scary.

"This place has a Rottweiler of a security system," he said. "God." Temple could see him glance to the house's side. "Six foot fence. Don't tell me I'll have to heave myself over it in this condition."

"The security system is still working?"

"Why not?"

"Molina said it had been breached."

"You'd think she'd know."

"Then again," Temple said, "the house was playing tricks on people, like me, the moment you disappeared."

"How?"

"Sleight of hand and household goods. I came out here to check after I hadn't heard from you in a few days, and every stick of your furniture and magic paraphernalia was gone. An aging chorus girl out of *Guys and Dolls* answered the door."

Max laughed so hard he fell back against the entry area's tiled side wall.

"Not funny to me," Temple said, irritated. "That's the first moment I knew for sure you were gone."

"Sorry," Max huffed as he caught his breath. "That's the kind of wholesale 'disappearing' act only Gandolph — Garry — could pull off."

"I deserved far more than a wholesale trick."

"So he told me." He straightened and grasped her arms. "Temple, you have to understand. I crashed feet first at God knows how many miles per hour when that tampered bungee cord at the Neon Nightmare broke. I was out cold and taken for dead. Gandolph — no, Gandolph is truly dead now — *Garry* was an old man, but he had to get me out of there and this house and Las Vegas. He had to make me disappear so whoever had attempted to take my life would think they'd succeeded. And the illusion had to be total."

She wrested away from his grip.

"Temple," Max said, pleading. "At the Swiss clinic I was accused of being drunk when injured, because only drunks are so

85

limber and relaxed they can survive fatal collisions, when their sober victims can't. I'd learned that doing 'death-defying' acrobatics as a magician: go limp if you fall. That's what saved me at the Neon Nightmare, if not my legs."

"I could have been told, Max. I could have been trusted. I'd never said a word about where you might be for almost a year when you were gone the first time, when Molina was harassing me. And that woman knows how to harass. Even hoods couldn't beat it out of me in a parking garage."

"Hoods? Beating? Did I know this?"

"No." Temple simmered down. "Matt did."

"Ah."

"It's not what you think. He caught me sneaking back to the Circle Ritz and insisted I go to an ER, where who happened to be there but Molina, implying I was a domestic abuse victim. Of Matt's."

"Sorry." Max swept Temple into an embrace despite herself. "I should have been there for you. That was humiliating, I know. And you never told the copper what really happened because the creeps were after me. Garry was right. You *had* to be deceived. You don't give up."

"Let me go."

Max released her to lean against the wall again.

"I'm doing this for — what's the cliché? — old time's sake," Temple said. "So you better figure out a way into the house, because I'm going home unless you need a tour of the premises."

He didn't answer, just returned to the security panel and torturing the door lock again, while Temple tormented her do-gooder instincts. That impulsive embrace had shaken her. Max hadn't been that effusive. This house, the night. Max. Being here was playing with fire. Old flames, to be exact.

"Remember," he admonished himself after a couple minutes of gashing the metal with the Swiss Army knife. His fingers played tune after tune on the keypad, and . . . "There!"

He pushed the broad door open.

Chill air wafted against their faces like the house's exhalation. They stared at each other, although the dark was fast becoming total.

Max cocked his head at the hum of air-conditioning units all over the block.

"This one's running, too," he said, pushing inside, the Swiss Army knife still clutched in his hand, now as a weapon.

The hall light rained down incandescence when the wall control was depressed.

"This stuff belong here?" Max asked, waving at a console table and mirror.

"From your time of residence, yes. Molina told me everything had been restored only a few days after I saw it gone. Garry should have waited longer to undo his vanishing act."

"Who knew a rogue homicide lieutenant would break in?"

"She wasn't the only one."

Max had felt his way deeper into the house and was too distracted to hear her. "Wish I had a flashlight."

"I think everyone who wanted to break in here has come and gone by now," Temple said.

Max doubled back to shut the front door.

"Let there be light," he announced, moving forward again to turn on any light fixture he encountered.

How strange, Temple thought — that the security system was on, the air-conditioning was on, the lights working, and the door had been locked. She hadn't thought to check on the house all these weeks, having been so dramatically turned away from the door and the thought of any future with Max.

That was just what Garry Randolph had wanted. Needed. He was protecting his foster son, she supposed. By cutting off all contact with the woman he loved?

Poor Max. Who would love him now?

An exclamation from down the bedroom wing drew her deeper inside. Had he found the opium bed . . . or the clothes closet?

She walked into the dazzle of the master bedroom, with its cove ceiling lighting and mirrored wall of sliding ceiling-high closet doors. Max stood by an open area, holding up shreds of black material.

"Silk. Cashmere. Featherweight wool. These are leavings fit for a moth's feast. Looks like a pack of feral cats have been at the contents."

"Try a butcher knife from the kitchen. Molina was concealed in the house when this slasher party went on. Someone hated you."

"Nothing new, I gather. I suspected my instinct on the run to avoid black clothing was worth heeding. Was I the depressive sort?"

"Not usually. You always said naked was the best disguise."

"And black's the best camouflage . . . unless it's your signature." He let the tatters drop from his hands to the floor. "I was letting myself be predictable. Maybe that's why Garry died."

"I don't think so, Max. You're a guardian. You don't slack up. Sometimes fate is bigger than even a magician's ego."

"Okay. I won't self-flagellate in front of you." Max stared at the huge, glitzy master bedroom. "Where did I sleep? It sure as hell wasn't in here."

"This house once belonged to Orson Welles," Temple explained.

"Ah. So . . . ?"

Feeling mischievous, perhaps because she was now firmly in control here — Max's "spirit" guide to his own house and past — Temple went down the hall and opened the door on the bedroom holding the opium bed and pretty much that was all.

An opium bed is like an internal gazebo, an exquisite, small room meant to be the central jewel within a larger room, an intricate fretwork frame of ebony and mother-of-pearl. Its silk cushions are miniature embroidered artworks.

Max stepped inside the room, feasted on the art object, and sighed. " 'A thing of beauty is a joy for ever,' " he quoted Keats, "but I never slept on this magnificent artifact, nor smoked dope on it."

"No, you didn't," Temple said. "And you would never blunt your perceptions with recreational drugs."

"But I did 'sleep' with you on it?"

"Nor would I blunt your perceptions with bawdy speculations." Temple smiled. "I can show you two more bedrooms in this house. Game?"

"Lay on."

She retraced their steps to another closed door, which opened, and again lights blossomed in a room.

This one was stacked with elaborately painted boxes reflected into invisible mirrors.

"Illusions," Max said, stepping into their midst like a late arrival at a cocktail party crammed with old friends.

His long supple fingers caressed the smooth wood and cool glass as if they were beloved childhood pets. Temple knew these boxes and mechanisms were the conjoined artistry of Gandolph and the Mystifying Max, years of experimentation and creativity boiled down into the mechanisms of magic.

"Has anything been — ?" Temple asked.

"No," Max said, his eyes and hands still devouring the landscape of escape. "Some things are sacred even to psychopaths."

Temple remained quiet. She guessed his touch remembered more than his mind at the moment — years of hearing Garry Randolph's voice on the stage, in this room, or on the run.

Max turned, done with reruns. "I didn't sleep in here either."

Without a word, Temple turned and led him to the fourth bedroom, opening the door with a theatrical flourish.

He stepped over the threshold as she depressed the light switch.

Bare walls. Bare wooden floor. A futon on the floor between two metal-shuttered security windows. A celadon vase holding a pussy-willow branch and a silk bird of paradise blossom. A low ebony table holding a Japanese blue-ware teacup. And thou.

"It must have seemed boring to a barbarian," Max mused, stepping inside and breaking the surface of peace that lay like a seal on the room.

"That's why it was safe. This was where you slept."

"Not you."

"I'm a social being, Max. You were always somewhat Zen. That's how you kept your sanity."

"I'm a monk?"

"You could be."

"Was that a problem?"

"Hell, no."

"You often talk like that?"

"Hell, no."

He turned with a smile. "I can sleep here safely tonight."

"Good. I can go."

"Can I let you?"

"You will."

They tell me my name is Michael Aloysius Xavier Kinsella, and I know I need to get the hell somewhere else fast. I guess there's only one question to ask or answer before I decide where.

He nodded. "Thanks for the tour. I'll see what my dreams dredge up tonight."

"Mine, too," Temple said, mocking herself. "Welcome home."

Is it possible . . . ? Do you . . . love me?

CHAPTER 6
HOME, SWEAT HOME

While my Miss Temple is playing tour guide on Mr. Max's homecoming trip down No Memory Lane, aka Mojave Way, I need to reconnoiter the exterior of the former Gandolph homestead, and fast, or I may face a long, lonesome hitch or hike back to the Circle Ritz.

Getting myself out of the tiny space between the Miata front seat backs and the door makes my much-put-upon limbs as shaky as Mr. Max's.

Call it the feline equivalent of a transatlantic flight.

I am really annoyed that my kind is kept out of restaurants. Just think of the wasted food that could be saved if every one came equipped with a "house" homeless feline on the premises.

(I realize that this system would not work for homeless dogs. Even when on their best behavior, they are hopelessly unmannerly.

Restaurant patrons would not put up with panting, begging, yapping, drooling, and all the other unattractive canine habits. Nor should they.)

However, I am living proof that the feline moocher is quiet to the point of stealthy and as subtle as a shadow.

So I shake out my cramped legs and gimp around to the house's shrub-sheltered side. This neighborhood is established to the point of being old, and the owners can pay for watering the greenery, although it is a matter of local ecological debate whether they should.

I make good use of the concealing options of oleander bush and canna lily plantings. I do not much go for the native thorny cactus plants, although I run into one of that ilk not more than ten feet along the house side. So to speak.

It whaps me right on the sensitive black nose leather I like to maintain unscarred, like Miss Temple's pristine caramel-colored leather upholstery in the Miata.

Of course, I am related to it.

"Nice of you to finally drop by, Go Daddy-o," Miss Midnight Louise says, welcoming me to the scene of *auld lang syne.* "While I had to hop a ride in a Vito's Vegetarian Pizza delivery car, you were cruising the Strip eavesdropping on Mister Max's traveler tales and visiting high-end dining venues. I could smell the steak on your breath from the moment you put paw and claw on the desert dirt up front."

Not one to hold back, our Miss Midnight Louise.

"Nothing rare, medium, or well-done has crossed my lips on this most uncomfortable trip, Louise," I answer virtuously, although a snicker flirts with my fangs. It is her bad luck to have to ride in a *vegetarian* pizza-mobile.

"I was forced," I add in an injured hiss, "to share the meager area behind the Miata's front seats with Miss Temple's unfortunately named 'doggie bag.' Fortunately, she sets her seat far forward."

"She has nerves of steel," Miss Louise says, purring with admiration. "She meets her ex-lover after he has barely escaped death and with his mind a blasted ruin, yet she does not hesitate to bring home tidbits from their first reunion feast together. That girl has her priorities right. Most humans in such a situation would have pled 'no appetite.' "

"Miss Temple is the pillar of practical," I say, with a certain pride. "She took him to a costly steak house at Planet Hollywood. Why should she not get all that she paid for?"

"Why indeed."

"And, my esteemed partner in private investigating, Mister Max's mind hardly seemed a 'blasted ruin,' from what I overheard. I myself would not mind forgetting to remember certain episodes of my past."

"My existence being one of them."

"Now, now, my dear Louise. I have grown quite accustomed to your skills as an expert 'tailer.' I will be able to rest easy after my cramped travels tonight in the Miata, knowing you will be on patrol here, keeping an eye or two on Mister Max."

"Nothing will happen here . . . if your Miss Temple decides to leave. If not, we have front-page news."

"I know you favor Mister Max Kinsella over Mister Matt Devine, but I see no signs that you are in for a happy ending there."

"It is not a matter of 'favoring' one human male over another. I strongly felt you failed to follow up on Mister Max's chilling fall at the Neon Nightmare and thereby let the trail of the Synth grow cold while you were swanning after another of your roommate's causes."

"It would not be wrong to state that your . . . doggedness . . . in considering the Neon Nightmare central to all our long-term concerns was well placed."

"I should think so."

"That is why I depend on you to keep an eye on Mister Max now, though the site and situation looks pretty barren from an investigator's point of view. Most of it is wait-and-watch work, Louise. You know that."

"I know that *you* know Miss Temple will give you her doggie-bag steak, cut into bite-size pieces served over your never-eaten eternally full bowl of Free-to-Be-Feline."

"Perhaps," I say, trying to avoid visibly salivating.

"And I will have a hot, dark night crouching among the fire ants and lizards while Mister Max goes beddie-bye alone inside."

"Ah. I heard the front door cracking open. I must be gone, anon."

"Oh, shut up, Shakespeare, Jr. I know you will have nothing to report in the morning but a full stomach and a long nap."

A consummation devoutly to be wished, but I do not say so aloud.

Miss Midnight Louise is not in the mood.

Chapter 7
Strangers in the Night

Max was beginning to wish he'd booked a room at Planet Hollywood and had stayed there.

The house was rambling and rang no bells of recognition with him. Instead, it felt creepy.

He wandered from the kitchen, which his memory had populated with a glimpse of Temple Barr sitting on the granite island like a ghost on a marble monument, or a Goth girl perched on her idea of a kinky sex site, to the bedroom closet with its hanging shreds of his knifed former clothes.

Where was Garry Randolph's presence? If he was going to be haunted by ghosts, Gandolph's was one he'd welcome.

Max began to realize that from the moment he'd awakened with amnesia in the Swiss clinic, he'd almost never been alone. When Garry hadn't been shepherding him, he'd been on the run with Revienne

Schneider, the Sexy Shrink, from the Alps to Zurich. Then there'd been Temple Barr, Girl Guide, awaiting him at the airport.

This Max Kinsella he didn't much know had been a lucky guy. For a loner with a double life as stage magician and counterspy, he'd had help from a lot of friends.

He hurled himself away from the symbolic carnage in the closet back to the kitchen. Garry had been something of a gourmet. Jerking open the door to the wine cabinet, he hoped to lay his hand on a bottle significant to his mentor's memory. But the labels were cuneiform script to him. Presumably he'd shared some of Garry's tastes, but that was gone, and Garry wasn't here to aim his hand aright.

Max pulled a dark bottle from the rack, feeling unsettled by the meat-rich dinner. He had to search six drawers to find the corkscrew. Pathetic! He slammed a flat hand down on the granite counter, his palm stinging like hell.

At least he remembered how to use a corkscrew. This had better not be a red wine. He stared down the round lip of the bottle. Bullet-hole entry wounds could look almost this neat and intentional. He'd seen the real and brutal results of Garry's head wound on the car window to his right, blood spattered like rain in a misty Northern Ireland night.

Max poured the bottle contents into a water glass from the first cupboard he'd opened. He wasn't going to search every one for a wine glass.

White wine, more like lymph fluid than blood. He gulped some down. Where would he sleep tonight? The futon had been fine for a man without injuries to nurse. Garry's former bedroom had obviously been turned into the paraphernalia storage room, thank heaven for that. He wanted no dead man's bed for a resting place. That left the opium bed, more of a stage setting than anything. At least it might spur memories of the nonresident sprite.

He was surprised to find his lips smiling as he thought of Temple. She had a lot of guts to take him on in this condition, with a fresh new fiancé to explain to. Or maybe she didn't answer to anybody. Maybe she'd bring him sweet dreams in that opium bed. That was one new thing he'd learned since coming back to Las Vegas. She knew his recent past as well as Garry had known his distant past. Max would have to probe her memories to regain his own.

Would the fiancé like that? Matt Devine could go to hell.

Max had finished the wine, drinking it down like the water that normally filled the tall, narrow glass, when a barely detectable sound chilled his veins.

Faint. So faint most people would dismiss it as a distant outdoor noise or the house settling. Faint as a single revolver barrel clicking a bullet into place fifty feet away.

Max set the glass down on a hand towel he'd whipped to the stone counter. He bet he'd used to know how to soundlessly traverse this furniture-scape in the dark. He moved stealthily toward the main room, his stance wide to keep his trouser fabric from hissing against itself, flat-footed to counter any shoe squeaks.

The scraping sound came again, from the front hall. What the hell? A key?

For a heartbeat he hoped that . . . Gandolph had pulled off another resurrection.

Max plastered himself to the living-room wall. He'd abandoned the shot-up car with the body near the Belfast address of a long-ago counterspy network contact. People didn't tend to move as frequently in the Old World as in the States. He'd hoped.

Maybe Garry had still been revivable, and found.

The hall was too narrow for an opening door and two people. Max's blood was pulsing through his carotid arteries, pounding in his eardrums. *Maybe Gandolph. Maybe Gandolph.*

Whoever . . . he needed to startle and control the body that came past this break in the house wall.

He heard the door open and shut. The newcomer paused, his or her senses routinely checking the empty house for any change. Max nodded mentally. A pro of some sort. Not the redhead deciding she wanted a return fling in the opium bed. He weighed the slow oncoming footsteps. As precise and cautious as his own.

This was interesting. Who or what would expect this empty house to offer more than vacancy? The white-noise hum of the air conditioner muffled the visitor's approach. Suddenly a presence blocked the archway, just oncoming bulk and darkness.

Max jumped into the opening, pounding a fist into kidneys, right on target, needing to disable the trunk before the struggle quickly came down to the intruder's hale legs against his weakened ones. He heard the man's grunts, but the guy torqued his torso away before Max could get in any more cheap shots. Max pushed his sharp forearm bone across the man's windpipe and used the opposite wall as his own buttress. Had to exercise some care. He wanted to overcome and question, not kill.

The guy's elbows were pummeling his ribs. Max slid aside, letting the intruder hit his crazy bones against the wall. During the expected cascade of curses, he spun the guy against the wall, knee to nuts, and let up on the windpipe.

"Enough already," the intruder gasped. "You know the turf, and you're tall enough to be Max Kinsella, in person."

"And you are — ?"

"Your damn house sitter. My contract with Randolph covers my medical costs, so ease off before you run up a bill even you can't pay."

Mention of Garry's name was like saying a password to Max. He lifted his arms and backed away.

"Mind if I turn on the living-room lamp?" he asked the unknown man.

"Hell no! I wanna see how much I can sue for. Freaking idiot. No one called me to say you'd be coming back."

Max turned and found the lamp he'd noted on his tour of the house, fumbling for what should be a familiar on-switch. He let himself sit on the couch arm, relieving his legs but still projecting the impression nothing was visibly wrong with them.

In the weak lamplight, he confronted a sturdy guy, five-ten maybe, 190, and enough five-o'clock shadow for a Latino, with a cop stance, more curious than pissed.

"Man," he said, "you look like death warmed over and served as sliced jellied aspic. Why'd you attack me?"

"I didn't know Garry Randolph had contracted for your services, whatever they are. Must be watering the yard and fine-tuning the air-conditioning. Can't be security."

"Now that's where you're off base. There was nothing to secure here but the house, until you showed up. Where's Randolph? He e-mailed me saying he'd rendezvoused with you in Switzerland and you were both heading to the British Isles, last I heard."

Max leaned his head against the wall. "When was that?"

"More than a week ago, U.S. time."

"Who are you?"

"The guy who helped Randolph get you out of the Neon Nightmare club and then the country." The man shifted his pummeled body. "I gotta say you recovered pretty damn well from that so-called 'fatal' accident in just a little over two months. I figured you'd never walk again, much less threaten the family jewels." He glanced around. "Where's Randolph?"

"Who are you?" Max asked again.

"You'd seen me around. Rafi Nadir."

Max just shook his head.

"My regular job is assistant security chief at the Oasis. Randolph did me a good turn and recommended me for the position, in exchange for maintaining the house so it didn't deteriorate while he was trying to get you back on your feet again at some fancy Swiss clinic." He glanced at Max's legs. "Guess that worked."

"Somewhat," Max said. "I'm still compensating. That's why I hit you like a ton of bricks. I'm still mostly bark and not bite."

"Pretty nasty bark. But why don't you know this? Where's Randolph? Where's the old guy? He's some character, but he knows his beans."

"Dead," Max said.

Rafi took a deep breath and leaned against the hall wall in his turn. "Shit. I liked that guy. He gave me a second chance."

"Me too," Max said. "A couple times."

"How did he die?"

"Shoot-out with the ex-IRA and alternate IRA in Belfast. Our car got caught in the crossfire. I lived and Garry didn't."

"Shit," Nadir said. "Nothing personal. I mean the situation. Bad. That old guy moved the world for you."

Max said nothing. Just took a deep breath.

Nadir said, "Sorry. I'm guessing the admiration was mutual."

That brought Max's head up, business on his mind.

"I don't know what Garry's arrangement with you was. I don't know you . . . who or what you are or how you're involved. My legs were smashed and my memory is . . . a vast wasteland. I know what happened after I woke up from a coma at that Swiss clinic, yet almost nothing of my life before, just the . . . static . . . of the inane march of pop culture. Nothing important."

"So you're a blank slate?" Nadir said. "I know some things. I know someone wants to kill you bad enough to follow you from Vegas to Europe. You say your legs are iffy and your mind is an empty playground? Cheer up, Kinsella. That's just the bad news. The good news is you have me to depend on."

The stranger named Rafi Nadir grinned.

"And my ex thinks I'm utterly undependable."

CHAPTER 8
DRY-GULCHED

Who would have ever guessed that Temple Barr would be grateful to Savannah Ashleigh for anything?

Not Temple Barr.

The annoying has-been actress who'd made Las Vegas her shaky second-career base seemed to embody everything that kept the female persona known as "bimbo" alive way too long into the twenty-first century.

Still, it was good to have a serious errand the morning after picking up what was left of Max.

After a fitful night with Midnight Louie in her California-king-size bed and a nervous morning wondering how Max had fared, Temple was glad to have something on her agenda.

She parked her Miata outside the Aloe Vera Drive address Savannah had given her, although no house was visible. She stared at a tangled web of mesquite trees and spiny desert shrubs and varieties of cacti, a desiccated jungle compared to the scruffy lawns and foundation-planting-bare neighboring house yards.

This was an older area, from the sixties, not maintained with watered Bermuda and landscaped plantings, as Max's house had been and still was. *Another oddity,* Temple thought.

En route here she'd driven by *really fast* to eye Gandolph's former home in daylight. The groomed yard looked as *Twilight Zone—* maintained as the interior house systems. No sign of Max, thank God. She would die to be spotted as "hovering."

Another fading car engine alerted her to the Saturn Sky convertible that had just parked along the crumbling curb. The vehicle's maker and model had been discontinued by the 2008 Great Recession, but the driver emerged in nineties glitz and glory, tall and thin and extreme, a blond Cher.

"Savannah," Temple said in a bit of a daze. "That car color almost exactly matches your hair dye . . . uh, your hair."

Savannah clicked over on four-inch-heeled mules, her designer jeans torn in all the right places. "Vegas Gold, baby."

"Vegas Gold what?"

"The custom car color."

"There's a color named 'Vegas Gold'?"

"Absolutely. It's used to convey the golden glamour of the Strip lights, the glitz, and the gold to be won at the gaming tables. And now it conveys moi." She turned back to claim the car with a possessive glance, just in case Temple hadn't gotten the idea.

Temple was, admittedly, a bit gaga at the entire entourage of one, but mostly she was miffed that ditzy Savannah Ashleigh knew something about Las Vegas, that she Temple, the public-relations professional, had never heard of.

Vegas Gold. She wondered if Gangsters car service had a limo of that color.

Meanwhile, Savannah had dressed for her usual riveting entrance. She wore a tiny ruffle-ragged silk top that played peekaboo with sheer transparency, and carried a designer bag the size of an old-fashioned postman's bag. From its side pouch peeked beady black eyes inset into a brown fur face mask. It would be easy to take Savannah Ashleigh's current purse pet as a . . . joey kangaroo. Captain Jack proved that tiny lap dogs were passé, and cats had always had too much dignity to put up with being hauled around everywhere.

"This is your aunt's residence?" Temple

asked, getting out of her car and nodding to the desert scenery. "I don't see a . . . house."

"Oh, yeah. This is the place, Temple. The yard is a mess, but Violet likes it that way. Doesn't want the neighbors peeping in her windows."

Judging by the burglar bars on the other houses' side windows, the feeling was mutual.

"Yvette and Solange live here now?" Temple asked, trying to picture the pampered Persians reclining behind this Sleeping Beauty hedge of thorny bushes and cacti.

"Yes, along with the strays Violet is always collecting. After that cat-food-commercial deal fell through, the Persian Girls just weren't earning their keep. And those long, thick coats are *soooo* hard to maintain."

Temple knew Louie would have a screaming fit if he ever heard the gorgeous shaded-silver and shaded-golden Persian sisters had been handed off so casually. He would give Savannah Ashleigh a brand-new face-lift . . . or reason for one, anyway.

"Besides," the actress said, "I've had to kick up my heels to earn a living and keep Violet and her Animal Farm going. She's become something of a recluse; doesn't have my outgoing personality."

"Thank goodness," Temple murmured.

As Savannah's pseudosympathetic simper turned into a glare, Temple added, "Thank goodness you can help out your aunt. Violet does seem to have some socializing . . . issues."

"Our family grew up dirt poor in Alabama," Savannah answered. "You know what that really means?"

Temple shook her head.

"Dirt was about all we had to eat."

Temple took in a deep breath, about to say she was sorry, she'd had no idea, but Savannah had always had enough to say, if not to eat at one time, and she kept saying now.

"It did keep my figure scrupulously slender. That's how Audrey Hepburn did it, you know, kept her slim figure."

"I didn't know," Temple said.

Savannah leaned down to impart girl talk. "Starved in a basement as a child in World War Two Europe. Best thing that can happen to a girl if she wants a film career. You could stand to lose ten pounds, you know."

Temple was momentarily in an altered state alien to her. She was speechless.

Not so Savannah.

"But you are going to *marry* that darling radio man, and once you've got that wedding ring on your finger, as well as that significant engagement ice, along with the *ceremony* that goes with it, you can be sure the new mister won't mind a few extra pounds, or if he does — and they so often do, even when they themselves are as obese as Fatty Arbuckle — will find someone who has the discipline to lose them later."

Speechless.

"Dis-sa-plin," Savannah spelled it out. "You're cute enough to pass now, but what will you be like after forty? Yes, forty! It is death, my dear, but Savannah Ashleigh is a death-defying act."

She spread her stringy, skinny arms to better frame her foot-wide torso. The creature in her purse climbed to her shoulder, revealing a body as lean and long as its mistress, only furry.

"Is your aunt as fashionably . . . skeletal as you?"

"Oh, my, no. She's just my mother's youngest sister. There always has to be one who'll let herself go. I don't blame her. It takes *ded-i-ca-tion* to be beautiful and successful. Remember that."

Temple was thinking it seemed to take more like *dead-i-ca-tion* to the point of anorexia nervosa.

"I'll never forget it," Temple swore, as

fervently as if a courtroom bible were under her right palm. "You should explain about the dead . . . employee before I go inside the house, wherever it is, and actually meet . . . er, Violet."

"Well, he up and died. Or rather, *down* and died. There is a concrete-lined ditchy thing behind Violet's property. He was found at the bottom, dead as a stranded fish in Lake Mead. The empties found him."

"The . . . empties?"

"You know, those good-looking young muscle guys who come with ambulances these days."

"You mean EMTs — the emergency technicians. And some are women."

"Everything is too, too technical these days, don't you agree? I mean, they take away the 'empty' body in that 'empty' ambulance, isn't that so?"

"In a manner of speaking," Temple said. "So the only reason you and your aunt think her life is in danger is because her yardman was found dead. How did anyone spot his body?"

Again Savannah leaned in and down, lowering her voice as well as herself to broadcast in Temple's ear, "Her neighbors all have *bi-noc-u-lars,* Violet tells me, and watch every little thing that goes on outside

114

and inside her house."

Which, Temple observed again, was invisible to the naked eye.

"Let's us go inside Violet's house," Temple suggested, scratching her neck. If there were this many pests outside, what would the inside be like?

"Don't be nervous, dear girl." Savannah also idly scratched her neck, but her fingers were wearing weapons. "You may just be a chubby, short, little overlookable thing, but I've heard people say you are a pistol at stumbling over crimes and criminals."

Still Speechless on Aloe Vera Drive.

Temple followed in Savannah's footsteps through the winding gravel and twisting carnivorous plantscape.

What do you know? A rounded, earth-toned stucco house lurked at the center of the lot, its style more Santa Fe than Vegas. Meanwhile, the clever masked face clung to the shoulder straps of Savannah's over-weight designer bag and regarded Temple with appallingly intelligent eyes.

"Where did the yardman die?" Temple asked, even more puzzled. There was nothing here that required a yardman to tend it, and no ditchy thing.

"Oh, out back by the control towers and the containment channel and the — what did they call it? — retainer basin."

"Are you talking about the control channel for the summer flash floods?" Temple asked.

"Something to do with planes or TV stations, I guess. I didn't know floods flashed," she added with a calendar girl pose and a wiggle followed by a giggle.

"I didn't know Las Vegas had 'retainer basins,' " Temple said dryly.

"That does sound very dentist-office-y."

"There are fields near control channels called 'retention basins.' "

"Why don't you settle all this confusion and hike back and look over the area?" Savannah eyed Temple's rope-fiber wedgies. "Your casual shoes can take it. I'd sink to my Nicole Miller ankle straps in sand if I left the street or sidewalk."

Savannah finished presenting her case by cocking a hip and pointing a toe to display a boney ankle and super-high-heeled sandal.

"You might have mentioned," Temple said, "that the terrain was rough for a city lot."

Savannah shrugged, her gesture making the head of her purse pet pop up from the outside pocket again like a prairie dog masquerading as a cat burglar.

"I figured a PI could cope."

"I'm in PR," Temple said.

"We'll wait here," the woman went on, "while you inspect the death scene. Then we can go inside and you can meet Violet. Captain Jack just loves to play with the cats."

Temple could well imagine. Meanwhile, she followed a slightly worn path of sandy dirt through the aggressively overgrown brush, shorter plants whipping her bare ankles. Who wore hose in Vegas except chorus girls and cocktail waitresses in overly air-conditioned hotel-casinos?

Cowboy boots would have been the proper footwear for this expedition, but Temple's sole pair was aqua-and-silver flamed leather, and not born to be scuffed.

Temple glimpsed stucco walls as beige as the sandy soil to her right from time to time. Quite a bit of house did indeed lurk in this wilderness. And when she broke through the last, bristly, face-whipping stand of brush, she gazed, like Balboa on the Pacific, on a vast, empty scene, in this case water-less.

A concrete-lined gash in the terrain was Savannah's "control tower," otherwise known as a water channel. Next to it lay what most people would take for an empty lot, the retention field used to soak up excess floodwaters.

Anyone who'd lived in Vegas even a very few years, as Temple had, looked on these vast and careful constructions with a small shudder. When the skies clouded over and thronged with storm clouds, their water broke in a cascade so concentrated that desert washes and in-town artificial washes like the control channel filled to their brims then overflowed to swamp roads and even highways, sweeping away vehicles and people in an irresistible eddy of terror and death.

This was the cusp of summer, and the floods came from July to September, but, according to Savannah, a man had died here in the dry belly of the flood-protection system.

It'd be easy to fall into a control channel, hit one's head fatally hard, and not be found for days. It'd also be easier to push someone into a control channel, counting on no one finding him or her for days. And if the body remained undiscovered long enough, a sudden flood could sweep it away miles down the system.

Temple made her way back to the so-called "front yard," savvy enough now to avoid the worst tangles, but her lower legs and forearms still looked like she'd been boxing a lynx.

"Tsk," Savannah said, when Temple finally broke clear into the broken-down front yard. "Those scratches are so unattractive. And your skin, especially that pale kind, tends to never heal deep down. That kind of damage is cumulative, you know, even if you wear sunscreen."

Temple regarded Savannah's golden spray-on tan. No doubt the airbrushing had a high SPF rate and protected Her Delicateness from deterioration.

"You could have warned me I'd be roughing it."

"I didn't think," Savannah said. "That's not my job. That's your job. What do *you* think, now that you've viewed the scene?"

"You haven't seen it?"

"Lord, no. I'd never risk my manicure or my skin or my best heels in that wilderness. The police said Pedro had probably been chasing one of Violet's critters that had gotten loose and fell into the control pit or whatever it is. Violet had reported people lurking around her house at night, but the police discounted that, too. Said it was just all this wild, scratchy stuff brushing on her screens and window glass."

Temple was starting to itch all over. Maybe it was sand fleas or cat fleas.

This did not seem like an auspicious

beginning for a Las Vegas PI.

Where were the night and the neon and the surly pit bosses and sleek and shady casino go-to guys?

Where was her Veronica Lake peekaboo long blond hair and gold lamé trench coat with the impossibly cinched waist and the front hip pocket with the revolver bulge? Where was the glitz and glamour?

CHAPTER 9
WHAT A LOUSY LOT

I pity poor Miss Temple.

I really do.

When she trots gamely off to view the site of the suspicious death, I am finally able to shrug off the black canvas tote bag Miss Temple keeps behind the Miata's front seats for hauling heavy books in the trunk.

Across the street I can hear Miss Savannah Ashleigh's steel-tipped stilettos sticking in the sun-warmed asphalt as she paces. They make a monster-movie sucking sound as she pulls them out. Say what you will of Miss Savannah Ashleigh, but that woman has calves of steel.

I poke Miss Midnight Louise, who had caught up with me this morning only as I was hustling my tail section into the Miata to accompany Miss Temple on a very important date: her first assignment as a paid PI.

"Hop in," I had told the more-than-somewhat-bedraggled and red-eyed Midnight

Louise. "We are going to examine a death site."

"Big deal," she mutters. "If you are into death sites, there are more surrounding the average Las Vegas household than in any Strip hotel."

"Vermin and crawling prey do not count," I say. "Please, do as I say. Hunker down and keep it shut. It is broad daylight now, and our dramatically dark coloring is no longer an advantage."

Thus it is that we broil together in the Vegas pre-noonday sun, which bakes down through our black canvas cabana roof and onto our solid black coats.

This is why desert-dwelling people wear white.

Cats do not pant often, but we do then, dedicated sleuths that Midnight Investigations, Inc., is. Are? Never mind. Thus, we have not had a chance to confer during the bouncy, "road feel" trip. People have odd tastes, and my Miss Temple likes to rip and roar in her small red car.

Being the larger, manlier member of the firm, I have risen to shrug off our canvas curtain first.

"Vito's Vegetarian Pizza car was a far smoother and cooler ride," Louise comments, while unbending her eyebrow hairs with dampened swipes of her mitts. "But I do have news from Chez Max that is as hot as a pizza-box warmer."

"Amaze me."

"He had an unexpected visitor soon after Miss Temple left."

"Not the ghost of Garry Randolph?"

"No. It was someone with a key to the place and the chutzpah to use it."

"Well?"

Miss Louise pauses to slap back her mangled vibrissae. My "whiskers," as humans call them, are snowy white, a distinguished and unusual marking for an otherwise solid-black dude. Louise's are just plain black, but daddy longlegs–fine and out-flung.

"Well?" I demand again. My curiosity is about to give me heatstroke, and she knows it.

"Mister —" she begins.

"A guy. Okay. Then Mister Max did not call the nearest private dancer as soon as he hit town."

"Rafi Nadir."

"Whoa. This is the big one, Louise."

I sit back on my haunches, feeling my heart blip with shock.

How the Hallelujah Chorus would Miss Lieutenant C. R. Molina's ex-cop ex-cohabitator know of the Randolph-Kinsella house or connection or any of the many mystery threads involving my Miss Temple that Louise and I have been following these many, many months like bloodhounds? Excuse the expression, but sometimes only a doggy comparison will do the job — speaking of doggy expressions.

"My vibrissae almost went as white as yours overnight," Louise agrees. "Even worse, Mister Rafi stayed about as long as Miss Temple."

"Twenty minutes or so you said. So it was . . . cordial?"

"Who knows? I only know that both visiting humans left the house under their own power. One would think, unlike our kind, they would not hunker down and glare silently at each other for many minutes."

"You will certainly not question the senior partner's instincts or orders again," I say.

"You have that wrong. This just confirms my instincts at the Neon Nightmare more than two months ago that Mister Max is the one to watch."

"And that is just what you will be doing again tonight."

Miss Louise's muzzle makes an annoyed moue, which is a French word for a dainty grimace.

I leap, claws in, to the sun-baked leather seat and then place my front "velvet paws" on the leather upholstery edging by the rolled-down window. Bast knows that scratched cowhide would not only give away the presence of feline stowaways but earn Miss Temple's swift dismay and wrath.

"What is happening?" Louise asks.

"Miss Temple has returned from exploring the back forty looking as if she has spent a month on the *African Queen* with Humphrey Bogart.

"Oooh! And she is always so smartly turned out. Let me see."

Midnight Louise has lofted up beside me without a claw prick and is blinking her old-gold-colored eyes in the bright sunlight, taking in my human's scratched legs and arms and limp curls.

Meanwhile, Miss Savannah Ashleigh has been sitting in the Sky's driver's seat with her earbuds inserted and her garish blond head bouncing in tune to some pop-rock drivel.

The world is not a just or kind place.

I stare at the pale adobe walls of a house barely visible through the overgrown scrub surrounding it.

"I am about to reverse myself, Louise," I say.

"At least you are just a backseat driver."

"We are coming back here in the dark of night and are going to bust into that illegal cathouse."

"Oh, you guys love to pile on the sleaze and pose as masters of sex and violence. This is a private residence, not the Sapphire Slipper ranch out in Nye County. I doubt we will find anything illegal inside besides too many cats."

"Which there can never be too many of," I get in as a final word.

CHAPTER 10
GATHERING VULTURES

On the sun-seared front concrete step spilling unpicked-up daily newspaper rolls, Temple eyed the rusted screen in the battered aluminum outer door and donned a mental suit of armor, not rusted.

She knew hospitals didn't keep the terminally ill around as long as, say, in her mother's day. The patient's home now was a bridge to hospice care at the point of no return. Temple braced herself for the sights and sounds of bedridden illness she had experienced among her extended family now and then as a child.

Savannah showed no such reticence or sensitivity.

Her spike heels kicked away any blocking newspapers as she used a key like a weapon to belabor the big but grungy-looking front-door lock. The wooden door cracked open on darkness and the tepid, wet indoor temperature likely created by an old-style "swamp cooler."

Temple didn't have to worry about bracing against the odors of bedpan and medicines. What hit her and Savannah like a tsunami was an invisible wall of litter boxes kept in a musty, closed-windows house.

"You'll get used to it." Savannah waved her free hand in front of her face. "My aunt did. It's worse now, of course, since Pedro Gomez kicked the bucket in the back forty."

Temple could only nod while holding her breath. Bless Midnight Louie for using the bathroom window to go outside to do his duty most of the time, and not the bathroom litter box.

Now she knew at least two things Pedro had done for Violet. One was to collect and recycle the daily newspaper, a rarity these Internet days. The other was to dig daily shallow graves for the sifted leavings in box after box of used, probably clumping litter.

Finding unsullied new ground to dig must have taken him far from the house and near the retention basin, making Gomez a sitting duck beside a deadly, man-made dry wash.

Temple also realized that Pedro burying cat litter by the light of the moon might have given someone criminal notions of buried treasure. That was another angle.

Why go to such lengths? Because . . . leaving so much used litter bagged for the city trash haulers would put them in revolt — and, Temple realized, tip off health officials to the fact that Violet was a cat hoarder. And just what was her last name? Surely not Ashleigh, a stage surname if Temple had ever heard one, and she'd heard many.

Meanwhile, Savannah exhaled a shallow breath and stalked on echoing heels into the house, which was floored only with bare concrete and some wood sections. Temple suspected any carpeting had long ago succumbed to litter-box overflow and been ripped out.

The main room was dim, thanks to deep adobe window wells. It was occupied by a bulky island that Temple's focusing eyes identified as a hospital bed. Around and on it lay a half dozen cats of various sizes and patterns, surrounding the sickly white shadow of a woman.

Temple stared at Savannah's aunt Violet, thinking of the portrait of Dorian Gray aging in an attic while the real man stayed artificially young in his everyday environment. That was the sort of resemblance Savannah Ashleigh's aunt bore to her niece.

"My aunt," Savannah introduced her to Temple, "Violet Weiner. I could attach a few ex-husbands' names to that, but neither

Violet nor I choose to remember those skunks. Now, Violet, this here gal may be young and look a little silly, but she is going to find out what happened to Pedro."

Temple threw Savannah a warning look as she approached the bed. She didn't need any extravagant claims wrapped in the disparaging word *silly.*

Violet lay half-raised on the bulky hospital bed, like a Lazarus in suspended transition between life and death. The old woman's hair was long, wild, and a dazzling platinum-blond color, but only because it was completely and magnificently white, naturally. Her bone structure was as camera-ready as her niece's, but the skin had collapsed onto it. Her lips were thin and pale, and her torso was paper-doll flat under the white hospital sheet. No collagen, no breast implants, just her unassisted form.

"Oh, Pedro," she murmured, her head tossing on the pillows. "He hasn't come to the house in two days. The cats and I could always depend upon him. I'm so worried. Is he here now? I want to see him. We miss him. It's terrible to miss someone."

Her low mourning-dove coos turned harsh with conviction. "He's dead, they say. I *know* someone did something to him, like they did to Alexandra. She died, you know.

Far away. A terrible accident, they said. Like Pedro. I don't believe what they say."

She glared at Savannah, but only because she was known to her, and handy. Violet was an old sick woman. Temple wondered how many years separated Savannah and Violet. How fascinating that Savannah's stage surname, Ashleigh, was almost an entire alphabet away from their shared maiden name.

Temple would bet *Savannah* was equally removed from the actress's christening name. She would love to know what that was, and probably would before this sad story was over.

"My name is Temple Barr." She put her hand out to the thin one that reached up from the bed linens in an automatic gesture. The wrinkled skin felt dry and hot. "I understand your concerns and must admit that Pedro's death looks suspicious, Miss Weiner."

"Call me Violet, dear." The woman's voice had an eerily light and girlish lilt, like Savannah's. Her wrist wore a string of purple beads the same color of the prominent veins in her claw-thin hands. "My name is a good omen," she added. "Amethysts and emeralds are healing gemstones for my kind of cancer." She looked to the other side of her

131

bed. "Isn't that true, Jayden?"

A figure sitting in the shadows beyond the bed stood to capture Temple's attention as much as the dying woman's. In the house's naturally dim lighting, he seemed to rise with the supernatural smoothness of an animated corpse in a horror film.

Savannah's heels stuttered forward a pace as if she felt compelled to challenge the man.

"Mister Jayden?" Temple went around the foot of the bed to shake hands.

She needed to get a quick fix on this guy, and was instantly assaulted with a theatrical costume, a white muslin Cossack shirt embroidered by way of Sedona, Arizona. He was heavily accessorized for a man, with a thick turquoise bracelet on his left wrist and a chunk of amethyst crystal at his neck.

"Just Jayden," he corrected her. "Surnames are required by bureaucracies, not our natural impulses. The individual outweighs the tribe. What a potent first name you have, Temple. You need use no more. In fact, your karma would improve if you dropped your surname. *Barr* is negative, implying barriers. And you don't like barriers, do you, Temple?"

"Who does?" she said. "Miss Weiner's employee was found dead in a big concrete gash in the desert — talk about negative barriers. I don't care to be taken for a place of worship, and I'm not that interested in being omnipotent, so I'll keep using my last name, thank you anyway, uh, Jayden."

She wondered if he'd ditched a plain-Jane surname like *Johnson.* He was too old to have been christened something as currently trendy as Jayden. Under that sun-worshipping natural tan his facial wrinkles were as fine as spiderweb lace. He was pushing fifty, at least. The package had a certain televangelist charisma without the obvious smarm. She found her eyes reluctant to leave his gaze for some reason. And she had two highly charismatic guys preoccupying her mind, heart, and conscience.

"The Earth is our place of worship." Jayden smiled at Violet as he dropped Temple's hand to circle around the bed's foot to Violet's side, deftly inserting himself between auntie and visitors.

Temple was shocked silent to observe in the better light that Jayden's left eye was an unearthly turquoise blue and the right was . . . purple. She'd seen semiprecious stones combine veins of both gems like that, and also color-enhancing contact lenses that were spectacularly unnatural. The teens today were all Lady Gaga about wearing

133

oversize contact lenses that made their eyes look as anime-winsome as the artist Margaret Keane did with cats' and kids' eyes fifty years ago.

Jayden bent over Violet like Dracula over a sleeping Victorian lady. "You must rest, dear lady." He laid his right hand on her forehead, the second finger wearing a silver ring set with an amethyst the size of a teaspoon bowl.

For an instant, Temple feared his nimble golden-brown fingers would retreat down Violet's pallid features and shut her eyes as a doctor might do for the dead. Instead, his hand lifted to make a dismissive gesture that seemed to start as a sign of the cross, but turned loopy.

Oh. His fingers had sketched out the crosslike form of an Egyptian ankh.

"It's time for our nap," Jayden said so softly Temple had to strain her ears. He regarded Savannah as his voice turned from molten to adamant. "You should leave."

"Hell's bells," Savannah said. "We just got here, and I'm kin. Closest kin that she wants to see or hear of, that is. *I* want to show Temple around. Maybe some of that first-name mojo you rave about might rub off on poor Violet. I'm not leaving unless Violet asks me to, Mister Jayden, and you've got her zoned out. What kind of tea have you been pouring into her now?"

"I ease her pain by psychic, not physical means, Sue Anna."

Sue Anna? Temple swallowed, hard.

"You don't want to upset her by making a scene," Jayden added. "From what Violet has told me, you were always good — or should I say bad? — at that."

Sue Anna Weiner?

Temple was struck silent despite the minor spat brewing beside her.

Savannah Ashleigh was really *Sue Anna Weiner?* Temple knew that double *n*s often read like an *m*. So *Savannah* could be *Sue am-a Weiner.*"

"You are a bigger phony than I am," Savannah was telling the equally artificial Jayden now. It takes one to know one. "And a worse actor," she added. "I am going to have you investigated by my PI."

"You'll never get in Violet's will. Trust me. I know."

"Unlike you, I don't care. I actually care about Violet."

Temple eyed the sick woman. She lay with her eyes closed, apparently hearing none of this talk. She spied a Garfield mug on the bedside table, but no tea bag tag dangling over its rim. Whatever Jayden was giving

Violet was home-brewed.

Her hand tightened on the tote-bag straps over her shoulder. These roomy carriers sure came in handy. The house was a monument to clutter and cats. That Garfield mug was leaving with Temple, and she'd at least give it the sniff test, or, better yet, take it to a tea shop for diagnosis. Many health shops in the suburban strip malls offered exotic tea varieties. Or . . . maybe the coroner, Grizzly Bahr, would be interested enough to analyze the stuff. Their similar surnames made the pair unlikely soul mates, as did loving the weird little details.

"I've brought some treats for the poor cats," Savannah announced, as importantly as if it were the Second Coming.

She extracted a sealed packet from her bag and rattled something Louie had never seen the likes of, interrupting Temple's plotting.

"There's plenty of kibble already set out all over the house," Jayden said.

"Pedro used to give the cats treats," Savannah answered. "I'm sure they miss that dreadfully by now. You are obviously not a cat person, which is very odd since you claim to be psychic."

"I claim to draw on the universal healing calm we all can tap into if we only will."

"Speaking of wills," Savannah said, "it's amazing how the ghouls show up when an old lady who's determined to cut out any relative is sick. Old Pedro was the only man who ever did look out for Violet, and it's very convenient for everyone but Violet that's he's gone now. I'd think it would be good karma for you to help give out treats to the cats."

She turned to Temple. "We're going to the kitchen," she announced. "You can get acquainted with Violet and bring her mug along later for a fill-up. Then we'll both leave Jayden to work more of his mental mumbo jumbo on poor, helpless Violet's psyche." She looked at the floor. "Watch out for random litter boxes," she warned Temple over her bare shoulder as they left the room.

Temple saw that aliens had indeed landed: aluminum turkey-roaster pans filled with litter and . . . leavings . . . lay like sand traps on the concrete floor. Who was going to deal with the cat boxes now? Jayden was far too elevated for such earthly matters.

"Oh, good. We're alone." Violet's clawlike hand clasped Temple's forearm with painful desperation. "They never leave me alone."

"Who?" Temple asked in the same loud whisper Violet used.

In the kitchen, she could hear Jayden and Savannah bickering over a chorus of meowing cats. What a perfect time to interview Violet. Almost as if Savannah had engineered this moment.

"Everyone," Violet replied. "You're such a pretty little girl, just like my Alexandra. I can tell you. You wouldn't believe what's going on here."

Temple's eyes got bigger and she leaned closer, though Violet's breath was very bad. Illness or Jayden's brews?

"Every night men climb in and out of my bathroom window."

"Aren't your windows locked?"

"They're very old, like the house. A child could get past them now."

"What do the men want?"

"My fine china and sterling silver place settings. Will you look in the dining room to see that it's still there? The burglars do stumble over the cats a lot, but they're disappearing, too."

"The cats? How can you tell?"

"How can I tell?" Violet's grip grew more painful. "Whisper, Alexandra's white shorthair, never comes to visit my bed anymore. I haven't seen Frederick, the mackerel tabby, since Pedro deserted me."

"Pedro didn't desert you. He had an . . .

138

accident and fell into the concrete canyon behind your house."

Violet's features puckered with puzzlement. "You're not supposed to swim there." Then came panic. "Maybe that's where the cats are going. None of them are supposed to leave the house. That's where they're to stay. And where's Alexandra's old girl, Little Doll? Where have some of my cats gone?"

"There're so many," Temple said, wondering if Violet was imagining things or . . . right.

"Oh, I know every whisker on every one. I've only been bedridden for . . . for a day or two. Or is it a week or two? Time! It's hard to keep track of, but I can keep track of my cats and my china."

"How do you know Jayden?"

"Oh. He has a New Age shop. He knew Alexandra when he lived in Sedona and he met her in Tucson when he toured the southwest. Then he moved here. I went to see his shop, for crystals and magnets. I have magnets on all my cat collars. And under my mattress. They're from Father Hell."

"Father Hell?"

"A funny name for a priest, isn't it? But he was a Jesuit healer. Father Maximilian Hell. He was a friend of the mesmerism man and knew how to restore your magnetic fluid."

"Is that what you're drinking, magnetic fluid?" Temple picked up the empty Garfield mug. Violet seemed spacey and erratic, and she was jumbling thoughts together. If her mind was going, were iffy potions helping it depart? "It sounds like something you'd put in an automobile."

"Hardly," came Jayden's jarring voice from behind her. "What has our Miss Violet been saying?"

"Just telling me about mesmerism and magnets," Temple said, pulling her arm from Violet's death grip. She turned to him and dropped the Garfield mug into her tote bag in one smooth movement when her body momentarily blocked his vision. "Apparently, you own a shop."

"I do." Jayden produced a card from his pale linen pants pocket. A slightly wrinkled card reading, HEALING ARTS, MAGNETIC AIDS.

"Very interesting." Temple studied the images of faceted gemstones and sunlike rays. "But I'd hate to sleep atop something dreamed up by a guy named 'Father Hell.' "

"It's more than merely interesting," Jayden said. "Magnet therapy goes back to the Egyptians and the Greeks. By the seventeen-seventies, Father Hell could heal people with a steel plate so successfully that Franz Anton Mesmer, the German physician and pioneer in hypnosis, studied Hell's devices and results and first identified the subtle magnetic fluid flowing through all creation and creatures. The correct placement of magnets on or near the body will restore the disruptions in the field we call poor health."

"Uh-huh." Temple had dropped the gaudy card into her tote bag also, where it landed inside the Garfield mug. She pulled the straps tight on her shoulder so no one could see in.

She turned to Violet. "I'll certainly do everything I can to help care for your cats now that Pedro's . . . not here."

"Do you have any cats?"

"Just one."

"Only one! So many need homes."

"He's a very dominant cat."

"Oh, you'll end up with more, my dear. I can tell the lone and wounded just flock to you."

"You may be right," Temple said, sweeping her gaze past Jayden's unnervingly odd-eyed face. In fact, she spotted a white cat with one blue and one gold eye on the bedside chair. "Is this your missing Whisper?" she asked Violet.

"Oh." She turned her head to view the animal. "No. That's her sister, Becky Sharpe."

Temple was startled to hear a cat named for the heroine of an old novel. Then she remembered that Becky Sharpe had been "two-faced." Violet was, or had been, pretty sharp herself.

"I'm going to help Savannah put out the cat food in the kitchen," she told Violet in farewell. "It was fascinating meeting you."

Temple couldn't help wondering if Jayden's differently colored contact lenses played on odd-colored eyes sometimes showing up in animals. It would certainly give him an "in" with cat and dog lovers. Did human eyes have that possibility too? Max had worn cat-green contacts when he'd performed as a magician. She wondered if he'd ever gone with one natural blue eye and one artificial green one.

It certainly was a distraction, and magicians are all about distraction. Like right now. Temple was thinking of her returned "lone and wounded" ex, when she should be figuring out what was going on at Violet's house.

She had to thread her way through milling cat bodies to reach the kitchen and found that the cat treats being distributed had attracted cats like a nucleus gloms on to protons. Or whatever. She was relieved to spot two other Garfield mugs on the counter. The one in her tote bag would not be missed.

"So," she asked Sue Anna — Savannah — "who will take over Pedro's litter-sifting and outdoor-burying duties? Surely not the devoted Jayden. And you don't have the footwear for the job."

"Oh, Rowdy will do it," Savannah said, pinching her nostrils shut and waving her free hand under her nose to indicate the distastefulness of the task. "He's been in town all these years since Alexandra died. Violet could never stand him, but she's been forced to call on him now and then since she got ill. Not that he'll get anything out of it but doo-doo."

"Rowdy?" By now Temple realized her nose was already adjusting to the overpowering odor of many cat boxes in close quarters. She desperately wanted to go outside to talk and breathe.

"You know I have a cat of my own, sort of," she told Sue Anna . . . Savannah. She had to forget the woman's birth names — first, middle, and last — because she would simply giggle at having unmasked the eternal starlet's unpretentious past, and this was not the place for inappropriate reactions.

"Oh, yes." Savannah gritted her ultrableached teeth. "I remember that rogue male well! I ended up owing my plastic surgeon a bundle for 'fixing' your tomcat with a vasectomy instead of a neutering. He was a very dumb doctor. And he threw in a tummy tuck for your Two-O'Clock Louser, while I certainly didn't get any freebies. I can't afford any more surgery with the stupid economy, and I desperately need Botox and collagen. And Violet won't leave me anything 'on principle.' "

"Do the cats inherit, is that Violet's issue?" Temple wondered as she helped Savannah open more of the treat bags the actress had jammed into her oversize Prada bag.

It was a metallic swashbuckler of a purse, buckled to the nines, nothing as old-fashioned and simple as Temple's ever-present tote bags. Captain Jack must have felt right at home inside all that hardware, but he still scrabbled from his out-of-pocket home to grab an entire bag of treats and rip it open with his tiny paws and claws.

Smelling the fishy-scented plastic packages in the adjacent section and having to be a good boy and cozy up to the mistress must have been torture.

As the packets were ripped open, cats appeared from the vicinity of Violet's bed and then many more from other house areas. In a minute, a milling, mewing carpet of cats of all shapes and colors swarmed the women's feet. Cats perched on tables and the wide adobe windowsills, meowing. They lofted atop the countertops, nudging human elbows.

"S-S-Savannah," Temple said, determined to inter Sue Anna Weiner forever in her consciousness, "is there a definitive count on the cats?"

"I never knew you stuttered. There is help for that, you know."

"I know! These cats can't continue to run all over the house. How could the doctors release Violet to her home?"

"It's obvious you've never had a terminal disease, Temple," Savannah lectured her.

Temple could only blink at the disconnect that sentence implied.

"Am I right?" Savannah obviously had to be.

"Right," Temple said in exasperation. "What would that have to do with it?"

"Well, the doctors and hospitals are happy to have you coming in and out for daily radiation that's costing your insurance or

Medicare thousands a week, and when they've made their bundles and you get so ill from the radiation you can't get yourself in, they release you to your 'home and caretakers,' until you're sick and out of your mind enough that they can stick you in a hospice for your final day, or days, hopefully just the one if they time it right.

"What is going on, do you think?" Savannah asked. "Violet's been hallucinating from the pain meds for the last week and a half. Taking these cats away would push her over the edge. Her whole deal was that the cats stay in the house as long as they lived, after her death. The person who will do that for her gets the money, and while the will still isn't signed, I figure that crystal freak will get it. I'm just trying to keep Violet going as decently as possible until it's out of all our hands."

Temple had never heard Savannah Ashleigh speak that many sentences, or sentiments, in a row. She'd obviously seen a tragically similar case to Violet's. Temple found it touching that the struggling, middle-aged actress would do so much for her difficult aunt, for no personal gain.

"And," Savannah added, "Violet has promised me I'll get Yvette and Solange back in the will. When I dropped my babies

146

off with her a few months ago, Violet had far more marbles and many fewer cats."

"I don't see Yvette and Solange." Temple gazed around, counting cats. At least sixteen.

Savannah sniffed. "They would be rushing to Mommy's arms, but I think Captain Jack's scent on me is a deterrent. That's them, on the kitchen table."

Temple looked over. She couldn't believe her eyes. It was more than ferret scent that kept Savannah's formerly favorite pets from approaching her. What about complete betrayal? Could that pair of scruffy gray and yellow cats with knotted coats be the Persian purebreds? No. Yvette was a shaded silver Persian like the beauty on the Fancy Feast TV ads, and Solange was a richly shaded golden version of same.

"Don't look at me like that!" Savannah said as Temple turned to her. Her guilty eyes kept shifting somewhere between the Raggedy Ann cats and Temple. "Violet is holding both of my girls hostage, and I can't get them to a groomer for a lion cut until she . . . well, gets to the bottom of her own bowl of not-so-Friskies."

"Lion cut?" Temple asked, fastening on the most bizarre phrase.

"Of course." Savannah shrugged. "My

Persian babies will have to be shaved to the skin except for their heads and ruffs, the 'boots' on their lower legs, and the tufts at the end of their tails. It's a cool clipping for this climate, rather adorable, and will allow their scrumptious soft, long coats to grow out smooth and knot-free. Until they start tangling again. Hasn't your Midnight Lounger ever been to a groomer?"

"*Nooo*. He'd take that personally. I mean, he attends to all his barbering needs himself."

"I suppose that's possible. He certainly doesn't have a show coat."

By then the treats had been distributed to the small saucers placed everywhere . . . Royal Doulton, Temple had noticed. Underneath the clutter and the cat hair lurked some wonderful and fragile things.

"So," she asked, "the will still hasn't been signed?"

Savannah nodded unhappily. "When Violet first got ill she sounded all certain and organized, but she's delayed doing anything final, and all the while the vultures have gathered. I'm terribly afraid that crystal-flashing crook will get the whole shebang. I'm no fonder of my aunts and uncles and cousins than Violet is, but her money would be better off with greedy relatives than with an outright con man."

"What about this 'Rowdy' guy?"

"He was Alexandra's boyfriend at the time of her tragic death. He came to Vegas for the funeral and never left."

"So Alexandra died far away from her mother. You said drugs?"

"Yeah. In Tucson. Alex was not one of those drug-abusing kids. That's what was so sad. What got her was one of those awful cases where some creep they never caught was putting bad stuff in pain-reliever bottles on drugstore shelves. Like playing Russian roulette with pill bottles. But Alex was far away from her mother for a reason. They'd had a falling out."

"And then Alex dies in a freak outbreak of anonymous murder? Poor Violet."

Savannah nodded. "I didn't realize at first, but that's when she started going cat crazy. She can't let one of them go. It's like she's searching for Alex to come back as a cat. Alex was the one who had cats. Violet took her four and the litter of kittens after she died, so I thought she could handle my two. This was before Violet got ill. How was I to know she'd been adding every homeless cat she ran across? She'd always wanted to lunch on the Strip when I was in town, so I never saw the house."

Temple could understand how Violet's pet population had multiplied. Most city codes were strict on pet numbers per household. She knew a lot of animal lovers and rescuers exceeded the stingy allowances. Temple had no problems with the codes. Louie would not tolerate even one additional cat on his Circle Ritz premises. Maybe not even a stuffed one. Temple wasn't about to buy one and find out.

"I need to leave," Temple told Savannah. "I need to think this over and probably come back and talk to Violet further."

"Why not? Duh. I come here almost every day now." Savannah imitated Temple by hoisting her bag straps on her shoulder. "Wait! My bag is too light. It's not just the treats that are gone, Captain Jack is!"

Temple scanned the cats, looking for a ferret in feline clothing. Most of them were short-haired, she noticed, and pretty sleek. Her glance fell on the woebegone Persian sisters, looking listless and lost. She tried to approach them, hand out with treat nuggets, but they hissed at her in unison. The poor things seemed half feral now, and forcing these pampered cats to fight for their places in this menagerie was outrageous.

Midnight Louie would bring the house down if he knew his former lady friends

150

were being neglected. Even as she thought of Louie, a lean, wiry form came barreling across the treat-sprinkled countertops — not Louie, for sure.

"Captain Jack!" Savannah welcomed the ferret as it raced up her arm and into the purse's big outer pocket, its tail vanishing last, just as it did a U-y and the masked little face reappeared over the pocket edge.

Captain Jack seemed very pleased with himself.

Temple and Savannah threaded their way back to the living room, hearing Violet on the cell phone that rested on a small square pillow by her right shoulder.

Jayden bent over the dining-room buffet table, lighting an incense stick that looked and smelled like the cinnamon ones people sometimes put in hot drinks. Temple couldn't help thinking that even a pot smell would be better than the odor of cat boxes. And she wouldn't put it past Jayden to give some of that to Violet. That would sure not make for clearheaded will signing. Nevada was not California. Medical marijuana wasn't legal, but it was easy to import.

"No, Briana." Violet was on the phone, her light, frail voice strained to sound emphatic. "You can't have my full-length Russian sable coat no matter how much you whine. What a thing to think of at a time like this — not me, but what I have that you want! That coat is far older than you are, not suitable for a young girl. Besides, I'm still alive. I might wear it in my casket. So there, you greedy little girl. I don't care that you're my grandniece. You didn't care that I was your great-aunt until I got sick. Go away."

Violet's thin hand clutched the phone. She seemed unaware that she could click it off. Briana's whining voice escalated until even Temple could hear it. She walked over and gently slipped the phone from Violet's fingers, shutting it off.

"She's gone now," she told the sick woman.

Violet's heavy-lidded eyes barely followed Temple's gestures, instead staring into her face. "You've got some red-gold in your hair, like I used to. Would *you* like my sable coat?"

"What a lovely thought, but you keep it."

"Can you believe the nerve of my grand-niece? She acts as if I was dying." Her focus became fierce. "I'm going to be fine. Jayden said so. Emeralds and amethysts will see me through." Her giggle was faint but harsh. "Briana and her parents can go to hell! Father Hell's magnets all under my mattress will shrink the cancer. Sue Anna . . ."

Savannah sighed with gusto and clicked over to the bed.

"I did leave you your two precious Persians and a few thousand for pin money," Violet told Savannah. "Maybe I'll even give you my sable coat, although it doesn't go with your bleached-slut hair color."

"It's a custom salon tint, Auntie. 'Vegas Gold.' Only Rolf at Hair Carousel can do it. It's the quintessence of all the glitz and lights on the Strip."

"You are the quintessence of stupidity, niece, with that thin résumé of what you call a 'career.' Meanwhile, you keep coming to feed the cats, do you hear me? Jayden has better things to do, and Pedro . . . Pedro went away."

Temple was taken aback by Violet's swift mood changes. She knew the sick can be difficult — heck, give her a stomach flu and watch her moan and whine — but Violet displayed a vengeful, mean streak. Maybe that was why she'd had a rift with her daughter before Alex died so tragically.

Hers not to judge a life she knew so little about. Already she was feeling sorry for Savannah, and *that* was a major change of heart.

The two visitors walked out of the door,

stood in the sunshine, and breathed deeply together, as if sharing the end of an exercise class. The wall of stuffy, fecal odor behind them still wafted past.

"She's my aunt," Savannah said with a grimace. "I don't like her sister and two brothers any more than she does. Luckily, they live in Alaska and are not about to pressure her on the will from more than long-distance calls she can refuse, like her bratty, spoiled grandniece. If they showed up, they'd have to do some things for her, and they're not the tending type. I guess I'm not either, but I'm here, and I have no stake in any so-called fortune."

"Do you have any idea what that is?"

"The house is old, but the land is good. She probably has mutual funds, life insurance. With the antiques and household goods, I'm guessing two hundred thousand. Not peanuts, and enough for someone greedy to covet. I can't say it wouldn't help me out, but I know the family rifts go back to her and siblings, and she somehow managed to drive Alexandra away, too. I've got nothing to gain here but grief, but I *am* here. What are you gonna do?"

"You're right. She's alienated the very people who might have had her good at heart. So she's been left vulnerable, and the vultures are gathering."

"So what are *you* gonna do?"

"Investigate Jayden, number one."

"That's all?"

"Uh, check with my police contacts on Pedro's death."

"Police contacts — wow. You gonna call your blond hottie in on the case?"

"He's out of town."

"*You* get outta town! You wouldn't let that guy loose on his own in some other city with other women, would you?"

"Other cities are full of other women, and so is Vegas. I trust him implicitly."

"That a relative of explicitly?"

The wink of Savannah's false-eyelashed eye indicated she'd understood Temple's phrase perfectly. Maybe she wasn't as dumb as she looked and acted. They were almost at the curb, about to split for their respective red and Vegas Gold convertibles (another appalling sign of sisterhood), when a guy in pseudocamos ambled up the walk.

"Miss Ashleigh," he greeted them, surprised, and giving Temple a bright, alert, Captain Jack look, only with blue eyes. "How's she doing today?"

"Off and on, as usual, Rowdy," Savannah answered, relaxing as she hadn't when Jayden was around. "The guru has got her in his grip."

Rowdy shook his buzz-cut head. "Losing Alex kinda unbalanced her. It's not nature, a daughter passing on before a mother, and now Violet's dyin' and still denyin'."

Temple needed to put in a sympathetic word, even though the necessary introduction really killed her.

"Hi, I'm Savannah's friend, Temple." Moving on. "Her aunt's situation is so sad . . . Rowdy. Oh, that's right. I remember. Savannah said you were with Alexandra in Tucson six years ago when she died so tragically. And now you're here?"

He winced. "Came up to Vegas to look after the old lady for Lexi, truth to tell. She and her mother had one of those spats that was hard on both of them. I was lost to have Lexi taken from me like that. She didn't die right away. They didn't know what killed her right away. I guess Miss Ashleigh told you."

"Horrible, horrible thing," Temple said with full sincerity. "Who would kill people randomly like that? Pointless."

"Yeah. Even serial killers at least have their crazy logic. I was kinda . . . at loose ends after Lexi died. I work construction, and until a couple years ago Vegas was booming, so it made sense to move from Arizona up here. I drove the cats up for Violet, but she never warmed to me whether Lexi was alive or dead. I kept an eye on her anyway. Helped Pedro outside. She never tumbled to the fact that I was concerned about her. But I lost my most significant person, too, when Alexandra died."

Savannah swayed from sole to sole on her painfully high heels while Captain Jack's little head followed the conversation.

"I know, Rowdy," Savannah said. "Alexandra was a beautiful girl. To die in her twenties of something so random . . ."

Temple had been studying the guy. A boyish thirty-eight or so. Short, maybe five-six, but wiry and strong, a wind-tanned face and sun-squinting eyes. A burr of brown hair, intense blue eyes. Not overeducated, but a solid, nice guy.

"Anyway," he told Savannah, "now that Pedro's gone, I come over after work every day to bury the litter. It's been neglected for a few days, and you know that pouf Jayden won't lift an amethyst pinky-ringed hand to do what really needs to be done around the place."

Savannah shook her head. "And you know Violet'll never put you in the will, Rowdy. She hated you when you were Alex's boyfriend, and she just tolerates you since you came to Vegas because you do things for her."

"It's not about the money, trust me," he said. "I know how she's always felt about me. No one was good enough for her daughter, especially me."

Rowdy turned to Temple, pulling a worn wallet out of his pocket-tiered pants. He produced a small portrait photo of a slim, well-groomed blond with hyperthyroid eyes, popping slightly as if she were surprised. She certainly had been, by life. And early death.

He ran a thumb over the matte surface. "That's Lexi. She and her mom didn't get along, but no way am I going to let Lexi down and do unto her mom as she did unto me."

"You dislodge that Jayden creep," Savannah said, "and I'll support you."

"It's Violet's house, her stuff. Her life. And death." He shrugged and moseyed up the walk.

"Violet has more people trying to look out for her than she'll ever realize," Savannah said.

"What's Rowdy's real first name?" Temple asked.

"Something uncool like Sylvester . . . no, I guess that turned out to be plenty cool for

Stallone. Um, Sylvan Smith. You know how parents with last names that are a dime a dozen always stick an embarrassing, different first name on their kids?"

"That's a very astute point, Savannah."

" 'Astute.' You commenting on my world-class ass? It's my own redistributed fat."

Temple refused to be grossed out. "I think you know what I'm commenting on. Your brain that isn't as disengaged as you pretend."

Chattering as if joining a *Gossip Girl* session, Captain Jack peeked out of his personal pocket.

"What's he got now?" Savannah's expression turned disgusted. "A hairball from Violet's house!"

Temple snagged the dry brown object from the ferret's paws.

"*Euww,* don't touch that," Savannah yelped. "Naughty, naughty Captain Jack!"

"Clever Captain Jack," Temple said, putting the tea bag into the inside pocket of her tote bag. Come to think of it, she had room for a purse pet herself.

Captain Jack had managed to filch one of Jayden's custom tea bags from the kitchen. Just what the doctor ordered . . . for the visiting PI.

"Mind if I keep this?" Temple asked

Savannah.

The actress made a very slight dismissive moue, so as not to overstress her facial skin.

"Keep it. It will hardly be in the will."

Temple had two thoughts as she left Aloe Vero Drive.

It can't be good for Violet to be living out her last days in this giant cat box.

And: who would try to kill a woman who was already dying?

CHAPTER 11
CRIME'S HER CUP OF TEA

Once Temple got back home, she made a tall glass of double Crystal Light cherry pomegranate and loaded it with fresh lime slices.

Mike Hammer may have tossed back double rye whiskeys but she was too petite to handle the calories a hard-drinking male private eye could swallow.

Sitting at her office desk, she stared at the framed black-and-white photo of film noir actress and director Ida Lupino on the bookcase opposite then looked up the numbers on her cell-phone list and punched one name before she could chicken out.

"Molina," that deep, dark voice spat out, sounding as if this exact phone call would "make her day" by requiring her to shoot her own phone.

"Ah, Barr here."

"Bar what? Is this a crank call, kid, because I can have it traced so fast —"

161

"It's Temple Barr."

"Temple Barr?" There was a sudden change of tone Temple didn't like. She'd describe it as too civil and way too sadistic. "Calling me in the middle of a working day? Lost another ring? Fiancé?"

"This is a business call."

"And those matters weren't? Never mind. What do you want?"

"I . . . need . . . some information about a man found dead three days ago in the flood channel behind Aloe Vera Drive."

"Well, that's so simple, Miss Barr. Just phone your seriously overworked, friendly neighborhood homicide lieutenant and chew the fat — not that we women have any excess of that. Wake up and smell the caffeine! I can't give you any police information, not even about a dead grackle found in Sunset Park."

"Well, all the private detectives on TV know somebody on the police force who'll fill in the technical details."

"That's because they only have forty minutes and three 'acts' to wind up a totally fictional case. Perhaps the *CSI* fad has totally corrupted the public mentality on just what boundaries the police really observe, but I thought you might be a tad more sensitive to the inanity of what you're asking."

"At least I know this probably isn't a safe line."

"Is this your PR person's way, TB, of forcing me into a P.M. coffee break?"

"Do you really get one?"

"No." Sigh. Another sigh. "There's a Sin City Caffeine Cache franchise two blocks from me. Be there in an hour. And what's the name?"

"Sin City Caffeine Cache."

"Not that! The DB."

"Oh, I thought you wanted me to confirm the, ah, assignation spot."

"Don't make it sound so romantic."

"And . . . DB? Oh. Dead body. Oh, yes. Pedro Gomez."

"*Hmm,* that name has a distinctly coffeehouse ring to it."

"*Gomez,* not Valdez."

Molina sighed again. "Or an Addams Family vibe. I can always expect the unusual from you, Miss Barr. Be there."

Temple clung to the disconnected phone. Molina always made her feel like a breathless junior-high-school newspaper reporter — nervy but eternally hopeful.

Temple supposed being female, tall, and blue-eyed with a Latino last name had been

163

both a curse and a blessing in a high-school life and a police career. Being short and smart and redheaded carried a Little Orphan Annie "vibe" Temple was only now escaping . . . until she tangled with Molina.

Still . . . Bingo! The cop was coming across. Temple ramped up her desktop laptop — the new Gateway — to check out the coffeeshop's address. Poor Starbucks, once king of the coffee-bean hill, now fighting new little independent chains in the Great Recession economy.

Somehow, Temple could identify more with . . . the SCCC. Sin City Caffeine Cache.

Maybe they served tea, too, and she could run the aroma of Violet's special "brew" past the expert witnesses there.

"First," Molina said, "tell me why you're interested in this noncase."

"A . . . friend asked me to investigate the circumstances of her rich old aunt. She was concerned that a pack of vultures were gathering around the ill old lady, Violet. Pedro had been Violet's yardman, but far more. He kept her and the entire establishment going."

Driving Miss Daisy," Molina said. "Shorthand, please. I don't ordinarily have time to

164

consort with amateurs."

"You know the man was found dead in the flood channel."

"He was seventy-eight years old, and it's hot here. Anything could have caused him to keel over at the back of an extremely rugged property, sustain a concussion, and die."

"Is that what Grizzly Bahr said?"

"Oh, you *know* the old goat? I should have guessed. He's a leg man, even with corpses."

"Lieutenant!"

"A joke. What's your footwear of the day?"

"Sensible Easy Spirit pumps."

"I *do* put a crimp in your operating system, don't I?"

"Yes, sir."

Molina chuckled. "That's the attitude, Private. Private Investigator, is it now? As it happens, the Gomez death report was buried in File Cabinet Limbo with a lot of other 'unexplained' and unglamorous deaths. My 'Bahr' — I doubt 'Grizzly' will ever be a nickname of yours — finds the cause of Mister Gomez's death 'vague.' He could have had a heart attack at the top of the concrete spillway and fell into it. His head could have been bashed in at the top, and then he fell into it, impact masking the initial, deliberate blow. He could have been alive when he was pushed into it and died from the impact.

"This is a case that will only be prosecuted and decided on a reasonable motive for killing an elderly yard worker. A wealthy disabled employer who might name him in a will could very well be one. I can't tell you not to interfere, except to note that if Gomez was murdered, as you suspect, you should keep yourself miles away from that invalid and that house."

Molina tapped the manila folder on the tabletop. "Violet Weiner is listed for lots of crackpot calls to the police in the past year, men coming in and out of her bathroom window, Peeping Toms, and suspicious neighbors. That would make her latest fixation on Gomez being killed sound overwrought and like more of the same."

Molina rose — towered — all almost-six feet of her.

"You know, Miss Temple Barr, PI, sometimes it also depends on a vic's last name how much attention an unexplained death gets in this town, or any town in the lower forty-eight. I'll have the case given a new look-see. Good work."

She left Temple clutching her cup of orange pekoe and blinking with . . . relief, exhilaration, and pride. Guess she'd finally made the senior-high newspaper staff, after all. So to speak.

Such unexpected recognition, the euphoria, and the cold cup of orange pekoe made Temple decide to visit an herbal tea shop familiar with more exotic varieties. She had Captain Jack's purloined tea bag from Violet's house in her tote bag, and a wise PI would never look a gift purse pet in the mouth. Especially with sharp little teeth like that.

The Teahouse of the August Moon in bustling Henderson had a quaint, ersatz-Asian exterior, and a man inside named Augie Moon actually ran the place.

"Which came first?" she asked the portly, silver-bearded proprietor after making a deeply scented tour of the shelves. "Did your name or the novel, play, and movie's title give the shop its theme?"

"Aha. A young lady with some long-range knowledge. However, if you're as perceptive as I take you to be, you'd know I pre-date the fifties play by about ten years."

"Really, Mister Moon?" Temple looked mock skeptical.

"Call me Augie. Even more perceptive than I thought. I'm following my life's obsession, so I've certainly shaved at least a decade off my years. Not enough to court you, of course, Miss — ?"

"Temple Barr."

"Now there's a name that already decorates establishments from the high and mighty and British to the low and Las Vegas."

She had to chuckle. "You know the territory pretty well yourself. You have a wonderful place here. You wouldn't be insulted if I told you I was led here by a ferret."

"A ferret? Great hunters, ferrets. What are *you* hunting for?"

Temple pulled the Garfield mug from her tote. "The original contents of this cup and this tea bag."

Augie seized upon the mug with as much relish as Captain Jack had retrieved the tea bag.

"You have to have a nose in this business," he said, burying his rather large red one in the mug. "I'll need to consult the shelves on both of these. Please step over to the tea bar and have a savory something on the house, the Teahouse of August Moon. I recommend a cinnamon-chili brew for one of your temperament and hair color."

"I can change my hair color."

"But never your temperament. Some paprika might do you very well, too."

That flustered Temple into blushing.

"*Hmph.* I see the spice is not new to you."

"Can tea have such exotic seasonings?"

"Tea can be made of anything."

"Including narcotics or poisons?"

Augie hoisted the mug and the tea bag in both hands. "As you suspect? Are you a private investigator?"

"Moonlighting as."

" 'Moon'-lighting. Then you've come to the right place. Sit and I'll search."

Temple perched herself and her tote bag on the cocktail-height chair while the slightly pierced girl behind the counter showed her a menu and offered a glazed ginger cookie to go with her choice.

Augie Moon was back with her items in a brown paper bag in fifteen minutes. He refused to let her pay and escorted her to front of the shop.

"I should let you pay for one of my greatest challenges?" He shook his head. "The tea bag was the easiest, but it was not what had been brewed in the cup. It's a soporific. I'm assuming a clever puss like you knows what that means."

"Inducing sleep."

"Exactly. Ages-tested ingredients. Chamomile, lavender, valerian, catnip, passion flower, skullcap."

"You pronounce those last three ingredients with particular zest," Temple noted.

"Catnip for the Garfield figure on the mug, skullcap because you are investigating naughty doings, and passion flower because you are young enough to find it stimulating rather than soporific."

"Augie, are you flirting with me?"

"I'm warning you. The tea bag is nothing you wouldn't find in the most innocuous herbal-goods chain. The cup holds faint traces of less innocent concoctions."

"Such as?"

"It's not on my shelves but it is in my impetuous youth. Yes, I had one. Cannabis."

"For medicinal purposes?"

"So they say now. I detect a slight milk scum. Cannabis in a water-based tea is weak stuff. With milk and its higher fat content, not so weak. In India it's been referred to as *bhang* and used for medicinal purposes, despite its name."

"I thought I smelled marijuana smoke in the house."

"Not from the tea. What I think has been in this cup — and is very dangerous — is poppy seed."

"*Ooh,* that knocked out Dorothy and everybody but the Straw and Tin Men on the way to the Emerald City."

"Exactly. Poppy pods give us morphine

and codeine for the ill as a sedative and painkiller, but it can be overdosed on."

"So neither item is harmless, and each could be lethal?"

"As with everything, so it is with tea, Miss Temple Barr. A little of it is bliss; excess is dangerous."

Temple allowed herself to be escorted out, still unsure whether Violet was being dosed for benign or malign reasons.

The custom blends in the bag and in the mug had been passed on, or under, the best "nose" in the house. They were strong combos of blends good at inducing sleep, which is what a sick old lady might crave and need. Nothing at all lethal.

Even the poppy seed was useful in the right dose.

Yet, she thought glumly, between Violet's own flaky moments and the flakes she was surrounded by, anything evil was still possible.

CHAPTER 12
RETURN ENGAGEMENT?

Morrie Alch pounced the moment his boss returned from her errand and knocked at the hard-won private office door then peeked in.

The room wasn't much wider than Lieutenant Molina's desk, yet having a hidey-hole at homicide headquarters had been invaluable when she'd been semiseriously wounded and had to keep it hush-hush.

"Don't pussyfoot," she told the veteran detective; "come into my parlor."

"You must be feeling better."

"Shut the door."

He did. Molina had no qualms that office gossip would buzz about her and Morrie, and nowadays she wouldn't have cared anyway.

"I *am* feeling better," she said. "The stitches are finally not pulling and itching with every movement, although my torso looks like an overlaced football. Mariah's home and behaving, so I don't have to lie by omission at work anymore. Other than the troubling, unsolved business of the former stalker in my home and the planted trademark of the Barbie Doll Killer inside my teen daughter's bedroom window, all's right with the world."

Alch settled himself onto one of her wooden visitor's chairs. "Feels good to get a weight off my . . . feet."

She nodded, puzzled. Morrie had settled into his fifties like a slightly graying Scottish terrier, comfortable but with plenty of chase and growl left in him. He didn't, uh, "pussy-foot" around like this, even when invited.

"You know those folks you were having me keep a casual eye on?" he said, casually.

She nodded. Two men, one woman.

"My free time for casual eyeing is hit or miss, Lieutenant, you also know that."

"What I know is I'm lucky to have one last man I can trust on call, Morrie. Whatever you come up with is appreciated."

"So get this: I was driving up the Strip last night and spotted Our Miss Barr's red Miata leaving Planet Hollywood."

"Not her usual venue, like the Crystal Phoenix, but nothing suspicious in that. Girls just want to have fun."

"Not this one. She drove out to an old

address that used to be in the boonies and now, with the years of housing booms, is alarmingly close in, when you think of it."

"What address?"

"It was already dark. I still kept my distance. She'd already tried to dodge a tail en route. Private house on Mojave Way."

Molina sighed, audibly.

"Yeah. Guy pried himself from the Miata's passenger seat."

"Pried?"

"He was a big guy and that's a small car."

Molina shut her eyes.

"I should say he was big by being taller, not so much wide."

She nodded. "Barr go in?"

"After he apparently jimmied the front door open."

Molina's dark eyelashes flicked wide.

"Yeah." Alch knew he had reached the core of the apple and it was a Golden Delicious. He grinned. "Dude jimmied the lock. He went in. She went in. She stayed . . . um, barely twenty minutes. I'd have mistaken her for a real estate agent if I didn't know better. No farewell smooching."

"Duty, not desire," Molina pronounced. The missing Max Kinsella was now accounted for.

She had to give Temple Barr credit for

character, for not staying to give her returning ex-lover the ugly modern courtesy of a pity screw, but then, if Kinsella had masqueraded as the Phantom Mage, who vanished from the Neon Nightmare after sudden impact with a wall, he must be a shadow of the lady-killer he had been. Whatever the story behind Temple Barr's stepping out on Matt Devine with her ex, it would be juicy.

"Good girl. Bad boy," she told Alch. "Interesting from a gossip-mag point of view, but what about our other . . . serious persons of interest?"

"Good boys both. In the routine groove, work and home, no carousing, no bad habits. Mind you, I'm not on either one enough to swear they're not busy plotting to knock off the Wynn Casino tomorrow."

"Okay." Molina produced a rare smile for their work environment. "Your personnel file is bloated with recent commendations, detective. Better get back to cracking your caseload so that doesn't look suspicious."

Alch rose, wincing as his knees creaked. "I don't suppose you want to know about the black stray cat I spotted in the Mojave Way house vicinity?"

"No, Morrie, no more cat tales around here, if you can contain yourself."

"And no more shadowing these persons of interest?"

"No. Don't bother your handsome head about them anymore."

"But . . . this new development is a killer."

"Yet . . . not illegal. You might still keep that . . . casual eye on Miss Barr. I worry about that girl as if she was a daughter."

Alch blinked. "Since when?"

"Oh, Morrie, you're so behind the times. Since it was we three girls against a berserk but well-hidden killer at the celebrity dance contest — me, Mariah, and Miss Barr's ever-so-trendy Zoe Chloe Ozone persona. If your name was Charlie, you could call us your angels."

"Yeah, right. Not a halo in that bunch." Alch went to crack the door open but turned. "You need anything else, let me know."

"Always."

Molina shut down her wide smile the minute the crack in the door went to six inches. The Iron Maiden of the Las Vegas Metropolitan Police Force had a reputation to keep up. And places to go and people to see.

Person. Singular.

One formerly missing person.

Apparently fate had dropped a shiny new pawn on her board.

CHAPTER 13
SHE SPAT, HE SPAT

"This site is dead," Miss Midnight Louise declares when I come to inspect her work. "All the juice has been squeezed out of it. We should be back on Aloe Vera Drive where all the cat action is."

"I am thinking that it is always good to keep an eye on Mister Max. Were you not hot to do that from the moment the Phantom Mage hit the wall at the Neon Nightmare? I am giving you your dream assignment."

"That is what will be going on here tonight. Mister Max's dreams. Now that I know he is all right — or at least alive and back where he belongs — I can concentrate on Miss Temple's first case along with you."

Phtchooey, I say.

"Dudes always give dames the 'scat' work."

"What is 'scat' work?" I ask, much amazed by the term.

"Where we are forced to hang around and twiddle our dewclaws and are finally shooed away by irritable humans yelling 'Scat!' "

"I trust you to keep a very low profile, Louise, and the reputation of Midnight Investigations, Inc., discreet."

"Besides," she says with a sly sideways look, "you would think the senior citizen of the firm would want the snooze detail."

Actually, I have been losing some sleep lately over Miss Temple's suddenly overpopulated private life.

To be honest, I do not have much expectation of anything worth a squib in the *Las Vegas Review-Journal* happening here, but I am keeping my personal private eye on Miss Violet's house with all those residents of the female feline sort and do not want a chaperone on my tail.

So I leave Miss Midnight Louise there, on discontented duty, feeling a bit smug in the knowledge that the lovely ladies on Aloe Vera Drive will certainly not be growling "Scat!" at their devoted protector.

What could happen here in one night?
Really.

CHAPTER 14
SHE SAID, HE SAID

The last time Molina had stood outside this address in the dark of night, she'd been wearing camouflage black, slinking around to the back of the premises to break in.

The last time she'd been *inside* the place, an unidentified intruder had paid a simultaneous visit, resulting in an eighty-six-stitch wannabe scar across her left rib cage and hip.

Now she stood at the front door, under the subtle entry light, ringing the doorbell.

Max pressed his eye against the peephole, cursing the long Black Irish lashes obscuring his vision, trying to ID the shadowy figure outside, a suited six feet with no other identifying features he could make out in the dim light.

Door-to-door salesmen hardly showed up at 9:00 P.M.

Was he an international counterspy or a

180

mouse? Might as well find out what lamb or lion had called at a house of mourning.

He opened the door, his hand on the SIG Sauer P226 butt now nestled in the small of his back.

It didn't help that he needed to lean against the wall after all the past four hectic days and nights had done to his recently broken legs.

"Mister Kinsella," she told the lurking figure in the dark hallway, rather than asked, when the door opened, "I'm here on un-official business."

"I'm here on official home ground," he answered.

"I know. I've checked the ownership of this property. Orson Welles, once upon a time. My, my. Garry Randolph is the resi-dent of record, but the paperwork had always listed you, Max Kinsella, as co-owner. In his absence, I'll assume you're the man of the house."

"I won't buy anything."

"I'm not selling anything."

"You still want to come in?"

"Oh, yes indeed I do, Mister Kinsella."

"A woman?" If so, she was tall and her vocal range was low. She sounded authorita-tive and . . . she didn't carry a purse. What did she carry? How did she know Garry was "absent"?

"I need some ID," he said.

"Turn on a light."

He liked the dark at his back, so he simply turned up the rheostat on the outside entry light as she pulled her blazer aside in a universally familiar gesture. Brass badge and gunmetal black at her hip played well in the improvised spotlight. A command performance, you might say.

"And you are . . . ?" he said, waiting for verbal ID.

She eyed him oddly. "Lieutenant Molina, Metropolitan Police."

"Come in." He leaned into the front door to shut it after her. The Temple harasser, in person.

"Head on in," he said. "The living room's on the right."

"I know."

What the hell? Oh, right. She'd broken in after he'd disappeared. Miss Temple was an informant worth her weight in eighteen-karat gold. And that cost the world these days.

Max managed to touch the walls from stride to stride and so make his way to the living-room arch without his feet making the betraying dragging sound of a limp. He trusted no one interested in crashing

Garry's house party, but Rafi Nadir had certainly been prepped and employed by Gandolph. Was there any way this was another prearranged Vegas contact? No. This is the lady who wanted to hang him for murder.

He leaned inside the living room to turn on the first table lamp within his long reach, but her forearm cut across his gesture to stop it.

"Just getting some light," he said.

"Are the light-proof shutters drawn?"

"Tight as a . . . well, it's not a fit comparison to make in front of a lady."

"I'm not a lady, and like you'd worry about that."

She walked into the center of the room as he turned on the overhead central fixture, all Craftsman bronze and creamy milk glass. She wheeled to confront him.

Now she believed in ghosts . . . not the vague, airy-fairy, sheet-draped ones, but the ones fresh from the graveyard after having clawed their way to some gaunt semblance of their former selves.

"You look like hell," she repeated.

"So you've . . . seen me before looking a lot better?"

Molina was stumped. First he wanted her

name, then he wanted an opinion on his previous condition? Did he think she was a damn doctor? Oh. Did he think?

In the overhead light, she spotted a healing slash peeking out like a murder weapon in a game of Clue from under the lock of black hair that brushed his forehead.

Vastly . . . shrunken physique. Head wound . . . She was a detective, wasn't she? Put two and two together.

"You've obviously been through hell," she said. "You've seen the shield and the piece. I get a drink? Because you could sure use one yourself."

"Do I know you?"

Now his disorientation was out of the closet. He'd worked for her briefly before, tracking Rafi. Why confuse the man? Or waste the gift of amnesia? She thought for a long moment.

"No, Mister Kinsella. You don't."

He couldn't argue with her instincts. Interesting that when he had gestured through the dining room she had gone straight on through and into the kitchen.

He caught up with her, laboriously, to find her staring at the countertop. All he saw there was an empty blender and a full knife block.

"Uh," he said, "I know where the wine cellar is, but . . ."

"No bar in the dining room," she'd observed. "Hard liquor and glasses are kept up here," she said, pointing.

"A lot of cabinets to page through."

They started a methodical search from one end of the kitchen to the other, opening the birch doors, Max leaning on them subtly. They ultimately opened a pair into each other's knuckles, saying "Scotch" and "Whisky" simultaneously.

"Why are you here?" he asked.

"I'm the law. You are a suspicious character back in town. And I want to hire you."

Max hadn't heard such a tasty come-on since some long-forgotten noir film.

She was glad he had poured the Johnnie Walker Black neat, the European way. Jerking open all those cupboards had irritated her midsection's taut, healing incision. Her right hand even quivered a little now. Ice would have chattered and given away her lingering vulnerability.

Maybe the nerves weren't just from her big-time deception. If everything Temple Barr had said about this guy's counterterrorism career was true, he was formidable — despite the shocking physical deterioration and the healing evidence of a nasty head wound. And she'd already tangled with him a time or two he'd so conveniently — for her — forgotten. *Maybe.* At least he was treating her like a stranger.

Clearly now, Kinsella was leaner and probably meaner, and had a pile of personal vulnerabilities. The perfect patsy.

They sat in the living room, sipping. It would not be unfair to say a contented air commanded the room.

"Why do I look like hell?" he asked after a while.

"You died."

He only bothered to raise his eyebrows, not his heavy Baccarat crystal glass.

"Apparently, you died," she added. "I'm willing to concede some semblance of life."

"What did I look like before?"

"More weight, more . . . arrogance, less like your last best friend had passed on."

"He did."

"Randolph?"

Max nodded, drank.

"Too bad. Where?"

"In a forgotten spot in Ireland."

"Northern Ireland, you mean?"

He shrugged.

"Nothing has come through on Interpol."

"It wouldn't."

"Why?"

"Doesn't reflect well on either ex."

" 'Either ex?' "

"The ex-IRA and the ex-anti-IRA. It never ends even when it ends."

"But you're home on sabbatical now."

"You could put it that way. What do you want done? I'm not an assassin. I'm not a snitch. I'm not a doctor, lawyer, or gentleman thief."

"What a disappointment. How do you know all that if you don't remember?"

"You don't forget soul." He looked into the empty hole of his glass. "Johnnie's run out on me."

"Sure has." She recognized that dark, lost mood. Recent events seemed to confirm his secret "good guy" counterterrorism history and had give her many fewer bones to pick at all with Max Kinsella. Even so, a memoryless Kinsella was still better. That put her in the driver's seat.

"I'll get the bottle," she said.

At least neither of them needed any ice.

CHAPTER 15
THE TROJAN MEN

At last!

Max was tucked away safely at his house, and Temple finally had time to stay home of a workday morning to catch up with her public-relations business on the computer. And . . . she could look forward to picking up Matt at the airport at the end of it. Work and pleasure in one bracketing package with a few unexpected butterflies of anxiety fluttering in her blue sky.

By 10:00 A.M. she had fielded six phone calls and twelve texts between updating the Crystal Phoenix's Facebook page, Twittering for a dozen clients, and checking that all Google ads were up and working correctly.

"Now what?" Temple demanded of the Fates when her doorbell rang at 10:10.

It couldn't be a solicitor. They never got past the lobby.

Savannah Ashleigh knew Temple was on the violet case when she had the time.

Matt had his own key now.

Max? He'd been unnervingly distant and quiet for almost two days. Temple might almost think she'd hallucinated his return. He had *her* cell-phone number, not vice versa. Temple gave a small snort of annoyance. Having Max back in town and incommunicado was like returning to junior high, waiting for the boy to call . . . only now he'd text. Or the girl would.

Temple jerked open the door, having worked herself up into being the injured party, and demanded, "About time!"

"I agree," her aunt Kit said, walking in. "You saw Aldo and I were back two days ago, yet I get nothing, not even an old-fashioned phone call wanting to know *all about* the honeymoon."

"I'm not one to pry," Temple said, shutting the door.

Her aunt snorted this time, a theatrical yet feminine snort of disbelief. "*Hah!* 'Pry' would be your middle name if my first name wasn't."

"I would love to have your nickname, 'Kit,' as a middle name," Temple said, embracing her aunt. "Who on earth named you Ursula? And why?"

"Apparently there's always been an Aunt Ursula in the Carlson family, but I never

189

met the woman ahead of me in the ugly-name sweepstakes. She died young," Kit reported in a dire tone, perching on the living-room sofa. "And unmarried. Unlike me, who is old and newly married."

"You don't look a day over forty," Temple said.

In fact, petite women like Temple and her aunt Kit Fontana, née Carlson, and Sally Field did seem ageless. Temple was very glad of that fact. Right now, she'd felt she'd aged twenty years in one transatlantic phone call.

Kit's head was poking into a chic Parisian bag she'd brought with her, her hair a soft silver-and-copper Brillo pad of loose chin-length curls. She still wore the large-framed, dated, fashion-editor glasses that made her look chic anyway. She hefted a wine bottle.

"I brought you a ton of Italian goodies, but this is a bottle from the vintage Aldo and I drank during our honeymoon at Lake Como. Scenery, water, flowers, swans, wine, walks, talks, nights of not talking. Since you're about to become a married lady as well, I thought we could share a good mother-daughter chat over this *vino*."

Temple took the gift to the kitchen to open it, calling, "You're not my mother" from around the partition.

"My sister Karen would never drink wine and talk at the same time. Very wise, but not much fun."

"So." As Temple came back with two glasses of red, Kit glanced around. "Looks the same. No Midnight Louie peering over my shoulder, though. No Matt doing likewise with you?"

"He's in Chicago," Temple said, sitting.

"Still?"

"Some things came up."

"Family? You said there were 'issues.' Maybe the Chicago 'Family' swarmed him and whisked him away, like the Fontana brothers here. Aldo is now off on some apparent 'Unbachelor party' with Fontana, Inc. That's why I'm here crying on your wine-soaked shoulder, a deserted bride already."

"You look in the pink for a deserted bride," Temple said. And then she sighed.

"What?" Kit asked, sitting up straighter, as alert as a fox terrier scenting fox. "You're not telling me something. I've felt it since you opened the door."

"Well, this time and place is not of my choosing. . . ."

"Don't tell me you and Matt —"

"Are fine. He's on the brink of some big-time career opportunities, that's all."

"Involving what?"

"The Big O."

"Are we back on my honeymoon topic again?"

"Decidedly not, Aunt. I was referring to Oprah. She's 'retired' from network TV. Even bigger news, if you must know. I've heard from Max."

"Max? What excuse did he have for disappearing this time? His nine lost brothers whisked him away?"

"Only one unrelated man," Temple said. "A gutsy old guy who's now dead."

Kit stared at Temple for what felt like a full minute. "Oh. I entered stage right in a romantic comedy and here I find myself center stage in an unfolding tragedy of some sort. Drink up and tell Auntie all, my dear, because who else knows the cast of characters, and you, so well?"

"Oh, Kit, it's a bloody mess." Temple hadn't wanted to dwell on this today, but Aunt Kit was like her big sister. She kicked off her heels and folded her feet under her on the sofa. "Max is a bloody mess."

Kit's eyes widened behind her magnifying lenses.

Temple related the sequence of his accident, his being spirited away by Garry Randolph, the coma, memory loss, and escape, Switzerland, Ireland, his tangles with the ex-IRA and alternative IRA, Kitty the Cutter's possible death and resurrection, Gandolph's resurrection and death. Max's disappearance and return.

"This is a three-play cycle, at least," said Kit, ex-actress-turned-novelist, after digesting "all." "I should have brought two wine bottles. Max is really and truly amnesiac? It's not just a sympathy ploy? No, drop that rebuking look. He *is* a master of deception."

"Whatever Max is, how am I going to convince Matt I couldn't just leave the man hanging out there among his mortal enemies, his mind blasted and his body in shock?"

"Max really does look and act that bad?"

"It's not 'acting.' He's been through hell physically, and the death of his mentor is devastating. He was at the wheel, Kit. He was driving. The bullet that killed Garry Randolph was meant for Max. It missed him by only a fluke . . . which was the seat belt Max insisted Garry wear. That's what killed him. Max had no time to take safety measures himself and was jolted free of the oncoming bullet."

"Dramatic irony fit for the Greeks," Kit mused. "Men will get all Oedipus Rex-y about battle guilt as well as that mother thing. Obviously, Max needed a sensible woman to talk him out of his self-destructive post-traumatic stress. And he knew just where to go. Don't worry. Matt, ex-priest or media performer, is a professional counselor. He'll have to understand the situation."

"He'll understand it," Temple said, "he just won't like it. He also understands the appeal of a lost, wounded puppy."

"You can't possibly be describing Max!"

"Don't laugh, Kit. He's weak, he's gaunt, maimed in body and soul. And he's still being hunted. We all may be if Kathleen O'Connor isn't dead. Oh, not you, Kit. I'm sure she doesn't know about you." Temple frowned. "Probably."

"Well, if that bitch does know and messes with me, she'll have Fontana, Inc., on her tail. I am *Family* now."

"Kit! I've never seen you so fierce."

"This is a fierce situation. There's only one way you can soften the blow for Matt."

"Keep this to myself?"

"Arrange a meeting between him and Max as soon as he comes back into town."

"Are you crazy?"

"The only way to meet impossible situations is head-on. I'll mediate, if you like."

"No," Temple said, taking a thoughtful sip

of bloodred wine.

"That's my job. Again."

CHAPTER 16
SOCIAL CATWORKING

Your average hard-boiled private eye of yore would not deign to eavesdrop on a couple dishing dames, even if they are dishy, but that is what makes me the more modern and effective sleuth.

I have already overheard enough phone calls around this joint to know that this is a second Very Bad Day for Miss Temple Barr and her Case of the Roving Romeos.

Much later this afternoon, she must again drive to nearby McCarran Airport, this time to pick up Mr. Matt Devine. I hope his long week in Chicago has left him in better physical and mental condition than Mr. Max Kinsella's longer recent jaunt.

I rather doubt it. Being the fond object of a large extended Polish family and high-powered TV executives hunting a hot property for a week is probably about as bad as dodging political assassins.

Meanwhile, I am aware she is also planning

a solo visit to Miss Violet Weiner's residence first.

Thank God! I am not eager to encounter Miss Savannah Ashleigh and her latest portable purse pet, Captain Jack, especially after I read up on the ferret kind over Miss Temple's shoulder. I was sitting on her desk, pretending to be slitty-eyed asleep, but, of course, my predator eyes were speed-reading everything about the breed.

It is commonly known that domestic cats were worshipped by ancient Egyptians, and we have been considered wise in all cultures and time periods. Few know that the cat god, Bast, gifted us with the ability to read some two thousand years b.c. Great Bast knew we would never again be so cherished by an entire civilization and might even be persecuted at times, as we were. Great Bast knew that hieroglyphics were not the future of human communication, although I doubt that Great Bast anticipated e-books.

I shudder to think how much more difficult our daily survival would be without some of our seeming "extrasensory" perception, although, alas, most of my peers have long ago lost my "secret weapon."

Also, being Miss Temple works at home alone, often with me beside her, she has taken to commenting on her online researches aloud to me in a conversational tone.

"Look at this, Louie. Huh. I thought they were a weasely kind. . . ."

My sentiments exactly! Vermin.

"Ferrets are related to polecats. They have scent glands and do all that catlike 'marking.' But . . . wait! They do the 'weasel war dance' while making soft clucking sounds, called 'dooking.' "

Oh, my scented grandmother!

"Imagine what one can do in the deepest recesses of Savannah Ashleigh's purse. I think she's gotten accustomed to her aunt's cathouse odors and isn't noticing that Captain Jack has a few bad habits.

"They can live in feral colonies," she adds, nodding my way, as if saying, *See, just like you cats.* "Although I doubt that polecats are your real relatives."

I should hope not!

"You know, they remind me of mongooses, which would be handy to have along in one's purse if you encountered any rattlesnakes. Not that I plan on doing that. I was lucky I did not meet any in that wilderness behind Violet's house."

That is what research does to Miss Temple, sends her off into the wild blue yonder of speculation. I can understand she would like her mind taken off Mr. Matt's imminent arrival and greeting him with the revelation that her "ex" is no longer conveniently absent, but very inconveniently returned.

"Well," Miss Temple says, shutting down the World Wide Web, "you can keep snoozing. I am going out and I do not need any extra passengers."

Actually, I have my own assignation this evening, so I need to stay home and get my beauty sleep. Or so I let her think.

Chapter 17
Up for Grabs

As she headed for Aloe Vera Drive that afternoon, for all the upheaval in her private life, Temple found herself worrying about the old woman in that half-hidden house surrounded by suspicion and rescued cats.

Confined to the island of her hospital bed and mind, Violet was helpless except for the weapon of her unsigned will. The moment she selected an executor-heir . . . who knows what would happen to her?

Temple's mind replayed her impressions of the sad, scary scene and the cats and people around Violet as she drove. And she couldn't forget the ghost who haunted the whole kit and caboodle, Alexandra, the tragically dead daughter who died far away and forever estranged from her mother, thanks to the actions of a freak random killer.

Alexandra was not like the victims of the Barbie Doll Killer. A killer with such a specific trademark was actually the more common kind. Drugstore tamperers were rarer, even more random, and, when Temple did a computer search, the hardest to find. The most notorious case involved potassium cyanide–laced capsules in an OTC painkiller bottle. When family members came for one of the victims' funeral, some stayed in the family house . . . and two died from taking the same contaminated headache remedy before anyone put the cause into focus. Tragically tripling the death toll for this one family alone.

Temple might find Savannah over the top, but her aunt's situation was a human tragedy waiting to happen. Temple realized her face had assumed a grim set, despite the ever-sunny Vegas skies and the convertible ride's breezy vim and vigor.

As she pulled to the curb in front of Violet's place, the Miata's small red snout was pushing at the solid white-fortress rear of a parked Chrysler 300. The muscular yet cushy model was a favorite of middle managers, or . . . *hmm.*

This time she noticed the overgrown driveway around the house's side, snarled with stubby mesquite trees and the rears of a tattooed Volkswagen van, which was probably Jayden's, and a dusty red Ford Focus, which made her think of Rowdy Smith. The name made her smile. He was such a home-spun guy. She could see why a pampered, neurotic flower like Alexandra had been drawn to him despite her mother's flab-bergasted objections. What a way to rebel against parental authority, before death took over the job.

Temple put up the Miata's top and ap-proached the house, tote bag and shoulders making a solid front of it.

Before she could knock, the ponderous door swung open.

A heavyset woman filled the open frame.

Her hair was dyed ultraviolet red, white scalp showing through. She wore eighties shoulder pads and peep-toe pumps. She was shaped like an inverted pyramid or an opera singer or ocean liner of the old school, all imposing shoulders and bust and slim hips on thin stilt-like legs.

"I'm Freddie LaCosta. Who are you?" she asked, nay demanded.

"Temple Barr." Temple bristled like a schnauzer. "Violet's niece asked me to look after what things I could for her."

"You're not going to be in the will."

"I don't *want* to *be* in the will. I want to see Violet and the cats, and that they're all right, and that I will do."

202

"Where do you live?"

What nerve! "In Las Vegas."

The woman's eyes narrowed. "House?"

"Ah, condo."

"Then come in, my dear." The door swept wide and the wide woman stepped aside.

Temple reentered the house of litter dust and shadows, puzzled even more.

Temple headed straight for Violet's bed, unaccountably worried.

"Hello, my little Legend of Ireland, Deirdre of Ulster, the redheaded girl."

Violet's voice was a soft rasp, and her pupils were as large as a cat's expanded iris. "I so hoped you'd come again. My Whisper is still gone, and the bewitching Rebecca, the tuxedo cat, too. Can you find them?"

Given where Max had just come from and what he'd had to say of Kathleen O'Connor using the name *Rebecca,* Temple felt a chill from her nape to her tailbone.

"Rebecca the tuxedo witch?" Temple said, thinking of Kitty the Cutter using the name.

"Oh, so enchanting. Black-and-white. My little baby dolls are dwindling. Savannah said you could help."

"I want to. I will." Temple looked up to see that Jayden and Rowdy had gathered around Violet's bed. Neither man could bear to leave the old woman alone with a visitor.

"You're just dreaming about cats being gone, again, dear lady," Jayden said. "Here's some sweet chili and chamomile tea." Jayden put the straw to Violet's mouth, effectively shutting her up.

He may not want her talking to anyone, but he couldn't stay on the premises all the time. Rowdy backed out of Violet's eyesight.

"She really doesn't care to see me," he whispered to Temple. "That phony bastard turns her against everyone, but she had a head start with me anyway. I've done the cat-litter straining and buried the evidence."

"You do it daily?"

"Once a day, like Pedro. Violet kinda cottons to you, that's why Jayden moves in so fast. I guess you remind her of something good."

"Alexandra?" Temple asked the former boyfriend.

"Aw, naw. You're a different type, nothing personal. Alexandra was, ah, more statuesque? 'Built' would be the word. And blond hair like on a Christmas angel. Yeah. I didn't know what a looker like that saw in me too." He glanced at the bed. " 'Cept I didn't have 'expectations,' like her old lady. Funny. They were awfully alike, but they didn't know it.

204

Perfectionists, you could say."

"Thanks, Sylvan," Freddie stepped in to say, muscling Temple away from Violet's bed and toward the entry hall where they wouldn't be overheard. "Now, you seem to be someone Violet can trust. No relation. Never knew her before . . . what — ?"

"Yesterday," Temple said.

"And you're only here because . . ."

"My, uh, friend was worried about her aunt."

Temple knew she couldn't say, "I'm Temple Barr, PR" and expect to be taken seriously. But when Temple thought about it, she'd been schooled in criminal surveillance by a master counterterrorist and in shrinkology by a vocational expert. Plus, she was a pretty shrewd judge of people herself. Freddie, she was sure, was a smooth operator.

"Well, your friend *should* be worried about Violet," Freddie said, bending to whisper in Temple's ear. "This house is pretty old and needs updating, but the land could be cleared and worth something nowadays."

"What about it backing onto the flood-control area where Pedro died?"

"I'm licensed to sell real estate, among other things. You never mention anything dying anywhere near a property, except maybe coyotes, and you're okay. I hate to say it, but ole Violet is a sitting duck, and it's hard to figure who's gathering round for her own good and who's hoping to profit big-time."

"You have a seriously pessimistic view of human nature," Temple said.

"And I shouldn't have?"

"What do you think Violet is worth with your name on the will?"

Freddie shrugged. "I can't talk her into any sense. I told her long ago to leave it all to an animal shelter, but there are so many she can't make up her mind now that she's ill and confused. That leaves everything she is and has to who wants it worst."

"How horrible."

"You got your will made, Miss Just-Wants-To-Help?"

"Ah, no." Temple was going to say she was about to turn only thirty-one, but Violet had probably been saying that for forty years. Suddenly, one day you realize you're not immortal and that you're unprepared for defending what you most care about.

"Do you like cats?" she asked the repellent but logical Freddie.

The woman shook her ridiculously dyed head. "Not a bit. Whatcha gonna do about it?"

Temple turned to look at Jayden, who was singsonging Violet into a trance, and Rowdy, who'd retreated to the kitchen arch to sling a huge bag of cat kibble into bowls he'd fill only as long as Violet lived and his duty to dead Alexandra was over.

Temple had been here just twice, but even she noticed that the cat population was reduced from her first visit.

"My baby is missing," came the weak keening from the bed.

Was Violet cognizant enough to know the awful truth, or was she speaking about her dead daughter?

Temple was just investigator enough to know she was dealing with an impossible situation. She was a stranger who couldn't urge Violet to end this impasse and name an heir, and meanwhile people who could be up to God knew what for God knew what reasons were freely coming and going to and from her house in the name of tending the sick.

"What about Violet's day helper?" Temple asked the savvy Freddie.

"Yolanda comes in early and does her best to keep the living areas litter-dust and cat-hair free, as she has for years."

"What kind of relationship did she have with Pedro?"

Freddie's already soaring red-penciled eyebrows almost hit her hairline. "Yolanda has a husband and three adult children. No hotsy-totsy potential there."

"Is she in the will?"

"Violet has left five or so thousand here and there, not to her relatives, I know that."

"What about you?"

"Oh," Freddie said, shaking her extremely coifed head, "we used to be great friends, but we had a falling out. That's the way it was with Violet. Like Alexandra, you find it's got to be her way or the freeway. She was just too demanding that Alex stay her mother's little girl. Even her niece Sue Anna came up a caricature of a girl-woman, caught up in looking like a supermodel, just like these kids today are all little Britneys and Lindsays, no matter how whacked those child stars grow up. That's why Violet's taken to you. You're just a little doll."

"I resent that," Temple said. "Height I don't have, and female I am, but I'm nobody's 'little doll.' "

"I'm just saying that Violet wanted to confine Alexandra in a box, always young and beautiful and shallow as ditch water, although she was smarter than anybody thought."

"You don't approve of a thing in Violet's

life, down to these cats."

"No, I don't."

"Yet you're here now."

She glanced to the bed, with Jayden hanging over it. "Violet always had a flaky streak. Mediums and magnets and New Age chicanery. It's sad to see her weaknesses instead of her strengths ruling her last days. Like this infestation of cats. The home health nurses who stop in to monitor vital signs and change the bedpans have a fit about the unsanitary conditions, but it's a free country, as long as you can remain sane enough to declare your wishes, and Violet won't leave her house until she's carried out of it."

"You know something about the will," she told Freddie. "Does she leave the bulk of her estate to whomever cares for her cats?"

"Not a few years ago when we were still buddies."

"She could have added that provision in a codicil more recently."

"And some scam artist could know more about that than I would," Freddie said, throwing Jayden a poison-pen look with a jerk of her head.

"Whoever inherits, I hope to get the job of selling the house," she went on. "It will be quite a challenge clearing out all the clutter, and the *first* thing to go. I'm betting that, despite Violet's violent wishes otherwise, whoever inherits, the second things to go will be the cats."

Temple stared into Freddie LaCosta's sun-damaged features and understood that she too was one of Violet's worst enemies.

These days, who wasn't?

CHAPTER 18
UNLIKELY BEDFELLOWS

I am ambling through the Circle Ritz parking lot now that Miss Temple and her Miata are off on errands of an investigative nature on the hot and seamy side of town.

I am heading for my favorite oleander bush, shade in Las Vegas being a rare and beautiful thing. I am expecting peace and quiet now that my recently discovered maternal parent, Ma Barker, and her feral clowder have pulled up stakes (rather like vampire slayers) and relocated to the nearby police substation, where they can get all the fast food the folks in desert beige can share with the homeless of one stripe or another.

I have found a vermin-free patch of cool, sandy dirt and have made the proscribed three full ritual circles in tribute to Bast before I lie down. My rear member has coiled around my limbs and body in the approved manner. My eyes have shut and my ears flick only once, at the rude buzz-by of a fruit fly.

211

Minuscule nobody. Away. I am not a fuzzy peach turning ripe.

So I am producing a lazy buzzing-bee sound to fend off other impudent insects and also to practice the meditative mantra of my kind when I become aware of more lurking shade than I need or want.

Master of the "eyes wide shut" discipline, I allow myself to see without being seen and discern a blurry black blot on my escutcheon, the ever-iffy offspring on my family tree, Miss Midnight Louise.

"I thought you were on watch duty at the house on Mojave," I say.

"Sorry to disturb your snores," she replies.

"I was not snoring; I was thinking. How and why did you leave your assigned post?"

"I hitched a ride with the mailman then switched to the nearest UPS truck until it crossed the Strip, and then it was just a long walk here. And what have you done today so far?"

"I saw off Miss Temple on her new investigative visit to Miss Violet Weiner's premises. We will have to look further into crimes against cat on that location tonight."

"So you are taking me off Mister Max duty?"

"Spotting Mister Rafi Nadir visiting the night before last was probably all the hot news you will get there."

"Yet you wanted me there for a second long night of observation."

"It never hurts to be overvigilant."

"I guess not," Louise says, deciding to bite a wayward toenail.

"Are you saying you saw something of interest last night? Miss Temple was safe at home in our bed here at the Circle Ritz, I can assure you."

"And I can say the same of Mister Max. He never left the house."

"What a relief. I must say these humans can be nocturnal wanderers, and we do not want any unsanctioned canoodling before the current favorite, Mister Matt, comes back and it really gets interesting."

"News flash, O Snoring Sage of the Underbrush. It already has gotten even more interesting. Who do you think visited Mister Max, bold as you please, now that he is resident in the Mojave Way house?"

"Let me think. Mister Rafi Nadir already shocked the footpads off of us by turning up there. It cannot be my Miss Temple. I can account for both the quality and celibacy of her sleep last night. *Hmm.* Even if Mister Matt happened to slip back into town early, he would not know the house was now occupied again."

I cannot help manicuring a nail of my own,

the big scimitar of dewclaw that would be a thumb if my kind but had them. In fact, I am so stumped I gnaw off a shedding sheath.

"Do not bite yourself to the quick, Pop, trying to figure out the jaw-dropping facts."

"I give up, Louise. Mister Max's return was announced only to my little doll. Now it seems half of Vegas is showing up on his doorstep after the sun goes down. This one must be a dame. We black-haired guys are irresistible."

After I spit out my nail sheath, to Louise's distasteful silent snarl at my manners, the light dawns and does a surprised spin *en pointe* in my brain.

"I know!" I hiss triumphantly. "It is that shiny European blonde who showed up in Vegas before Mister Max returned. She was a former schoolmate of Crystal Phoenix manager Miss Van von Rhine in Switzerland. You told me about her visiting out of the blue, and we both saw her during the recent Chunnel of Crime case. She is too hot looking to be up to any good. Miss . . ." — I search my slightly lulled data bank — Revienne Schneider."

"I must say you do remember the person in question, and I do consider her a questionable lady."

Louise settles herself down on her haunches, her folded forelegs assuming the "mandarin position" that hides her long nails and makes her look contemplative.

"But — wrong, Daddy-o!" she spits out with younger-generation sass. "Mister Max's visitor last night was Miss Lieutenant C. R. Molina."

I could swear she was just saying that to shock me — you know the younger generation — but I can tell by the slits of her pupils that she is shiv-serious.

"So did the lieutenant take him out of there in ankle chains?"

"No. She left. But not in twenty minutes, like your Miss Temple and then Mister Rafi Nadir the first night. What is going on at the house on Mojave Way? Some sort of anti-Synth secret conspiracy? What I was able to hear through the windows was conversational, not confrontational *or* cozy."

"*Hmm.* That house does seem to be a place of pilgrimage since Mister Max came back to town. We definitely need to keep an eye on our sometime-compadres as well as all of Miss Violet's feline favorites.

"If you want to put your house pets into a perilous position, make sure their care is the condition of a human inheritance. That really makes the poor things objects of jealousy, abduction, and homicide."

CHAPTER 19
SHOCK AND AWESOME

Temple waited by the baggage-claim area as people surrounded the carousel, jumping up every now and then to compensate for her lack of height. The light started blinking, and baggage came banging over the end of the conveyor belt onto hard metal, but no blond head she recognized appeared on her high jumps.

The first tick of alarm reverberated deep in her stomach. *The Amanda Show* flew Matt first class for his appearances. No sense in having travel-frazzled guests. He was usually first off.

Temple started circling the people clustered thick as vultures around the rotating carousal, peering through akimbo elbows, around big indifferent shoulders, avoiding successful bag grabbers who turned so fast to leave they could mug her with their hard-shelled Samsonites.

Life was a cabaret when you were short.

Over what appeared to be a tattooed linebacker, who had no business being in Las Vegas since it was one of the largest U.S. cities without any Major League teams, a still-unfamiliar head of highlighted blond appeared and circled her way.

Temple backed out of the crowd and started waving her left hand, her engagement ring attracting sudden interest ranging from awe to avarice.

Before anyone with criminal intent could accost her, Matt pushed the linebacker and his matching-size bag out of the way to capture her hand in his and bring it down in his custody.

"You're here," Temple said. "I was beginning to worry."

"You should worry about letting your ring cause a feeding frenzy."

Matt grabbed her in a hard "I'm back" embrace. Nothing too Public Display of Affection.

"I missed you." He shook his head. "The insanity. The show. My family. I've had it with solo schlepping from Vegas to Chicago. You're coming along as my personal assistant until we get married."

"And then?"

"I'll leave you at home so I can flirt with fame." He grinned.

"*Hmph.* You think. What are we waiting for? And what kept you?"

"Small roll-on and a suiter. I was too beat to bring anything on board. And . . . the crew wanted me to sign autographs before I deplaned."

"That happen before?"

"No. It's just as Ambrosia and the radio station management dreamed would happen. That silly *Dancing with the Celebs* reality-TV show made me instantly recognizable. A new crown of thorns for the local media freak show."

"Speaking of crowns of thorns," Temple said, leaning back to eye him, "looks like *The Amanda Show* wants to build on your dance-show redo. Blonder hair, tanner skin, whiter teeth."

"Yeah, I look like a *Baywatch* rerun escapee. Don't you pick up where my family left off."

"Next they'll want to give you aquamarine contact lenses. That I put my foot down on. Your brown eyes do not make me blue."

"It's all very head spinning," he said, interrupting his report to grab the last two lone pieces of luggage. "This'll put your Miata to the test."

"Nope. I brought your Crossfire. Still not the trunk-space king, but roomier."

"What would I do without you?"

"Don't even think about it." Temple grabbed the rolling bag, but Matt resisted.

She was an equal-opportunity helper, but men needed to keep building their upper-body strength, she supposed.

"It seems like I've been gone an age," he said as they trotted and escalated through the vast airport. "How am I going to update you on so much so fast, when all I want to do is —"

"Ditto. My problem exactly. Which is why I've booked dinner at the Crystal Phoenix. Almost a home away from home, but a good place for us to come back to earth and catch up."

"You're brilliant, Temple. I'm starving for some one-on-one time on a scale that lives up to the way I've been wined and dined almost blind in Chicago. When I wasn't being berated by family."

"Poor, suffering media hottie. You need a private PR person to make it all better," Temple said, wincing even as the words came out of her mouth.

What Matt needed was a couple glasses of wine before she told him of her . . . their . . . new reclamation-and-redemption project. The PR whiz did reclamation every day in her job. The ex-priest hopefully had a few more freelance redemptions left in him.

One thing she did know. She and Matt, and now Max again, knew separate pieces of a years-long puzzle that could redeem — or destroy — every one of them and what they most held dear.

"You look wonderful," Matt said, when they were seated at the isolated table they'd requested in the Crystal Carousel rooftop restaurant. "Purely objective opinion."

"Thanks." She had tossed the tissue-thin circle coat she'd worn to the airport over the back of her chair. "I spent two hours before I decided on this fifties ballerina dress."

"What do they call that color? It matches your eyes perfectly."

"You're going to have to learn all this arcane stuff to live with me and my wardrobe. Changeable taffeta. Goes from lilac to blue."

"Yeah, they do. Your eyes. And that neckline?"

Temple shrugged. "Off the shoulder."

"Your bare shoulders are sexier than Angelina Jolie's . . . you know."

"The fifties was a more gracious, flirtatious, feminine era. And, frankly, I can compete on shoulders and waistlines. On bustlines, not so much."

"So why are you regaling me with the competitive you and keeping me at table's length?"

"I've been making the rounds of the vintage-clothing shops while you were gone and wanted to show off. And . . . we have a lot to talk about."

"Yes, I know," he began, contritely.

That's where she needed to have him before it was her turn to be contrite . . . big-time. He of all people would understand guilt.

"This Chicago media stuff is sudden, I know," he said. "It was all show-and-tell. Nothing will get serious until my agent gets in on it. I was in phone contact with Tony Valentine all along. He told me to bask in all the perks and pretty talk and commit to nothing."

"Oprah already retired."

"Just from network TV, so everybody's still trying to fill the gap." He named a mouthy female celeb.

"And for a vote in favor of only one, I'd bet," Temple said, "she's abrasive."

"Humor often is."

"But Oprah's appeal is being a sort of overlady of everything family and psychologically dysfunctional and physically healthy and fashionable."

"That's a wide swath to follow in," Matt said. "A lot of new shows will try until something clicks."

"Or someone." Temple smiled as a waiter wafted a couple tall, footed glasses in front of them.

"The newest house signature cocktail," he announced, "compliments of Mister Fontana."

"Which Mister Fontana?" Temple asked, craning her neck, though it was most likely the owner, Nicky.

But the donor had deserted the dining room.

"What is it?" Matt asked, more to the point.

"A Silver Zombie," the waiter said, happy to have a bit part. "Silver tequila, of course, lime vodka, Blue Curaçao, et cetera."

"It's those 'et ceteras' that get your head turned around," Matt commented.

Temple was thinking that a zombie was the perfect drink to numb Matt's sure-to-be major reaction to her news about Max.

"Smooth move," Matt said, making Temple start. Was he reading her mind? "The drink matches your dress and your eyes."

They clicked rims and sipped. *Not bad,*

222

Temple thought. Like a Moonlight Margarita on steroids.

"Before we order," she said, "I need to . . .
address a certain change in status."

"Believe me, Temple," Matt put in, "this
Chicago talk-show notion is just that — all
talk so far. I've had time on the plane to
think straight, and I realized I couldn't just
whisk you out of Las Vegas, where your
business and home are now."

"Yes, you can. In fact, I'd prefer to be out
of town and with you in Chicago right now."

"You're serious?"

She nodded. "While you were gone, there
was a murder connected to the Crystal
Phoenix."

"You're right." Matt had sipped the Silver
Zombie a third down. "You do need to leave
this town."

"It also involved the . . . Synth. I found
their hidden headquarters at the Neon
Nightmare club. And Kathleen O'Connor
may still be alive, Matt."

"Kitty the Cutter? Can't be. I identified
the body."

"You saw her, what? A couple times, and
she sliced you with a razor on one of the
occasions. Besides, she may have had a . . .
body double."

The waiter wafted a sampler tray of hot

223

and cold running hors d'oeuvres down on the middle of the table.

"Somehow," Matt said, "this is not the most appetizing conversation."

"Dig in or drink up," Temple warned him; "this is going to be a bumpy night."

"Why?"

"Max is back."

CHAPTER 20
SET 'EM UP, MAX

"Max is alive?" Matt looked like he'd been poleaxed. "You've heard from him, then?"

Matt's expression remained puzzled. "Wait. You said 'back.' In Las Vegas?"

She nodded.

"So . . . ?"

"We were right. Someone tried to kill him."

"Now he's back, and the first person he contacted was you?"

"Actually, he called me from abroad and I told him to come back."

The waiter arrived and handed them menus, waiting to deliver a long, lavish list of the night's specials.

"We'll order from the menu, thank you?" Matt said.

"Another round of cocktails, sir?"

"No." Temple.

"Yes." Matt.

She eyed their half-full glasses after the

waiter left.

"We'll make short work of these, I'm sure." Matt grabbed his footed cocktail glass.

"Matt, I told you bald truth, but there are a busload of extenuating circumstances. You would have done the same thing in my place."

"I kinda doubt that. We're just getting our new life together . . . together . . . and the last thing I — we — need is Max Bloody Kinsella popping out of the woodwork."

"He's not Max anymore."

"Oh, that'd be a real magician's trick."

"He has no memory since he came out of a coma a couple weeks ago."

"He found you fast enough."

"His, um, counterterrorism cohort, shall I call him? — Gandolph the Great — told him about me. And you. Max didn't remember us at all. Still doesn't."

"You've seen him already? While I was gone? And isn't that Gandolph guy dead?"

"His real name was Garry Randolph. He and his magician persona were presumed dead after that séance at the haunted house last Halloween, but he wasn't. He *was* shot dead in Northern Ireland about a week ago days ago. In a car. With Max at the wheel."

Matt shook his head and worked on the

226

Silver Zombie. "And you say Kitty the Cutter may still be knocking around somewhere, too? Everybody we presumed dead . . . isn't. Except for poor Gandolph?"

"That's about it."

"Chicago's looking better every second." Max buried his face and expression behind the tall padded menu.

"Matt," Temple said.

"We'd better eat to offset the drinks. And think." Matt clapped the menu shut so definitely, Temple jumped.

He sighed and shook his head. "That's why I love you. Wounded birds will not be left flapping on your doorstep, even when they're hawks. But I am not deliriously happy."

The waiter edged toward them. Matt ordered New York steak, medium. Temple wanted to order crow, but settled on flounder.

Matt picked up the "discussion."

"I see why you wanted to lay this on me in public."

"No. I wanted you to be relaxed from the flight and the hullabaloo in Chicago and whatever your family's been up to."

"You are a born referee, Temple. You want everyone to get a fair chance before they tear each other part. Where's the resurrected

227

Wonder Boy now?"

"I left him at the house he inherited from Garry Randolph, where he'd lived in hiding after his, um, first return to Las Vegas."

"After his *first* abrupt, unexplained disappearance," Matt said.

"I haven't seen him since."

"And that's been?"

"For two days."

"And you couldn't have called me? Warned me?"

"You'd want this over the phone? Look, Matt, you're not really jealous, are you?"

He thought about it. "No. The counselor in me realizes you're better off knowing what happened to him. You need the closure, but me, I just want a past that's laid to rest."

"As with your stepfather." Temple nodded, remembering Matt's tenacity in tracking down the louse. That's what had brought him to Las Vegas and the Circle Ritz and her. "Laying a past to rest can't always be literal," she argued. "Your stepfather is truly and sincerely dead, and he was also pretty harmless by then. If Kathleen O'Connor is still out there . . . not the case. She seemed to have it in for you as well as for Max. He and Garry found out all about her in Ireland."

228

"I wish they all had stayed there," Matt said as their salads arrived.

The pair of Caesar salads were too lavish to be ignored. They came with a Crystal Phoenix twist, capers instead of anchovies in the dressing. Temple didn't remember ordering salad. She guessed they both had mechanically OK'd the first item on every course the waiter had thrown at them.

"So," Matt said, picking at the greens, "Kinsella knows nothing of his past except a lot of juicy stuff about Kathleen O'Connor that he and the late Garry Randolph uncovered in the last week or so?"

Temple nodded. "I didn't press him for details. He's . . . not the same. Both his legs were broken as well as his head in that arranged Neon Nightmare accident. I thought the new revelations were something we should discuss together."

"You and me."

She nodded.

"And Max Kinsella?"

She nodded.

"Because . . ."

"I don't think any of us will be safe until we lay the mystery of Max's past with Kathleen O'Connor — or Kathleen O'Connor herself — to rest."

Matt literally chewed it over.

"You're the girl gumshoe," he said. "Look. Here comes our second round and we've just killed our first Silver Zombies. Too bad ghosts of the past aren't that easy to get rid of."

CHAPTER 21
THE CACTUS GARDEN
CHA-CHA

It is a sad day — I should say night, in this instance — when the senior partner of a firm is forced to follow the druthers of the junior partner.

That is exactly how I find myself on the hard concrete of a flash-floodwater-control channel, sneaking up on a tangle of ungoverned desert scrub with Miss Midnight Louise leading the slomo "charge," so to speak.

I voice my objections again.

"We will have more stickers in our soft underbellies than a porcupine's back has spines if we crawl over all that unfriendly terrain to the house."

"Obviously, your night-assault skills have suffered sadly from La Vida Lazy at the Circle Ritz condo of your currently conflicted roommate," Louise says. "I know when to zig and zag to find the soft sandy aisles between this Inquisition of cactus plants."

"Cleverly put, my would-be flake off the

paternal monument, but you forget — *yowl!* — one thing."

"Keep down the noise! And what is that one thing?"

"Mine! My underbelly is a lot more complicated than yours, and I am a tad broader of beam. If I had wanted to be curry-combed I would have come back as a horse."

"That is you, all right, the old gray nag," she hisses over her shoulder. "There may be persons of evil intent lurking about, so keep the objections to yourself."

Just then I spy an incandescent glow to my left, behind a tall scrawny mesquite tree. Enough with being a lowly grunt! I spring toward the slender trunk and ratchet up it with my built-in pitons.

Mesquite trees may make twenty or thirty feet in height. They are more an ambitious shrub than a real tree and thus not built for taking much weight. You do not want to mess with the young shoots, not only because of the weight problem. New growth has nasty protection — three-inch thorns that could deflate the tire on an SUV.

So I am up the tree, out on a limb, and leaping toward the light like a would-be saved soul before you can sneeze "Midnight Louise." As I suspected, I spy a window and am soon perching claws-out on a sill.

These old adobe-style houses have thick walls and wide sills. I can relax and stare right into the living room. I love being on a high perch in a power position.

I know as I contemplate my next move that nothing bad is going down in my little corner of Vegas now that I am on the job.

As for the rest of the city, that is up to the two-foots on the official force.

The smart money is on me.

CHAPTER 22
ALL DOLLED UP

The victim's body was laid out like a corpse on an autopsy table, stiff-armed and -legged, like a horrible life-size doll.

Homicide Lieutenant C. R. Molina stalked around the body lying on the pavement. The night was warm and dark, the shopping-mall parking lot empty except for the circle of police vehicles.

Forensics had done its grisly duty. Every iota of evidence had been photographed and collected. The meat wagon was waiting, along with Coroner Grizzly Bahr at the end of the ride. Then would come the Y-cut of the torso, the circular saw through the skull-top, and the corpse wouldn't resemble a molded plastic doll anymore.

Molina could already hear the saw's whine, scent the Febreze-laden, icy air of the city morgue. She was not quite ready to release this corpse from its state of suspended wholeness.

There was not a mark on the girl's form. She was twenty or so, high-fashion-model thin, with her hipbones as prominent as an undressed department-store mannequin's through her thin summer skirt, her small breasts supernaturally firm under the lacy top.

Her open-eyed face, though, was a mask of distortion and anguish. Most corpses, even victims of terrible accidents, even horribly damaged ones, were blessedly expressionless.

This girl, though, had stared death in the face and struggled to the moment of her last breath.

Molina was betting the Cause of Death was strangulation, from the inside out. Not a crime of passion, except for the ghastly repetition of these circumstances.

Beside the victim lay a naked Barbie doll — a tiny mini-me — its El Greco–lean torso and limbs an equally stiff version of the victim's.

Unlike the dead girl, the Barbie doll wore marks of violence. Scarlet nail polish circled Barbie's elongated neck at the throat, visible even beneath a tiny, throttling chiffon scarf. Scarlet nail polish dotted her tiny wrists, slashed across her slim-hipped, big-breasted torso. Her feet were half severed at the ankles, and screwdriver-size dents had impacted her face.

"Turns your stomach," said an unexpected voice beside Molina.

She glanced at the man in shopping-mall civvies who'd appeared out of the black nowhere that was her crime-scene mind.

"What brought you here?" she asked the undercover narc called Dirty Larry.

"Heard it on the grapevine," he answered. "Thought about your daughter."

Molina's hands fisted in the pockets of her khaki blazer.

"You are not a detective," she told him in clipped, superior-officer rebuke. "You are on temporary traffic-accident duty. You have no reason to be here."

"It *is* a parking lot, Loo," he said.

"Not amusing."

Molina walked away to quiet the hyper-heartbeat he had kicked up by mentioning her daughter, waving at the morgue attendants to claim the body. She'd wanted to be alone on the scene with it longer, but there'd be film and photos at 9:00 A.M. tomorrow.

Dirty Larry had bulled his way into her professional and personal life on sheer nerve and a smarmy hint of sexual interest. She'd let him ride that wave because she'd needed

236

someone to do off-the-books investigating on Max Kinsella for her. She'd never trusted D. L. Now she had a disabled Max Kinsella for that kind of work, who was probably a lot better at it even without his former strength and memory. She harbored a huge need-to-know about Kinsella's history since his spectacular fall from good health, but she could wait.

Dirty Larry was the impatient type. He followed her, still an irritant.

"You showing up at my crime scenes is getting old, Podesta." She stopped and eyed the empty lot, wondering what the security cameras would reveal. "The first time was enterprising and ballsy. Twice gets irritating."

"Kinda like your love life?"

Molina spun to face him. "Don't tread on me. Or bring Mariah's name into this crime scene. Thank God her disappearance was a misguided teen scheme and we found her quickly. You don't have any children. You have no right to play on my parental concerns. What are you up to? It sure isn't getting into my bed, the way you're going."

"No. I don't have kids. I never married. Not with a job you can never bring home. Doesn't mean I haven't seen lots of kids wounded or killed by the drug trade. It

237

doesn't mean I don't care as much as you do about catching this Barbie Doll Killer."

"As much as me? Don't you have enough grief fighting the drug wars? Why?"

"Look. I was there several nights ago when your daughter went AWOL and the mutilated Barbie doll was found in Mariah's bedroom. She's young for this perp's preferences — thirteen — but how old is this dead girl? Seventeen? Twenty, tops? You've gotta admit to the facts."

"Which are?" Molina used her lowest "show-me" tone.

"The Barbie Doll Killer has been circling the Southwest to the California state line for years, targeting young women who audition at shopping malls for reality-TV shows that offer them a grab at fame. Vegas is at the center of the pattern now, with two shopping-mall Barbie murders, and so is your daughter."

"You think I need assistance putting patterns together, Officer Podesta? I'm the homicide cop. You're moonlighting. Undercover narcs are not needed or wanted on my crime scenes."

"I might have some offbeat insight."

"Mentioning my daughter is not going to get me to listen. I take it as a distraction."

He leaned close, took her elbow. "I know

you've got to concentrate on your objectivity, Carmen. Let *me* look out for Mariah. You're too close, too professional."

"*You*'re too close," she said, jerking her arm out of his confidential custody.

"You're losing it," he grumbled under his breath.

"Get off my crime scene."

"I know this guy. He operates like someone high on cocaine. He can't stop himself. We've got to do it."

"He's on my turf now," she said. "For the second time, yes, and he's come out of the Malibu Barbie closet. So far he's left a dead body and mutilated Barbie doll images. This time, this crime scene, it's come together, doll and human victim. Go play with your shattered headlights and tire patterns. I'll do what my gender is supposed to do best from birth — play with dolls."

All the lights were off at Molina's modest bungalow near Our Lady of Guadalupe Church and School when she pulled her old Volvo into the driveway. The time must be snagged close to either side of midnight, she thought, too tired to check her watch. She was even too weary to maneuver the car into the garage and weave her way through the laundry room into the house.

She'd use the front door and her key.

Mariah had a new overnight "house keeper" now, Angela Ortega, a single home-owner in the neighborhood and former beat cop going for a law degree. What a find! Angela could burn the scholar's midnight oil while watching Mariah and was young and attractive enough to earn Mariah's teen fascination. Angela made a great role model, and she'd been tops on the firing range.

Molina let the heavy driver's door slam shut. *Gotta find time to shop for a new car someday soon,* she thought. *Get Mariah in on the hunt. Something "cool" she could drive in . . . gosh, learner's permit in two years only? Dread.*

"Got a minute?" a low voice asked.

Molina didn't think; she just spun, GLOCK out of its paddle holster to face the male voice at the level of her head, which was about six feet. Big guy could mean big gun.

"Tough night." The voice hadn't tensed at all.

Her shoulders dropped. A little. "Kinsella. Don't you know better than to sneak up on a cop?"

"Didn't want to wake the house. Figured you wouldn't either. Smooth, fast draw, though. Very Wild West."

"When you said 'Tough night,' just now. It wasn't a question."

"No, I followed Podesta to your crime scene."

"You were lurking in that parking lot, too? You *want* to be considered a suspect?"

"Nothing new for me with you, I'm told. You wanted him followed."

"So . . . where did Larry come from?"

"I'd hesitate to call it stalking . . ."

"Pot calling the kettle black?"

". . . but he keeps a close eye on your movements. Is it love or is it something else I should know about?"

She looked over her shoulder toward the house. She wasn't ready to bring Mariah into yet another semisuspicious man's knowledge bank.

"If letting that car door slam shut didn't wake the house, our talking won't," he pointed out.

"I was . . . thinking." She wouldn't admit to the crime of "tired."

"So was I. You don't trust either this Dirty Larry guy *or* this Rafi Nadir. *Why* is your business, but major crime is your business, too. You think either one of them might be your Barbie Doll Killer?"

"Remote possibility."

"Yeah. One's your ex and one's your . . .

241

wannabe current."

"I didn't hire you for background checks, just keeping an eye on their whereabouts."

"You know 'the past is present' in all police work."

"In Shakespeare, too," she said. "Don't get fancy on me. So where *were* the boys earlier this evening? From the time it got dark?"

"As assistant security chief at the Oasis Hotel, he gets assigned mostly night shifts."

"So he was there?"

"No. He alternates from the three-to-eleven-P.M. shift to the eleven-P.M-to-seven-A.M. turn. He went out for dinner about eight."

"Not at the Oasis? He'd get comped."

"Nope. Nice restaurant in Henderson. Offers this fancy fondue of several courses, steak to strawberries."

"I know the place."

"Then you know the spread takes a couple hours or more to eat."

"Rafi has an alibi. How nice for him. Still, was he alone?"

"Nope."

She waited for him to say more, but he didn't, and she wasn't going to ask, man or woman? They both knew Nadir was her ex, ex-live-in anyway, and the last thing she wanted to look like in front of Max Kinsella was insecure. If you're going to be a rattlesnake handler, don't blink.

"What about Dirty Larry?" she asked.

"Love that street name. He's more interesting than Nadir in another way. I got on him as soon as Rafi was settled down with his appetizer course of exotic dipping vegetables, rutabagas, and snow peas."

"That sounds so disgusting," she said.

"The place is all the rage. Lots of couples get engaged there." Molina bit her lip. Was Rafi courting some . . . woman? Good! Maybe he'd forget his shared custody hopes for Mariah. Not likely. He'd have better luck if he was "settled" and married. Unlike a working mother with a demanding 24/7 job.

"Dirty Larry was another story," Kinsella went on. "As soon as Rafi was snuggled in with his flame-melted cheeses and chilled wine courses, I looked up Podesta. He has a police radio in his car, which was sitting on the fringes of that mall parking lot when you pulled into it after the uniforms had answered the alarm.

"He has a police radio in his personal vehicle?"

"Yeah. Big old Impala. Kinda cool. Almost *Barracuuudah*."

"Only to overage juvenile delinquents."

She peered toward the street. "What are you driving now?"

"You'll never see it. Ditto Nadir and Podesta. Isn't that what you hired me for? To be an unseen man of mystery?"

"I hired you to report without any fancy frills. So Larry was on the crime scene before I got there? For how long?"

"Long enough to have done the deed and faded into the wings until you saw him arrive later."

"But you were there at the same time, too."

"Ay, there's the rub."

"Not Shakespeare again."

"Appropriate for the tragic death tonight."

"Yes. It *is* all about the victim. Wait? Are you leaving?" The dark near her seemed less dense.

"I'm going home," his voice said, fading, "to put Elvis on the sound system."

"*You* listen to Elvis?"

" 'Suspicious Minds,' " Max Kinsella said. "Classic."

CHAPTER 23
BREAK DANCING

Imagine my surprise to see myself mirrored in the window.

Not exactly mirrored.

The dude is the same species and gender as me, but his vibrissae are black and his brown tabby coat is longer than mine, forming a lionlike mane around his face. His eyes are as narrowed and his pupils as dark as mine.

If I had wanted to have a mirror-go-round, I could not do to better to come up with a worthy opponent. So imagine my surprise when he lays a set of hooked claws on the window crank inside and makes it do the boogie-woogie.

In an instant a wave of fully feline occupation wafts into my sensitive black nostrils as the window swings outward. We are talking clowder here, and indoor.

"Let me in by the hairs of my chinny-chin-chin," I order. "You need outside help. Something very dark and dirty is going down here, and only I —"

"Cat burglar!" my doorman screeches. "Black as sin and hanging by his dewclaws from our doorway."

Immediately there commences such a caterwauling as has not been heard outside a Disney animation.

The inner watchcat rolls out the window sideways, so I am almost knocked four feet back and eight feet down on my keister.

It is only by the scrabbling of my claws that I am able to dodge the opening window and to eel inside, not without plummeting down two feet to a countertop.

"Reach for the cupboard handles and identify yourself, stranger," the big hairy dude demands. "Maverick is my name and guardian is my game."

"Louie, Midnight Louie. Founder of Midnight Investigations, Inc."

Immediately, hordes of housebound kitties loft up to greet me, eager for news of the outer world.

"So you are a detective? Detect. Where is our wonderful Mister Pedro?" they mew plaintively. "He always brought us Fiesta Feline bits and tended to the indoor plumbing."

"We miss him," a quartet of calico kittens croon. "He was our schnooky-wooky, hunny-bunny, daily-waily do-the-doo-doo kinda kind and special dude."

"I hate to break the news, crew." I crawl atop a cookie jar for a podium. "Your daily-waily guy-to-go-to is gone, a victim of what may be Mother Nature — as are we all — or the all-too-common Foul Play."

The wails turn into boos and boo-hoos.

"I am here," I howl, to overcome the winsome kitten choruses, "to make things right. But I need your cooperation and testimony."

Several males shrink at my mention of the last word.

Maverick stares them down. "Miss Violet has always seen us properly tended, so there would be no untoward breeding. We are all righteous dudes. You do not come in unless you are litter-free. Right, cat burglar?"

I am not about to admit to this politically correct crowd that I have an escape clause, namely my involuntary vasectomy. It is too big a word for them, anyway. It is too big a word for me, too. I am not much excited about having something to do with a pansy container like a "vase."

Wouldn't you know that Miss Midnight Louise picks this moment to finally claw her way onto the windowsill and into my persuasive pitch?

"He and me, his essential partner in Midnight Investigations, Inc., are litter-free," she announces, making all the female ears in the area, which are numerous, perk up. "Midnight Louise is the name."

The females inside commence to caterwaul themselves hoarse, since they always stick together, much to male detriment. Or they do not like competition. Although I do not admit the kit-chit is an offspring, I must admit she got a share of my striking good looks from somewhere very close to me. The motives of the female of the species, any species, are always multiple and subtle.

"Maverick," I howl, "I rely on your guidance."

Having thus named my inside man, I leap to the kitchen floor.

Ook! It is covered with niblets of dry kibble and maybe dingleberries and ear wax. Despite the best intentions of humans and civic animal-control acts, there may indeed be "too many cats" here for one indoor clowder.

My poor Miss Temple! She is fighting a losing battle. Unless we organize these cats to protect their helpless defender and keep Miss Violet alive, we will not be able to prevent her losing her feline friends to the merciless disposition of the law, and, even worse, whatever friends and family she has who want the whole kit and caboodle . . . by which I mean money, not formerly feral furs.

While the resident mob gathers to look us

248

over, I convey all my concerns to Miss Midnight Louise through soft whispers and body language.

"None of that here!" a tortoiseshell of size says, boxing my ears.

I stare into malevolent, squinty green eyes and about twenty-two pounds of muscle, fat, and fur soaking wet after a tongue-bath.

Louise's whipping longhaired tail smashes me in the kisser as she leaps between us.

"Lay off of my aging partner, Moby Mama. He has just had a very tough climb, and we were simply conferring. Get your mind out the alley it was born in."

"Dumpster-diving snit," the tortie hisses right back. "We are all street people in here, except for the Persian castoffs."

"You got something against Persians?" I demand, that being a personal sore point with me. "They have more moxie in their smallest vibrissa than you have in your whole . . . um, Suma-wrestling-worthy body."

Which she is about to throw on me, wholesale. Which I cannot allow, as my daintier daugh . . . duh . . . partner would be in the way and possibly smashed.

Maverick flips his tail tip over all our faces, so we are forced to blink.

"Calm down, ladies and gentleman. I run an easy establishment here. No unsheathed weapons or yawning maws on site. Number one, I say so. Number two, you will get one of our dear lady's visitors coming in to check on the noise, and you know what we all think about them."

The intense hisses that fill the room remind me of a snake pit. No one here is venomous, thank Bast, but I am facing a sea of unified and viral dislike. We of the cat clan are not loud and obvious in our hatreds, but that makes us all the more dangerous to cross.

A rangy half-year female calico dances into the middle of the kitchen floor, as young ones will.

"Our beloved Pedro went outside and never came back," she mews. "What do the strangers know about that? Our food trays are empty and our . . . indoor sandboxes are overflowing. We came inside for shelter, but now —"

"Hush, youngster," Maverick hisses. "Keep your cries below human-ear level. Our only indoor friend needs us more than we need her now."

"This is a hostage situation," Miss Midnight Louise growls in my ear. "These are half-domesticated homeless. Their real caretakers are both out of service — one sick and one dead. And the vultures are circling."

"Are not they always?" I ask no one in particular.

Something is nagging at me. Besides Miss Midnight Louise and Moby Mama.

"Say, Maverick," I begin, blowing a confidential question in his spidery-furred ear. These longhairs always make me wish I had an electric-powered nose-hair clipper. Even humans know to keep their ear hairs under control.

"Yeah, Louie?"

I have not given him permission to get past calling me Mr. Midnight, but given that he runs this gang and that my Ma Barker and her police substation posse are far away, I put up with his familiarity.

"What is this about Persians? Frankly, besides you and Miss Midnight Louise, I see few even semi-longhairs in this house."

Maverick shakes his head. "Sad case. I do my best to run a clean clowder, but females mightily outweigh the males here."

"Yeah." I glance at Moby Mama, who has subsided into a Jabba the Hutt–like pile against the kitchen island.

Maverick is still shaking his head, which drifts way too much flea powder into my sensitive sleuthing nostrils. My Miss Temple manages to anoint my shoulder blades monthly with some vermin-dispensing potion that does not contribute to air pollution, although I understand care must be used.

However, I have the luxury of a one-feline household.

"So these supposed Persians?" I prod Maverick with a well-sharpened but friendly shiv. It is more of a brush than a thrust, but only because I have exquisite control when I want to, as the ladies will attest.

"A sorry lot," Maverick said, shaking his big head. "I can only do so much as a peace-maker. They just do not fit in. How would you like to control a mixed bag of cats in a burlap sack whose Noah's Ark is sinking? Those two do not have the basic survival skills. Look at them."

I look around, following his on-the-floor focus.

I spot a pair of beige dust bunnies under the kitchen table, behind the wrought-iron curlicue legs, which form a briar patch of sorts.

I spot Sleeping Beauty in a thorn forest. Two of them, only they are more like Rapunzels who've fallen from their tower.

I look into the huge, sorrowful green eyes of the pair of woefully knotted outcasts against the wall and recognize . . . the Divine Yvette and the Sublime Solange.

CHAPTER 24
MAXED TO DEATH

"What's the big surprise in the parking lot you texted me about?" Temple asked as soon as she burst through Matt's unlocked unit's door at 11:00 P.M.

They'd gotten back from dinner after ten, both self-conscious after all the talking about Max had left the ghost of his love affair with Temple hanging over them like ectoplasmic halitosis.

Following some discreetly illicit-feeling necking in the hall leading to her door, they'd agreed that Matt needed rest before getting to the radio station at 11:30.

"Especially," Temple had said sensibly, "with such an unexpected high-pressure week in Chicago to recover from."

Matt had agreed, uneasily. He still felt crummy about Temple wasting her seduction-worthy dress on a half-baked hallway interlude and had stopped after climbing the stairs to his own place a floor above, thinking about going back down instantly.

Then he noticed someone loitering by the short hall to his door.

"Mister Devine?"

The guy was about twenty-four, dressed in an expensive business suit to pass as at least thirty, his hair lightly gelled into an upward eager beaver do.

Matt nodded slowly. He didn't look like a thief, more like he was selling something. Door-to-door, at 10:30 P.M.?

"Craig Coppell." He thrust out a tentative, moist-palmed hand that smelled of . . . Old Spice? "I'm sorry to disturb your evening, sir, but I've been waiting here since six and was instructed not to let a day pass until I gave you this. It was supposed to be here before you got back home."

He pulled his spongy hand from Matt's grasp and replaced it with . . . a set of keys.

"Is this some . . . sales promotion?" Matt asked, feeling steel prongs poking his palms.

"Promotions? Oh, no, sir, Mister Devine. Maybe for me. Someday. Just look down in the parking lot. With the compliments of Harvey Klinger and Dave Eckstein. Good night, sir, and, *whew,* sweet dreams."

The guy was gone before Matt could react. Harvey and Dave sounded familiar, like the Harry and David mail-order catalog of fruit arrangements. . . .

Duh! Matt turned, but the last echoes of the determined Craig's running footsteps were wafting up the two stories from the lobby.

If he could forget his new Chicago acquaintances so fast, he guessed he could let go of a formerly presumed-dead guy with a whacked-out memory chip. So, a bit later, he texted Temple to come up to his parlor for a parking-lot surprise.

"What is it, Matt? You're looking stunned."

"Like your outfit wouldn't do it?"

She'd changed into some pink skimpy-topped pajama set with silver chocolate kisses all over them and looked good enough to put over vanilla ice cream and call it a sundae.

He nuzzled the halter straps near her neck then put an arm around her bare shoulders and marched her to the balcony off the living room. She spotted the new feature of the parking lot below instantly.

"The liquid-silver Jag is yours?"

"Maybe. Call it a perk. Bribe. Whatever."

"What? Who?"

"The Chicago producers. Can you believe I'd forgotten their names already?"

"No. No more MIA memories around here. How could you forget?"

"It's all a blur."

"They must really, really like you. I love the car. While you were ogling it, did you notice that clowder of feral cats hanging around the parking lot? I haven't seen them recently, and I'm afraid Louie has driven them off, poor things."

"No, I did not see any cats." Matt turned her to go back inside.

"Why are you frowning?" she wanted to know. "I know you're tired and don't want company just before racing off to WCOO. All that daytime-TV business in Chicago must have been exhausting. And, say, we never discussed the family matters you said were kicking up."

By then they were back inside and she was hanging off him like a fond climbing vine.

"Temple, you've got enough questions to keep the WCOO call-in line busy for the whole *Midnight Hour.* Yeah, it's a bit disorienting to be back after all that's happened, and that's why I'm afraid I blew it tonight."

Her sudden silence reminded Matt that he wasn't the only one who'd returned after an absence, after a much longer and more dramatic absence than his own week-long jaunt.

"I don't know what's got you wired," he told her, "but the last thing I'm going to do with the rest of the hour — before I have to leave to listen to everyone else's troubles — is sleep, so maybe you could get me some hyperdrive, too."

"Just get comfy on the infamous Communist couch, and I'll bring us two Diet Cokes with lime."

"The 'infamous Communist couch'?" he asked when she returned to put the glasses on the matched small coffee tables fronting the sinuous length of red-suede couch.

"This is where WCOO had you do that barefoot lounge pose for their first *Midnight Hour* billboard. It's by the fifties designer Vladimir Kagan, and it's red. Red as in 'Communist,' back in the day. So assume the position and I'll cozy up."

Matt laughed as he kicked off his casual suede loafers and made room for Temple to curl up alongside him.

"When you're on TV," she said, "you won't get away with wearing polo shirts and chinos, even if they come from men's shops on the Strip."

"You mean I'll have to dress on camera like Regis Philbin? Then it's no deal."

"Okay," Temple said. "We can discuss the details of your media future in full daylight.

For now, back to my questions. The cats."

"I didn't spot any feral colony before I left town, and didn't see a whisker since we got back tonight. Not even Midnight Louie's."

"Me neither, not in the past twenty-four hours, anyway. Which is odd. Usually he's patrolling the Circle Ritz at night. He's very territorial, you know."

"I know," Matt said, untying the soft knit bow at her nape that held up the loose top.

"I'm forgetting all those questions," she warned.

"I think I'd like that about now."

"Wait. This is most important. What's up with your family?"

Matt leaned back, pulling her atop him. "The good news is our getting married would hardly ruffle a Polish feather."

"Yeah?"

"Yeah. It's my *mother*'s getting married that has the extensive extended family in an uproar."

"Your *mother*? Remarrying? That's wonderful. Maybe we can make it a double ceremony."

"Temple." He put a hand over her mouth. "Temple, Temple. Always the PR hotshot. No, we do not want to be involved in any way in my mother's marital plans. I did mention that a distinguished older guy

258

seemed to be sweet on her at the tourist-spot Polish restaurant where she's a hostess?"

"Yeah, I guess. You said she was coming out of her self-imposed shell after punishing herself for having you out of wedlock — *wedlock*, that does sound mandatory and icky — by marrying that abusive loser, um, Efflinger, Essing. . . ."

"Effinger. Cliff Effinger."

"Right. Effinger. But he went down with the Treasure Island's old pirate-ship attraction, when someone bound him to the bow to go to a watery grave when the ship was sunk during the evening spectacle. So your mom's free to remarry, even by the Catholic Church's standards."

Matt shook his head in disbelief. "That's not the problem. She's perfectly free to marry. I think it'd be wonderful if she did marry someone. I would even give her away, since she's old-fashioned and probably willing to be given away. . . . What would you do about being 'given away,' Temple?"

"Oh, I'd let my father waltz me down the aisle. I *am* the only daughter. I really couldn't deprive the old folks at home of their traditional roles just because the custom is sexist."

"That's very sweet of you," Matt said, kissing her just as sweetly.

Temple was not about to be diverted from the latest news as soon as the kiss ended.

"You still didn't tell me what's bad about your family situation. Sounds peachy to me. Postmenopausal romance, like my aunt Kit's. Marriage to a guy who sounds like a pillar of the community, if not a Fontana brother. Don't you think your mom deserves a second chance?"

Matt sighed and explained. "It's not peachy. Mom's finally met her restaurant Romeo's family. Her new guy happens to be my birth father's brother."

Temple gasped and put her own hand over her mouth before it outpaced her mind. "Wow. When you tried to arrange a meeting after you found your birth father, your mom walked out, refusing to meet him. She must hate him."

"I've left them all alone since my brilliant attempt at failed mediation," Matt said. "My real dad is married, but not happily anymore, though he never said so. I don't know if he married in the Church. And my mom — they were teenagers who met in a church, for God's sake. He was bound out of the country for service the next day, so the attraction must have been instant and intense. . . . I figure they both never got over it and they're scared to death of each other. The whole situation's impossible."

"That family meeting must have been horribly awkward. And your mom told her strict Catholic relatives?"

"She didn't. She just broke off the relationship with my father's brother, and they all think she's crazy."

Temple shook her head. "What a tragic mess."

"Mister Midnight here doesn't know what to tell anybody, except to get off each other's case."

"Matt." He looked hard at her because of the "more bad news" tone of voice.

"I hate to bring this up, but if this . . . family tangle got out, couldn't it hurt your reputation as an advice-giving talk-show host?"

He looked dumbfounded. "I never thought of that."

"And that's why I love you," Temple said, "but PR is my business. I have to say if your media presence is due for a huge upswing, the paparazzi and Internet rumors will be all over you and everything about you. Especially your roots and family."

"Even us, Temple? Even you?"

She fake-punched his bicep. "I'm a media girl. I can take it, big boy. I just think you better get the situation with your mother and the two brothers straightened out before this deal goes public."

"Or goes through," he said. "Meanwhile, tomorrow is another day." He pulled the knit straps down past her elbows, tangling her in his embrace.

Temple looked surprised and very pleased. "Oh. We, uh, don't have a lot of time before you need to leave for the station."

"I've got a fast car and I'm from Chicago. We do everything fast and hard there," he said, rolling her over and under him, "and Chicago girls like it that way."

CHAPTER 25
WAIT FOR *THE MIDNIGHT HOUR*

Matt got into his new car in the Circle Ritz parking lot, settled his body into the multiply adjustable setting of his choice, and said an Our Father.

His "daily bread" was getting way out of hand. Still, he enjoyed sitting back in the cushy leather, almost asphyxiated by "new car" smell. If this was a pot-sweetener, the producers were beyond serious. So was the current situation in Las Vegas. Dare he even consider leaving now? Keep the car and Chicago, and lose Temple. Or lose the car? No contest.

Matt put the luxury car in gear, glad he was slinking away unseen in the dark of pre-midnight. He could put a put a few miles on the odometer and still return it as a loaner.

The Jaguar prowled into smooth street speed like its animal of origin, and Matt made WCOO's parking lot in record time.

Also unnoticed, since the lot was pretty empty as local programming switched from Ambrosia's show of classic comfort songs and her down-home style of advice to the lost and the lovelorn.

The Midnight Hour, his advice show, which was all talk, ran two hours now due to the continuous call-ins, but the producers clung to the magic of the original name.

Both he, aka Mr. Midnight, and Ambrosia, whose real name was Leticia, were profitably syndicated. He grinned as he *whoop*ed the gift car locked, thinking of her reaction when she came out into the parking lot after ceding him the mic tonight. He'd given her the "Blue Suede" Elvis VW Beetle he'd won, and she loved the headroom, but this glittering Baked Alaska of a car would really rev her engines.

Inside the small building with the big radio tower he passed the lit but empty reception room and went to the studio, watching Ambrosia coo into the mic as she dished out solace and songs.

She sounded like an exotic siren escaped from some noir movie. Maybe she played the sultry big-band singer, her voice soothing as melted caramel.

"Now, baby, don't you get down. Tonight is the turn of a new day, and I'm going to play a little traveling music just for you while you're waiting for Mister Midnight to warm up my hot seat for a while and for your chilly little hearts to lift with more sage advice than should be slung by a young, hot guy like him. So hang on this dial, girls and boys, and prepare to be inspired."

Leticia nodded as the commercials began and doffed her headphone muffs.

"Here's my man," she greeted Matt as he came through the door. "Great to have you back. Your superlarge sparkling water awaits, along with all those adoring ears out there. You already had a fan asking me for a song in your honor."

"A fan?"

"Called herself your 'biggest fan,' but she was forgettin' about *me,* baby."

Leticia shimmied her red zebra-striped three hundred pounds out of the broadcast chair to give him a hug. "Welcome back from Chi-Town. The phone lines are already lighting up."

"No rest for the wicked." Matt slipped into the upholstered swivel chair. Yup, it was still warm. Leticia was his literal mother hen.

"Wicked?" She made a skeptical face. "You? About time."

"Eyeball my new car when you leave."

"You just got new wheels a short while back."

"Not gratis like this."

"What could be foxier than that silver Crossfire? It's even a limited edition now."

Matt shook his head and smiled, settling into the "cockpit" of headphones and mic and lighting call-in lines. He felt as alone as a soloing pilot once the show was running on night voices in the unseen distance.

Leticia poked her head back in, bead-decorated black plaits rattling just before airtime. "I'm waiting around for a ride after, believe it," she warned. "And to see if Miss 'Are You Lonesome Tonight?' from my program shows up on yours."

Matt felt the frown lines forming. "Are You Lonesome Tonight?" He hoped Ambrosia's guest wasn't anyone with delusions of being Elvis. That would-be King caller last year was eerily accurate. Not even the FBI voice techs could say it wasn't the Memphis Cat himself.

He also felt a figurative shiver. Max Kinsella as good as back from the dead, and now intimations of Elvis were resurrecting at WCOO-FM radio?

Naw. Matt just wanted to marry the woman he loved, do the right thing in the job market, and get along with her ever-present alley cat and his own sort-of name-sake, Midnight Louie.

"Where were you the past week?" asked the caller.

Matt stirred uneasily in his adjustable chair. Lots of callers had already said they'd missed him for the last week. None had asked him to account for his whereabouts. Not that anybody couldn't tune in *The Amanda Show* on their Internet connections. Usually radio listeners liked the call-in intimacy but didn't cross the line.

"I ask the questions," Matt said. "Don't I get a vacation?"

"From me, Mister Midnight? No. Never. I'm your biggest fan."

"I appreciate loyal listeners," he said, "but I don't think of you as 'fans.' More like fellow travelers in life."

"Night fliers," she said.

"Like night owls?" He tried to reference the cliché, because her tone had gone deep and seductive and dangerous.

"Yes. Hunters of the night."

Oh, great. One of those vampire groupies. He'd done this gig long enough to recognize the occasional crazy.

"We're all birds of a feather," he said, switching to another lit line. " 'The Mid-

267

night Hour,' " he intoned into the mic. He'd learned to speak softly and be wary of kooks.

"Oh, Mister Midnight, I've been waiting a week to ask this. What can we adults do about school bullying? If a parent intervenes, it can make it worse for the kid. What's the matter with kids today?"

And that launched an evergreen topic, with the call-board lighting up. For a moment Matt flashed back to his bad moments at the *Dancing with the Celebs* local reality-TV program, when he'd been bowed over a light board bleeding, alone in the dark in the wee hours, at the mercy of a masked attacker.

"Mister Midnight, did you hang up on me?"

The vampire groupie, back again. Was that so surprising? No.

She rolled on without pause. "That's not polite. I just wanted to know if the rumors were true."

He thought of his major TV offer and wondered how this creepy call-in knew about it.

"Are you really going to be doing a *razor* commercial on television, Mister Midnight?"

"I'm not getting or taking any commercial offers."

"But you're so good at bleeding."

The air silence was Matt catching his breath, wondering how she knew he'd been stabbed by a sword recently.

"Bleeding heart," her mocking voice continued.

And not so recently as well. Months earlier. More memorably. By a razor.

For the first time he'd detected the whisper of an Irish brogue in the voice, on the word *heart.*

And his blood ran cold. That cliché was true.

A diet-scam commercial blared in his headphones, so loud his pulse spiked with shock.

Leticia's face appeared in the studio window, her expression furious.

Matt felt like he was in a movie like *The Matrix,* everything happening in fast, dislocating film cuts.

Then Leticia burst through the door and his senses snapped back into real-time and real-place mode.

"I am babysitting the technician until this show is over, Matt honey." Her anger seemed to add ozone to the stuffy studio air. "I will make sure that crazy bitch doesn't get through again. Don't say a word. Save everything for the real call-ins. You the man. We talk after."

Matt checked his watch. Forty minutes to go. For once, he was looking forward to the usual problems — dumped lovers, backstabbing co-workers, adoptive children seeking birth parents, unwed mothers seeking and sought by lost children, drug-addict brothers — all-American dysfunction with a capital *D.*

Leticia was right. He couldn't let a crazy stalker make him blow the show. Especially not now. He gave her a faint smile and took the next call, welcoming a dose of ordinary, home-grown angst.

"Love, love, love the Jag," Leticia said as she led him out of the station like a defensive lineman obscuring a quarterback. "It's so you. Of course, you're going to take me out for a drink in it."

They neared the sculpted hunk of high-end metal, and Matt murmured "Maybe not."

The front driver's side tire was flat, obviously . . . slashed. An ice pick lay beside it.

"*N . . . ice.* What a way to treat an artwork." Leticia shook her beaded braids until they *tsk*ed. "How'd you ever afford this baby?"

"Didn't. It was a . . . gift," Matt said, sickened by the vandalism. He wasn't a

Material Guy but he appreciated beauty. " 'Cashew leather interior with truffle trim.' So said the owner's manual. Very fattening to the wallet. Obviously out of my class."

"At least she didn't key it." Leticia was on her cell phone, reporting the vandalism to the station security service and requesting a night guard for what was left of it while Matt looked up the dealer service number. Apparently, Jaguars weren't allowed to languish.

"They'll fix it and have it back to your place pronto."

"You're sure?" Matt asked.

"Hon, you get a twenty-four-hour nanny with cars this classy. It looks like you'll have to ride in my Elvis Beetle, then I'll drop you off at home. Better this way. You can drink, and you need one right now more than I do. Good thing Vegas is a twenty-four-hour town."

The guard's car was already entering the parking lot, and the uniformed guard who exited it was the usual middle-aged and thirty pounds overweight.

"Whew," she whistled when she saw the XJ and the flat. "Pure jealousy. I go off duty in four hours."

"That's okay." Leticia fished her set of station keys from her humongous designer bag.

"Personnel comes in at five A.M."

"A shame," the guard told Matt. "Looks brand new."

"One day. Be careful," he told her. "The person who did this may still be lurking and must have had a lot of anger, and strength."

She patted the holster on her hip. "So do I, if necessary."

Las Vegas thronged with corny bars and lounges all trying to live up to the Strip's glamour.

Leticia didn't take him to one of those but to a freestanding building with a vintage blue-and-magenta neon sign outside.

"The Blue Dahlia," Matt said, sounding as surprised as he felt.

"You know it?" Leticia went on without pause. "Great little club. I like the jazz trio, and sometimes a kick-ass torch singer sits in with them. Really rocks good for a white girl."

Matt beat back a smile. Molina would get a kick out of that "review." But the sometimes singing cop known at the Blue Dahlia as Carmen hadn't come out to add vocal riffs to the music lately, as far as he knew, and she'd never perform this late. She had someone to watch over — not her; she was unattached and always had been since he'd known her — but her teen daughter at home needed protection.

"We close at three," the waiter warned.

"We only need one drink — his," Leticia said, pointing.

Matt wanted this fast and simple, so he ordered Scotch on the rocks.

Leticia was even faster on the draw when it came to getting down to business.

"Okay, Matt. Who was that woman caller who abused our shows?"

"A psychopath."

"*Ya-uh.* How'd she get to be *your* psychopath?"

"By proxy." Matt leaned back as his drink arrived. "She was someone else's psychopath first, only he was harder to find than I was."

"This is really creepy. I'll have a Doctor Pepper," she told the departing waiter. "And what's the supercreamy, polyester shiny, Eurotrash, über-cool car about?"

"I'd rather discuss the phone stalker."

Leticia's big brown eyes grew bigger. "Am I smelling bad news here? You said that car was a gift. I can't imagine your redheaded girlfriend letting you take anything compromising from . . . Madonna, say."

Matt had to smile. "You're right, but I'm not sure I'm keeping it."

"I saw the temporary license plate. Is it insured?"

"By the dealership right now."

" 'Cuz those tires are mondo pricey, Jagboy. It's not the free original investment, it's the upkeep. So who's giving you my salary in cars?"

"You know your syndication deal pulls down a lot more than mine. The car is . . . a bribe, maybe."

"You, take a bribe?"

"There's a possibility of a daytime talk show."

"Oh, my sainted seat at Oprah's last network show and all my loot! It's orin she gave out VW Beetles when I already have a cooler one. You were in Chicago to visit family and do your occasional *Amanda Show* gig. They want you to do a solo."

"*Try* a solo. Yeah. With Oprah heading her OWN cable network, the legacy network talk-show feeding frenzy is on rolling boil. OWN, Oprah Winfrey Network. That takes chutzpah. I don't know, Leticia. Do I have the hunger for it? It would turn my life upside down just as Temple and I are planning to get married."

"Good timing. Marriage means changing cribs, maybe even baby cribs. Producers on the level you're dealing with would move the world for you."

"I could bomb."

"Yup. But my money would be on you. You got the chops and the voice all honed on radio, the most demanding form of talk show. And you got the looks. Is that why this spoiler babe showed up, just to rain on your parade?"

"Of course not," Matt said. He didn't say the thought that zapped his mind: *Of course! Max Kinsella is back and so is Kathleen O'Connor. Both back, back from the dead.*

Leticia downed half of her freshly arrived Dr Pepper, dressed up in a tall, footed glass with a sprig of mint.

"My advice?" she said. "Finish your Scotch and prepare to blast home to the Circle Ritz in my 'Blue Suede' Beetle-rocket. What a combo! The King and the Brit bug-boys who usurped him . . . for a while. Betcha that fiancée is waiting up to greet you on your first night back on *The Midnight Hour*. You two have a lot to talk about, much more than me and thee."

"That's the truth," Matt said, toasting her before draining his lowball glass.

On the small stage behind a similarly small dance floor, two couples were slow-dancing. The trio was riffing on a melody that got more familiar with every note, "One for My Baby (and One More for the Road)."

"It's quarter to three," Matt told Leticia. "I've got to be getting home."

She nodded and produced cash from her bottomless bag, nodding at their empty glasses.

"I guess we had the 'one' for your psycho 'baby' and one more for the road. I just hope you're not the one being set up."

CHAPTER 26
YVES OF DESTRUCTION

What do the letters *YSL* mean to you?

If you are a fashionista or keep abreast of *au courante* lists of Who's Who in the world celebrity-name sweepstakes, you would promptly say, Yves Saint Laurent, of course, the twentieth century's most celebrated high-fashion and therefore highfalutin French dress designer.

Alas, YSL died a couple years ago, although his fashion brand lives on.

But the YSL I am referring to is not a fancy label flaunted on a handbag. It is that immortal trio (besides the Three Musketeers) of Yvette, Solange, and Louie.

Of course we all have more than a single name. It is the Divine Yvette, the Sublime Solange, and Midnight Louie.

However, as I stare upon the startled faces and almost unrecognizable forms of the Divine and Sublime ones, I fear I am going to have to find new sobriquets for the darlings of the purebred Persian set . . . such as the Disheveled Yvette and the Shredded Solange.

"Yvette!" I yowl in disbelief. "Solange!"

"Louie!" they wail in echoing chorus.

The Persian formerly known as Divine turns her face from me. "I have not had my hair done in ages, Louie; you must avert your eyes."

The Persian formerly known as Sublime is more practical. "We have been taken out of solitary confinement and put into a common holding cell full of ruffians and bullies and shorthairs. You must save us!"

This is a tall order, even for Midnight Louie. Not only R & R — rescue and release — but C & C — coiffure and comb-out.

"How did this happen?" is all I can ask.

"Our mistress sought to enhance her failing career and profile," Solange says, idly running a clawed forepaw through her bedraggled golden ruff, "by forsaking the reigning breed of the cat world — we luxuriously furred Persians — for the chic but déclassé bug-eyed, bony, nearly naked purse pooch of the dog world, the Chihuahua."

"Dyed pink, no less," Yvette wails. "As if my tender pink ears and pads and rose nose were not enough!"

I can testify that the formerly Divine Yvette's witnessing is true. Her silver-gray coat was

278

formerly so soft and lustrous that she almost looked faintly lavender in some lights.

Who would kick out a lavender cat for a faux-pink dog? Someone very mentally disturbed, but what does one expect from Miss Savannah Ashleigh, who tried to have me totally de-tommed?

Solange brushes near so I can feel the wadded lumps in her once full and smooth shiny coat. Her huge green eyes fix on mine.

"Overnight we were considered passé by all society, Louie, even *Excess Hollywood.* Our mistress left us here as a temporary shelter, but she never considered that we were not suited to push and shove for our places in the world.

Granted our mistress was facing a fading career of her own, but she did not understand the degree to which Miss Violet was declining both in health and mind. We had no one to aid us, to even know of our plight."

Miss Midnight Louise is pushing past my shoulder to inspect the sorry sight. "Did it ever occur to you pampered showgirls to save yourselves?"

This challenge drives She Who Was Formerly Known as Divine to spin, hissing and spitting.

"We cannot," the Divine Yvette answers with

some of her usual, charmingly adamant
hauteur. "We are French."

CHAPTER 27
LIES AND ALIBIS

"Watson. Come here. I need you," said the voice on the Temple's desk phone.

For a moment, she wasn't sure if Sherlock Holmes or Alexander Graham Bell was calling.

However, Sherlock Holmes would never have admitted to needing anybody, not even his faithful friend and chronicler. And Alexander Graham Bell had famously called his assistant, Watson, on the first-ever phone, all right, but he'd called him "Mr. Watson."

Besides, the voice was female.

Temple put it on speaker, an option she used to take computer notes with the phone far enough away that the keyboard's rapid chuckling wouldn't make the caller self-conscious. Knowing your words are being recorded in any fashion is stifling. Temple had learned that when she'd been a TV news reporter in Minneapolis.

Meanwhile she'd placed the contralto

voice putting the kink in her workday. Luckily, she'd gotten a lot done in the morning.

"You 'need' me where, when, and why?" she asked Lieutenant C. R. Molina. "Is this, like, official?"

"Semiofficial," came the answer.

"You're doing a lot of that lately."

A long pause. "Want to make something of it?"

"Dying to."

Another pause.

"You're acting pretty sassy," Molina noted, "for a woman in a seriously awkward situation between her resurrected, injured ex and her impatient fiancé."

"You're acting pretty high-handed for a homicide lieutenant who's been AWOL from work for dubious reasons."

"I guess we're both in hot water," Molina said. "This is for Mariah."

Temple was surprised by the almost maternal clutch of anxiety in her stomach at mention of the policewoman's daughter. "Is she all right?"

"So far, but the mystery of that mutilated Barbie doll in her bedroom the night she ran off is unsolved. I want to recreate that night, and, Miss Temple Barr, you . . . were . . . there."

"So were a lot of people, starting with that

creep, Crawford Buchanan."

"You're right to despise the man. I never want to see him again unless I'm arresting him." Molina's voice softened. "This is a private party. Just you and me and Detective Alch. You don't have to worry about Max Kinsella showing up. I need people with memories."

"How did — ?" Temple was glad she wasn't holding on to a phone; she would have dropped it.

"By now, Miss Barr, you should be quaking at my preternatural grasp of your most intimate situations. Just shut up and come as you are. My place. Two hours. Put on your thinking cap."

"I . . . might have an appointment."

Temple had planned to visit Aloe Vera Drive to check on Violet's condition and observe her hangers-on, that is, any possible-heirs and/or homicidal maniacs. Meanwhile, she had to stage-manage the momentous meeting of Matt and Max. . . .

When did a PI get to work her first case? Molina was about to tell her.

"An appointment?" The hard-edged cop emerged. "Now you really do."

Silence.

Molina was gone, leaving Temple baffled. She had until 4:00 P.M. She reached over to hang up the old-fashioned desk phone and glanced at Midnight Louie, who'd soundlessly lofted atop the desk, the way cats do, even large ones.

"That night Mariah ran off was a zoo," she told him. "People were coming and going in Molina's house — me and Awful Crawford, Detective Morrie Alch, Dirty Larry the narc. . . . Molina must be nuts to think I can help her figure out how the Barbie Doll Stalker got a foot-long 3-D calling card into her daughter's bedroom. And why is it so urgent now?"

The rogue Barbie doll was one of the loose ends from Mariah's recent unauthorized — but excellent to her — adventure helping a disadvantaged girl win a place in the junior division of a televised show.

Temple made a face at herself and decided to think about the night Molina had ordered her to find and bring Crawford Buchanan to her house, counting on her to know where to find her fellow PR flack. In the later flurry over capturing a murderer at the dance contest, she'd forgotten that sinister object found in Mariah's typically overfurnished teen bedroom, a Barbie doll. Of course the kid's cop mother hadn't, not for one moment.

Who knew what game Molina was playing

284

now? She must suspect somebody, Temple concluded as she locked her unit door and went down a floor in the tiny elevator's elegant wood-lined box, which for the first time reminded her of a vertical coffin. Hers.

In half an hour she was parking the Miata in the shade of Molina's well-aged neighborhood near Our Lady of Guadalupe. Molina's almost-as-well-aged Volvo was not in the driveway for once. Instead, a white Crown Vic showed Detective Alch had beaten Temple here. Or had been here even when Molina had called.

Temple sat in the Miata for an instant. She'd left the convertible's top up for the drive. This part of town wasn't a fun drive and wasn't as safe for a small woman in a small car as public streets around the Strip.

She recognized a pang of guilt for the conspicuous rides she and Matt owned when a public servant drove an old beater. Considering, Temple decided Molina was more pressed for time than money. She worked her job as if it were a religious vocation, but Temple not only had a high-pressure job in a never-stopping town herself, she also had an accidental avocation so ingrained now that Molina had asked *her* for help.

Well, ordered. But the fact was really

something. She thought of Max's blasted memory and shivered with sympathy in the heat. Someone had to have put that mutilated Barbie doll in Mariah's bedroom, and it hadn't been the Barbie Doll Killer. It had been someone with one weird motive, maybe even the unknown stalker who'd entered the house before, the one Molina had always, and bitterly, believed to be Max.

Aha! Max hadn't been here when that Barbie doll incident had gone down. For once, he had an unbreakable alibi — two broken legs and a coma — which might not even stop the Max Temple knew, but the nearly six thousand miles to Switzerland would.

Max had been a convenient suspect physically and emotionally for the "old" Molina. Now the woman had to know if it hadn't been Max, it very likely had been someone even more supernaturally elusive.

Usually, Temple felt she *had* to help Molina for Max's sake. Now, she mused, she had to help her for everybody's sake.

Alch opened the door when she knocked.

Off a crime scene, he was a fifty-something silver fox with kind eyes. Even he was looking frazzled and weary. Temple recognized the survivor of a too-long boxing match with worry.

"Hi, Detective Alch," she said. "You look wilted off the crime scene."

"Wilted? Oh. You mean instead of looking 'fresh off.' You're always fresh, Miss Barr, and not always in a good way."

"I know I can be painfully perky at times, but I'm here to help. Or so I was told."

"Me too." Alch stood holding the front door open, or maybe it was holding him up.

"Hey, may I come in? I *was* invited."

"Sorry." He swept the door fully open with a slight bow. "I've been pulling a lot of overtime lately."

"I'll bet," Temple said, stepping in curiously.

Why wasn't Molina here to greet her? She did an open survey, craning her neck up and down and around. Being short, she always risked missing something. No Molina or Mariah in sight. Not even the two rescue cats. Just a lot of slouchy kid-friendly furniture.

Alch was chuckling.

"What?" Temple asked, turning his way.

"Miss Pussyfooter. You look just like a cat stepping over a threshold, anticipating turning around and running at any second. The soles of your sandals won't burn, and Molina won't bite."

"*Hmph.* Maybe not for now."

Alch was shutting the door, forcing her to take a step forward and commit. "You know something you're not supposed to?" he asked.

"Probably." While Alch frowned, visibly torn between saying something more and not, Temple added, "I can guess how much you did for her these last couple months. Merit badge time."

"Yeah, maybe, but she's well now."

"I guess. What's the rush here? Why do we need to relive the night Mariah disappeared, especially me? I was peripheral to all that."

"Nasty new development." Alch studied the carpeting. "It's under wraps, but there was another parking-lot Barbie doll murder last night."

"Oh, my gosh. Here? In Vegas?"

"Yeah. Again. And, given the weird incident of the Barbie doll left in Mariah's bedroom . . ."

"Molina needs to solve that freaky fact fast for her own peace of mind," Temple finished for him, "and maybe to unlock the whole case. So here we are — lieutenant's little helpers."

Alch nodded and waved a hand toward the couch.

Temple still felt leery about sitting down

when Molina was not there to OK the hospitality. The last time she'd been ordered into this room she'd had that weasel, Crawford Buchanan, in tow, on Molina's orders, and Mariah had just gone missing.

A wild, scrabbling sound erupted from around the kitchen eating bar. Two brown-striped streaks bounded over the sofa back and seat, and then to the floor and down the hall.

Alch shook his head at their vanishing tails. "I'll never understand why adult cats will suddenly act as if a black widow had bitten them in the ass and take off like kittens," he said.

"We'll never understand feline behavior." Temple felt free to sit on the couch now that the cats had run roughshod over it. "What's up? Where are the human inhabitants? Are we for dinner, literally?"

"Mariah's doing an overnight at a friend's house," Molina's contralto voice said from the unlit hall down which the cats had vanished. "For real this time. This time *I* wanted her out of the way. I was printing some things out in the home office."

Temple had leaped to her feet like a guilty schoolkid at the sound of Molina's voice, and Alch corrected his tired slouch.

Maybe Molina was what had bitten the

tiger-cat girls in their fluffy rears, but she was coming from the wrong direction.

"Sit," Molina said. "This is not boot camp."

Alch and Temple exchanged a sympathetic look. If either had heard a more contradictory statement, it would be a long shot.

They sat.

"I'd offer you some refreshment," Molina said absently, shuffling her papers, "but this is an exercise in a game of Clue." She looked up. "Maybe afterward, if you've been good."

Again Temple and Morrie Alch exchanged glances.

Molina was moving slowly, probably more from mental abstraction than recent physical problems. She was dressed casually, but Temple noticed that the khaki denim slacks had tight, fashionably wrinkled legs at the calf and that Molina's buckskin flats were fringed around the ankle strap. Her loose leopard-print linen top was astoundingly fashion-assertive for the laid-back lieutenant, and her functional brunette bob was caught back on one side with a tortoiseshell barrette — a small tortoiseshell barrette, but the first jewelry Temple had ever spotted on C. R. Molina.

Maybe not so astounding, Temple decided

on second thought. The policewoman's alter ego, the torch singer Carmen, who'd been in retrograde for months, had worn a very forties silk flower in her hair.

Alch was still frowning, detecting a change but way too male to read the small-print signs. Obviously, however you looked at it, Molina was finally feeling better . . . and back!

Temple wondered why. Time and healing . . . or something else.

Molina sat in a chair opposite the device-cluttered coffee table — Mariah's trail — and spread the letter-size pages over its length.

Temple blinked to see her Web site head shot blown up. Alch was next, with a ten-year-old ID shot that looked focused and jaunty.

"No comments?" Molina asked.

"Wish I didn't need Just for Men now," Alch said.

"As if you'd use any subterfuge for anything," Molina chided. "Distinguished gray works. Trust me."

Molina eyed Temple.

"I need to update my Web site photo," Temple volunteered.

"Why? You wouldn't look any older or wiser."

Temple made a disrespectful Zoe Chloe Ozone face.

"You've got that teen persona down," Molina conceded.

She laid out another glossy sheet.

"The tiger girls aren't banishing rats from the house?" Temple asked as she recoiled from the gleaming visage of Crawford Buchanan.

"Nice shot." Molina leaned back to study him. "You've known him for as long as you've been in Vegas?"

"It seems like aeons longer than three years."

The photo was truly as oily as Buchanan was, taken at that old "Hollywood slant" so his stringy neck was hidden and his jaw looked stronger, his smile pasted-on phony, and his hair a monument to trendy-until-two-hours-ago male vanity.

"I believe you call him 'Awful Crawford,' " Molina said. "You're not very subtle in your dislikes and likes, are you?"

"No, I'm up front and honest," Temple said. "What's it to you?"

"It may be a very lot."

Temple felt her flippant, defensive gaze caught in the searchlight of Molina's electric-blue concentrated stare and found herself saying . . .

"He's sexist and sleazy, and everywhere I've gone there's always been one guy like him trying to do me dirt."

Molina nodded, her lips taut but smiling satisfaction.

"Snitch," Alch said, dismissing the photo and Buchanan. "That's what this guy strikes me as — sneaky, lying snitch."

Molina tossed down another image.

Rafi Nadir. Her ex-lover, father of Mariah, long ago abandoned, or fled from, in L.A.

"I like Rafi," Temple said.

Molina's head reared back in surprise.

Temple smiled to herself to have shaken the cool authority figure this woman had created as much as the hot jazz singer Carmen. Talk about bipolar! Then again, "woman cop" had been an impossibility in her mother's generation.

"He seems okay," Alch conceded. "Still has a chip on his shoulder."

"Still has a daughter who doesn't know who he is," Temple told Alch.

Alch nodded. "Fathers and daughters. It's a . . . special relationship."

"Will you two shut up?" Molina had lost her cool control. "I asked you here because I want your memory banks and your objective considered opinion. If I'd wanted personal snipers, I'd have asked . . . some-one else."

"Asked?" Temple asked Alch.

"It's her way," he told Temple. "Guys wouldn't listen if she wasn't emphatic; then they called her a . . . you know."

"I've been called uppity," Temple admitted.

"Funny. You don't look black."

"Same biased principle."

"Shut up!" Molina bellowed. "You two aren't listening to me as much as any sexist pig."

"Do you mean 'pig' in the sense of an unattractive female?" Temple began.

"Or a cop?" Alch finished.

In answer, Molina slapped down the next and apparently last head shot.

"Dirty Larry all cleaned up," Temple said in surprise.

The guy had what used to be called a crew cut, his skull shape exposed under a blond-ish mowed lawn, and such a beard-free shaved jaw it would have appeared naked on HDTV, which was saying something. His gaze and features were clear and sharp. He looked like the class valedictorian.

"He must be a terrific actor," Temple said. "He totally owns the Dirty Larry persona now."

"He's a cop," Molina said, eyeing the photo with an odd, almost rueful distance. "Under cover, but a cop. Probably a good one once."

She shook off her mood and gestured to all the mug shots.

"These are the five people who were here, besides me, the evening I discovered Mariah had run off. These are the people who were here when we found, and didn't find" — she eyed Alch — "the mutilated Barbie doll in Mariah's bedroom. I've ruled out you two as having anything to do with the . . . manipulations that night. I want you to remember everything, every detail your naturally observant brains saw but didn't process in the one, wacky way that would explain . . . everything. I'm convinced we three know something we don't put much importance on, but it's the key to why this house, and perhaps me and Mariah, have been targets the past few weeks.

"I want you to put your thinking caps on, study the photos and sit here until they light up and you proclaim, 'Bingo! Eureka! Jimmy Choo-choos!' — or whatever rings your bells."

"Jimmy Choo shoes," Temple corrected.

Molina stared at her.

"They call them Jimmy Choo *shoes.*

Details are important to get right, lieutenant. I believe that's what you're telling us. I will bet you a pair of Stuart Weitzman flats for Louboutin platform heels that we will crack this conundrum in an hour flat."

"And I want a beer," Alch added. "A bottle of Tutankhamun Ale, available for a king's ransom."

"Dream on," Molina said. "I can offer you both a cold Dos Equis after the job's done." She scanned the rogue's list of suspects. "One of these people had to have left the Barbie doll in Mariah's bedroom that evening. It had to be an inside job."

"You're missing someone you didn't even think of." Temple leaned back with a smug expression.

"Who?"

"You."

"Like I'm going to . . ." Molina unbent from leaning over the photos. "You're right," she told her captive guests. "Everyone should be accounted for. Back in a minute."

Molina did a rapid soft-shoe back down the hall, which startled Temple. On the job, Molina walked with an emphatic low-heeled-boot stomp.

"You can be annoying," Alch said, with a sigh. "Carmen's been seriously aggravated enough by personal matters lately. I wouldn't push it."

Temple just shrugged. She saw where Molina was going. "She's set up this game of real-life Clue, detective. We need every piece in place to play it."

"Does anyone even play board games anymore?"

"On computers."

By then Molina had returned with one last printed-out eight-by-ten.

Molina threw the last "card" down on the table, her own straightforward police ID mug shot, her expression dead serious because a woman had to mean business 24/7 in a man's world.

That reminded Temple why she so enjoyed working in a liberal-arts area, with words, where being small and smart and female was not a triple handicap. She had to wonder how much Molina's height — whether you considered it mannish or high-fashion-model tall — had helped her career.

Temple had seen archives on the first women in police work a couple decades back. They tended to be petite, entry-level officers with ultrafeminine hair, makeup, and nails, who made cop wives uneasy. Had they been law-enforcement groupies, or had they just not known *not* to use feminine wiles? Not Molina's problem!

"What do we do now?" Alch asked in the lengthening silence as Molina studied the row of faces.

" 'Try to remember . . .' " Temple sang from the sentimental song.

"That kind of September . . .' " Molina dropped the singing voice and finished, "is months off."

" 'September Song' is my theme nowadays," Alch said, and leaned forward to contemplate each black-and-white face. "You must have forgotten you could put the HP printer on color, Carmen," he told Molina, "but the starker likenesses will probably shake up our memories more. This feels like a film-noir showdown, only all our suspects are mute."

"Yeah," Temple said, sitting up, refreshed and alert. "They can't talk back, confuse the issue, or issue lies and alibis. Okay. You two were here when I dragged in Crawford Buchanan, per my instructions."

"We need to go back to before you arrived, hard as that may be for Miss Zoe Chloe Ozone's ego to take." Molina snatched up a photo and waved it. "Dirty Larry Podesta was also here when you arrived. Do you remember seeing him?"

Temple nodded. "I remember thinking I

couldn't decide if he grew up as military brat or a plain street punk."

Alch chuckled.

Molina glowered.

"Carmen," Alch said, "I never figured why you were letting that insubordinate loner hang around."

"I needed someone to do what you've been doing for me lately, Morrie."

Temple sat forward, all ears and eager hopes. Just *what* had Dirty Larry and Morrie Alch been doing for Molina lately? If only it was something juicy that proved the hard-boiled homicide dick had female hormones.

Nothing further was said. The next photo Molina had snatched up was . . . Awful Crawford's.

"You arrived with this piece of . . . garbanzo beans," she told Temple, "and I needed to do a private interrogation on him, so I dragged him down to Mariah's room, sat him in front of the computer, and showed him his questionable lecherous kiddo-performing site, which Detective Alch had found on Mariah's 'Favorites' list."

"Wait a minute," Temple said. "Could Awful Crawford have planted the Barbie doll during your bedroom interrogation? Wow, that sounds as sleazy as he is."

Luckily, Molina had found Temple's idea

arresting and ignored her editorial comments.

"Mariah's room is the usual ten by eleven and piled with girlie mess," Temple went on, "with clothes and school materials and makeup and stuffed toys and posters. It'd be easy to sneak one more item in."

"I'd smacked him down right in front of the computer," Molina said.

"Precisely." Temple stood to make her case, like a prosecuting attorney, pacing on the couch side of the coffee table, while Molina paced on the outside.

"You'd never seen Crawford's teen-star promotion site before. Never knew that Mariah had posted photos of herself online — glamour photos, or attempts. That she yearned for a kid-star future. Were your eyes on Crawford, or the screen?"

"You're saying that little weasel could have pulled a mutilated Barbie doll from his suitcoat armpit and tossed it onto one of Mariah's girlie nests without my noticing?"

Alch put in a suggestion. "You were major upset, Carmen, and not in top condition from that long slash wound and always hiding that you'd been wounded. Buchanan is a born sneak. I know *I* didn't see it where it was found an hour later."

Molina corralled her nervous energy and

stood her ground.

"And you're telling me, Morrie, you weren't distracted from guarding my back at work and at home for weeks, supervising Mariah morning, noon, and night so she didn't suspect I had anything more than the flu?"

"Whew," Temple said. "Way too old married couple fighting, for my sanity. I get you two were working under a lot of strain. And, remember, Mariah, being a teen, could have not cared less about your comings and goings. She was plotting a star-making career and totally involved in her own secrets."

"What about Crawford Buchanan?" Molina asked her. "Could *he* be the Barbie Doll Killer? Two of the victims were in Vegas, and it looks from the other Southwestern murders that the killer has circled back here. Could Buchanan be the killer and right under our noses?"

Temple had to sit down to contemplate the big picture. She stared at the photo-studio head shot of the guy who'd intruded on her new career in Vegas from the first. He'd been smarmy and sexist, but that was hardly unheard of, or a crime. He'd crashed her women in media meetings, demanding they "integrate." Cookies with Crawford. Corny but also . . . contemptible.

She started thinking aloud. "He's always had this downtrodden girlfriend."

"Abusive?" Alch asked.

"His whole personality is an affront to women. One of those sleazy, lechy guys who won't shut up and be politically correct. Who need to challenge civility. And the way he encouraged his girlfriend's teen daughter to take on questionable 'modeling' jobs, like being ring girl at prize fights and playing up her sexuality to get attention . . . Then we discovered that he had a site devoted to luring girls into 'auditioning' for all these reality-TV shows that exploit them."

Temple jumped up. "That's who the victims were — girls near malls wanting to audition for every singing, dancing, cat-fighting reality-TV show that comes along. Maybe Mister Entrepreneur wasn't getting his jollies running their so-called careers. Maybe he was . . . oh, my God . . . amassing victims!"

By now Temple's pacing had taken her behind the couch and into the kitchen and back out again.

"I've always, always hated and distrusted the guy, and he was always picking on me, but I never thought he could be really . . . dangerous."

Molina nodded slowly. "Such a loathsome

little worm. We think of serial killers as powerful because they seem to come out of nowhere and do so much damage. Yeah, we could all be underestimating Crawford Buchanan. That radio-DJ shtick allows him to go everywhere pretty young girls are, and Vegas is Casting Central for that type."

Alch and Temple nodded in concert.

"We'd stayed out here in the living room, out of your way, with Dirty Larry," Alch said. "Then you came down the hallway, propelling Buchanan ahead of you like a push broom once used by Typhoid Mary."

"You," Molina told him, "had searched Mariah's bedroom before that and never found the doll. I shook Buchanan free of all his contacts out here in the main rooms and sent him on his way. I doubt he could have done anything with me there, no matter how upset I was."

Temple almost jumped up and down with a new suggestion. She really "liked" Crawford for the Barbie Doll Stalker.

"Maybe he didn't leave," she said. "Someone could have snuck around the house side and opened the bedroom window to throw the Barbie doll in while we were all out here."

Alch eyed Molina. "This old house must have sash-style windows. Easy to break into.

You reinforce them?"

She shifted her weight uneasily. "Everybody knows this is a 'cop house.' The locals don't foul their own nest, and the neighboring gangs know to stay off their turf."

"That's good enough for break-ins," Alch said, "but for a stalker? Didn't those earlier incidents get your guard up?"

Molina's head shook so hard her hair shimmied. "That stalker made a point of getting in and out without leaving a trace of a break-in, like he had a key or was a —"

"Magician?" Temple asked. "That's why you thought it was Max. The seamless entry and exits."

"That and . . . some other reasons."

"What?" Temple wasn't about to let go of past motivations on a subject she'd always wondered about. "You thought he was after you because you were after him for that Goliath Hotel murder, right?"

"Right," Molina mumbled.

Molina never mumbled. Temple knew the woman was hiding something. Something embarrassing. Molina was never embarrassed.

"What exactly did that stalker in your house do?" Temple demanded.

"None of your business."

"Yes, it is. You made it mine when you

ordered me here to remember. How can I remember anything if I'm not fully informed? One wild idea leads to another that leads to a productive advance. Nothing happens in a vacuum."

"She has a point, Carmen." Alch folded his arms. He wasn't budging.

Molina pushed her short-nailed hands into the hair at her temples. "You two are worse than Mariah when she really, really wants something. Okay. I made a big mistake. I thought the incursions were aimed at me. They happened in my bedroom first."

"And naturally you thought that was Max," Temple said, pouncing.

"First, it was just my closet being rifled. Then one of my performance gowns seemed to be . . . new."

"You mean those wimpy pre–World War Two velvet numbers you wear to sing in?" Alch asked.

"I think he means 'skimpy' or 'slinky,' " Temple translated, wickedly.

"Alch means neither," Molina declared. "He means that bias-cut vintage silk velvet is so . . . thin and compact in a closet. And they are. The lot barely takes up a foot of rod space. And they're all dark colors, so I can't be sure to this day that the one that seemed new wasn't one I'd bought and forgotten about. It's not like I did the singing gig every day. Once or twice a month, tops."

Temple raised and waved her hands. "Wait another minute. You think a stalker went out and found just the right vintage dress to slip into your closet? Vintage shops have gone all eighties and nineties now. You can't find those really old thirties and forties treasures anymore. Trust me, I look. Who are we talking here being the Good Fairy of your closet, Bob Mackie? Send him over to the Circle Ritz. He can stalk my clothes rack anytime."

"This is not about me or my wardrobe." Molina's voice was edging into bellow again.

"It is," Alch said. "You've been doing some mighty crooked thinking a lot longer than I thought."

"Okay. The stalker seemed very adult and focused on me," Molina said between her teeth, loss of control seeming a syllable away.

"Because it was sexual, you assumed it was Max?" Temple wouldn't let go. "What do you think you've got, girlwise — which I've been using all my life while you've kept it in cold storage for years, like a fur in Las Vegas — that would attract Max or any other man in that way?"

"I have been way off base for a long time, on everything. All right?" Molina's cheeks flushed a dusky burgundy. She truly did look beautiful when she was mad. "I've been a bad cop, and I've been a bad mother."

Alch shook his head. "Not for lack of trying to be great in every venue."

"The point is," Molina said very slowly, "the last . . . sign of the stalker was the most deviant. Rose petals through the house and down the hall. A radio playing. Not in my bedroom. Mariah's."

"And *that*'s," Temple said, "when you first thought your suspicions of Max might be wrong."

"On the stalking charge. Not on the Goliath murder, and not on deceiving you."

Temple rolled her eyes and swallowed the B word. "At least you don't have his photo on your suspects table."

"He has a cast-clad alibi. What I want to know, and you two are here to help with, is *who doesn't?*"

Temple and Alch sighed in tandem, exchanged glances, and began again. They would almost make a vaudeville act, Alch and Barr. No. Barr and Alch.

"Why don't you move the photos around for where the people were?" Alch said. "So Buchanan is outta here, but maybe not off the exterior premises. Dirty Larry is still on the couch. Does that guy ever sit up straight?"

"Drug dealers don't," Molina said. "You have to realize D. L.'s undercover persona has become second nature. He's not such a bad guy, just a good cop with too many years on a rugged beat."

"He showed up out of nowhere, to hear Detective Alch tell it," Temple pointed out. "Could he have been your stalker? He did act kind of boyfriend-y during Mariah's reality-TV stint."

"I let him act 'kind of boyfriend-y.' " Molina looked at Alch, not Temple. "Frankly, I was using him to check up on my ex, and on y*our* ex." This time she eyed Temple. "Just an all-round handyman."

"Kinda cold, Carmen," Alch said.

"He's a kinda cold guy, Morrie. Cold nerve is what keeps you alive in undercover. I don't know what he wanted from me. I'm not as naive or" — she eyed Temple — "as self-deluded as you two think. He wanted something I don't think he got."

"Yet . . ." Alch pronounced, slumping Dirty-Larry-deep in the upholstery.

Ooh, Temple thought, *ye olde faithful guard dog is ready to bite someone.*

"So," Temple said, being the good PR

woman and discharging the edgy emotions around her, "the lovely and enterprising Crawford Buchanan is off the scene, perhaps to do dirt outside, perhaps not. He was in his Hummer H2 and on the cell phone when I came outside to leave."

"A Hummer H2?" Alch questioned with disgust.

"Orange," Temple added.

For a moment they all mused on whether the driver of an orange Hummer H2 could be a stalking slayer of young women.

Much too recognizable a vehicle.

A glum silence prevailed.

"Wait a minute!" Temple said.

Blue eyes and brown eyes regarded her with equal resignation.

"Dirty Larry *left* the main room." Temple took a deep breath. "He's always so low-key you automatically 'erase' his presence. That's his day and night undercover job. *Not* to be noticed."

She had their attention and went on.

"During all the sound and fury of Crawford Buchanan being given the bum's rush out, I think Dirty Larry got up and faded . . . down the hall to Mariah's room."

"Can you swear to that?" Alch asked.

"Can you swear you saw a ghost? You were sitting on the couch," Temple told Alch, "and Molina joined you after Buchanan was escorted out. So. Where was Dirty Larry?"

Alch jumped up. "That's true. I try not to see the jerk, he's so annoying. He's got that act down good."

"Why would Larry do it?" Molina asked.

"Mine is not to reason why," Temple quoted an old nineteenth-century military poem. "Mine is to say there's something rotten in the cast of characters on your coffee table, lieutenant."

In the ensuing silence, the tiger-stripe girls came running through again. Barreling out from the kitchen, they touched down on the sofa back and seats then took off for points unseen.

Midnight Louie followed in semihot pursuit, slip-sliding across the coffee table and pushing off the photo of . . . Dirty Larry Podesta. Louie skidded to a stop on the slick surface, clawsout as four feet stapled it into the carpet.

Dirty Larry's photographed face slip-slid away, shredded like a horror movie monster's victim.

"Where did that cat come from?" Alch asked.

"Apparently," Temple said, "he hitched a ride with me and snuck into the house, maybe through an old, insecure sash window?

"Clearly," she added, "Midnight Louie 'likes' Dirty Larry for the dirty deed. Or deeds. Any objections?"

Molina had one. Or two.

"I told you to put your thinking cap on," she told Temple. "Not your 'thinking *cat*.' "

"We go together, like Mickey and Minnie, like oregano and olive oil, like spunky and funky."

"Okay, Zoe Chloe. We're done. Get the hell out, with your tiny red shoes and your big cat, too."

CHAPTER 28
HOME INVASION

Lieutenant C. R. Molina sat on her homely couch after everyone but her housecats had gone.

She'd cleared the decks, had Mariah safely away for the night, had rerun the night in question, and had ended up in an unpleasant place.

She wished she smoked. She wished she'd cultivated some vice besides generating an impressionable daughter for whom she felt she had to supply an impeccable model. Which Mariah's father certainly wasn't. Or was he?

She got up to fetch a beer from the fridge, listening to the two visiting vehicles depart outside as she leaned on the breakfast bar. Was the person who'd planted the Barbie doll on her premises Dirty Larry or Crawford Buchanan?

The next, almost laughable question? Was either one of them a serious Barbie Doll

Killer candidate? Molina pressed the beer bottle's cold glass against her forehead.

Larry made the more believable serial killer, yet she'd never gotten that vibe off of him. Lots of minor warning blips, but no serious suspicion. Was she slipping? Not a subject for debate. She *had* slipped.

A deep but easy breath told her the long and winding slash scar had finally settled in. Her own damn fault. All she'd learned from that insane B and E at the house on Mojave was that she and Max Kinsella might share the same enemy. Who?

Or . . . had Kinsella *wanted* someone to think that? Had his mentor, Gandolph, arranged for a watchdog as a diversion? Anything was possible.

A sharp pounding on her door made her heart jump. She put the beer down and got up to grab the GLOCK in her kitchen drawer. With Mariah out for the night, she hadn't needed to use the gun safe that was in her closet and was suddenly glad.

The police-invasion-level pounding resumed.

Molina stuck the firearm down the back of her beige denims and pushed her face against the door's peephole. Too dark.

"ID yourself," she shouted loud and hard.

"Carmen, it's me," came a male voice.

Not many would say that. Alch or Rafi. And this wasn't either voice.

She opened the door and stepped back.

Dirty Larry, looking particularly sullen, burst in . . .

. . . in the firm custody of Max Kinsella, the evident pounder.

"Who the hell are you?" Larry snarled at Kinsella.

"I don't know. If you put it existentially. Or aren't you feeling too existential now?"

What a bizarre nightmare! Mr. Light and Mr. Dark making a home-invasion duo with two faces.

"What's going on here?" she demanded as she swept all the coffee table photos into a pile, which she moved to a hall-table drawer.

Kinsella propelled D. L. to the sofa like she'd propelled Crawford Buchanan to the door a few nights before. She had to admire his total control, despite a forced, stiff-legged gait. It still served for a perp walk. She understood now why his pounding had been so urgent. He hadn't expected to maintain control of a pro like Dirty Larry for long.

"You have any idea," Kinsella asked, breathing hard after dumping D. L. on the couch, "how much time this bozo spends tailing *you?*" He paused for more breath and to smooth his hair with his fingers.

Dirty Larry wouldn't have been an easy takedown.

"That's what you're paid the big bucks to find out," she told him while regarding Larry, who was massaging his right shoulder and keeping his eyes down.

"What was Temple doing here?" Kinsella asked.

"Okay." She returned her weapon to the drawer, a gesture Kinsella saw, but not Larry. Molina shook her head. "Even without a memory, you're her self-appointed guardian angel. Now we know why you broke your cover and muscled Dirty Larry inside. Did I want this degree of disclosure? No."

"Look." Kinsella eyed her beer. "How about one of those? I've been getting as buggy and sweaty as Podesta eavesdropping on your big confab. You know this old house's windows are doors . . . and listening devices."

"Just another thing I was going to fix someday," she said. "Okay, I'm going to let you two duke it out in my living room to do what I seem to do best tonight — fetch beer."

She got two bottles from the fridge, put them on the breakfast bar, and returned to the living room.

Then she eyed the two men. Kinsella had collected the beers and was handing Dirty Larry Podesta one. Had she ever dreamed of such a day . . . ?

"There's no one here but us and the cats," she told them, "so . . . spill. Guts would be nice, but explanations will do for a start."

Dirty Larry cracked his shoulders and accepted the cold brew from Kinsella. Even Temple Barr could handle twist-off tops, so the opening ceremony offered no macho one-upmanship.

"I was just protecting you," Larry said, after his first long pull on the beer.

"From what?" she wondered.

"Yourself, maybe."

Molina eyed his angular face with the faint glint of gold beard growth and the slitted, defiant eyes. She remembered Temple Barr's comment: *grew up as a military brat or a plain street punk.*

"You had no reason to be lurking outside now, Larry."

"I came over, saw you had company. Figured you didn't want your underling and that Sally Field on K-9, er, Kat-9 patrol to know too much about me."

"And what would be 'too much' to know about you, Larry?" Molina braced an elbow

316

on one knee and her face on her hand. "That you transferred to traffic from undercover at your request, not your superiors'? That you weren't 'burned out' on drug casework? That even a distracted, concerned mother like me figured out you had some hidden reason for worming your way into my office, my confidence, my life?"

"You'd listen to a freaking cat? These old walls are Swiss cheese. I heard that black devil's owner saying that he 'liked' me."

Larry's burning blue gaze fixed on Kinsella's deceptively casual figure upholding the low wall between the kitchen and the living room. "You'd listen to this questionable guy even you pegged as a killer?"

"I agree he's questionable, Larry," she said, "but so are you."

She eyed Kinsella, not fooled. He'd braced his back to the wall, legs straight out. That's about all they'd do after the exterior tussle. He looked like he'd taken a stance far from the fray, but his injuries had forced it.

Molina sighed. She had a gimp and a cop with a lot of gray areas on her hands. Both were probably armed.

She resumed her interrogation of Dirty Larry. Kinsella had faced her with that prematurely, the bastard, and had forced her to conduct it in his presence. On the other hand, he wouldn't have been able to do that if she hadn't hired him to tail the man and if Larry hadn't been lurking.

Just like on the night Mariah had disappeared?

Tabitha and Caterina came tearing through the room again, rushing past Larry's back and making him duck.

"Just the thunder of little cat feet, Larry," she told him. "Nothing to be nervous about here but me. So. Did you plant that messed-up Barbie doll in my house?"

"God, no, Carmen. Sure, I sniffed around the place. I was trying to help. I've had a lot of experience with runaways. The drug beat is filled with them."

"That night you told me that Mariah wasn't a runaway. Not the type, you said. And you were wrong."

"Not really. She wasn't running away from home, or from you. She was running *to* something — that constant media and Internet hype that kids can be stars. Look at Justin Bieber, the pre-boy-band phenom, and the preteen wannabe Pussycat Dolls freaking out on alcohol and drugs and S-and-M fashion. I don't blame you for being a hard-ass about your kid. You're right."

Molina eyed Kinsella, drinking beer standing up.

He shrugged. "You want me to leave, since you two are so in tune on the horrible state of teendom nowadays? Not my field."

"I want you to shut up and sit down." Molina saw his eyes flare with defiance. Max Kinsella didn't *need* to sit down, not him. "Sit," she spat out.

She jerked her head at the breakfast bar with its high, hard stools. He could manage that better than a mushy upholstered chair, and she sure didn't want him on the sofa with Podesta. This smelled of her first, horrific days of seniority on the force, when every guy "under" her needed to prove a point. To prove his superior force and masculinity.

"Larry," she said. "I don't see any reason why you'd want to hurt my child or my career."

"Swear to God, Carmen." His voice was hoarse with emotion. "Never. I have the greatest respect for you as an officer and a detective. You have always laid it on the line for the job. Never a gender thing with me. I wouldn't be here if I didn't think you had the drive and the stones to catch the Barbie Doll Killer. Me, I just put away scum who kill people slowly with drugs. You take down murderers."

The sound of two hands clapping, slowly,

ended the *Law & Order* moment.

Max Kinsella, of course, ever the cynic, even without a functional memory.

"I believe you, Larry. Every word," she said.

And she did.

"Get along now. It's been a long, nasty night. I'll set Kinsella straight."

Behind Podesta's back, Kinsella toasted with his beer bottle and a crooked grin. No one could have "straighter" legs than he did.

Dirty Larry fidgeted on the couch, rubbing his neck and alternating with slugs of beer to finish the bottle. Molina understood his reluctance to leave the scene to this iffy newcomer at the breakfast bar. She had to swallow a grin. Setting up these guys against each other was the smartest move she'd made lately.

Dirty Larry finally stood and heel-dragged out of the house as if his dingy Reebok sneakers sported steel cleats. He'd been so sure he'd had her confused, wounded, and alone, like a stray dog, so he could play the hero.

Only after the front door had slammed shut did Kinsella move.

First he held the beer bottle to his forehead. She could get that.

Then he finally rested his rear on the stool

she'd sent him to. The only thing missing was the corner and the fool's cap.

"He's a low-life wrangler and a midnight tangler," Kinsella said. "You choose your stalking horses well."

She lifted an eyebrow with her Dos Equis bottle. "What's the difference between a 'stalking horse' and a 'cat's-paw'?"

"A horse has steel hooves. A cat has a steel ego, assuming you're referring to Miss Temple's Midnight Louie."

"Why'd you force the issue with Dirty Larry? Bring him in?"

"Because my legs were getting damned tired of following him around shadowing you. You knew when you asked me to watch him he was up to something."

"I asked you to watch Rafi Nadir, too."

"Not to knock your taste in men then and now, but Nadir is truly not as interesting as Dirty Larry. In a criminal sense."

"You think Podesta is criminal?"

"No more so than this Crawford Buchanan character I heard you talking about."

"And you're going on . . . what? With legs that threaten to capsize you and a memory made of cheesecloth?"

"Instinct. That's why I'm still here, and why you still want me." He made a deprecatory gesture before she could jump on his phrasing. "Alch won't cut it anymore. You need someone more ruthless, without a life and a career to ruin. Your conscience wouldn't allow that. Enter *moi,* just in time. We didn't get along, did we?"

Molina couldn't stop a low, confirming chuckle. "An understatement."

"You made a mistake about me, yes? So now you need *me* to vet and uncover your current mistakes."

"Simple job. I wanted a discreet report on a couple guys normally not objects of professional police interest. I may have a personnel problem, but you've got personal problems, too."

"There's nothing personal in my life, or my memory. Except . . . Garry Randolph."

"Are you sure? I bet you're finding that you like Temple Barr a lot more than you thought you would."

"That's odd about what I remember. I do recall my druthers."

"And?"

"Not my type."

"What is?"

His smile was reminiscent. "I'll know it when I see it."

"You already did," Molina surmised. "Men. God, you're like Stephen Hawking, committing infidelity from a wheelchair."

"As I understand it from the lady in question, and her very-present fiancé, I was and am free to commit whatsoever I choose with anyone of my choice."

"I'm sure women the world over rejoice. Back on topic, why the hell did you out Dirty Larry? I just wanted him followed, not confronted. You put him on notice."

"When a guy is Johnny-on-the-spot for a murder scene one night and skulking outside the investigating officer's the next, he *should* be put on notice. That's when mistakes get made. Also, I overheard the byplay about your underage daughter. I get why you went supernova when she disappeared. You want me to investigate that Crawford creep, too? If Temple loathes him, he must be scummy."

"You're doing too much as it is." She collected the empty bottle from his hand and weighed it to match her mental processes.

Max Kinsella waited.

"Anything else you want me to tell you?" she asked finally.

"Anything and everything about Larry Podesta, from the moment he showed up, and your stalker, and the Barbie doll killings."

"That's very restricted personal and professional territory." She dropped her hand with the beer bottle, moving from hostess to challenger.

"That's the beauty of it. I have no restrictions. I've got a totally fresh outlook on the facts. I'm not emotionally attached to anyone involved, and I find the whole sequence of events I've heard so far seriously troublesome."

Molina considered. "I suppose you'd take another beer. I can't interest you in a cushy chair?"

"Beer is fine, but I need to stay as close to vertical as I can be these days."

"Most pricks do," she tossed behind her back as she went for the fridge, walking straight into and out through the probably unintended implication.

She slammed two fresh beer bottles on the breakfast countertop and took an opposing stool.

"What did I ever do," he asked, "to make you an enemy?"

"Left town before I could interrogate you."

"Interrogate me." He opened his hands to prove he had nothing to hide.

"Too late. I guess I'll have to let you interrogate *me*."

"Okay. Dirty Larry. I already know you never trusted him. As you don't trust me now that I'm playing the same role for you

324

— undercover investigator. The only man you really trust is Detective Alch."

"True enough. As you only trusted Garry Randolph."

"After what he did for me through the years, just the past two months of *this* year . . ."

Molina turned the now-damp beer bottle in her hands. Her palms had already been wet with career memories. Losses. Cops would die for each other, but civilians weren't obliged to. She wished she'd met "Gandolph the Great." Her sympathy for Kinsella's unfading grief at losing him made her respect both men.

Temple Barr had believed to that terrier-tough core of hers that Max Kinsella was a "good guy." Still to be proven to Molina. And now she was about to do what she'd never done with Dirty Larry. Tell Kinsella her secrets. Admit that she'd been so obsessed with him as a cop she'd believed he could be obsessed with her as a woman. As Mariah would moan in her melodramatic teen way, "*Tres* embarrassing, *mo-ther!*"

"All the chalk has been wiped away," Kinsella said to get her started. "It's that old cliché, a fresh slate. Maybe now I am the murderer you always thought I was, by default."

"Quit whining. That was never in your jacket. Randolph's shooting was the universe's fault. We've all screwed up. Whatever was wrong about my assumptions these past two years, about you or Temple Barr or Dirty Larry or my stalker or my daughter — or my ex — is my fault. My watch."

"Okay." She saw her hands — large, strong, plain — clutching the thick bottom of the beer bottle. "I decided to 'use' Dirty Larry as an off-the-books investigator because I couldn't find you. I knew Temple was seeing you regularly, that you were out there. When Larry did it, when he tracked you to your hidey-hole, your house on Mojave, it happened to be just after your Phantom Mage persona had crashed and burned at the Neon Nightmare club. Randolph must have been an even better magician than you."

Max just nodded. She had to credit him with being a good listener.

"Getting you out of the Neon Nightmare wall-banging scene as a DOA, and then, presto, you never got to a hospital on the other end — I didn't believe it. But I didn't know about that incident when Podesta followed you home from a rendezvous with Barr and got an actual, genuine street address for you."

"What did you do with it?"

"I didn't trust anybody. I went over myself."

"The house is equipped with embassy-level security," he said. "It almost managed to spit me out when I returned.

"I had to do a B and E."

"Illegal."

"Naturally."

Kinsella lifted his beer bottle. "I like your style. Hard on a police career, though."

"Even harder on me was the stalker inside."

"Already there?"

"Maybe. The biggest butcher knife was missing from the kitchen block when I went through the back. One of those now-you-see-it, later you-really-"see"-it, bite-you-back situations."

A rueful grimace. "I hate it when your instincts are ahead of your brain."

"I heard someone else there not much later and ducked into the hall closet."

"Not the greatest cover. Shallow. Louvered wooden doors like toothpicks. Not much in there, but not much protection either."

"I didn't know the house. Then I . . . heard what I later knew to be the sound of a knife shredding someone's wardrobe.

Yours. It sounded like a big cat on a rampage."

"Very *Psycho.*"

"Exactly. That's when I knew I had to get out of that closet. I heard someone coming, tried to surprise the intruder by banging through the flimsy louvered folding doors."

"You had a weapon."

"GLOCK. Of course. But I didn't want to use it randomly. I fended off the perp with my right forearm, but the knife was already sweeping down in the darkness."

"Ouch," he said. "If it was a Norman Bates–type attack . . ."

"No. Slashing, not stabbing. And I was a moving target. The cutting edge did a bouncing glissando on my ribs, left a blood trail, but didn't damage any critical organs."

"All pain and no glory."

"You got that right."

"So there you are, in the dark, bleeding, hurting, armed, and alone."

"Don't I wish."

"You saw the attacker?"

"You tell me. I figured my attacker was gone, got myself to the living room, and discovered someone was still in the house with me."

"Not the attacker?"

"So he claimed when he explained himself."

"At the barrel of a GLOCK?"

"And in the light of a lamp."

"First lamp in the main room off the hall?"

She nodded.

"Dirty Larry." He said the name thoughtfully.

She nodded.

Max Kinsella whistled softly, but waited.

"Larry said he'd been watching the house and came in after me."

"So might the attacker have done."

"Right."

"Or the attacker might have been lying in wait, quietly, until you were fully committed to . . . housebreaking. In a vulnerable position."

"Right."

"Anybody admit to seeing the attacker leave?"

"Larry, you mean? No. I was bleeding a lot. He had to get me out of there."

"How'd he explain being there?"

"He thought I'd stood him up."

"You were on dating terms?" The slight-disbelieving tone in Kinsella's voice was either flattering or insulting.

"I'd used Dirty Larry to find your address and then didn't invite him to the B-and-E party. He figured something was up and followed me. Ironic, huh?

"Oh, better than that, lieutenant." Kinsella actually grinned as he considered the Vegas police version of "Spy vs. Spy." "Maybe that's how my wardrobe ended up shredded on the closet floor. It looked expensive."

"It certainly looked like someone hated your guts, and your Guccis."

"I must have made a lot of money on the Strip. I notice I have expensive tastes."

She shook her head. "So you're rich. Big sin. Can you access any of that wealth?"

"Haven't tried yet. Don't remember where, actually. Wanna help?"

"Your tough luck."

"You wouldn't have to pay me anymore. Have you done any digging into Podesta's background?"

"His record's with us. He worked in Flagstaff earlier."

"I mean, where he and his people came from, family, and school — all that jazz?"

"No. I suspected he had some self-serving scheme going, but nothing truly shady. His file jacket here as a narc is impeccable."

"His recent behavior sure isn't. Cops aren't immune from over-controlling women. Maybe he wanted you freaked about danger to your kid and depending on him."

"But I didn't."

"Who did you depend on during that challenging time when your daughter was missing? What? You look like I'd handed you a pickle for a Havana cigar."

"*Ugh.* What a distasteful figure of speech either way."

"So who?"

Molina made another pickle-smoking face. "My ex, Rafi. And . . . a crazy teen alter ego of your Miss Temple Barr called Zoe Chloe Ozone."

"She's nobody's Miss Temple Barr but her own. 'Zoe Chloe Ozone'? That sounds rather . . . disturbing."

"It is. Check the Web. I guess ZCO caught some buzz. Anyway, we caught up with Mariah and her little dancing friend. There'd already been another Barbie doll killing at a mall audition out of state. The captain wanted all of us under cover at the dancing competition, which was being sabotaged. Larry was among the security and police forces there."

"And the Barbie Doll Killer wasn't behind anything, or caught?"

"No. Actually, the saboteur was after Matt Devine."

"Why would anybody be after an ex-priest radio counselor?" When he saw she wasn't talking about the case, he added, "I suppose no public personality is safe these days. Mister Midnight or Zoe Chloe Ozone. Well."

Kinsella put his finished beer bottle on the countertop as if planting a flagpole. Firm and targeted. "It'll be harder to shadow Podesta now, but I'll manage. I'll also look into the deepest and darkest corners of his past. You?"

"Larry's games are just a distraction. I'm going over all the Barbie Doll Killer incidents, lethal and just creepy, until I squeeze a viable suspect out of those files. There's got to be a loose end somewhere."

Kinsella stood, wincing. "You're surrounded by loose ends, including me."

She watched his stride stretch out after the long time sitting, as he moved to the front door. He was walking pretty damn well for two months off two broken legs. She needed to keep in mind that magicians were often athletes.

Once he'd left, she allowed herself to remember their one set-to, when she'd tried to subdue and cuff him. He'd been frantic to get to Temple, rightfully worried, it turned out.

But while Temple was waltzing with the Stripper Killer and a can of pepper spray in another local strip-club parking lot, she and Kinsella had been tangoing in closest quarters with matched skill and strength at Baby Doll's.

Recently, forced to watch *Dancing With the Celebs* with Mariah and Temple/Zoe, seeing the five competing couples do the tango, including Matt Devine with unsuspected macho fire, she'd felt her face heating with memory.

To break her hold and concentration, Kinsella had begun taunting her about her Iron Maiden nickname. She'd recognized a ruse to distract and anger her, but for just a furious moment, she'd thought, *I could show you a thing or two, you bastard, just like I showed all the sexists on the force. I could heat you up and then shut you down so fast your brain cells would go nova, if I wanted to.*

Luckily, his desperation to get away had ultimately ended that old Argentinean tango she/he impasse. He'd folded, let her take him down, hard, cuff him, and haul him into her Crown Vic while they headed for the other strip club. Only he'd slipped the cuffs off like Houdini and left *her* cuffed to the steering wheel. He got to the other club first, but Temple was already safe.

Loose ends, Molina thought, smiling as she locked the door after him.

Max Kinsella was completely up for grabs now, and he didn't remember how he'd tried to seduce her in the heat of battle. She still might like to show him something, after this case and its other loose ends were dead and buried. She had the mental advantage now, although they both had been through the wars. She had a memory.

With Mariah out for the night, she had the bathroom to herself for once. She headed down the hall, now glad that Dirty Larry had been outed. Progress on the case.

She needed, and could get in blessed peace, a muscle-relaxing, pulsing shower. *Umm,* too *Psycho.* Why not a long, luxurious soak, courtesy of Mariah's perfumed Hello Kitty bubble-bath set?

Even Iron Maidens had the occasional day, or night, off. And Mama had a lot of eligible men worrying her mind, some of them even deliciously dangerous.

CHAPTER 29
BIG PUSSYCATS HAVE SHARP EARS

Mr. Max Kinsella is not the only expert "tail" in the shamus business.

Everyone assumed that I would meekly follow my Miss Temple out of chez Molina and go home of a night.

Hah!

The night was my basinet and is now my beat and my business.

Some people barhop. I carhop. Not as in serving fast food to anybody but myself. I am a high-level low-ender. With my natural coat of cat-burglar black, I can enter pretty much any vehicle on the planet. Not to brag. So I got there with Miss Temple but I felt no obligation to leave with her, even if she "brung" me, loathsome expression.

I had a quiet corner chat with the hiss-and-run combo of Caterina and Tabitha and arranged the artful chase that allowed me to literally point out that Dirty Larry has been skulking around crime scenes far too long for anyone's good.

Some private dicks would dust off their trench coats and say, "My work here is done."

Not Midnight Louie. Have coat, will travel. Or stay put. I got these feelings that put more than my neck hairs on parade salute. Tonight my hunches raised my hackles all the way down my spine to the end of my second-most-valuable member.

So I hunkered down during the farewells to settle into a quiet evening with Miss Lieutenant C. R. Molina and her two somewhat dim-witted rescue girls.

Not everybody can be the brains of the operation, and I do employ freelance assistants at Midnight Investigations, Inc., when necessary.

So not only did I get the chance to alert my Miss Temple and associates to the suspicious lurking behavior I have long observed in Dirty Larry — not that lurking is suspicious when I do it — but I got to see and hear Mr. Max Kinsella come along after my revelation and give the same warning, if at more tedious length. I am always short and to the point. I was born that way.

Moreover, I did not alert Larry to anyone's being on guard about him, as Miss Lieutenant certainly chewed out Mr. Max for doing.

Plus, I overheard lots of juicy back-and-forth

that would have had my Miss Temple salivating, could I but convey long narratives to her.

Let us just say I have more insights on all sorts of actions and reactions among the human sort. One cannot underestimate the usefulness of on-scene snoopery.

Miss Midnight Louise will be so burned up about what she missed.

CHAPTER 30
BOYS' NIGHT OUT

"I'm not sure if it's a good idea to get to know each other," Max Kinsella's strong, familiar voice told Matt over the phone the next day, "but since I'm not sure of much of anything, including my past, I'll have to take Temple's word on it. And yours. You're the professional shrink."

"Not a shrink. A counselor, and I think it's best we meet on neutral ground."

"Not your place or my place, then?"

"No." Matt couldn't stomach seeing Max back at the Circle Ritz. And although Kinsella's residence might reveal things the man himself wouldn't say, Matt wasn't curious enough, or stupid enough, to venture onto his territory.

"The Crystal Phoenix?" Max suggested.

Matt mentally rejected that idea. Too much 'Temple" all over that place. He got a wicked idea, and it was out of his mouth before he could weigh it.

"How about a jazz club called the Blue Dahlia? The background music keeps conversations private without being strident."

"What an intriguing name," Kinsella said. "Let's try it. Have I ever been there?"

"Not that I know of."

"But you have?"

"A couple times. My WCOO producer took me out for a nightcap there. Actually, early this morning."

"Male or female?"

"She also has her own syndicated show under the name *Ambrosia.*"

"Ah, the after-dark Siren of Sympathy and Schmaltz."

"She helps a lot of people. You've heard her, so you must remember that?"

"You must remember this: I only remember trivial things from years ago and only a couple weeks in Europe from before I came back to Vegas. The house I . . . inherited here . . . is . . . empty."

Matt held a pause that would be far too much "empty" airtime.

Of course, Matt thought. The man who'd owned that house and to whom Max owed so much was dead now. Kinsella must have been checking out *The Midnight Hour* and caught Ambrosia's show, too.

"I'm sorry for your loss," Matt said. "And

Ambrosia, she's less siren than sister," he added, "to everybody."

Now Kinsella kept quiet for too long.

"Yeah," he said finally. "It's easy to be cynical if you haven't suffered. I hope they serve cool drinks at the Blue Dahlia, along with the hot jazz."

"Of course."

"It's six now. How about dinner at eight?"

Matt had his marching orders, as he imagined Kinsella did, so the connection was broken with mutual but gruff, "All right"s.

Except nothing was "all right," Matt thought as he pocketed his cell phone.

And it was getting wronger by the minute. He'd checked his latest messages and recognized the several megs of a pictorial porn solicitation from RazorGrrl666@hitmail .com and deleted it. Again. He'd have to figure out how to block it. He wasn't ready to declare that Kitty the Cutter was on his trail again, until he had better proof.

Maybe the Blue Dahlia wasn't the best rendezvous site. Temple had mentioned that Max was drinking hard the night he came back, but he'd just run out on that homicidal mess in Belfast. He'd had his reasons.

Matt had some reasons, too.

What rotten timing that his talk-show career was going stratospheric just as Kinsella made his dramatic return. Max had pried Temple loose of Minneapolis and her family to follow him to Vegas. Did Matt have the moxie to pull Temple away from her new Vegas home to follow her man? Did he want to? He now had family "issues" in Chicago, and any new life for him and Temple — and Midnight Louie — would have to deal face-to-face with that mess.

That couldn't be as bad as dealing face-to-face with the new Max. Tough for him, but really rough on Temple and her sympathetic soul. Matt had to forget his insecurities and do what was best for Temple.

First things first.

Matt agreed with Temple that all three needed to discuss their interlocking pasts and possible mutual enemies, and that he and Max needed to meet before she became involved.

Still, they hadn't discussed bringing Molina into the case. Molina'd had a lot of family business on her mind and had stopped performing under cover as Carmen, the Blue Dahlia's come-and-go torch singer.

Temple would be the first to swear that Matt didn't have a mean bone in his body, but he felt a distinctly wicked tingle in his funny bone right now.

What if Molina showed up at the Blue Dahlia to sing for some insanely remote reason and saw her most elusive suspect sitting in the audience?

Now that would be a psychologically satisfying confrontation to mediate.

Matt pulled the Jag into the Blue Dahlia parking lot two hours later, wondering if a law-enforcement pro like Molina remembered, every time she arrived, the dead body found near her car here, many months ago. The words *She left* had even been painted on her Volvo. No wonder "Carmen" hadn't been on the Blue Dahlia menu lately. Now Molina had "left."

So she probably remembered, but with less of the sudden sadness that Matt felt. That killer had been caught. Her job was done on that case. Or maybe not.

He checked the parking lot for a car Kinsella might have driven, but spotted nothing in the Mystifying Max's trademark black. Matt turned to punch the lock button and jumped, less at the sharp bleep the device made than at the voice so close behind him.

"Look who won the lottery."

He turned to find Max looming, looking gaunter and therefore even taller than his six-four.

"How'd you recognize me if you don't remember me?" Matt asked.

"WCOO Web site. You're all over it. Ambrosia, on the other hand, is just an exotic set of dark eyes, close-up."

"Radio personalities are usually camera-shy."

"That's usually because they've had a lifetime of designing their personalities to be heard, not seen. You're not that type."

"You can tell?"

"I'm not *that* good. I was told you were an ex-priest."

"By Temple?"

"By Garry Randolph."

"I'm sorry I didn't know him," Matt said, walking toward the club entrance. "Temple said he was a great guy, and your mentor."

"Yes, and yes."

They were inside, where Max was sizing up the place like a gunfighter picking the best back-to-the-wall seat. The Blue Dahlia wasn't a family draw. Its small tables held mostly couples, or foursomes of friends, all fairly mature.

The hostess in Max-black from her flats to her leggings to her short dress and the matching menu cover eyed the room.

"The corner table all right, gentlemen?

343

You look more like talkers than listeners."

The spot she led them to was perfect, isolated on the side wall, with a 180-degree view of the musicians' small riser and the tiny dance floor in front of it.

"We *are* here to discuss business?" Matt commented as they followed the hostess to the setup.

"You've been here before, haven't you, sir?" she asked Matt as both men took room-facing chairs, putting each other at right angles.

Matt was surprised. The hostess had already gone home by the time he and Ambrosia had hit the joint in the wee hours of today.

"It's been a while," Matt said, referring to an earlier prime-time visit. "You have a remarkable memory," he added with a smile. She was old enough, in her fifties despite the youthful dress, to appreciate that compliment. And she reminded him of his mother.

A brooding silence at his right made Matt realize he'd just uttered a dirty word — *memory.*

The hostess smiled wide enough to be on a tooth-bleaching commercial. "Oh, there's a reason I remember you. I also saw you recently on *Dancing with the Celebs* and recognized you, Mister Devine. Well, I almost didn't. Those were some wild costumes the celebrities got to wear."

"*Had* to wear," Matt said, sitting and opening the menu to end the conversation.

Too late.

"*Dancing with the Celebs*?" Max repeated, on the verge of disbelief.

"For charity." Matt kept his eyes on the menu, forcing the hostess to be on her way. "Complete disaster. It attracted a homicidal loony, but he's awaiting trial." Matt had worn his long T sleeves pushed up, so he flashed the inside of his left wrist.

Max stared at the thin, vertical, shiny pink line of the scar alongside his veins. "A suicide slash, not self-inflicted. Someone meant business. That must have bled like crazy."

"Yup. Almost as bad as the razor slash Kathleen O'Connor carved into my side a year ago."

"So you're a two-time knifee. I guess radio-show hosts attract a lot of hostility these days."

"Not usually. The dance-show stalker bore a grudge because I'd talked his abused wife into leaving him. He'd killed her just days before I was announced as a contestant."

"Sorry," Max said.

"And I owe the cat slash from Kitty the Cutter to her fixation on *your* hide, not mine."

"Sorry again. Maybe we'd better order some food and drink for a mellow rerun before this exchange gets too dark to deal with."

Matt kept his eyes on the menu, not really seeing it. "I guess you've had a lot of grief lately."

"At least I can't remember most of it," Max said, lightly. "What goes with jazz?"

Matt found himself focusing. "The, uh, the sirloin tips are good. That's what I had here. Grilled Chicken Picata."

"Sounds like a Temple Barr preference," Max said, of the chicken entrée.

"Actually, I was here with Lieutenant Molina. I'll have the Salmon Fettuccini."

"You're a brave man." Kinsella let his comment confuse Matt for a long moment then continued: "artichoke, purple onion, and garlic all in one go."

"I apparently like to eat dangerously. They have a great pale ale here, even Guinness stout."

"No beer, ale, or stout for me," Max said. "I'm allergic now."

"Oh. Well, you don't look like a wine guy."

"Not like you were."

346

It took Matt a second to realize Max Kinsella had been reared Catholic and understood *ex-priest* almost as well as he did.

"No," Matt said, "sacramental wine hasn't been on my menu lately, either. Why not just skip the well-aged angst and order the hard spirits of our choice?"

Max laughed with genuine appreciation. "Gandolph didn't tell me you were easy to underestimate, too. Scotch whisky it is for me, a double. A doughty drink. Neat," he added, to the now-hovering waiter, whose brow furrowed. "No ice," Max added in explanation.

"I'll have . . ." Matt observed that Max had ordered the most manly drink first. ". . . A vodka gimlet. Ice, no sugar, and a lime wedge."

"So she's sweet and you're sour," Max commented.

"Are we talking about Kathleen O'Connor or Temple?"

Max chuckled softly again. "You're not what I expected."

"And you expected — ?"

"Mister Nice Guy."

"I am."

"You won that." He glanced at Matt's wrist.

"Not by much."

"Doesn't matter by how much, trust me."

"I can't."

"On that you can. Listen. I don't like this any more than you do."

"What's not to like?" Matt asked. "Guys night out. I can . . . help you with a lot of those blank areas in your memory. It's my business. Trust me."

"I can't."

"You should."

The waiter brought their drinks and waited like an expectant chipmunk for their food orders. Even food-service jobs in Vegas were hard to come by nowadays. Matt ordered his salmon and Kinsella his Caribbean Spiced Prime Rib of Pork, just to be left alone for a while.

"Talk about eating dangerously," Matt said. "Pork with habanero-banana salsa and Diablo Sauce?"

"Have to keep up with the competition."

"Look," Matt said. "I'm glad you're alive, but I'm not happy about you coming back to Vegas from the dead. Temple is a true-blue soul. She'd never leave you out there, twisting in the wind with serious losses to deal with and no memory."

"And you?"

"Me neither," Matt heard himself almost snarl. "So you're our pet project. I want to help you on your merry way to mental health and new places and faces, okay?"

Max took a long slug of Scotch, nodding. "Self-interest I can buy. Meanwhile, chew on this: I don't remember much, Devine. Frankly, I don't *know* much, but I do know that Temple is not my type."

"How do you know?"

"I encountered it . . . her . . . on my escape route."

"You're with another woman?"

"I was."

Matt let a lot of gin and lime fill his throat before he answered. "That's . . . crummy."

"What? You'd want me back, whole, picking up where I'd left off?"

"No." Matt sipped some more of his mixed vodka-sour feelings. "Temple shouldn't be that easy to get over."

Max lifted his amber glass. "I've made my point. I'm a cad without a memory. You have nothing to fear . . . but Kathleen O'Connor. I'm here not because of Temple or any memory or feelings I have of or for her. I'm here because we all three have a mutual enemy. And Kathleen's like that vengeful wife abuser from your once-innocent airtime advice show. She won't go away and stop hurting people, mainly us, until we catch her and stop her and put her away. *Sláinte.*"

Max held out his glass. The word *predestination* crossed Matt's mind before he chimed rims with his second-worst nightmare. Kinsella was right. Handicapped but right.

It would have to be a battle to the death with the banshee from Max's past and Matt and Temple's future. Matt had been uneasily relieved to hear his attacker had at one time been declared dead, by Max, at the end of an attempt to hound the object of her twenty-year vendetta into a deadly auto accident. The deadly auto accident had just happened months later and five thousand miles away . . . to another man.

None of this was what it appeared to be, and not so simple. They needed to collaborate, again, Matt and Temple and Max, to find out what had really happened, what hadn't, and what was in store for them.

Kathleen O'Connor rides again.

CHAPTER 31
EVERY SILVER CLOUD . . .

Temple sat at home alone on a Friday night, her only companion a cat, and racked her brain to pick some neutral territory where she and the M&M boys — Matt and Max — could meet to discuss their precarious physical and mental situation.

She'd heard about last evening's raw and recent M&M rendezvous at the Blue Dahlia from Matt. She didn't want to risk Carmen showing up for the 10:00 P.M. show, if the trio met there. Matt and Temple and Max and Molina would not make a "fantastic foursome."

Temple was too well known at the Crystal Phoenix.

And Planet Hollywood was suddenly "too Max."

Anyone's place of residence? The Circle Ritz condo address that all three had shared at one time was also the only place she had slept with both men . . . at different times,

Temple reminded herself.

She couldn't help being a serial monogamist — life threw love at you as unpredictably as a twenty-one dealer threw players aces — but she certainly wasn't a two-timer, and her fiancé and ex would probably gang up together on anyone who implied that.

Wait! What about that commodious old house Orson Welles had once lived in? It looked bland but was supersecure. No. Max was living in it again, out of perversity or penance, and its forever-link to his slain mentor Gandolph was too memory-laden.

So, Barr, you're a PR whiz kid. Come up with the perfect location.

No more restaurants They were impersonal and noisy, especially in Vegas, fine for breaking bad news to the men in your life so they couldn't go too postal in public, but not for serious strategy sessions complicated by deep-seated male competition.

Another good controllable environment skidded to a premature stop in her mind. No. They could hardly reserve Electra's in-house wedding chapel. . . . True, the only ears in the place were on Electra's imaginative soft-sculpture "congregation," including Elvis. But the connotations of wedded bliss hit way too close to home.

Temple was totally flummoxed.

This was unheard of.

She prided herself on being the Go-To Guru for whatever or whomever you needed to know in or about Sin City. She was the PR concierge for the whole damn city. The Vegas Magus. The Sage of the Strip. The Info Icon. The utterly In-the-Know Nabob. She of all people would intuit where to take your ex and your current fiancé to solve mutual mysteries without devolving into past issues and public spectacles.

Not a clue.

So she called her aunt Kit.

"Don't whimper," Kit said, when she'd heard Temple's complaints of failure to be innovative, or even sensible. "You're simply too emotionally involved."

"Not news," Temple said.

"A cooler head would list the necessities."

"A sword for my own hara-kiri?"

"Nonsense. Suicide is gainless. You need to control the horizontal. You need to control the vertical."

"I don't believe in attempting to 'control' men," Temple said loftily.

"Not the men, silly. The circumstances. What do you need for this 'meet'?"

" 'Meet'? Kit, you've been hanging with the Fontana family too long already."

"Answer my question."

"Uh, privacy," Temple said. "So a restaurant won't do. It's a busy Friday night anyway."

"And — what else?"

"Liquor should be available as social lubrication, but in moderate amounts. Matt doesn't drink much — yet, but Max is a melancholy Celt in mourning and fresh from the Ould Sod. So a bar is too tempting as well as too public."

"What about a pub? Ale is less intoxicating."

"*Auntie! Pub?* Max lost his best friend, twice, two decades apart, in Irish pubs. Or near them."

"Oh." Kit sounded stymied. "No, beer would not be good. Champagne is all right, though?"

"I doubt anybody will be celebrating this reunion."

"Privacy, limited liquor . . ." Kit repeated.

"And nobody can see us."

"I was an actress and I am a writer, but I can assure you that cloaks of invisibility are not only fictional but a very difficult stage effect. Maybe Max could —"

"Max is not the mastermind here. I am."

"And your mind is out to lunch. Hush. No protests. You're so emotionally unstrung. Two wonderfully eligible bachelors on your hands. It would make a terrific reality-TV show."

"Been there, done that. Bloody murder resulted. Two of them. It may be awkward to have present and past guys in my life, but I can't afford to risk both of them being killed."

"And so you shan't. Lovely verb, isn't that? *Shan't.* So British. Thank you for allowing me to feel very Emma Thompson. I'll handle it all."

"You're *not* coming along, Kit."

"Certainly not! And make it a foursome? I'm a married woman now, Temple, to a hot-tempered Italian who brooks no rivals and springs for no free drinks for other guys. I just happen to have thought of the ideal solution. I'll get back to you in a lickety-split moment."

Temple shut off her cell phone.

Midnight Louie jumped up beside her, rubbing his nose against her arm.

He was a very nosy cat.

"You remember Aunt Kit?" she asked him. "From our magical, mystery Christmas trip to Manhattan a while back?" Her fingers circled his ears, the way he liked it. "You were on the brink of stardom as a spokescat, and I —"

Temple suddenly clapped her palms to her

355

ears. She just remembered that their jaunt to the Big Apple had ended with her being suddenly whisked away by Max for a night of sex in the city.

What woman on earth wanted to be "caught between the moon and New York City," between an old lover and a new one? *Oooh.* That sounded so tacky. Like she was a Material Girl who couldn't make up her mind.

Stop whining.

Kit was right.

Max was now a memory-impaired mess, and Matt was too earnest for his own good.

Both of them had been targets of Kitty the Cutter's most homicidal rages. Someone had to make up for male gallantry and take the bad "grrrrl" down.

Temple didn't believe in calling women "bitches." She did believe in fighting evil of any gender tooth and nail. Well, with her tenacious teeth and — she eyed Louie — his ferocious claws now and again.

A half hour later she was leaving cryptic messages on both men's cell phones.

"The Kitty the Cutter Club meets at eight P.M. In the Circle Ritz parking lot." She left that message for Matt and hung up.

"The Kitty the Cutter Club meets at

356

eight-twenty P.M.," she purred into the unanswered ether of Max's cell phone. "On the corner of Mojave and Juniper."

Temple left the message, as instructed, and hung up.

This mission was like those animal riddles about how prey and predator cross a river. Kit decreed that the men shouldn't be left alone with each other.

What a diplomat Kit would have made. Actually, as the latest famous bachelor-brother Fontana bride, Kit already had to be one. Temple pictured Kit Ursula Carlson Fontana and Vanilla von Rhine Fontana, wife of Nicky, the youngest Fontana brother, at odds.

It was not a pretty sight.

Good thing they were all "Family."

Meanwhile, Temple waited, mystified, on the corner of Las Vegas Boulevard and Flamingo in front of the neon row of dancing flamingos at 7:40 P.M., as ordered by her aunt.

The sunlight sinking behind the western mountains faded as the facing chorus lines of Strip light works intensified. Temple loved these magical minutes when natural and artificial light duked it out for mastery of the night.

She stood there like a schoolgirl in her

demure navy fifties suit and vintage clear-Lucite-heeled red pumps, a modern version of the Ruby Slippers, with her large red patent-leather tote bag — or should she think "Toto" bag? — clasped in front of her.

The last time she'd met with both Matt and Max, she'd still been Max's girl.

She bit her lower lip but forbore to chew, and vowed not to pick at her cuticles. This was crime-and-punishment business, mutual self-protection stuff, deadly serious business they all could handle like the civilized adults they were.

So why did she also feel like Alice about to attend a Very Mad Tea Party?

While she was putting herself into every girl-empowering scenario she could muster, she realized something was blocking her view of the iconic hotels across the Strip and even of the mountains' gentle sawtooth peaks.

Oh.

Something long and pale and metallic and, well, slithering had obliterated everything but her gliding close-up view. Its arrival so much resembled a movie-camera pan that her mind went into slomo and she only tardily ID'd the apparition as a Rolls Royce stretch Silver Cloud limo to die for. Or to ride in as one wheeled directly into automotive and vintage heaven.

Temple had been woolgathering so hard in the children's literature of an earlier day that the driver had already stopped, de-planed, and come around to open the very, very distant back door for her.

Even the driver's shiny-billed black cap couldn't disguise a glossy full head of Fontana-brother razor-cut hair. As he bowed to open the door, Temple wracked and rolled her brain cells. Obviously not Nicky. No solo earring, therefore not Ralph nor Emilio. No discreet thread of silver in that coif, therefore not Aunt Kit's new consort, Aldo. That left Rico, Ernesto, Eduardo, Julio, Emilio, and Giuseppe.

Temple realized the Fontana brothers had individual differences. They just so often appeared in well-tailored, Italian gelato smoothie, six-plus-pack that they over-whelmed the female ability to discriminate, and a woman usually fell head over heels "in like" with all of them.

"Miss Temple," the chauffeur said.

"Gracious Gertie. I didn't expect Gang-sters to provide the ride tonight, and even to have the honor of one of the owners at the wheel . . ."

"Emilio, Ernesto, Giuseppe, Eduardo, Julio, and I did resort to gambling to earn

359

this honor."

Aaah. He'd cued her, just like a Fontana brother would. Always in command, even when you, the mere mortal, were not.

"Thank you, Rico," Temple said, taking the long lunge she needed to get inside the huge passenger compartment. She was short and the Silver Cloud was *soooo looong.*

A bit of warm Vegas sidewalk heat entered with her, at calf level.

It was not only a sensual waft on her bare leg, it was butch-cut black fur on the clawed hoof.

"Louie," she hissed in a whisper. "You were *not* invited. You must have tailed me here, you . . . sneak."

Fortunately, he blended so well with the black carpeting underlining the Silver Cloud's ivory leather upholstery and fancy wood interior that Rico stared in vain past her ankles for the object of her surprise.

He did look in the right direction. Down.

"Nice Gianmarco Lorenzis." His voice dripped approval of all things Italian. For a moment, Temple thought he was naming three cousins. Oh, her designer shoes.

So that's what they were. Like the Rolls Royce, they'd been "previously owned," by a resale shop in her case.

Then Rico stood up straight as a staff sergeant and got all serious and squinty-eyed before he shut the door on her.

"This vehicle is a nineteen-sixty-one Rolls Royce Silver Cloud One. That 'One' is written as a capital *I,* to indicate the Roman numeral one, because it is fit for an emperor. There are very few stretch Rolls Royce Silver Clouds in the world, Miss Temple, because the model is so revered that only the most profligate and fashion-conscious purveyor of rides would dare to stretch one. Gangsters is one of the ballsy few, so only a handful of people have been so conveyed. You have to ask yourself, do you have the chutzpah to deserve such a world-class ride, Miss Temple? Well, do you?"

"Absolutely," she said, "and I feel *very lucky* to have one, too."

At that the door shut with a soft but firm *whoosh* of hot night air and absolute cool.

Louie had come out of flattened, belly-down-to-the-black-carpeting camouflage mode and was sniffing around the handsome curly-maple bar with its dazzling armada of cut-glass decanters and Baccarat glasses.

Temple recalled the recipe for détente she had recited to Kit. Absolute privacy. A controlled environment that called for self-control. A certain amount of high-proof liquidity to file off any raw edges. *Presto!*

Rico lowered the tinted window between her and his capped self, fourteen feet away.

"Ready for the next stop, Miss Temple?"

Was it Matt or was it Max?

The story of her life.

No. The order had been dictated beforehand. Her aunt Kit was fiendishly efficient.

"Drive on, Rico," Temple said, settling into the channeled ivory leather upholstery that flattered the hair colors of blonds, brunettes, and redheads alike. She fixed her gaze on the reflective green eyes blinking from the black carpet. "Louie, you've already chosen sides. Watch yourself, Blackie, and stay discreet, or you'll be walking home from . . . wherever."

"Temple," Matt said in surprise as he bent to enter the low-rise living room of the Silver Cloud. "This limo is amazing. It sure has my new Jag beat."

"The Silver Cloud is not entering a contest," she said. "It's acting as a rolling conference room."

"Then there's at least a third coming," Matt said, eyeing the vast seating arrangement.

"I'm in the center-back spot," Temple

said. "You take the left bench. Max can sit on the right."

" 'Sit down, sit down, you're rockin' the boat,' " Matt muttered as he bent to take the long bench seat. "Max, being the third pickup, won't have to do the Marx Brothers walk across the limo."

"He's taller," Temple said. "Also, more to the point, injured."

"Mea culpa," Matt said. "I forgot. He's a handicapped person."

"This is nothing new." Temple leaned forward with a piercing look. "You guys talked just yesterday. Wasn't a dry run useful?"

"Yeah, but having you here ups the ante. At least for me. Why couldn't you board with me at the Circle Ritz?"

"I'm worried Max will assume we're ganging up on him."

"I'll tell him we're not, Temple. He's already a bit paranoid, right now. Rightfully so."

"Very thoughtful, Mister Midnight. Did I tell you that you look to-the-manor-born in a Rolls as well as a Jag? Is this a taste of the Chicago life, or what?" Her voice had sunken to a sexy rasp. She couldn't help remembering their recent roll on the Vladimir Kagan. Next, a Rolls. Why not?

"A truly clever roaming conference room, Miss Barr," he said, obviously recalling the same incident. "Did I tell you, as a late-night chitchat expert, that these ivory leather seats are just right for a rolling tête-à-tête? Let's open that champagne bottle and ditch the last stop."

Temple sighed. Deeply.

"I'm tempted, but it would be really mean to leave Max standing on a corner waiting for the Kitty the Cutter Club to come by."

"Yeah. This way no one eavesdrops on us. What about the driver?" Matt jerked his head toward the capped silhouette beyond the tinted-glass interior window. "A Fontana brother, I presume. Won't he tattle on us to the whole family?"

Temple shook her head. "His new sister-in-law would have his shorts in a sling."

"Sister-in-law? Oh. Your aunt Kit is back from her honeymoon with Aldo."

"Right. It's nice to have my own blood kin as muscle inside of Fontana, Inc. Not a word will go beyond this limo. Here. Looks like Scotch is the, uh, car-bar favorite. Isn't this adorable mini-fridge with ice and mixers cute? The decanters sparkling like a chandelier in the center make this rolling luxury vehicle a maxi-bar, though."

Matt took the cut-crystal lowball glass she

extended, giving Temple that intensely significant glare he'd recently mastered doing on the Paso Doble on *Dancing with the Celebs*.

"You don't know what you just said, do you, Temple?"

Temple did an instant rerun of her admittedly distracted mental processes.

Oh. *Maxi*-bar.

"Honestly," she said, "that's like the faux fuss kicked up when the Apple iPad debuted and geek guys immediately associated the name with a feminine hygiene product. Talk about euphemistic phrases. Matt, you've got to quit personalizing this. If Kathleen O'Connor is still out there, she's not going to care which one of you she has a chance to off first, although she'd probably prefer it be Max."

Matt shook his head and sipped the Scotch. "You understand why I'm worried. Max is ahead even in the Most Wanted To Be Killed category."

"See. If you can joke it takes the social awkwardness away."

Matt stretched out his khaki-trousered legs. "Once Max gets in here, there won't be a lot of leg room."

Temple crossed her ankles. The limo seat kept her feet firmly on the carpet. Without the high heels, they wouldn't touch and would be swinging like a kid's.

"What the — ?" Matt lifted his beige suede shoes as the carpet beneath them rippled like asphalt in an earthquake.

"It's just Louie, the sneak!" Temple said, assuming the ramrod-spine posture of the disciplinarian. "I should drop you off wherever we are now," she lectured the cat, squinting hard out the tinted glass windows. "Circus Circus neon. Crawling with kids who'd probably pull your tail. Serve you right."

Matt was laughing as Louie hopped up beside her and began rubbing his chin on her tote bag.

"Hey," Matt said. "A ride-along referee. I was afraid your tender heart would make you a sap for Max in his current condition, but Louie accepts no guff from anybody."

"You think I have a tender heart?" Temple asked.

"Yeah, you do. It's your biggest flaw and your greatest gift."

"Aww."

"Cut the sentimentality, babe," Matt suggested in patented tough-guy-ese. "Our party is about to pick up the third man."

"There are only two guys in our party."

"You'd leave out the house cat?" Matt

366

asked. "What does he drink? White Russians?"

"Oh. You're right. There's a nice carton of cream in this adorable mini-fridge."

By then Louie's uniquely white whiskers were deep within the small cavity and bent back, so he looked like a windblown cat.

"The only thing I could put Louie's cream in," Temple said, frowning, "is a champagne glass. And I'd have to hold it."

And that's the tableau they presented when the Silver Cloud eased to a smooth stop that lived up to its name and Rico stepped out and around to open the door to a waiting Max Kinsella.

A Fontana brother and Max standing side by side was pretty intimidating, Temple had to admit to herself, but it also emphasized how . . . diminished Max was.

There went her tender heart again. Matt, as usual, had been perceptive.

What's a girl to do?

She concentrated on the only uninvolved alpha male present right now. Louie.

"There's champagne on ice," she told Max, "and ivory leather to lounge on, but the man of the hour has long white whiskers, not entirely due to cream."

Max ducked into the low compartment and lowered himself into a corner so his legs could stretch past the central bar.

"Devine," he said with a nod. "Temple. You can explain the cat, I hope."

"Hitchhiker."

"I admire his taste in rides." Max smiled, managing to include Louie, Temple, and Matt. "I'll have what he's having." He nodded at Matt.

"A grade of Scotch probably way better than I know," Matt said.

"I'd trade what you know for what I know in a heartbeat." Max flashed a rueful smile.

There was no answer to that.

The luxurious cabin — for the vehicle was sailing along again like an ocean liner, afloat in its uniquely powerful but tranquil way — moved into the anonymous dark, far from the Strip's glitz and glitter.

"Where are we going?" Matt asked.

"Nowhere," said Temple, "until we all exchange information and figure out what the Synth is or was; why K the Cutter is involved with Las Vegas; what the tunnels under the Crystal Phoenix, Gangsters Hotel-Casino, and the Neon Nightmare club mean; and what the attempt on Max's life has to do with it all."

After another long silence, Max spoke. "Which attempt on my life?"

"You've had that many?" Matt asked. "I've

only had one."

"Kathleen's introductory slash doesn't count?"

Matt waved that minor assault away as Max leaned forward to dilute the melting ice in his drink with more Scotch.

"You must not be a very interesting fellow," he told Matt. "One serious attempt. Minor league."

"That one almost got Temple killed instead," Matt said, leaning forward without refilling his drink.

Max glanced from him to Temple. "Obviously there's been a very fresh attempt I didn't remember, or know about. Sorry. I was trying to lighten the tone here."

"Why?" Temple asked.

"I feel responsible for the general air of angst."

"You've been a sick man on the run for your life for the past two months," Matt pointed out. "Why should you be responsible for anything?"

"Because my troubles, my literal 'Troubles,' in Northern Ireland years ago have brought everyone I know pain and death, all right?"

Matt glanced at Temple. "Definitely a savior complex."

She nodded. "He'd shown tendencies

before he lost his mind."

"Wait a minute," Max said. "I am not here to be . . . psychoanalyzed by a pair of amateurs — an armchair shrink and a PR sleuth, not to mention limousine riders."

"Just trying to lighten the tone," Temple told him.

"Now that I've insulted you two," Max said, "maybe we're done with the preliminaries."

"What makes you think," Temple asked, rubbing her ankle absently against Louie's solid, reclining bulk, "Kathleen O'Connor is still alive?"

"The alternate-IRA men in Belfast said she'd still been sending money from abroad to 'the Cause.' "

"But the Irish 'Troubles' have been over for years, haven't they?" Matt asked.

"Except for the usual diehards. And both sides believe any money previously raised for either side of the conflict is due to them only, for those wounded or widowed by the decades of civil strife. And most of that money during the active IRA years came from the Irish in America. Not that much from South America, where Kathleen had been rumored to be working even a few years ago."

"Always money," Temple noted, shaking

370

her head.

"Maybe not." Max eyed Louie. "What's with the oversize furry ankle bracelet?"

"That's Louie." Temple was startled. "Midnight Louie, my . . . furry Valentine. Max. You don't remember Midnight Louie?"

"He follows you everywhere like a dog?" Max asked, incredulous.

"Not just her," Matt said. "He has a knack for being where the action is."

"I don't remember you having a cat," Max said.

"I don't, Max. Louie is 'had' by no one. He's half alley cat and half bloodhound."

"If you say so. I trust he won't repeat what we say here."

"Only in cat," she assured him. "Why are you asking Matt about the time Kathleen O'Connor attacked him? She was really after you, wasn't she? And you were so elusive. You weren't even living at the Circle Ritz —"

"I lived at this "Circle Ritz"? Was it above a country-western bar or what?"

Matt remained silent, letting Temple talk her way out of this.

"We invested in a condo there," she said, watching the high-heeled sandal slip off her foot as her toes massaged Louie's shoulder, "after you had whisked me away from my family and job in Minneapolis to accompany you to a big magic act at the Goliath."

"What happened to our happy home?"

"Some bad guys from your counter-terrorism past showed up, I guess. A man ended up dead in the Goliath gaming-area ceiling, and you ended your expiring contract by . . . vanishing without a word."

"And you took up with an alley cat."

"Not then. Not right away."

"And," Max said, "I assume Mister Midnight Two came into your life a lot later, too."

"You were gone a year, Max," she said, meeting his eyes. "I waited, but new people and a cat still came into my backyard."

"All ancient history." Max leaned forward to refill their ebbing glasses. He eyed Matt so sharply that Midnight Louie uttered a low growl.

"Quiet, Kitty. You're not the one we're all worried about," Max said. "Devine, I think Kathleen's approaching you, what she did, is a key to her poisonous presence in all our lives. I need to know exactly what happened."

"She accosted me leaving the radio station," Matt recalled.

"Wait," Temple said. "Did you know why?

372

What did she look like?"

"She was a knockout, I bet," Max said.

Temple was shocked. "You don't remember *her* either?"

"Garry filled me in on her so vividly I almost feel I do, but no. Not this woman, this girl then, who ruined my life, destroyed my connection to my family, as I hear it."

He stared hard at Temple. "She may have killed that man at the Goliath on my last performance night, forcing me to run and ruining our condo dreams, Temple. So why did she literally lash out at our mild-mannered ex-priest here?"

"Oh, come on," Matt said. "You may not remember anything of your relationship with Temple, but you are not a man who lets go easily. Neither am I. I didn't just duck out on the priesthood, I went through the whole 'repatriation process,' you could call it. I jumped through every hoop —"

"Climbed every mountain," Temple put in.

"Honorable discharge." Max nodded. "Not a piece of cake in that Church. I salute you. Seriously. I apparently tend to cut and run."

"It's funny," Matt said, sipping soothing amber. "Kathleen O'Connor was not somebody you'd suspect came with claws. Not that tall, almost delicate. Attractive, seductive in a classy way, which I wasn't buying. And then . . . she stung with her words first. The razor she used for a bloody underline was a complete surprise."

"How, with words?"

"She knew about my past. She seemed to have something against me, my ex-vocation, the Church."

"Oh, Mama," Max said, his blue eyes glittering with comprehension. "Drink up, Master of Understatement. This is going to be a bumpy night."

"I've gotten used to that," Matt said. "Explaining why I am an ex-priest. Why I was a priest. Some of the older relatives in Chicago still don't accept my leaving. I'm not going through that Inquisition again with you."

"It's not idle curiosity." Max breathed out audibly. "We've all got a piece of the puzzle, only I've lost five-sixths of my pieces."

"It's not that bad, Max," Temple said, leaning forward to put a hand on his arm. "The best one-sixth, your survival instincts, are still there."

"Not enough to save Garry."

She backed off. Reaching out made Matt edgy, and Max was beyond consolation.

But . . . he was on the track of some very

tricky pieces that were almost a fit. Temple sensed that from how he questioned Matt.

"So," Max told Matt, "Kathleen dissed you because she thought you were a wuss —"

Major testosterone surge from Matt's side of the aisle. Temple's fingernails creased her palms and held on tight. Louie was up on his haunches, although who he'd go for as out of line in her presence was anybody's guess.

"— or *because* you'd been a priest." Max finished.

Temple had seen Molina use that whiplash interrogation technique to startle an insight out of a witness. So had Matt, but he was not happy with this new triumvirate nor, unlike his usual temperament, feeling and not thinking first.

"She wasn't real pro-priests, no," Matt said, his expression fierce. "After the international scandals of child abuse by churchly authority figures, a lot of people aren't, including me. The hierarchy was as bad or worse than any stonewalling government or corporate badass. 'Mistakes have been made.' Children abused. Lives ruined. Faith destroyed. 'Mistakes have been made.' In my own archdiocese."

"Whoa, Father Matt," Max said. "I apparently came up in the party line. I know my gut gets utter betrayal. What I'm here to tell you, which may make your unlikely *Fight Club* night more understandable, so did Kathleen O'Connor. Which is why she razored an innocent bystander like you only a year ago, and slashed my teenaged heart into broken shards in Northern Ireland seventeen years ago, and maybe why she could be behind my head being broken into tiny shattered bits, too."

Silence prevailed at the end of that speech. Shock and silence.

The Silver Cloud sailed into the dark distance like the *Queen Mary,* captained by a deaf and distant man in a chauffeur's cap, while Temple and Matt breathed deeply and slowed their respiration until no one in the compartment could hear them.

Midnight Louie rose and went to rub on Max's ankles. Unfortunately, he left a slash of black cat hairs like tar on Max's pale linen pants legs.

Like the sticky, dark residue that old sins not forgotten forever leave on the psyche.

CHAPTER 32
THE KEY TO REBECCA

Matt was the first to break the lengthening silence.

"I've seen many instances of galloping guilt in my church and in my counseling career, including my own," he told Max, "but you probably have the world's worst case. You always have to be a world-class contender, Kinsella, with memory chips or without.

"How do we find and get this 'Typhoid Mary' out of our lives before she hurts someone we really care about? Or at least I do."

Max leaned forward, intent. "Here's what I learned in Belfast, when I was in a condition to not forget a thing: Rebecca."

"Rebecca," Temple echoed. "You know I loved that novel when I was a kid." She knew it was connected to the young Kathleen O'Connor, but she'd let Max bring Matt in on the mystery. It would help the

two men bond. Listen to her! Did she want a happy ending to her own life story or to be a playground monitor? Or, maybe there was no separating the two elements.

"Rebecca," Matt echoed. "I guess I should read it?"

Temple lifted an eyebrow. "It's a dark, romantic novel but way less sloshy than *Wuthering Heights.*"

"It's on my iPad," Matt said. "Or will be in a heartbeat, if the great Max Kinsella says it's relevant."

" 'The great,' " Max mocked himself.

"Legendary, then," Matt said. And grinned. "It's quite a . . . kick to be more together than you are at the moment, even if that won't last. I'm sure your memory loss will fade as you follow the leads you got in Ireland. You're right. We should unite to exorcise this female demon whose venom has touched all our lives."

"I applaud your gutsy imagery," Temple said. "I don't think female transgressors should be spared a thing just because they're women."

She noticed Max's face looked both bitter and rueful.

"What if they're transgressors *because* they're women?" he asked.

So Max told them what he'd briefly mentioned to Temple, that Garry Randolph had tracked gorgeous-but-lethal IRA moll Kathleen O'Connor to her roots.

Temple couldn't watch Matt's face during Max's terse recital, keeping her eyes on Louie, who looked back and forth between the two men as if watching a tennis game. He didn't want to miss a nuance. Cats are always masters of subtlety, their own or their neighboring human's.

"A Magdalen asylum?" Matt repeated, unbelieving.

He obviously knew about these Church-run industrial institutions that incarcerated supposed "fallen women," including girls, for life. Many were put to hard labor in these places, named after Mary Magdalene, and there they lost their real names and became "lost" to society.

"Holy Mother of God," Matt murmured. "Those places were hellholes of Old World 'discipline,' otherwise known as mental and physical and even sexual abuse. Ireland's and Scotland's were notorious and operated until late in the twentieth century. No wonder a young woman labeled 'unholy,' as Kathleen was, would come out twisted. The motives were cultural; they go back centuries and aeons and appear in all societies and religions. It's why the human animal is so hard to defend. Hypocrisy. Bred in the bone and soaking the soul until it drowns."

"Beautifully stated, prosecuting attorney," Max said. "But no."

"No?" Matt was on a righteous roll. "We shouldn't pity Kathleen as victim as well as our personal villain? The young women were incarcerated for life — for *life* — and considered unholy creatures unworthy of the smallest kindness or sympathy, not even allowed their own names. . . . Why wouldn't anyone strong enough to evade that fate be a monster?"

"You don't understand," Max said in a mild tone.

Matt's fists were bunched, white-knuckled. "That's my job, to understand."

"You don't have all the facts," Max said.

Temple stayed out of it. This was where the rubber hit the road. For all her desire to negotiate a decent truce between the two men who were rivals for her in their own minds, they had to throw it all out there and learn this was about them, not her.

And about Kitty the Cutter, above all.

"Then tell me all the facts," Matt said, demandingly.

Max smiled slightly. He had played this to get Matt going in one indignant direction then another. He was testing the level of passion and commitment Matt would bring to the hunt for the real Kathleen O'Connor.

Temple knew he'd be surprised, but she was thinking of the old Max, not the maimed man before them. She eyed how he angled his stretched legs across the central space of the limo "living room." He needed to take the pressure off his body so his mind was up to handling a tricky situation.

His eyes found her fascinating — as a missing piece of his past. They no longer held the look of love. So she breathed a sigh of relief even as the two men jostled in the closeness of the limo compartment for position, a place they each could stake out without losing face.

Not an easy "guy" thing.

"Listen," Max said, talking only to Matt. "You're a good guy, by intention. I hear I was a quasi-good guy, always trying to undo my past by hunting the future in the form of Kathleen O'Connor. Gandolph the Great. There's where the word *great* really comes in. I was always just the 'Mystifying.' He was my mentor, my father in absentia, my 'great' friend. Garry Randolph. A second-class magician, maybe, but a first-class human being."

"Don't you blame Kathleen O'Connor for his death?"

"I blame myself. She's been an easy out for my entire life, I'm thinking now. Yeah. She needs to be stopped, for her own sake, maybe. That much hate, even justified, is ultimately self-corrosive."

"What do you mean by 'that much' hate?" Matt asked.

"You see, she wasn't just put in a Magdalen institution as a teenager. Her mother was."

"Her mother? Who was that?"

"Who knows?" Max said. "I saw the mass graveyard of unmarked, unnamed burial sites at one such place near Dublin. The point is that the woman who called herself Kathleen O'Connor and then Rebecca, our mutual enemy who won't die, was born in a Magdalen asylum. Her mother had been consigned there. And there Kathleen grew up to have her own child."

"Child?" Temple couldn't contain herself. "Kitty the Cutter has a child?"

"She had one," Max said, eyeing her for the first time in several minutes. "She ran away as an unwed mother, one of very few who had the will to escape."

"To become the femme fatale who seduced you in Belfast?"

"I wasn't her first, but she was mine, my aching bones tell me that much. And my instincts."

"She must have been incredibly damaged." Matt shook his head.

"She is," Max said. "Beyond what any of us can imagine."

"The rings," Temple said.

Both men eyed her.

"Matt. She forced you to wear that big ugly snake ring for a while."

"Not a snake. The worm, Ouroboros," he said, looking unhappy to share the incident with Max. "It's an ancient eternity symbol. A 'worm' or Medieval dragon eating its own tail."

"Rather like Kathleen herself," Max said. "What about such a ring, Temple? She forced it on Matt?"

"When she was stalking him."

"After the razor attack?" Max wanted to know.

Matt spoke for himself. "Yes. She'd marked my skin. She wanted to mark my mind and soul. I had no option, but she finally stole the ring back, as if she'd tired of the game. She'd threatened Temple. Every woman I came in contact with." Matt hesitated. "I was counseling a call girl who fell to her death. I never knew if Kitty the Cutter had done that or not."

Max drew back to coddle his glass of

Scotch. "She's really put you through the 'Guilt Gavotte,' too, hasn't she?" He looked at Temple. "You're being quiet. Am I right to think that's not typical?"

"The ring business is beyond . . . eerie. I found the Ouroboros ring in my scarf drawer not long ago, and I don't know where it came from."

" 'Your scarf drawer," Max drawled. "Is this a place of pilgrimage? An inner sanctum? Who has a scarf drawer these days?"

"Temple collects vintage clothing," Matt explained. "She stores shoes, gloves, hats. And scarves."

"Any of my magician's unending rainbow of linked chiffon scarves?" Max asked with a fluid gesture that almost made that hokey trick seem visible in his hands for a moment.

"You didn't do the scarf trick," Temple said. "Way too expected. No, the fact is I'm not good with scarves. Some women are. I'm not the drapery sort of woman. Too short." She looked down. "So is Louie."

"He's not too short to impinge on my pants legs." Max frowned at the horizontal bar of black hairs.

"Louie impinges on everything," Matt said, not sounding regretful about Max's impaired wardrobe.

"Including Temple's scarf drawer." Max was trying to brush off the hair, which stuck like barbed fishhooks to the textured linen weave.

"You need tape loops for that," Temple told him, glad they had skirted the issue of Louie once upon a time impinging on their California-king-size bed. "No. There's nothing in my scarf drawer that Louie would find worth the effort of opening it. It's a lost and found for things I don't feel I can throw out but don't know what to do with."

"Kinda like me."

Matt groaned at Max's quip. "It's not all about you anymore."

"It's a stupid scarf drawer!" Temple said. "Can you guys keep on point? Which is . . . that Ouroboros ring turned up in it, I don't know how."

"Exactly when was that?" Matt asked her.

"It was after we think Kitty assaulted you with an aspergillum on the crowded down escalator at TitaniCon at the Hilton."

Max shifted to restretch his legs. "I know my misfiring memory may be a bore, but can we speak about the same planet at least?"

"Yeah." Matt frowned, trying to rerun his own memory track. "Mini-Molina was there. She was really kiddish then. They

385

grow up fast."

Temple nodded at Matt. "Mariah was chubby and half bummed out about being 'watched' by us . . . and half totally crushing on you. Now look at her, all teenybopper. No wonder Mama Bear has been getting unraveled lately."

"Look," Max said. "This cozy trip down memory lane isn't helping my recall or my nauseous feeling. What was TitaniCon? What is an aspergillum, which sounds vaguely familiar, like a medication name . . . or some kind of flower? Why would Kathleen try to assault you on an escalator?" he asked Matt. "And why were you two wandering around the Hilton with a bratty kid in tow like *The Simpsons*?" he asked Temple.

Temple took on the task of answering. "TitaniCon was a huge science-fiction convention. Murder was afoot, but Matt got suckered into taking Molina's kid, who wasn't there when Matt was going down an escalator and felt something hard, like a gun barrel, pressed into his back.

"When he got to ground level, he heard a metallic roll and found this funky object on the hotel floor. The thing looked to me like a baby rattle with a wooden handle and a silver ball, the kind of fancy, nonfunctional nonsense people without kids give as baby gifts. Matt explained it was an aspergillum."

"You've seen one," Matt told Max. "Whether you remember or not. It's a ceremonial holy-water dispenser, and the officiating priest does indeed shake it like a baby rattle at the most solemn rites."

"I *do* remember that." Max waved a hand in front of his eyes. "Just a vision. A pale cloud of incense and chanting and crowds . . . and me being short." He made a hasty sign of the cross. "You're saying Kathleen has collected these mystical or religious artifacts, an Ouroboros ring, an aspergillum? And used them to taunt you? That is really sick."

"It may be sicker than you think," Matt said. "She was after any woman I associated with, like the call girl I was counseling, whose death was never solved."

"Interesting." Max's eyes narrowed. "Looks like Molina's kid wasn't the only one who had a crush on you."

Matt was not taking on that role.

"I think, from what you just said," he pointed out, "she just wanted to hound people the way she and her Magdalen-asylum mother had been hounded. Kathleen's 'haunting' presence in my life did stop shortly after that aspergillum incident. She

387

was able to get in and out of my unit. One day the ring was gone. What's sick is that she somehow got it into Temple's possession later. I never thought I'd say this about a human being, but it's a pity she wasn't dead, as you thought. As you said you saw."

"Few people really want someone dead," Temple said. "You may not be sorry they're gone, though, like Kitty the Cutter." She eyed Max. "How could you have made a mistake about something as definite as a dead body with all your counterterrorism experience abroad?"

"I swore she was dead, too, don't forget," Matt said. "I ID'd the body through a morgue window."

"Everybody thought Gandolph the Great was dead when he wasn't." Max turned to Temple. "How could that have happened?"

"That wasn't so hard to pull off," Temple said. "He was disguised as this ditzy, turbaned, overripe female medium."

"Looking dead isn't the problem," Max said. "It's being carted away by the coroner's office. In my case at the Neon Nightmare, I had the services of a fake ambulance and hired EMTs to whisk 'the body' away."

"And a past-master at faking death in Gandolph, now that we know about that," Temple said. "Besides, after impact, your condition was severe enough to fool Rafi Nadir, Molina's ex-boyfriend, who was working security at the Neon Nightmare when you fell. He'd been a cop."

Max hesitated before saying more. Temple supposed he might be reliving the last moments before he hit the wall.

"The crash was authentic," he said, "and pretty spectacular to witness, I imagine. I was unconscious, in a coma for weeks. At the Swiss clinic they suspected me of being a drunk driver, because the impact ordinarily would have killed me," he explained to Matt. "What saved me then was what saved me when I braked that car in Belfast so hard to avoid bullets. I wasn't drunk, and I wasn't wearing a seat belt, but I've trained myself to go limp at any oncoming impact. It minimizes the damage if you don't tense up. And you said I'd used bungee cords before in my official act."

Max reported all this to the limo carpeting and Midnight Louie's unblinking, upcast eyes. Temple caught Matt's somber glance. Time to move Max past dwelling on his latest case of survivor's guilt.

"Gandolph must have stage-managed some sort of exchange, then," she said, "after he got you off in the hired ambulance."

"From what I saw of his impressive contacts in Ireland and Northern Ireland," Max said, "he'd have plenty of Vegas help to call on. He was the wizard who helped me develop the Neon Nightmare act as the Phantom Mage, and he whisked my unconscious body out of the Neon Nightmare and Las Vegas all the way to a Swiss clinic."

"Without any on-scene treatment?" Matt sounded incredulous. "That would be barbaric."

"Not if Max had really fallen on a mountain," Temple pointed out. "It can take hours, even days, to get to and carry out a victim. Gandolph didn't dare leave any kind of trail here in the U.S. In fact, officially, the Neon Nightmare 'accident' was written off as unreliable reporting from the scene. It's not like the onlookers were sober."

"Except for Nadir," Max put in wryly. "Little did he know his ex would have killed to get her hands on me for once."

"Poor Rafi," Temple mused. "So close to making points with Molina and getting access to his kid."

"Poor *Max!*" Max put in. "I guess you and I really were exes by then or you'd be a teeny bit more solicitous about the almost-murder victim."

"Oh! I'm sorry to be so insensitive. I was

390

just caught up in the dramatic irony, and you don't look like that much of a victim now, and . . ."

Temple caught the first momentary glimpse of a twinkle in Max's eyes. He was just teasing her. And, ironically, you tended to forget about his gigantic memory loss, he was so good at looking like he was in complete control, of himself most of all. Poor Max indeed.

"Next you'll get around to 'Poor Louie,' " Matt said, "and maybe finally me."

"It's hard," Temple said, "to feel sorry for a guy whose business associates just gifted him with a new Jaguar."

"Really?" Max commented. "That ride was a gift? Good going."

"That's the trouble. It would mean 'going.' Leaving Vegas for Chicago."

"Matt's been offered his own TV talk show," Temple explained.

"Good show," Max said in the Brit way then laughed at how literal he'd been. "Brave man. I don't remember hearing you on the radio except for a spin through the dial lately, but you seem adept at that."

"Yeah. If you need any counseling on your memory loss . . ."

"I need someone who can bring it back."

Matt said, "That would be someone you

had a deep emotional connection with."

Awkward silence.

"Midnight Louie," Temple said with a pointed forefinger. "You two were always 'soul brothers.' "

Max crossed his arms on his knees and bent down to fix Louie with a stare. "Those unsmiling Irish eyes of yours have hidden depths, do they, Louie, old boy?"

The cat's expressionless face shook with a sudden sneeze, which broke the building tension as they all laughed.

"Maybe he's developed an allergy to you while you were gone," Matt twitted Max.

Louie pawed his muzzle like a dazed boxer while everyone sat back and sipped their drinks.

"Speaking of jogging memories," Temple said, "I could use professional help on dredging up exactly how I might have gotten the worm ring. If it was near the aspergillum incident, I might be able to check my PR date book and get some ideas."

She almost went on to say that Molina had returned the semi-engagement opal ring from Max, but . . . assessing both men's politely guarded air, she decided the topic of her affections and any rings that resulted from them had gone on about as long as reasonably possessive and competitive-but-civilized men could stand.

"Okay," she said. "Homework for Temple. Track down the when and how of Evil Kitty's hate tokens."

They'd dipped their heads for a silent sip to that resolve when the limo sped forward so fast they all had dripping chins.

The limo swung into a wide left that made it lurch like a swamped boat.

"Bottoms up," Max shouted, downing the contents of his glass and reinstalling it in the rack.

Both he and Matt reached for the same button in the *Starship Enterprise*–complex panel installed in the upholstered ceiling.

Temple had ridden in limos for her job before but not the latest tricked-out models.

Matt won the button war. "What's going on, driver?" he asked.

"Sorry!" came Rico's angry voice over the intercom. "We've got a . . . wasp on our tail. I so much as blur the wax finish on this baby, it's my ass on the line. Crazy biker kid!"

With that, the limo sped up and screeched around another corner.

"The windows are tinted so dark we can't see out," Matt complained, pushing more buttons until the side passenger windows descended, revealing a speeding panorama of off-Strip shops and importing a blast of warm, pollutant-laden streaming air.

Both Matt and Max had their heads out opposite windows.

Midnight Louie leaped up beside Temple. What a good guard kitty. She was about to pat him, but his shiny fur skimmed her palm as he jumped to the rear window ledge and stared into the dark as if he had laser eyes.

Temple got on her knees and joined him.

"It's the Vampire," Max and Matt shouted as one.

Really, Temple thought, *that vampire fad was now at the point of overkill.* If she never heard about another one . . .

Then the shrieking whine of an overtaking engine so shrill and loud that it inspired the name of a mechanical beast came through with the wind, and Temple saw through the black back window a blinding Cyclops blur that darted off to the side like a UFO.

Next she'd be seeing Elvis.

Or . . . she leaped to Matt's side of the car, but the passing traffic and buildings were only a blur, even with the window down.

Temple glanced over at Max and his open window and saw a gun butt balanced on the door padding. Of course he'd be armed these days.

"Speed Queen," Max muttered in determined fury.

Something was coming up alongside them, overtaking them. Someone in a space suit. There was that UFO imagery again. The speed, the road cinders flying into their eyes — Temple thought she was coursing through the Chunnel of Crime ride between Gangsters and the Crystal Phoenix again, only it had been put on crystal meth.

Max was aiming the gun at the rider.

"No!" Temple shouted.

She must have leaped across the limo's conversation-pit middle, because even as she screamed, what looked like a dark arm brushed Max's braced elbow. The firearm flew out the window.

"Holy freaking flying cat!" Max shouted, leaning far out the window, hair windslicked, eyes squinted almost shut.

The limo was finally slowing. Max slumped back in the cushy leather, wincing. He'd heaved himself up on his knees, folded and twisted his legs like he used to, and hadn't felt a thing in the excitement.

Matt was hair-ruffled and bleary-eyed too as he pulled himself back into the seating.

"The Circle Ritz Hesketh Vampire motorcycle," Temple said, dazed. "I don't get it."

"Using Electra Lark's Speed Queen hel-met," Matt said, eyeing Max.

"You or Electra been riding it lately?" Max asked Matt.

"No. Not lately. It was my only transporta-tion for a time, a while back. I started get-ting shadowed by another rider. You know anything about that?"

Max's laugh was weary. "If I did, I don't now. Could have been Kathleen or a traffic cop. Seeing and hearing that bike brought a lot back. All of it just about the ride. I gave it to Electra as collateral, I think."

Temple nodded confirmation when he glanced at her.

"Then I got irritated when I saw she'd gotten that corny helmet. And I seem to know . . . somehow . . . that you rode it, Devine. I've had visions or dreams of Kitty the Cutter crashing on another motorcycle, being dead. And that's all I know, but it's more than I knew a few hours ago. Maybe there's hope for my memory."

Matt nodded. "The motorcycle literally jolted your brain cells. Probably the intense high-pitched scream. And it was something you loved and wanted. That leaves an indel-ible mark, too."

Another awkward silence.

"Where's Louie?" Temple asked, searching the black carpeting.

Max turned to Temple. "I'm sorry. I hardly understood what was happening when it was happening, and you probably didn't see it. My shrimp-breath 'soul brother' was determined to stop me from shooting at a moving target.

"The weight of his leap knocked my arm away. That forestalled my shot, but not his own momentum. He landed on those leather saddlebags behind the rider like he was on a bungee cord that worked.

"He's tailing that Vampire in the riding pillion position at seventy miles an hour to God knows where."

CHAPTER 33
IN THE HOT SAUCE

WHEE! If I had a headdress I could be the Flying Nun.

Not that I'd sign up for the chastity part. Or the obedience part. Poverty I could handle, having been born in the streets.

Meanwhile, the Hesketh Vampire and I are flying down side streets lurching to the left and to the right, the metal foot-peg caps sparking on the pavement. I am at my claw-hanging, balancing-like-a-butterfly, screaming-cat-spat best, vocalizing in counterpoint to the engine.

I realize my Miss Temple must be a trifle worried by my absence and means of egress from the limo, but I did not want Mr. Max doing anything intemperate with a firearm. He is not quite himself, as you may have noticed.

I am sure that he believes the person in biker leather in front of me is Miss Kitty the Cutter. He may be right. Such a sneak attack would be up her alley. But does he really want her dead before he can have a nice long heart-to-heart with her about then and now and why and why, why, why?

In this way, Mr. Max is sort of a Hamlet person. I am a just a ham.

So I bask in the double-takes that pedestrians shoot my way as we zoom past.

By now we are down to street-legal speeds, say forty-five miles an hour. It is getting so a guy could almost jump off and just skin his shins and chinny-chin-chin. Not that I want any scars.

The Vampire slows to glide into the service area behind a row of one-story businesses. By now I am hanging by a single nail, preparing to drop off where I can shelter in the shade of the handy cat's best friend, a dumpster.

The rider is dragging the soles of — what else? — motorcycle boots, which I judge to be a size 6 or 7. I am looking for a woman a bit taller than my Miss Temple. Five-three, I heard long ago.

My unintentional driver drops the kickstand and dismounts. This lean, slight build looks womanish, but then the figure doffs the silver helmet. I hold my breath and snick out my shivs.

No need.

This nefarious knight of the road is an Asian man, small, wiry, and black-haired. He has a cell phone to his ear before you can say "brain damage."

"I am leaving the ride behind a Chinese restaurant," he reports then snickers. By this I gather that he is Japanese. "Yeah, the dorky helmet, too. Glad none of my bros saw me in that thing; I might have had to defend my honor." Another snicker. "I will walk a couple blocks away and call another biker for a ride. I really rattled that snazzy limo's tailpipe. I am sure the contents were well shaken up."

His motorcycle boot soles flash the overkill of steel cleats, so I hear his scraping steps fading away out front.

First, I check to see that I am alone, then I leap upward to the seat and start working out the saddlebag flap latches with my bare shivs. My improvised hitch on the saddlebags has more than somewhat marred the leather, but I know my Circle Ritz acquaintances would prefer to lose some anonymous cowhide accessories over my well-groomed turf of shiny black fur.

Alas, the stuffing inside the saddlebag is just a Red Hat Sisterhood sweatshirt decked out with sequins and rhinestones, most likely belonging to Miss Electra Lark.

I certainly have no use for it, since my breed does not sweat.

I look around from my solitary perch, planning my necessary next steps. First, I need to guard this valuable vintage motorcycle. Then I need to guide my handicapped humans to where it is.

The second step is the easiest. I spot a Wong Ho's coupon on the littered asphalt behind the restaurant, which smells of fried noodles and . . . fish.

Now I have also settled problem number two.

Just as hobos left marks on places good for handouts during the Great Depression, so we survivors of the Great Recession have our own marking system. No, it is nothing so crass as inappropriate littering. Even our homeless members know enough to bury our eliminations if we can.

It is an auditory signal, aka a mew news line.

In no time, local alley cats come pouring in from all directions, left, right, and up.

I make the proper paw gestures and gang signals, adding a few choice audible calls. The moniker of my mama, Ma Barker, is like a passkey on the mean streets of Vegas. Even bulldogs tremble at the mere mention of her name.

Soon I have the coupon in my fangs and twelve hardened street fighters at my back, three remaining behind to guard the "undead" bike.

I lead them from the back alley onto the nearest main street, retracing the way the Vampire and I have come. We all make quite a sight, though it takes some nerve for these retiring, dark-of-night slinkers to do a public cat-pride parade under the streetlights. Luckily, most establishments along here are closed and traffic is thin.

Soon I see the cruising Silver Cloud approaching at a stately crawl then veering wildly to our side of the street. I halt the clowder and wait. You do not often see thirteen of my discreet breed gathered in a docile pack with a solid black dude with white whiskers at their head.

The limo's back door opens without the polite offices of Rico.

Miss Temple Barr comes barreling out, Mr. Matt right behind her, followed by a slightly gimpy Mr. Max.

It is a good thing I have my cat pack cowed. I have learned the Ma Barker theory of management from the old dame herself. Gruff voice, clear orders, and cocked shivs.

Before my Miss Temple can reach me and undermine my leadership position with an avalanche of sloppy human sentiments, another gang arrives — a silent-running confluence of the sleekest red, black, and red-and-black sports cars I have ever laid eyes on, and I have laid eyes on a lot of pricey cars in Vegas.

Seven or eight surround the Silver Cloud, and they arrived faster than special effects in *Avatar*. Even I am blinking with surprise, but then I do the math. It helps that lots of long, tall dudes in summer-pale Zegna suits unbend from the low, futuristic cars, talking on cell phones and doing things with GPS devices.

It is, of course, Fontana, Inc., in their new fleet of electric Tesla Roadsters.

The absence of *vroom* in their descent en masse unnerves me, but is most reassuring to my troops.

Miss Temple brings herself to an equally silent dead stop at my feet and looks down, rebukingly.

Yeah, it was a bold move, but all is well that ends well. I drop the Wong Ho coupon at her Gianmarco Lorenzi-clad feet, which she passes on to Emilio or Eduardo or Ralph.

Two of the brothers hop in an unnervingly silent idling Tesla Roadster and vanish. Another Tesla driver dismounts.

(These are really low, two-seater sports cars, with just room enough for a guy and his girl and a lot of high-end audio equipment that will be way louder than this cool green expensive electric car will ever be.)

Boys must have their thundering bass one

way or another.

Pretty soon I hear the siren song of an engine that will not tiptoe. Eduardo and Emilio return, one driving the Tesla, one steering the recovered Hesketh Vampire. Sans helmet, which is tied on the back facedown. No Fontana brother will don a helmet that reads Speed Queen.

I notice that Giuseppe has collared Mr. Max and handed him something bulky in a plain brown-paper wrapper. Obviously, he has retrieved the lost handgun. I know Mr. Max meant merely to blow out a tire and catch the rider, but I cannot permit such a risky maneuver with my Miss Temple present.

After all, she is a jewel, and she immediately understood the import of the Wong Ho coupon I laid at her feet.

"I feel," she says to all within hearing, "in need of a wonton special dinner at Wong Ho's. I also spy a fish special that is too good to pass up."

She thanks the gathered brothers and various vehicles, which scatter to deliver the Vampire back to the Circle Ritz.

The Silver Cloud shadows my three human companions at about five miles an hour as my feline escorts swagger back to Wong Ho's.

By my observation, it is hot, crowded, and sweaty inside the humble eatery as my humans sit elbow to elbow at a tiny table filled with large platters of Asian delicacies.

Me and my new street gang enjoy the night air behind the place with a dozen orders of the fish special.

Koi it is not, but it *is* ambrosia to my home-less kin.

CHAPTER 34
POOLING RESOURCES

Temple parked in the Circle Ritz lot under the recently installed row of carports, where Matt's gorgeous new Jag sparkled like a "big rock candy mountain," even in the shade.

It seemed to have the word *Chicago* superimposed on it, a perfect billboard for the glitzy musical.

Maybe it was time for them to be leaving Las Vegas.

The weather was almost always hot and hard on her skin type — pasty and prone to freckles. She was getting tired of bathing in sunscreen. And coming from the Midwest, Temple was no stranger to the cold: think of the new outfits that she would need.

She'd tried to reach Matt, but he wasn't answering, so she went up to her condo, looked for Midnight Louie to be taking an afternoon nap in the air-conditioning, and found him AWOL again as well.

Temple swung her heavy tote bag to the

kitchen counter and sighed. Two lovers in town — one ex, one not — and she'd spent the morning catching up on PR matters all over town when she was thinking she was alone, confounded, and not doing well with her first "case."

She went searching for Louie, through the living room to the tiny triangular patio that made a corner to her unit in the round building. That's when she spied a lone figure swimming midday laps in the usually deserted pool below.

The building was adults-only, simply because fifties apartment units had been under 1,600 square feet, and the Circle Ritz residents were older adults at that. Electra Lark had converted larger units into condos to keep the building full, but the wedding-chapel business on the side kept her solvent. The business was literally "on the side" of the building, because nowadays a drive-by wedding service was even more popular than the charming chapel inside.

Honestly, Temple thought, *people couldn't wait for anything in this Internet era.*

What *she* couldn't wait for was to get out of her lonely, catless condo and down by that pool to observe and interrupt those powerful clockwork laps.

■ ■ ■ ■

Matt suddenly sensed a presence and surfaced, blinking chlorinated water from his eyes.

Swimming was his form of meditation, like martial arts was his form of exercise, although too many things in his life had been hopping in the last few months to get to class.

His first blurred glimpse of the silently watching female figure reminded him that Kathleen O'Connor had confronted him here, face-to-face, that he was the "beneficiary" of the only two true personal appearances she'd ever made in Vegas. Both times she'd cut him with words, and once with a razor.

But it was Temple squinting back at him in the hot sun, her vibrant peachy-red hair a waving, curlicued sunset out of an Alphonse Mucha print of *Summer.*

He turned in midlap and made the pool edge in one underwater bound.

"No splashing on my new leather sandals," she warned, stepping back.

That forced him to regard the fretwork of leather and laces both baring and snaring her feet to well above the ankles. Fetishwear made fashion, and he totally got why.

"I'll splash more than your shoes," Matt said, "if you don't run up and slip into some sunscreen and a suit and come back down here."

"You know I never use the pool."

"Why not?"

"Natural red hair. White skin. Freckles. Burning. Melanoma, which sounds like something pretty, but isn't."

"The sun's going over the building and you wear nothing but sixty SPF. You may wear nothing much as a bathing suit, but I wouldn't know, would I? Something as strappy as your shoes?"

"That would be possible. I can't remember. It's been a long time since I've been swimming."

She walked back and forth along the pool's length while he paced her in the water.

"I miss your *Dancing with the Celebs* spray tan," she noted.

"Pretty remarkable stuff. All the network anchors are wearing airbrush these days. I still have some. I could give you an all-over sample. Up in my rooms. After we swim."

The high heels paused. "I don't do well in bikinis, except for waxes," she had to add, to be provocative back.

"Why not?" he asked.

She rolled her eyes. "I'm not a thirty-six C, as you well know."

"I'm like a nonsnob art lover. I know what I like. I don't need caliber."

"Oh, Matt, I've had a bummer day. I've been hired for a real PI job and I'm totally flunking it. I don't tan, I don't swim, and I don't fill out a bikini. I'm just a short shoe freak with a curiosity bone instead of a funny bone."

"Come in," he reassured her. Tempted her. "The water's like aquamarine silk. I can hold you up, and so can the water. You will feel like a thirty-six C, as you always have to me. You can also explain to me what exactly a thirty-six C is later."

"You've seen Victoria's Secret ads on TV. You know it's all about false packaging."

"Nothing to do with you, then," he said. "Just join me. I'd really like it."

She sighed heavily and scampered back into the building.

Matt leaned his chin on his crossed elbows at the pool edge and smiled. All his cares and indecision were floating away. Temple needed a TLC break, and he was free, willing, and able to give it to her.

"This is really cool stuff," Temple called

from his bathroom two hours later. "And it really stays on in water?"

"Longer than I wanted it to," Matt answered from the bed. "Of course, they used tanning spray booths at the dance show."

She came out dressed and looking slightly toasty all over. "I prefer the personal touch. I'll never coax you to put sunscreen on me, but a spray-on tan — that felt like a great massage." She went over to strip back the sheets.

"Amazing!" She wasn't eyeing him. "There's hardly any rub-off on the sheets."

"There is some only because you weren't patient enough to lie still, like I told you."

"And why should I be patient with you about that? You've been gone a week. You haven't even asked if I missed you."

"I was trying really hard right now not to be insecure."

Temple perched on the edge of the bed while Matt got dressed. The sheets had long ago dried him indirectly.

"Will all these shoe straps rub off the tan when I walk?" she wondered, inspecting her feet.

"I don't know, Temple. I don't wear strappy shoes."

That made her laugh. "You have nothing to be insecure about."

Then she got serious, addressing something she'd left unsaid for the four days he'd been back.

"I hope you understand that my getting a call from Max as if I was his last lifeline was like you talking to a lost soul on the WCOO call line. All he knew at that point was what Garry Randolph had been able to tell him in their last, short time together. I couldn't let him go blundering around without anchors of any sort in his past."

"I know you couldn't, "Matt said, sitting to pull on his shoes. "I couldn't have either."

She got to her knees on the mattress and plastered herself against his bare back. "We're both fixers, aren't we? And insecurity makes us human. I shouldn't have felt so . . . superior . . . to Savannah Ashleigh that I thought I could fix her family feuds and banish a bunch of vultures."

He turned to take her in his arms. "But you did and you can. You just aren't used to sleuthing without a partner."

"It's true. Louie's been annoying and seems to be up to something on his own these days."

They didn't mention that Max had been her invisible partner when he lived in town before.

"What's really bugging you about Savannah's case, Temple?"

"Other than that there's this irresistible distraction back in town and I can hardly find the time to make progress on it?"

"That *is* me you're referring to, right?"

"No one else," she promised, and sealed it with a kiss.

"Maybe I'm too young for the job," she said when they'd settled into a comfy embrace. "Her aunt Violet is an elderly lady. I don't know if she's getting senile or someone is messing up her mind to make her act that way. Expecting anyone to live in that oddball old house until all the resident cats die of natural causes is crazy.

"Once Violet dies, the people around her have no stake in honoring her wishes. She used to be shrewd in business, and I'm sure she has some money socked away in mutual funds and insurance, but she's hardly a Rockefeller heir. I just don't get why she has this cadre of suspicious people around her."

"Let's go find out."

"Let *us?*"

Matt checked his wristwatch. Temple's eyes saucered to see it was new, like his Jag, not only expensive but exquisite. Those producers were heavy seducers, but she doubted Matt even knew what the watch

413

was. A Rolex would have tipped him off. Clever people. She needed to meet them. He was a babe in the woods, but he was *her* babe.

"Sure," he said, the laugh lines around his brown eyes making rays like the kind kids draw around suns.

She watched him, soothed, satisfied, blissed out.

"You've got me, babe," he said, "from eleven to eleven — Eleven A.M. to eleven P.M. That's not counting any sack time you commandeer. So use me. We'll go over to Violet's house and figure out together what's what."

"I love you," Temple said, following it up with a long, luxurious kiss. "Give me five to hop downstairs and get changed into kitty-litter-kicking shoes."

"For a moment I thought you were going to say 'Kitty the Cutter–kicking shoes.' "

Temple didn't hesitate for a second. "That too."

CHAPTER 35
CANDLE IN THE WIND

Temple got out of her Miata across the street from Violet's house, resigned when she saw Savannah's Sky parked right in front and the fishnet leggings and corset-attired actress returning from the house to the curb.

"You do remember Savannah Ashleigh?" she quietly asked Matt as he unpretzeled from the car's passenger seat.

He wasn't entirely naive. He'd been wearing his usual Timex when he'd come to collect her for this investigatory outing.

"She's all revved up about something," Temple told him. "The animal shelter people want Violet to give them a bequest."

"Are you sure Savannah Ashleigh's motives are pure?"

"*Um,* normally I'd say she's too stupid to be crooked, but I'm beginning to think her eternal starlet act is crazy like a fox."

Matt eyed the silicone-enhanced vision on

six-inch platform heels heading toward them. "She *is* such a fox."

"I didn't know that you knew that expression."

"I mean the 'sly' version of the word. You're the only true fox on my horizon."

"Purr," Temple said. "Speaking of which, prepare yourself for cats."

"And you're not speaking of Savannah Ashleigh this time?"

"Why are women always compared to animals?"

"A man can be called a 'wolf' and a just plain 'animal.' "

"True," she said. "It might be interesting to see Savannah interact with Violet's estate suitors."

But first the Scarlet Starlet had to interact with Matt, whom she greeted with a snarky grin.

"Say, Mister Midnight. I saw you bossa nova–ing on *Dancing with the Celebs.* Lookin' good. And bad."

"No bossa novas," Matt said. "They're a dated dance."

Temple watched Savannah's seductive facade glaze over and crack. She wasn't used to impervious.

"What's the excitement about?" Temple asked.

"There's some cat shelter hoping to get Violet to sign on the dotted line, at least for a bequest if not the whole schmear. Violet is so confused, the place reeks and —" Captain Jack's masked face popped up from Savannah's purse, shocking the heck out of Matt. "— and that big longhaired cat inside named Maverick showed an unnatural interest in eating Captain Jack," Savannah went on in her usual sultry but aggrieved way.

"If," said Matt, " 'Captain Jack' is that marsupial in your purse, I can see why."

"Jack is no . . . Mar-soopial. He is a fixed ferret, but still not about to take kindly to pushy other males. Not even," she told Temple, "your alpha fixed cat."

"Thanks to you," Temple said. "If you recall, Louie is sterile, not impotent. And speaking of kitty-food commercial spoke-cats, how are Yvette and Solange these days?"

"You know darn well." Savannah stamped her solid-steel spike heel in the heat-mushy asphalt, where it stuck. "I wanted to smuggle the poor things out in my purse, but they're hiding somewhere inside that hellhole. I can't find them."

"Maybe they're hiding from you," Temple suggested, as Matt knelt like Prince Charming to free Savannah's impaled heel. She simpered prettily and balanced a hand on his shoulder while cooing, *"Ummm."*

"Are ferrets pursebroken?" Temple asked. "Captain Jack seems to be making too many happy wiggling motions for a fixed male."

"He's upset, and why not? Violet's place is a circus."

Meanwhile Matt had freed her heel and stood, leaving her without support.

Savannah staggered, trying to pull Captain Jack from her purse. As she extracted the wriggling form, it dribbled on the pavement.

"Eek!" Savannah struggled to hold Jack as far from her as possible and still keep standing on her fashionable stilts.

Matt took pity and stabilized her flailing elbow while Temple pulled Savannah's expensive purse free of the ferret's aiming range.

"When have you last given him a bathroom break?" Temple asked.

"He's trained!"

Matt picked up Savannah's wrist with its glitzy watch. "Six o'clock? Is that A.M. or P.M.? Your watch has stopped. It's only one P.M. I don't think the cats inside will appreciate ferret markings. You'd better get home for a make over. Leave the lowly chores to us."

"Oh! Oh! Oh!" Savannah stood still except

for limp-wristed, taloned hands shaking off ferret pee as if she were a slasher-movie beauty queen ridding herself of drops of blood. "Captain Jack has been a bad, bad boy. We will have to wait for the sun to dry us before we go in Mommy's pretty car."

In the desert heat, that wouldn't be long.

Matt and Temple headed up the cracked concrete walkway.

"This may be tricky without Savannah by our sides," she told him. "I've only met Violet twice."

"On the other hand," he said, opening the rickety screen door that covered the heavy wooden door, "we might find out a lot more without Savannah there."

A knock produced a harried-looking Rowdy Smith, running a nervous hand over his crew-cut head and focusing on Temple.

"You're Savannah's friend," he identified her, frowning. "Where'd Savannah go?"

"She had to attend to a small animal crisis," Matt explained.

"And who's this guy?" Rowdy asked Temple, as if they were old friends.

"Matt Devine." Matt captured his hand for a quick shake and also managed to get into the darkened house by taking Temple's elbow in the other hand and ushering her inside. "I do counseling work. Maybe I can help with the insistent visitors."

"I was just here cleaning cat boxes. Violet's getting pretty confused. She thought Savannah was Alexandra today."

"I imagine there's a family resemblance," Temple said.

Rowdy blinked hard. "Uh . . . maybe so. Maybe so. Alexandra was so young and pretty, though, nothing fake about her. Meanwhile, the crystal con man and some old friend of Violet's are both here, selling themselves as the ones to move in and keep the house and cats going after she's gone."

The usual suspects were gathered around the island that was Violet these days.

"Mister Midnight!" the sick woman exclaimed when Temple introduced Matt Devine.

"You know my radio program?" he asked, taking her frail hand.

"Oh, I listen to you every night you're on. Tell Ambrosia her voice and the music she plays just float the pain away."

"That'll mean a lot to her," he told Violet.

"Oh, you're wonderful, too. I can only think that if you'd been on the air when I'd had my little spat with Alexandra you might have talked me past my . . . selfishness and anger. She died so tragically and so young.

Could Ambrosia — ?"

"She'll dedicate a song to you and Alexandra tonight," Matt said.

Temple was glad she'd told Matt Violet's family history.

Meanwhile, Freddie had pushed herself into place behind Matt, so when he turned to give Violet breathing room, he was flat up against her formidable form, and trapped.

"Mister Midnight, wonderful to meet you. I'm a dear friend of Violet's. Freddie La-Costa." She drew him away from the bed and Violet's hearing. "If you could publicize the All Creatures Arc, it's a very worthy cause. 'No Needy Creature Turned Away' is our motto. And, of course, Violet's leaving her estate to a cause instead of a person would be so wonderful. You might mention that on your show."

"It's not 'my' show, Miz LaCosta. The producers have all the say on that. I'm sure I can talk to them about your idea, though. It's a hot-button topic, animals suffering on the home front when people are spiraling out of financial control."

"I've done some talk radio myself," Jayden said, extricating Matt from Freddie's clutches into his own expert hands.

Temple took advantage of Matt's celebrity

and people skills to occupy everybody in the house — except for the cats — while she explored deeper into the terrain.

Furry feline sides massaged her ankles all the way into the kitchen, but they were fewer than during her last visit. Gleams of reflective irises from hidden cats led her through the dim dining room, as she sought to get a firmer sense of Violet, her house, the many cats, and what anyone would really want here beyond the opportunity to become an instant heir.

Older Sunbelt homes tended to be dim interior mazes that beat back the heat. She was glad when she finally found a light to follow, a flickering flame.

The source was a huge, fat, decorative candle, maybe nine inches tall, on a black wrought-iron stand.

Hearing the steady murmur of voices from the main room, Temple found a round plastic control on the nearby wall and turned up the rheostat until there was light enough to see by without alerting the residents. She stood in an octagonal hall between the public rooms and bedroom wing, where one wall was a "shrine" to Alexandra.

The exquisite custom candle was diagonally striped in soft pastel shades, with white butterflies drifting upward against the watercolor hues.

Its strong flame illuminated the life-size stylized color portrait above it of a young woman's face and shoulders. She seemed to breathe in the flickering light, making Temple jump a bit, as if she were meeting a ghost.

As she examined the photo, she saw that Alexandra's face was perfectly made up, the thin eyebrows and lips both sharply arched, eyeliner and eye shadow and lip gloss impeccably applied. This must be what a twentyish Savannah had looked like.

The expensive candle sat on a carved Asian chest. Behind the doors elaborately inset with mother-of-pearl, she found several photo albums. A quick flip-through showed childhood photos of Alexandra, tapering off in young adulthood. In many photos, Alex was dressed in glitzy dance-recital costumes, always an ultrafeminine child, although in a more wholesome way compared to today's tweens, who emulated the ultrasexy Pussycat Dolls.

This "little doll" of a child and young woman reminded Temple of Savannah's doted-upon "accessory" pets.

Oddly enough, there were no cats in any

of young Alexandra's photos, no pets of any kind.

If Violet and her daughter had become estranged, as the boyfriend, Rowdy, had said, Alex's sudden death would have been doubly devastating. Hadn't Savannah mentioned that Violet's cat "collection" started when she took Alexandra's cats after her death, that Violet even thought Alex could "come back as a cat," and started taking in strays? Probably that conviction was the first sign of mental failing.

So now, facing her own death, Violet wanted the cats she believed might "forever" harbor her daughter's spirit to be kept in this house for as long as they were alive, to the last one. She must hope something of the love mother and daughter had once shared would survive through them.

Temple shook her head at the futility of family feuds, between Violet and her siblings first, and then with her daughter. Now, the bereaved mother had made herself an easy target for the takers of the world.

Temple replaced the albums and lifted out a box, the kind of pretentious packaging that expensive stationery comes in. When she opened it, she saw newspaper clippings and two slim leather-bound diaries, items she needed to read, not skim.

Still crouching below Violet's shrine to Alexandra, she followed an instinctive investigative urge. She stuffed the box into her tote bag to examine later, when she had time, and stood.

Violet's mind had begun unraveling with Alexandra's death. Someone had wanted Violet alone and isolated in her house and had likely pushed Pedro that night, intending at least to injure him and get him out of the way.

That could have been any man or woman. Maybe among these souvenirs Temple could find a motive more personal than grabbing a confused old woman's estate.

Because she knew one thing: regardless of whoever among the current candidates Violet was persuaded to make her heir and executor, once Violet died, the cats would be the first to go.

CHAPTER 36
THE FRENCH RESISTANCE

Since some unknown person or persons has been making it easy for the inside cats to slip out, I am happy to find that it is just as easy for an outside cat to slip in.

So I am already the inside dude when my Miss Temple and Mr. Matt pay a visit to Miss Violet. I also witness my sweet and straightforward roommate making a surreptitious survey of the house's nooks and crannies, specifically the hall leading to the closed doors of the bedroom wing.

I must say that I am shocked — shocked! — when I see her prying inside a chest of Asian design under the icon of some saint with a candle burning in front of her. You would think that an intimate associate of a former priest would not tamper with religious artifacts, but then she is an intimate associate of a former priest, and I am not sure if that is kosher. Great Bast never expressed herself on rules of personal conduct. She is a Rules of Prey sort of gal.

However, the search and abstraction of evidence is smoothly done, thanks to the fact that humans can tote objects in other than their mouths. That gives them great versatility.

So, once she and Mr. Matt have made their adieus to the folks in the front room and are gone, I resume my mission.

First off, I look up my inside guy, Maverick.

Being shades of brown, he comes and goes in the dimly lit interior like a shadow.

"Psst!"

I nearly jump out of my best satin-lapelled suit down to my skin when he ambushes me in the kitchen.

"How goes it," he asks, "with our exterior brethren?"

"And sisters," I add. Or is that "sisthren"? One never knows when Miss Midnight Louise is listening, although I have her stationed outside.

Maverick shakes his head impatiently at the fine points. He would not be so rude were my own fine points at his throat.

"What do you want in here?" he demands. "There are no resident black cats. You will stick out like a sore dewclaw."

"I need to get the Ashleigh sisters out now. It will be a delicate extraction. I have scouted a work-crew outbuilding near the flood channel where our homemade clowder can shelter until the evil afoot here is rooted out."

Maverick eyes the heaped bowls of Free-to-Be-Feline that now outnumber the cats around the place.

"What can they all eat and drink in the wilderness?" he asks.

"We have scouted a leaking water pipe near the flood channel, and Miss Midnight Louise is a very vigorous, ah, cook. If you like desert sushi."

Maverick nods sagaciously. "Sushi is good. Miss Savannah has brought us boxes of it lately."

"Where are the sisters?"

"With the greater number of people coming and going, they have hidden."

Oh, Great Bast's earring! I will not only have to convince them to accompany me into the great outdoors, I will have to find them first.

In minutes, Maverick and I have searched the house, floorboard to furniture, to no avail. Even the occupied main room, which he covered because he's a known resident, is not hiding the Persian sisters. We are stumped.

Then I realize rule number ten of feline behavior. If a door is opened, you are through it, and the less you are noticed, the better. That is how all Miss Violet's cats are wandering out of the house, through deliberately ajar exits. The Ashleigh girls would never venture outside alone, though. I rush to the hall and employ my street-sharp shivs as a crowbar under the Asian cabinet doors.

Presto, pussycats! Four fluorescent green eyes blink back at me. They slipped in when Miss Temple turned her back to slip the purloined goods into her tote bag. I was so busy watching her, they even evaded my keen private eye.

"Bonjour, chéries," I say. "I have come to escort you out of this unhappy domicile to a fine new nightclub down the street. It serves sushi."

"Oh, Louie," says Yvette, forgetting her snarled hairdo. "You look very handsome in your freshly washed tuxedo."

"And," says Solange, "Miss Savannah often brought us sushi when we were with her."

"Well, you are with me now, *mademoiselles,* and we have only to slip outside and be on our way."

Solange's pretty face looks worried. "Oh, Louie. I do not know if we can, without permission."

"Of course you can," I say, nudging each along by the shoulder. "You are French. And so am I."

CHAPTER 37
PRIME-TIME TAIL

Max sat in the rented winter-gray Prius almost as dark as the night itself and wondered if he'd ever had this thought before: *Molina had been right.*

Grabbing Dirty Larry and marching him into her house had had its satisfactions, but following the undercover narc now that he knew Molina had him under surveillance made the job much harder.

Nobody ever expected a tail to be driving a Prius, though, making an ecological statement. Max also wore a funky little tweed cap, one that a guy who played golf or listened to folk music might wear.

"Layers," Gandolph had always said. "The best disguises have layers."

If Podesta was in danger of noticing the guy in the Prius, Max could doff the cap, circle back from a different direction, and still get in some useful tailing time.

One thing he knew: Dirty Larry was

indeed dirty. He'd lied to Molina three nights ago at her house. Not all the time, about everything, but about a lot. Max could hear a lie the way musicians hear a single sour note.

Cynical C. R. had taken everything either of them had said with a grain of salt. Max wondered what the *R* stood for. He could see someone with a first name like *Carmen* had to be kicked off the law-enforcement career ladder. He thought of the opera. *Opera? Did he like opera?* Most men would think of some hot Latina chick.

Larry had been visiting the scenes of the Barbie Doll Killer's two Vegas crimes. Max saw the pattern early and kept the Prius on the farthest circling shopping-mall roads. Larry's big, bruising seventies Impala made him easy to be seen despite the deep-bronze-brown body color. D. L. expected to be predator, not prey. Visiting crime scenes was an uncool thing to do, especially now that he knew he'd been watched. Serial killers did that sort of thing. They couldn't keep away from the stage of their secret triumphs. They drove around at night.

So did cops.

And ex-magicians.

Max noticed the Impala disappearing between rows of parked cars and toddled the Prius — not his speed — along the access roads toward an exit.

He caught the car's taillights accelerating onto the freeway and had to goose the Prius's gas pedal, cheered by the swift, if quiet, response. Dirty Larry was either trying to lose any tail or was feeling a need, an intense need.

Holy St. Mackerel! Was he following a killer to a new crime site?

Ten minutes later he was playing catch-up, as Larry left the freeway on an exit he'd never taken before. Max's heart wanted to race in time with his car engine, but the damn thing was too quiet. He was on the trail of something dark, something secret in Dirty Larry's life, he knew it.

The scene at Molina's house had made Larry *less* cautious, not more. Max sensed an emotional ebb and flow in the man's driving that said he was losing control. Max was Irish; he understood how charm and fury could coexist. Podesta. Dirty Larry's father had to have had Italian or Sicilian blood, but something stubbornly Celtic was in there, too. Maybe Scots.

They were driving through a gently aged neighborhood, passing the occasional corner church or convenience store at the bigger

432

intersections. Max doffed the hat, sat it like a memorial on the Prius's passenger seat, felt a moment of grief too dark to bear.

Not too close, a voice in his head cautioned. *Not now.*

He forced his hands to relax their strangling grip on the steering wheel, even as Dirty Larry's wallowing Impala took a wide, sloppy left into a small parking lot.

Max and the Prius cruised on by, eyes and headlights front. Max glimpsed a long, mostly one-story building, institutional yet in a residential neighborhood. New, but pre–Great Recession. Blond brick, lots of outside security lights, damn it.

Max checked his watch: 9:30 P.M. Even late suppers are over and TVs are on prime time. He spied the flickering, cozy halos in almost every window. An apartment building? One-story?

He parked the Prius on a side street and shut down everything, silent-running motor, headlights. No radio. And waited. A half hour later the bad-neighborhood rumble of Dirty Larry's Impala notified him his subject was leaving the property.

Max knew he was now trailing a "subject." He waited ten minutes then guided the Prius around to the front portico and the central two-story core of the building, where matte steel letters over the entry doors read ST. ROSE'S NURSING HOME.

Max frowned and parked the Prius right out front, where it looked very at home. He paused in leveraging his legs out of the driver's seat, still a slightly hard physical — and a very emotional — move for him, when he paused to lean back to reclaim the tweed hat.

A wee dorky look would do for him here, he thought.

If things had worked out differently in Belfast, he might have been visiting Gandolph here, or vice versa. Garry, I hardly knew ye. . . .

The large lit circular lobby echoed his footsteps, magnifying the minor hesitation in his gait.

The woman at the desk looked up with compassion on her face.

Every little bit helps, Max told himself. "Dashing" was not his high card at the moment.

She had soft, pretty features and was in her late fifties. Her name tag read BARBARA. Max checked the clock above Barbara's head: 9:40 P.M.

"Yes? Visiting hours are almost over," she told him, "but you have a few minutes."

"Sorry I'm late," Max said a bit breathlessly with the shade of a brogue. "I'm from out of town . . . the country, really. My international flight was late and I missed meeting my cousin Larry at his condo to drive here together."

"What a time you've had of it, Mister — ?"

"Randolph. Larry's last name is Podesta. I don't know the room number —"

"You just missed Larry. He's such a regular. Most people would give up after a couple years. Not Larry. The room is in the left wing. Follow the green stripe in the tiles. She's in room six."

"Thank you," Max said. "I'll, uh, catch up with Larry later."

He began hustling down the hall, his mind going faster than his legs. *She? A couple years?* An ailing mother with Alzheimer's? He did not want to feel sorry for the man or feel like a creep for faking his way in here.

"Mister Randolph," the receptionist called sharply.

What the hell? He turned. Had Podesta come back for some reason?

She was still alone at the desk and smiling at him. "Do you need a cane? We have plenty."

"Ah, no. Thank you. You're very kind and perceptive, but I need to learn to do without."

She nodded. "You don't need very long with Teresa, just to feel better that you've seen her and can tell your cousin so."

Max moved on toward room six.

Creep, he berated himself. He was glad he couldn't recall what ruses he'd used in his previous life of counterterrorism. Sleeping with the enemy had probably been one; Molina had been right. Certainly he'd done just that accidentally his first time out, with Kathleen O'Connor. And maybe again, with his partner in escape, Revienne.

This was a top facility. Spotless. No usual urine smell — and he had empathy for that now. Only Febreze, as in a modern morgue. Cheery decor and colors, an air of attendants near but not hovering. Just the kind of place he'd put Garry in rehabilitation if . . . he'd survived.

Max slowed to approach the door numbered six. It was always hard to seem normal around the gravely ill, but he guessed this lady's comprehension was pretty nil, and his visit wouldn't alarm her. Old people can be as trusting as children if their minds have decamped.

In fact, he almost jumped a little when he spotted some stuffed animals inside — a pink tiger and a blue whale. Could this be a *child?*

He paused in the open doorway, aware that a nurse would be doing a bed check soon. Any minute. He'd have to do some fact-checking himself, on the patient's relationship to Dirty Larry Podesta, for instance. The sly nickname seemed obscene in this pleasant place, with its very serious reason for being.

He let his eyes pan up from the foot of the bed to the frail patient in it, her thin hair still showing the morning's brush marks, her face funeral-parlor composed, only her arms visible under the flowered hospital gown, as thin and angular as a high-fashion model's.

He recalled Revienne's anorexic sister, the suicide.

For this girl was not a child, but she was wrenchingly young, maybe in her late teens.

And cradled in her left scarecrow arm, wearing something sassy, shiny, purple, and Lady Gaga, lay a late-edition Barbie doll.

Max Kinsella could have used that cane now. He sank onto the visitor's chair. And just looked.

"I tried to prepare you, Mister Randolph," a voice said behind him.

He turned to find the receptionist in the doorway. Those rubber-soled white nurses'

437

shoes had come up behind him as silently as an assassin's. Did she suspect something?

"Aren't you supposed to be at the desk?" he asked.

"I had someone watch it. Not everyone who visits can deal with patients in a coma. Did you know her?"

"Not since she was a child." *Liar.*

"I was worried," she said, "the shock might impact your injuries."

"Now I see," Max said, realizing she considered him a sort of patient, too. "The cane."

She eyed his legs. "Was it an accident?"

"Ye-es." Not quite true either, but "murder attempt" was not a useful conversational gambit.

"Both legs?"

"Yes." What a relief to be honest with this damn saintly woman. "A couple months ago. I was, ah, in a coma for several weeks. In . . . in Europe."

"You came out all right?"

"Memory issues." Another honest answer. *Wait!* He could use that to pump her.

"I don't even remember Teresa's full name. Just saw her as child. Playing. Running." *Scum.*

"Oh, such a shame. Teresa Paddock. She only has a disabled grandmother and her stepbrother left. Horrible case."

"Accident?"

The nurse's eyes avoided his.

Max knew just what to say. "Larry's not aware of the extent of my injuries. Coma. The memory loss. I don't want to ask too many questions, make it worse for him. I've been overseas on a job, for, oh, before Teresa was struck down. What is it now, how long?"

"More than five years. She's been here two years."

He joined her in regarding the girl, shaking his head. "Somebody . . . did this, didn't they?"

"It was in all the papers. Horrible. In the west shopping-mall parking lot. Attempted strangulation. Someone came by. She lived. Just."

Max's recent memory dominated mind trolled for his former deductive processes. Eureka! He visualized puzzle pieces dropping like manna from the heavens above, assembling visually above his head. Dirty Larry. His stepsister. Attack. Mall parking lot. Barbie doll.

Dirty thoughts assembling. Beautiful young starstruck stepsister. Hanky-panky. She had to be shut up. Had to hide a motivated murder inside a storm flurry of mystifying ones. D. L. went into undercover police work, could go anywhere, un-watched . . . unlike an ordinary partnered cop. Oh, my God. Looking at this . . . broken doll of a young woman in her pink-and-blue nursing-home bed and thinking these things brought a fog of pollution into the room.

"Mister Randolph? Maybe the facts are too much for your own condition."

"No." He shook his head, violently. "The facts are never too much. Has the attempted killer not been caught?"

"Never," she said, sighing deeply. "And there've been more deaths. The papers call them the Barbie Doll Killer's work." She nodded at the doll in Teresa's arms. "She had a big Barbie collection. Dreamed of stardom the way kids do these days. *American Idol.* Anybody can be rich and famous in an instant. It's so innocent and tragic. Young girls today have no notion of the dangers in the world. They go from Barbie dolls to Pussycat Dolls."

"So her parents were absent?"

"I don't know the particulars."

I will, Max thought. He checked his watch.

"I need to go," he told her.

"I give you a lot of credit for having the will to see her when your own strength has

440

been so compromised."

He stood, stumbling a little. His limbs liked to "fall asleep" on him still.

She offered a shoulder.

What a woman!

"If I felt twenty years younger, I'd ask you for a date," he said.

She chuckled, being the one with twenty years on him. "I don't date younger men."

They walked out together, the clock above the reception desk showing the big hand on twelve and the small one on ten.

Max pulled out the Prius Smart key with the car-rental logo on it.

He had a feeling this was an occasion when his old self would amp up the charm, leave the lady with a false sense of almost flirtation. Charm was a tawdry bauble compared to compassion.

"Thank you, Nurse Barbara," he said. "My friend . . . in *my* accident . . . died. On the spot. Head trauma. If he'd lived to recuperate, this is the kind of place I'd have hoped he could have come to."

"What a lovely vote of confidence, Mister Randolph. I do hope I've been of help to you tonight."

"More than you'll ever know," Max said.

And than I deserve . . .

Max sat outside in the car, brooding. Gandolph had teased him during their journeys about Irish dark nights of the soul.

That veteran nurse had been right the moment she set eyes on him. The recent trauma marked him and had affected him far more than he'd been willing to believe or admit.

Apparently, he'd developed quite a conscience while in his coma. He'd recognized a certain automatic, ruthless survival instinct in him while on the run in Switzerland. Now, supposedly "safe," he recognized another restless, driving need . . . for honesty. And . . . connection.

Not gonna happen in Las Vegas as the odd man out, he told himself. Too little too late. All you can do is work for the "man," who in this case is a woman, keep out of Temple Barr and Matt Divine's way, get the guy who put that girl into permanent Barbie dolldom, and save the only people in town he did know from the walking, emotional kill zone that was Kathleen O'Connor.

He pulled out his cell phone and checked the last photo, luckily taken before he'd sat down by the bedside and the receptionist had come in. The camera had captured a head shot perfect for ID purposes, a sleeping Teresa who looked almost normal.

Imagine being tucked away for eternity with only a Barbie doll for company.

CHAPTER 38
RAFI, WITH FRIES, TO GO

"McDonald's?" Molina frowned up through her sunglasses at the familiar golden arches over the outside eating where they sat.

"At least," she went on, between sips of the chain's Starbucks-busting McCafé Latte, "Matt Devine would meet me someplace atmospheric, like the Blue Dahlia, when he's asking me to give him special information. Temple Barr even shows up at headquarters politely asking for an audience."

"The Blue Dahlia, huh?"

Max Kinsella's secretive smile was meant to rattle her, and it did. Who the heck had been talking to him about that place?

"I picked someplace cheap because you're paying." Kinsella kept his own sunglasses cast down to his paper cup, his eyes, like hers, slipping sideways to check out the other customers.

"And what's with the Hawaiian shirt?" she

444

asked in a retaliatory attempt to annoy. "The midday sun forcing you to abandon your signature black?"

" 'Loud' is always the best disguise. Besides, I lost my wardrobe in a hunting accident."

"Most amusingly put."

"I'm glad you and the home closet confirm black as my signature in my previous life. I've been instinctively avoiding it since I got my second lease on a memory."

"So 'Las Vegas clown,' aka rainbow vomit, is your new look?"

"I'm making sure not to have a 'look,' especially now that Larry Podesta will require my constant attention."

"Since when? What about watching Rafi?"

"I suggest you put him on Dirty Larry, too."

"Oh, he'd like that."

"That's why he'd be good at the job." Max made a face at his strong black coffee and set it aside.

"Since when are you directing my surveillance needs?" Molina asked.

"I've, ah, found out something pretty damning about our mutual object of suspicion. Until this, I'd thought it could be some misdirected mini-obsession with you personally."

"I'm so flattered."

"Well, you had me pegged for that role, and I don't find myself so inclined now, so I must not have been then."

"Not necessarily. Anyone with a police-work history would not confuse sexual stalking with romance, Kinsella. I always knew those home invasions were threats."

"You weren't too plain about the incidents. Better come clean now."

"Why?"

"Then I'll shock you to your menswear socks and tell you the truly horror-movie discovery I made about Dirty Larry. First the incidents.

"So," he said, enjoying the topic, "you sing somewhere in vintage velvet. The singing detective. Not new."

"I'm not doing that anymore."

"But your first sign of home invasion was when an extra vintage velvet gown showed up in your bedroom closet.

"Right."

"Too bad my memory's on the fritz. I have a feeling I'd know where to get more of those velvet gowns for you, wholesale. I don't suppose you have any photos of you got up as Carmen. That would be worth a thousand words."

"Sorry, no souvenir pics. Carmen was a

live, private gig. I didn't even allow them to use one of those cheesy chanteuse portraits behind glass outside the place."

Max framed her face with his thumbs and forefingers like a director. "Taken at a noir angle, red lipstick, and a black Dahlia kissing your . . . left cheek, like an exotic jungle spider."

"You don't need a memory. Your imagination is off the chart to begin with. I sang, all right? The band was cool and the jazz was hot and I had an unused talent."

"I bet you have many."

She ignored the smoldering look. Kinsella had always challenged her dignity and need to be utterly professional at all times, only now he didn't remember that. She did know he'd been relentlessly stubborn then and was now.

"Okay." She was eager to finish this humiliating confession. "The next 'invasion' was a lot more personal. The bedside radio playing when I came home, a box on my bed containing lingerie, Victoria's Secret or Frederick's of Hollywood. Then —"

"Which lingerie hustler? There's a big difference, even Mister Memoryless knows that."

"What? Red and black and filmy has degrees?"

"Oh, yes, *cher* lieutenant. You've never worked prostitution?"

She held off a retort. They'd put her on hooker duty in L.A., stings to humiliate the rookie who towered over some of the johns, tall enough to be mistaken for a transsexual. Some of that fury at those sexist games rose to choke her for a moment. Her hands resisted strangling the crushable, smooth-coated paper coffee cup.

"Sorry," Kinsella said. "I honestly don't think enough. Provoking reactions gets my own brain going full speed again. That was tacky."

"Agreed. Provocative was always your modus operandi." She decided to proceed because she really, really needed his info on Podesta. "There was a note inside."

"That read . . . ?"

" 'You dress like a nun.' "

"*Hmm.* Why wouldn't you? Smart, and you are that."

He started a psychoanalytical riff on her right then. "You wear Las Vegas Metropolitan Police Department street-cop khaki in the heat of the summer. I bet it's navy and other dark neutrals in what passes for winter here. Pantsuits, like our shrewd secretary of state. Both khaki and navy are military colors, subtly authority-enforcing, desexual-

448

izing on the job. Also, you wear the men's socks with your low-heeled boots that keep you from towering too unduly over inferior and superior male officers. Women's knee-highs are hot and cut off circulation at the . . . er, knees. Guys always dress for comfort. You adapt to be as neutral as humanly possible. That's why you needed to let Carmen out to play."

"How did this become about me and my working wardrobe?"

"Because it is." Kinsella leaned across the cheesy plastic table. "It was always about you. At least the home stalking incidents were, even the Barbie doll planting job. I wish I could assure you that your daughter's okay, but it could escalate to involve her. We've got one, maybe two, very sick minds loose in Vegas."

"Dirty Larry?"

"I'm not ruling him out. Give me Rafi. He's a good man."

"That I don't need to hear from you, Kinsella! I'll be damned. Memory or not, I've never trusted you. I've always believed you capable of anything."

"Thanks. Then you know I'm the man for the job."

"What freaking job?"

449

"Finding and stopping the Barbie Doll Killer, and saving your butt."

CHAPTER 39
LIVING DOLL

"Max?"

"You sound surprised enough to be hearing a voice from the grave," he told Temple over the phone. "Didn't I used to call you all the time?"

"Not lately. That's why I'm surprised." Temple blinked at her computer screen. "I'm just lost in a multimedia world. Let me save some stuff."

In truth, Temple had been more than surprised. She'd been almost shocked off her ergonomic office-chair seat. Until this call, Max had stayed away from her, solo, as if operating on another planet since his return.

"What stuff?" he asked.

"Podcasts, Tweets. Web site updates. The public-relations world is getting to be less paper and more screen every second."

"I'm impressed — and depressed — to hear that, if that makes sense."

"I get that reaction," Temple said. "I'm updating constantly."

"Kind of like me."

"Yes." She kept quiet, waiting to hear what Max wanted. He must have called for a reason.

Her silence did the trick.

"Look, Temple, I've resolved to stay off your radar, out of your hair, whatever. But I gather your 'career path' has made you good at 'ferreting' out information, and I need some fast."

"About the shootout in Belfast?"

"Nothing about me or any of my works. I can manage that on my own. Listen, in my quest to er, look up my own past around town, I've encountered some earthshaking possibilities involving the Barbie Doll Killer."

"I see. Why call me? Molina's really mellowed toward you now that you've got your own one-man soap-opera plot going. You should be talking to her."

"Maybe so. But I need to have a credible case by then. It's something I've stumbled over. I don't want to accuse an innocent man."

"Really? You think you have a lead on the killer?"

"Yes, really. What I'm asking isn't danger-

452

ous, Temple. I need information about a nursing-home patient who may have been victim one. Teresa Paddock. The anniversary of her attack is coming up, so the media would likely do an update."

"Depressingly, probably not, Max. Media has to be so 'now' now."

"And if you could arrange a visit with a nurse-receptionist named Barbara, you'd have it made."

"I'm supposed to fake an interview with a woman, a girl, the Barbie Doll Killer *may* have put in a nursing home?"

"No interview needed. She's in a coma."

"Max!"

"I know it's a tough thing to see. I've already been there, but I figure you can find out more on the case way faster than I could."

"Why not use Molina? She has access to police files, not just news trails. Or even Alch? I might be able to persuade him."

"No. Nothing official. Yet. I can't tell you why. I was thinking of the time you spent playing girlfriend with Molina's daughter. Mariah could be in danger. She fits the victim profile. You know that's been a constant worry."

Temple tapped a fingernail on the glass-covered desktop. Louie liked to lounge by her computer when she was working, and his nails were death on wood grain. She was tempted to tell Max the new suspicions about who had planted the Barbie doll at the Molina house. She couldn't. She had no idea what angle he was working, or how much it might conflict with Molina's concerns.

"Temple?"

Max sounding uncertain was just not right.

"If this girl's condition made the news," she conceded, "I can find the basic facts pretty fast. No need for me to visit the nursing home."

"I want your opinion on the setup there."

"You've seen it, you've said."

"Not from a girly point of view."

"No wonder you can't go to Molina."

"You had a Barbie doll once yourself, didn't you?"

Temple hesitated. "Yes and no. One. Once. One day."

"What do you mean?"

"My older brothers commandeered her the day after Christmas for target practice."

"You have older brothers?"

"Four."

"No other siblings?"

"Nope."

"It's a wonder you're not following a career in the World Wrestling Entertainment franchise."

"Or maybe obvious why I didn't." Temple brightened. This was her second serious investigative assignment in a few days, this time from an all-pro. "I'll get back to you as soon as I have all the info."

She clicked Max off after he gave her the nursing-home address.

By then Louie had appeared from somewhere and leaped atop her desk with enough "English" to spin some of her papers askew.

"Nothing you can supervise, big fellah," she told him. "Just boring research and a sad visit to a bedridden girl. Must be my week to comfort the sick."

His huge forepaw batted at her hand, perhaps to offer consolation, but more likely inviting play.

Temple sniffed, now that he had her attention.

"*Oooh,* boy. You smell like you've been laid up in mothballs or something. I hope you haven't been getting into trouble with that feral colony at the police substation."

He was not about to answer her, so Temple cleared her screen and started her search engines.

She subscribed to the Las Vegas daily papers, so she easily accessed the archives. The actual search was frustrating and time-consuming. Newspapers had such vast archives, going back to off-line years. She kept calling up long lists of loser leads. And local crime reporting was not the front-page star it once had been.

Temple decided she had time to accede to Max's strong request that she see the victim, and might as well make it a cheery evening by stopping in at Violet's, with all the litter and cat kibble the Miata could hold.

She laced up her working tennies and toted a couple grocery store visits' worth of ten-pound Free-to-Be-Feline bags down to the parking lot.

Midnight Louie seemed to sense she was on a mercy mission to his kind, because he seemed very excited to see the Free-to-Be-Feline bags going out and started supervising the operation. He watched her load up three tote bags at a time, used his private entrance via the guest bathroom window and leaning palm tree to beat her down to the lot, where he sat and watched her unload the totes and load the Miata, with an air of superior satisfaction. Or an over-seer.

By the time she got up to the condo for a new load, he was already present there to play major domo.

"These are *your* people, Louie," she told him through gritted teeth. "Surely you could do more than show up, show off, and lift a majestic white whisker or two."

In the end, Temple decided to shower and change before starting her rounds of mercy.

Louie had disappeared by the third time she got down to the Miata, so she pictured him lolling by his personal Free-to-Be-Feline bowl in the air-conditioned condo while she relied on convertible wind power to keep her cool en route in the waning rush-hour traffic.

It was again a gorgeous Las Vegas twilight, caught between sunset and moonrise behind the valley's western mountains, with the blossoming neon and Vegas Gold lights bursting into being like hot-lava fountains. This was when Nevada nature and Strip showmen collaborated to prove why they belonged together.

Temple sighed as she drove the Strip, let-ting the wind style her freshly washed curls, thinking about a really relaxing dinner out with Matt after her investigative errands were done.

Best of all, the first errand was a hands-off Max operation, so she didn't need to feel guilty about doing him this secret little favor. After all, he'd wanted *her* to do this, not Molina. *Hah! Take that, copper!*

Temple's peep-toe pumps with modest platforms and a skinny skirt and silk-blend cardigan set looked business-casual for Vegas, so she'd pass as a reporter. She soon pulled into a tight space near the nursing-home portico. Tight for some, not for Temple's small car.

She'd brought a separate envelope purse that would hold a reporter's narrow note-book and papers, and with it tucked under her arm, she entered the fluorescent-lit atrium surrounded by leafy plants.

The late middle-aged woman at the reception desk was indeed the Florence Nightingale of St. Rose's Nursing Home, Barbara by name tag.

"I called earlier," Temple said, introducing herself. "I'm with the *Review-Journal.*" Which was perfectly true; she had a folded copy in her handbag.

The woman shook her slightly silvered head. "I suppose it's good that someone remembers the anniversary of the attack that as good as ended this girl's life."

"Her parents don't visit?" Temple got out her old notebook and pencil, jotting down details.

Barbara ran through the short, sad details.

"Her mother ran off when she was eight. Her father remarried, but the family was hardscrabble, poor and uneducated. Lived in motels, worked the temporary jobs at the low-end of the Strip, handing out flyers for 'private dancers.' Let the kids fend for themselves."

"Kids?"

"The father had a son from a previous marriage. He went into the military later, was quite a bit older than Teresa. Lord knows what chances this girl ever had in life. She's a ward of the state now. No wonder she was living in an area where such a brutal fate overtook her. I suppose there's a kind of peace in her current state. You'll want to see her, I suppose."

She started to lead Temple down the hall, then paused to stare hard at her. "Have you ever seen anyone in a coma?"

"No, but someone I know was in one recently for a few weeks."

"And recovered and became functional?"

Temple nodded, carefully. "Memory loss about almost everything before the accident, though."

"Not uncommon, but the rest . . . a miracle. Cheer up. Those memory issues can be temporary."

Somehow Temple was not cheered. Things were complicated enough as it was.

They'd paused beside one of those super-wide hospital doors needed to accommodate gurneys, a big blond-wood slab with brushed steel hardware.

"You never saw your friend during the coma?" Barbara asked in a hushed voice.

"No. It happened out of the country."

Barbara frowned. "Your friend doesn't happen to be tall, dark, and gauntly handsome?"

"No. No way. No such luck." Darn that Max! He could make a lasting impression on a Tempur-Pedic mattress.

"His story is oddly familiar to a recent visitor's case. Well, dear. Sometimes long-term coma patients can look pitiful, but this one's a regular Sleeping Beauty, a little Kewpie doll, sixteen forever. Pale and peaceful. Is that a comfort or a greater tragedy? I don't know."

On that ambiguously encouraging note, Temple stepped into the room.

And stopped.

That damn Max could have warned her. But he wanted her immediate, unvarnished reaction.

"Teresa does look peaceful," Temple softly told the nurse-receptionist. "Very cared for." She approached the bed, silencing her heels by tiptoeing. She felt like she was attending a wake. Max could have ended up looking like this, forever.

"She only has one regular visitor, the stepbrother," Barbara said. "I don't know if he left the doll for her, or if her parents did before they disappeared. She's always had it, it seems like. No one has the heart to remove it. We undress and bathe it now and again, just as we do her, daily. They're a team."

Temple nodded, hoping her pounding heart wasn't audible or visible.

"Victim one," Max had said.

Teresa looked younger than her sixteen years. Had she somehow set off a serial killer? Or had she just happened into someone's path when he'd gone psycho for some reason?

"Very sad," the nurse said, the cliché really the only comment possible. "I imagine a reporter must see a lot that is."

Temple nodded and backed away, noticing the vase of fresh flowers on the bedside table. She smelled the small tea roses nestled among bigger scentless blossoms,

461

daisies, and carnations.

She didn't take an easy breath until she was back outside and under the well-lit portico, trying to recall which slot in the dark parking lot beyond held the Miata.

Parking lot. Parking lots, plural.

They were the favored killing ground of the Barbie Doll Killer. The news reports said Teresa had been attacked at a shopping-mall lot, and that was five years ago, before the current fad of auditions for reality TV were everywhere.

Temple skittered fast to the spot where the Miata was barely visible between two oversize pickup trucks. It would be murder backing out past those behemoths without getting her taillights dusted by some passing speed demon.

Parking lots were unsafe in so many ways.

Temple was glad she always put up the car's top when she parked. She was happy to be back in her small automotive cave, safe, awake, too old to attract the Barbie Doll Killer. Of course, everybody took her for younger. At least her hair wasn't the blond it had been dyed during the teen reality-TV show, speak of the devil.

She backed the Miata out of its slot, cautiously, slowly.

And a good thing.

A big ole car from the gas-guzzling decades rumbled past with its self-advertising engine. She didn't know if guys who drove giant trucks or road-hogging rust buckets irritated her more.

She braked to watch the arriving car cruise by in her rear-view mirror. The portico lights made the driver's profile into a sharp silhouette, a familiar one. There was nothing wrong with *her* memory. What was *he* doing here? Following her? Creepy.

And then Temple knew. It was the anniversary of Teresa's attack and the faithful stepbrother would be visiting, for sure.

Dirty Larry Podesta had a very close connection to the disabled girl.

That was why Max couldn't use Molina or Alch to research her background and the case. He needed to know more before he brought the police in on it. So he had used ever-eager-to-crime-solve Temple Barr.

Dirty Max!

CHAPTER 40
BOXING DAY

Dirty Larry and his truly disturbing connection to what might be the first Barbie Doll Killer victim was best left to pros like Molina and Max, Temple decided.

She had her own case to solve.

When she returned to her place she left a long phone message for Max, with the particulars of Teresa's background and attack and a sarcastic "Thanks" for sending her in blind.

Teresa's history, though, had uneasy echoes in Alexandra's life and death. Temple was starting to get a vague vision of a possible nightmare: two young women, one dead and one as good as, both within the geographic operational area and time frame of the Barbie Doll Killer. Vegas and Tucson. And maybe Jayden's Sedona, Arizona, too.

Alexandra, though, had died from a fluke and had been much older than the BDK's teen victims. Somehow, though, Alexandra

464

still felt like a victim to Temple, of her mother's ambitions and control, if nothing else. Could Alex have had a secret advocate who was bringing grief to her mother in revenge?

Temple decided to reexamine the "treasure box" of Alexandra's life that she had "borrowed" from the hall shrine. Taking it had been a dumb move. Who did she think she was, Nancy Drew?

Well, yeah.

Violet's health was so fragile. Temple should return these keepsakes fast if she couldn't find anything productive here. Once the will was signed, everything in the house would belong to whomever would inherit on Violet's death.

Temple settled on the living room sofa, Louie by her side. She frowned sternly at him. He never did her the courtesy of lowering the Free-to-Be-Feline bowl a few healthy nuggets while scarfing up the tasty seafood toppings, even though she changed the Free-to-Be-Feline twice weekly. Not one nugget.

She certainly hoped to find a missing nugget of a clue in the box she'd left on the coffee table.

Temple picked it up with a forbidden thrill, knowing she was acting on her nosy

465

reporter's "need to know" instincts. That was why she loved vintage clothes and objects. They all had a history and told a story and sometimes hid enchanting echoes of their past and their owners' lives.

This box was the size of a ream of paper, but much lighter. The heavy cardboard was covered in a cream-colored textured paper, so the box was tailor-made for holding heavy cream stationery . . . and then mementos after the letters and notes had been used and forgotten. Temple let her fingertips caress the surface.

Nobody bought items like this except when stumped for a present for someone you didn't know. Temple remembered being fascinated as a kid by the decorative boxes that notepaper and envelopes came in. She'd claimed them for holding her own treasures when they were empty.

Nowadays, greeting cards talked, sang, and showed minimovies, and people sent e-cards or "gifts" via online social-network sites.

Still, there was nothing like opening a sensual-feeling box, wondering why it had been kept for so long and what was inside. Poor Teresa was almost a human treasure box, hiding the last thing she'd ever seen, the image of a murderer.

Temple had already leafed through the loose photos of people she didn't know, but now she carefully opened the two leather-bound diaries with gilt-edged pages and weighted satin ribbons for bookmarks. The first entries dated from Alexandra's death, or, more accurately, her funeral, but they tapered off in both books after twenty pages to sporadic notations, mostly when Violet found a new stray cat.

Again and again the hard-to-read handwriting — in actual ink, probably from an expensive fountain pen bought just for these diaries — expressed love and loss and regret. Violet begged forgiveness for that "disastrous trip to Tucson," for being "wrong."

Temple sensed a terrible break between mother and daughter just before Alexandra's sudden and tragic death. No event or other person was mentioned, just how, after her daughter's sudden death, Violet had taken Alexandra's Whisper and tuxedo cat, Rebecca, and Buttercup and her four yellow kittens back to Las Vegas, where Violet pledged to keep them together and cherished in her house until her death and beyond, so they all — cats and mother and daughter — could be together until the last one left "to go to the place you are and

467

where I hope you are happy and getting along well."

Later entries, Temple found, were all about adding cats to the retinue.

"I know you sent this poor homeless tabby to me." "I love them so, as I love and miss you so." And finally, the latest entries: "Did you come back to me as Pancake? Let me know. She is a lovely taupe stripe and so sweet and came home a day after her surgery. Sadly, she had four kittens coming, but she needed to be fixed. I hope — oh, I didn't think! Were *you* one of her kittens? Oh, my darling daughter, I never dreamed you would leave me."

Temple had to set the volume aside to avoid blotting the ink. Now that she'd read how much the cats meant to Violet, she understood why the old woman was trying such far-out ways to fend off death. That someone was already letting the cats out showed no one could be trusted to follow Violet's wishes and keep the cats together in that house until their natural deaths, will or no will. It was an unrealistic hope.

It also showed Temple that Violet was not only surrounded by indifferent strangers or greedy hangers-on, but by someone truly *mean*.

Someone vindictive. Someone who

wanted Violet's last moments to be ones of repeated losses as, cat by cat, her beloved charges vanished. And she could do nothing about it. The dirty tricks were like tormenting a paralyzed person.

In pushing the diary away to save it from her tears, Temple saw something slide askew from the endpapers.

Opening the book again, this time from the back, Temple discovered three four-by-six-inch photos, printed the old-fashioned way. Two were of a beautiful blond young woman, slender and smiling, her face and hair and fingernails perfectly done, playing with a yellow-striped cat and its four tiny kittens.

The third photo was of a Barbie doll in the original box, the familiar features smiling through the cellophane window, hair blond, face perfectly made up under a cotton-candy cloud of shiny, wavy, Vegas-gold blond hair. That was the only photo with identifying writing on the back: "For My Beautiful One and Only Angel Barbie."

Temple shuffled the photos back to the two showing Alexandra. Long neck and blond hair, blue eyes. Violet had not only started confusing her daughter with stray cats, she had always equated her to Barbie. Her own collectible precious baby doll.

Temple grabbed her netbook and did a search for "angel Barbie doll" that led her in seconds to the exact image in the third photo, the 1988 Happy Holiday Barbie. That explained the huge eighties silver bow in Barbie's hair with its dab of red-and-green decoration. Mistletoe.

According to the Web site, this model had the "typical 1966 superstar face" and was considered the first "collectible" Barbie, setting off a buying frenzy among adult collectors, which would raise prices to incredible heights that later declined. Still, Temple saw that a 1988 Happy Holiday Barbie without the all-important *Antiques Roadshow* "original box" was worth two hundred dollars.

Had Violet begun collecting Barbie dolls for her baby daughter and kept collecting them, like the cats, even after her adult daughter's death, as somehow embodiments of Alexandra, as she thought the cats were?

How crazy-sad.

That didn't mean that someone crazy and not-so-sad didn't have it in for Violet.

Temple rounded up possible suspects in her head.

Violet had made her money selling real estate and could have made enemies there. Someone burned in an old real-estate deal, say. Maybe the person had overpaid for the house Violet sold them, and that's why they were haunting hers during her last days.

Or one of Violet's spurned family members could resent not being her heir and had come secretly to Vegas to take revenge on Violet's helpless rescue cats. Even a school rival of the impossibly pretty and perfect Alexandra, done up like a little doll from her earliest years, could harbor a hatred of the doting mother. Those folks would be hard to track . . . unless they had left clues.

If it *was* murder, the death of Pedro Gomez also seemed mean, almost childishly so, like a hard school-yard push. He was the last long-term employee loyal to Violet and her cats. So he was both a barrier for getting at Violet and another great loss during her last days. Where *were* the cats going?

What would be the object of killing Violet? She was already dying.

The motive had to be tormenting Violet, taking everything she had, with her knowing and hating it even in her foggy state. It had to be a personal vendetta.

That scheme would involve the moment she agreed to name an heir-executor and signed the will, which could be happening right now. And then that homicidally mean someone would lean close and tell Violet that no cat would be saved, that her house was history, an on-the-market property. That any assets would be given not to the family members she felt had betrayed her, but to the chosen person she had selected to carry on her hopes and dreams, who had been betraying her far more.

Who would that someone be, and why so vindictive? Freddie, the former great friend who'd known Violet long enough to build up a grudge? Jayden, the New Age con man who had spent several years operating in Arizona before coming to Vegas a year before, and who could have some hidden personal connection to Alexandra? Violet had come to depend on him most, so knowing he'd most manipulated her would hurt the worst.

Temple grabbed her car keys from the coffee table and headed to the parking lot and the Miata. She had to get the "treasure box" back and check on the situation.

Whatever evil under the sun and the moon was going on, it was happening now in the house on Aloe Vera Drive.

CHAPTER 41
CONVOY: BEWARE OF BEARS

Max spotted Temple flying out the side door of the Circle Ritz, short skirt swirling, low-heeled mules practically skidding off her feet as she headed for the Miata wisely parked near one of the lot's three security light poles.

Her headlong commitment and those lithe bare legs made him smile.

Miss Mini-Tornado.

He was driving his previously owned black Volkswagen Beetle, now that Garry's laptop computer had coughed up the names of his banks and numbers of his accounts. The humble Beetle offered surprising legroom for a tall guy. Max had read on an airline magazine that Tommy Tune, the six-foot-six (and a half, supposedly, sans cowboy boots) Texas tap dancer and Broadway star, drove one.

That had given him the idea, now that legroom was an issue. Also, the Beetle provided a literal low profile for tailing work. Max figured he'd be spending a lot of time getting up to date on his history in Sin City. But he wasn't here for testing the Beetle's legroom. Or legs.

Idling throatily along the side street was a much more serious car than either he or Miss Whirling Dervish Barr drove. A deep-bronze vintage Impala.

Max had always figured Dirty Larry Podesta for a man with an agenda that went far beyond police work. He'd followed the guy here on his own instincts, not Molina's instructions. And he found this destination as sinister as that possible personal link through Podesta's stepsister to the Barbie Doll Killer.

He especially didn't like that Impala waiting in the dark to pounce on the Miata. He might not remember his ex, but, by God, nobody was going to mess with her. Including him.

And, he was thinking, she hardly fit the profile for the Barbie Doll Killer victims. She'd left him a message saying that she'd seen Larry, not vice versa, at the nursing home. Still, he couldn't help worrying now that sending Temple to the nursing home Dirty Larry had visited had somehow drawn the undercover narc's attention to her.

Maybe something the receptionist had said on Larry's next visit had tipped him off to who "visiting reporter" might have been. Had he "made" Temple as a likely possibility for uncovering his real aims? Or as a likely victim? Was Larry an avenger or a serial killer? His job description well suited him for both roles.

No more deaths on Max's conscience, that was his obsession now, besides finding Kathleen O'Connor.

The Beetle swooped out of the lot after the Impala got into line behind the Miata. Max loved being invisible and underestimated, not doing the magician act out front, but pulling the strings from behind the curtain.

He hoped the sainted Gandolph had been right, as usual. Miss Temple Barr was too easy to underestimate. He hoped so with all his heart and soul, if he had any left, because his instincts told him this unintentional auto convoy was headed on a straight line to Showdown City.

He'd observed, at least, that Temple had her seat belt on. Good girl! It was going to be a bumpy ride. He had his on, too. You couldn't save someone else if you didn't care enough to save yourself.

Bitter lesson learned.

Chapter 42
Little Girl Lost

"Do you know where your girlfriend is?"

Matt blinked at the cell phone. He was already getting into that Zen place for the *Mr. Midnight Hour* tonight and didn't recognize the incoming number — or believe the voice he recognized.

"Carmen?"

"Molina. 'Where is your favorite fiancée?' I should have said. I'm in a squad car on my cell phone. Well?"

"Temple? Where is she? Uh. We're not a Siamese-twin act."

"Yet. Are you at the Circle Ritz?"

"Copy that, lieutenant."

"Don't bother trying to be cop show–ish. I need you to check her condo and then her parking space. Don't hang up."

By then he was shouldering through his door and racing down the exit stairs one floor and along the curved hall to Temple's door, which was locked. And then clawing out his key and using it, and shouting as he raced straight through to the balcony with its view of the pool and parking lot.

"She's not here. Nor the Miata either. What's wrong?"

"It's what *might* be wrong. I'll be swinging by in two minutes. Be down in the lot, and meanwhile be thinking of where she might have gone."

By the time he got to the street exit from the Circle Ritz parking lot, a black-and-white had pulled up parallel, blocking it.

"Hop in back," Molina ordered through the slightly opened passenger-door window.

Matt did, disconcerted by the hard plastic bench seat and the thick aluminum and Plexiglas barrier separating him from the front seats. He was starting to feel like he'd put on a mobile RoboCop suit.

Molina's face came close as she opened a small sliding glass window in the barrier. Now Matt was feeling like he was in a high-tech confessional.

"Two damn CIs I've got on shadow detail," she told him, "and they both go off the grid. Not answering contact. Kinsella at least left me a cryptic message to check with you on Temple's whereabouts. Tell the officer at the wheel where to go."

Matt took in the back view of a uniformed

cop with white-knuckled hands on the steering wheel. Kinsella was acting as a confidential informant for Molina? Who was the other one?

Molina prodded him. "Where did she go? I'll bet Temple's little lambs will be right behind. And one could be a big bad wolf, not to mention what's likely waiting dead ahead."

"She's been visiting a sick old lady lately."

"Specifics, please. Where?"

"It's 1405 Aloe Vera Drive," he yelled out, glad Temple had taken him there once. The driver wheeled away, punching buttons on her computer for the best route. Matt could see the computer better than the cop, but Temple's advertised "bumpy ride" had finally materialized.

Molina's fingers curled around the side of the open Plexiglas window between them. "Sorry for the lousy accommodations. A yardman was found dead a week ago at that address. Which precious 'friend' asked PR woman Temple Barr to get involved in a murder case?"

"Savannah Ashleigh."

"Get serious."

"I am. Savannah Ashleigh hired Temple to find out why her dying aunt's yardman ended up dead."

"Pedro Gomez."

"I don't know his name. He was found dead at the bottom of a concrete flood channel backing onto Savannah's Aunt Violet's property."

"Coroner says that could have been accidental," Molina said. "Or maybe murder. And you let your future bride run off and get herself involved in such things?"

"She's her own woman. And . . . I was out of town."

"At least you will stay out of this when we get there."

"No. I've a right —" Matt pushed against the back car door. It was locked, from the front seat.

"You have a right to remain silent, after I'm through with you," Molina told him. "So. What did Miss Barr think she was investigating? She surely didn't think she could solve a man's death?"

"Weird things were going on at Savannah's aunt's house besides the old guy's death. Violet is terminally ill and she rescued a lot of stray cats. She hates her relatives and plans to leave her house, her assets, all her worldly belongings, to whoever will swear to keep the house and its animal residents going after her death."

"Until the last dog is hanged."

"Cats. They're all cats. Until the last cat has gone to its reward."

"Which could be years, during which any tangible assets of the estate would be burned off."

"It's an addled old woman's dying fantasy."

"It's a con artist's dream. They don't usually murder, though. Anything more than cats, that is."

"Temple says some of Violet's cats have been let loose, but none found killed. Nearby or visibly. That Temple knows of."

"What Temple knows of would fit in a thimble on this case. Like I said, Devine, you're confined to quarters when we arrive. You wouldn't even *be* here if you hadn't had clues to what your loopy fiancée thought she was up to."

"It's more than money and cats and old ladies?"

"Could be."

Matt had been watching the route. He kept his mouth shut because he'd been there once and couldn't think of a faster way to go.

The car lurched through the night streets far from the Strip. He couldn't help thinking of Max Kinsella's recent, last desperate race through the streets of Belfast that left him bereaved. Oh, God. Was it his turn?

"Pray," Molina urged in an undertone. "That may be the best break we get tonight."

CHAPTER 43
GOLDILOCKS BOXED

Temple parked the Miata three houses short of Violet's.

A housebreaker doesn't pull into the driveway in the light of day, and it was nicely dark here. She'd never noticed before that the streetlights ended long before Violet's house at the end of the block, the end of the line. Maybe someone with a softball aim had knocked out the nearest lights.

Temple needed more sensible shoes in this desert-dusted area, and was glad she had been wearing kitten-heeled mules when she decided she had to make a house call. Easier to tiptoe in.

Supposedly, a night home-health-care aide was on duty. Temple spotted a faint glow through the deeply shadowed windows as she approached. Of course she wouldn't disturb Violet at this late hour, 9:00 P.M.

She couldn't see into the dark around the

side of the house or if any vehicles were parked near the abandoned garage.

Temple wasn't sure how she'd enter without disturbing the residents. If she had to, she could come up with some song and dance for visiting so late, but she really wanted to slink in. She needed to revisit the Alexandra shrine now that she knew more about the strained relationship between Violet and her daughter, and to return what she'd taken.

She grabbed the tote containing Alexandra's memory box and soft-shoed her way up the street. She imagined she resembled someone visiting the sick with gifts of cologne and hand lotion maybe or, in this case, cat treats.

While Temple paused on the stoop in the dark, weighing options, the front door swung soundlessly open.

A pale feline muzzle peeked out and then a calico cat eased out, more white than red, black, and orange in the interior light.

That was how some of the cats vanished! The front door was left unlocked.

Temple knew from Louie's window and door-massaging ways that a cat's hopeful rub back and forth could sometimes edge them both open wide enough for an escape. She ached to corral the elusive calico, but a protesting cat in her arms windmilling all four clawed limbs would not aid her mission.

Reluctantly, she moved the surprisingly well-balanced door open with her forefinger, wide enough to slip through sideways. She turned to pull it almost shut, just to the point of making a telltale noise, then eased off.

A television cast a flickering rainbow of light in the main room, turned on for a sleepless Violet or the night attendant's diversion.

Temple was able to tiptoe through the few slumbering cats into the dining room and then through to the hall, led by the flickering light of the eternal candle lit in Alexandra's memory.

She bent to open the chest doors so she could replace the box. Nothing looked disturbed since she'd last seen it. Violet, unlike the sleeping cats, had not been ambulatory for some time.

Temple straightened to regard the three closed doors that led off the back hall. A bedroom for Violet. A guest bedroom. And . . .

She felt so Goldilocks for a natural redhead.

The door to the left opened as easily as

the heavy-looking front door. They made houses true when this one was built. Level. Doors and windows opened easily, were not off-square and prone to stick or to make unseemly noises.

A huge Spanish bedstead declared this the master bedroom. The mattress was far too high for an invalid, hence the hospital bed in the living room.

This was Papa Bear's room.

She tried the far right door next.

Mama Bear's lair, the guest room, not crowding the residents' area. The candle-light, amazingly helpful, showed a queen-size bed without a headboard, with a cro-cheted comforter and two piled pillows per side.

That left the middle bedroom. In this case, Baby Bear's?

Temple turned the doorknob and pushed. She wasn't surprised to find it locked.

Satin place ribbons had bookmarked the two diaries she'd spirited away. One had a key tied on to weigh it down between the pages filled with Violet's lines of love, regret, and despair.

Temple had a hunch and had appropriated that key.

It fit exactly in the middle locked door.

Temple turned it after much jiggling, as if

485

it hadn't been unlocked in a long time.

The door edged open and she walked through, feeling she might be violating a sacred place. Even without any interior light, the candle flicker from the hall reflected from all three visible walls surrounding the white wicker "crown" of a single bed headboard fit for a princess.

Temple's vision was confused by a surfeit of pink and white and walls that were an eye-dazzling surface of myriad miniature windows.

And through each tiny cellophane window shone the face of a differently coifed and appareled Barbie doll. All exquisitely tiny and beautiful. All frozen faces of Alexandra, the perfectly imagined daughter who'd fled her controlling mother to lead an imperfectly imagined life and death. Far away.

Barbie doll boxes towered alongside and over the girly wicker headboard; they covered every wall, floor to ceiling, row upon row.

Temple stepped into the weird reflected aura of shining blue eyes and glossy red lips and Vegas Gold locks to turn and examine the door wall, also paved in Barbie doll boxes.

Mint condition.

In the box.

Temple recognized several of these blond babes from her Web perusal, spotting a few brunettes and redheads and bronze-haired later models among them. Even redhaired Deirdre of Ulster, from the Legends of Ireland sequence. When Violet had called her that, she took it for raving until she checked the Barbie sites. This was a complete collection, lavished on Alexandra as tributes and role models — and every last one of them never opened.

Not by Violet and certainly not by Alexandra. Temple guessed Violet had surrounded her daughter with temptation and forbidden her to open it. This entire room was a tribute and a tomb to a princess in a tower of her mother's making.

And . . . this was the prize of Violet's "estate." A collection worth a couple hundred thousand dollars or more in its pristine completeness. These tiny boxed showgirls were Vegas Gold, but they'd never been anything a real girl could play with or live up to.

While Temple stared up, turning around and around, the bedroom door had opened wide without a sound.

She turned to face full into it.

And the human figure it now framed.

CHAPTER 44
AWAY ALL CATS!

Of course I am stuck eight feet up in the air in the faithful mesquite tree outside Miss Violet Weiner's house.

In the dark of night.

I pass the time by counting the varieties of predatory desert nightlife that come out when the sun goes down. Coyotes. Bark scorpions. Tarantulas, now in their mating season, and giant desert centipedes, both about six inches wide or long, however you want to reckon it. I reckon it as too big to tango with. Then there are rattlesnakes and my big brothers, mountain lions and bobcats, not to mention an endless variety of lizards.

Some of these my kin can eat. Some are poisonous and we would not want to. Most of them can eat us.

I am uneasy about leaving our makeshift cat clowder alone on the retention-basin land, but at least human predators do not usually go there. In fact, more of that lethal ilk is inside the former safety of Miss Violet's house, now that someone has been leaving doors and windows ajar so that the feline population has been steadily declining, much to her somewhat foggy dismay.

At least so my inside dude, Maverick, reports.

Hark! What light at yonder kitchen window breaks?

"*Psst!* Daydreamer. Here's a youngling for you."

Maverick's longhaired face has side whiskers like a Victorian gentleman does, or Brother Bobcat. Under it peeks out a smaller, striped version.

"Succotash," Maverick reports, "is afraid to climb down the tree. This is the first time I have gotten him to the window."

Even the most dim-witted human knows that getting a cat or kitten down a tree is a trying task, but this is the most concealed exit route from the house and we do not want the ill-intentioned human inside, or Miss Violet, to know we are removing the feline residents for their own safety.

If they make it down the mesquite tree.

By now the youngster is crouching on the broad adobe sill, claws out.

Succotash. What kind of moniker is that? You do not want to be named after something that is eaten when you are going out into the untamed desert.

"Come on, Pops," Miss Midnight Louise harries me from the ground below. "If you cannot coax a kitten down a tree, make way for someone who can."

The astute observer will see that I am caught in the middle here. Maverick is the trail boss. Miss Midnight Louise is the cowcatcher, so to speak. And I am the cattle prod.

I lean over the unnerved tiger-stripe. "Hello, Suckie, my lad. I know the ground looks far, but I use a tall old palm tree to enter and exit my exclusive condominium near the Vegas Strip every day. Do you not want to grow up to be a big dude about town someday? So take one little pounce to the tree trunk like it was an unwary mouse, and Uncle Louie will have you on your way to rejoin all your pals in no time."

"No!" the little bugger yowls. Its small claws curl tighter, seeking purchase on the hard adobe.

I see the next customer already in line, a sleek shorthair dame wearing skintight solid gray velvet and winking at me with one emerald-green eye.

"Come on, Junior. No time for cold feet and fingernails."

"Uncle Louie lies," he squeaks. "I have never

seen such a scary, dark, and horrible place
—"

"Survival of the fittest," I decree, ducking my
head to pick up the impudent kit by the nape
of the neck, like his mama had, and flinging
him onto a fork of the tree just below me, hind
feet first.

"Now, just pretend it is a giant scratching
post and skedaddle down."

By then I am looming over him. His eyes
become as round as SpaghettiOs, but all four
feet start "swimming" in concert. His tiny claws
sound like a very loud zipper opening lickety-
split all the way to the bottom of the tree and
into the indignant embrace of Miss Midnight
Louise.

"He is just a baby," she hisses up at me, her
eyes gleaming as lurid green as a demon's in
the dark.

"He is down, is he not?" I turn to the next
customer.

"Now, young lady," I purr. "Obviously, you
will need to put your mitt in mine to bridge the
gap from sill to trunk, but I can see that you
are no stranger to performing alluring acrobatics on a pole."

She coyly marks the side of the window
niche with her sleek cheeks.

"And what is your name?" I inquire.

"Sirena."

"And so appropriate. Here you go, Sirena. Just take the elevator to the main desert floor. I will join you later when all my rescue work is done."

I watch her undulate down like a very furry snake.

When I look back up to the window, Maverick is shaking his head and long spidery vibrissae.

"What?" I ask. "You know the house is no longer safe for this crew."

"I just hope you know what you and your semiferal partner are doing. My associates are confused and upset at the condition of one caretaker and the sudden absence of another, not to mention the strangers trooping in and out of the premises. Taking all these hot house homebodies into the wilds is risky."

"I am experienced in the perfidy of the human animal, and I tell you again, this house is raising all the hair on my haunches. Letting domestic slaves out one by one to drift off and get hurt or killed is not simple mischief. It is malice designed to hurt your beloved caretaker. The other caretaker has died already over that. These sorts of benign humans are hard to come by, trust me."

"I know things are turned upside down, and our dear lady is unable to pet and feed us, and it is very bad," Maverick admits, furrowing the faint stripes on his brow.

"At least I have an inside woman."

"Miss Violet's niece?"

"No. My faithful red-cream. She is not a partner in Midnight Investigations, Inc., but I have trained her well. She can handle anything, trust me."

CHAPTER 45
SHOWDOWN AT THE SHRINE

Jayden, his pale clothes looking luminous in the bedroom's odd, rippling-underwater light, stepped inside.

"You?" He sounded truly amazed. "Savannah's 'friend.' How did you get in?"

"The doors . . . opened for me. I think it was the cats. They seem to be jumping ship."

"Maybe, but you're trespassing. You shouldn't be here. This is a storeroom. Violet keeps it locked. She's very sick. She could go at any time."

"Then shouldn't you be there, for the signing of the will?"

"That was done this afternoon."

"So I guess you've got nothing to lose now."

Temple tried to figure out how to push past him. He ignored her accusation and seemed disinclined to move. He, too, was mesmerized by the walls of Barbie dolls in their store packaging.

"What *are* these things?" he asked. "Astounding. It's very Kachina–doll, in a totally Vegas sort of way."

"You've never seen this room?"

"Violet had her boundaries. I respected them."

"As long as they included you, in the will."

"I witnessed it," he said, frowning. "You're a terribly cynical young woman. That attitude will impede your path through life."

"At least I've got a life."

She regretted pointing that out as his odd-colored eyes fixated on her.

"You'll be sorry . . ." he started to say.

And she couldn't disagree.

Then Jayden bounded forward.

And tripped.

He fell facedown on the hard wooden floor, a ghostly Kachina doll with a dark arrow impaled in his back.

A paler shadow-figure behind him began to weave martial-arts motions Temple recognized from a zillion movies and TV shows and Matt's shadowboxing by the Circle Ritz pool.

In the faint, flickering candlelight, the arrow in the back she thought had felled Jayden was starting to look a lot more like a . . . kitchen knife.

"Oh," Temple said, backing up in the

room of Barbie dolls, the cul-de-sac of Barbie dolls, the dead end of Barbie dolls, and probably her.

"Aren't you pretty?" The man in martial-arts pajamas stepped around Jayden's bleeding body to follow her retreat step-by-step, advance-by-advance.

"You're almost as pretty as Miss Angel Alexandra," he crooned in a phony, scary-soothing way. "Her momma's joy and puppet. You all just belong in a box, don't you, girly? All fluffed and frozen perfect, freeze-dried, like Mama's Alexandra. In a box so they can put you in the ground where you all can rot."

Oh, my God, Temple thought, *who would ever connect the Barbie Doll Killer with Violet and her estranged daughter and her massive and valuable and hateful doll collection?*

The man glanced up at the tiny Barbie faces wallpapering the room in 3-D.

And came closer.

"So here you are, too. Up against the wall, like these untouchable dolls. Who said it's better to have loved and lost? Lost is better."

"That would be Alfred, Lord Tennyson," Temple said, her mind flying in three different directions.

One: this man was a killer, *the* killer. Two:

496

Jayden might still be alive and needed emergency attention. Three: she might not be alive long enough herself to be in a position to help anyone.

"Huh?" the guy said. Lord Tennyson and his poetry had always been quite a mouthful.

"Just saying who said it," Temple said, retreating. Babbling. "A dead English aristocrat. You might be related. You have a fancy first name. Sylvan. Very . . . dead English aristocrat."

Her left leg had stopped against the wicker headboard, beside the piled small pillows in lacy, embroidered shams. For show.

"So." Temple's wandering gaze tried to fasten on a better defensive option than a heart-shaped crocheted pillow. "When did you get hooked on Barbie dolls? Aren't you a bit old for them?"

"Never," he said. "I play with them. I muss them up, all their pretty perfect looks. You all need mussing up."

"No thanks." Temple grabbed a couple pillows, clutched them to her chest like they were a Kevlar vest. "You play rough, Rowdy. When did it start? When Violet told Alexandra she was too good for you? And she left you?"

"Alexandra. No."

The name seemed to put him off track.

"Oh, wait." Temple began to see when the anger and madness set in. "Alexandra *didn't* leave you. She was *taken* from you. She died from poisoned drugstore painkillers."

"We would have been fine," he said, ignoring the tragedy that had probably set him off, "if the old bitch hadn't had her claws into her."

"Like, you were better for her?"

He lunged, as she had hoped.

Temple dropped the pillows to grab the bedside lamp, a ruffle-shaded, Barbie-like accessory, and smashed it into his momentarily parallel back.

"That cut!" Rowdy complained, brushing off the shattered lightbulb shards and pushing himself upright, looking around, not sure which doll had claws.

"It 'cut' when Alexandra rejected you after Violet warned her about you."

Temple grabbed a couple more pillows. There was nothing behind her but walls of insubstantial dolls in cheap packaging.

Rowdy was unarmed now, but she remembered he'd always worked in the construction trade. His short, stocky body must be all muscle, as his mind was all vengeance and spite, nursed for years and acted out in the meantime on all the pretty Alexandra dolls who also dreamed of auditioning for fame.

Temple was betting that Alexandra bought her own Barbies after leaving home and moving to Tucson, ones she could take out of the box and handle and costume. And she also had acquired a cat and kittens she *could* play with. And somehow she'd acquired a very *loco* local admirer whose seemingly simple, earthy ways had intrigued her for a time but who wanted, needed, her complete attention, sans dolls, sans cats.

Or . . . Rowdy may have never been her serious boyfriend, just someone she saw that she could flaunt at her mother, to reject Violet's quest for perfection in her daughter's life.

Temple had to wonder if Violet breathed yet in the main room.

She had to do something.

So she scrambled across the pile of pillows on the bed, pushing them into a white dotted-swiss avalanche behind her. She made the floor on the other side of the bed and ran for the bedroom door, leaping over Jayden's red-streaked form and out into the hall.

She was halfway through it when the stomping sound of Rowdy's weird white Oxfords, like forties hepcats and male dancers wore, caught up to her. Her ankles were clutched in two hard, tight, grasping hands. She went down, all at once, facedown, Jayden-fashion.

Temple kept her legs churning like a cartoon character's, but her hands and wrists had taken the brunt of her weight and burned with sharp, scraping pain.

She kicked loose and scrambled up onto her skinned knees and crawled toward the table where Alexandra's photo was enshrined. Maybe seeing his "lost love" would slow Rowdy down.

Maybe she could shove the table in front of him and escape to the front hall and through the big, heavy front door and into the dark and lonely street that stretched into desert beyond where Violet has lived and Pedro and maybe Jayden had died and maybe where Temple Barr would be found as another Barbie-accompanied serial-killer victim.

Not while she could stand and shove. Violet was alone now for real, in the main room, with only Temple between her and this madman.

She pushed one side of the chest into Rowdy's path, slamming it into his hip bones hard enough to jar the contents and knock the breath out of the guy.

500

With all the cats in Violet's house, you'd think a few of them could have congregated to get in the man's way, but Temple was spoiled by having Louie always around as her guardian feline.

Apparently he was out to lunch, and she was on her own.

She spun to rush out of the hall when a flare of . . . flame caught her eye.

The tall, thick candle flickering in front of Alexandra's eternally youthful features had fallen to the floor, rolled and . . . caught the bottom edge of Rowdy's flared martial-arts pants on fire.

Liar, liar, pants on fire.

The fabric was simple cotton. The flame climbed his pants leg, but Rowdy was fixated on claiming Alexandra's Barbie doll face. He lurched up to grab the photo off the wall, clasped it, then turned to the Barbie doll–lined bedroom, running back into it, reaching for and knocking down any Barbie doll boxes he could, a figure amazingly fast and furious . . . and quickly being consumed by fire.

Temple stood there panting, torn between where to go, what to do. Violet in the main room? Jayden on the floor, forgotten by his assailant? Rowdy only had eyes for Barbie. For so many Barbies, to be hated, mutilated, destroyed. Even with himself. He was screaming, with pain or triumph, or maybe they were the same thing. The entire room was a bright, crackling backdrop to Sylvan Smith.

Temple dropped to duck as much heat as possible and knee-crawled to Jayden's feet, half out of the bedroom door. She grabbed his ankles and pulled. Backward, backward. Out of the burning Barbie doll room. She really didn't have the strength for this, and he might be literally dead weight, except that she'd misjudged him and she could only budge his body a couple inches at a time.

When she looked up for Rowdy, she could see the cardboard and cellophane and plastic and tiny bits of satin and velvet and nylon hair erupting in a final blaze of glory. She could hear the dying Barbies screaming. High-pitched, tiny voices that rose in a silent smiling chorus as they shrunk into floating bits of ember in Alexandra's girlhood bedroom.

Rowdy's howling white figure turned black, dancing with transformation and death, and then it was all ashes, like the old nursery rhyme, and all fell down.

The screams continued for a long time, until someone lifted Temple up by the elbows and dragged her out of there with her heels trailing — *ouch!* — while big moonwalking spacemen smelling of smoke blocked the view of the bedroom and poured out a flash flood of epic Las Vegas proportions into the flames and on the room and all its contents.

CHAPTER 46
BURNED OUT

The spinning red lights of three ambulances and two fire trucks, along with the carousel of red, white, and blue flashing lights from two cop-car headache bars made an insane wonderland of the street outside Violet's house.

Temple had somehow been taken outside, a shivering, bloody, drowned rat. She wasn't too out of it to spot the coroner's van among the confusion of vehicles.

Emergency technicians had her sitting on the back edge of one ambulance while they sprayed her with stinging antiseptic and applied gauze pads to all her visible joints.

"Oh, my God. Temple. I couldn't come over to you sooner. They had me in custody."

Matt was suddenly beside her, all reaching concern that couldn't touch any part of her. Only his eyes, which were as burned-out as Rowdy's last-glimpsed figure.

"Who?" she asked. "Where?"

Then appeared the looming figure of Molina, no Barbie doll she, with news.

"Violet is alive, smoke-inhalation-free, and en route to a hospital. The man in the pale clothes is also alive."

"Jayden? Or Rowdy?"

"I don't have a cast-of-characters list, Miss Barr. That will have to wait until tomorrow. The one you were found clutching by the ankles is en route to the hospital. The stab wound in his back missed the heart and vital arteries. The firemen were too late for the other man. Grizzly Bahr has a new Crispy Critter."

Temple winced. She knew what medical examiners and staff called dead burn victims. It helped them disassociate from the inhumanity of seared muscle and skin.

"She's hurting." Matt's voice challenged Molina. "And she's the hero of this scene. Get off your high horse and act a little human."

Temple could have hugged him, except it would hurt too much. Instead, she pushed her lips into a grin and was amazed to find them obeying. Man, she needed moisturizer!

"After all," Temple told Molina, "I did help ID D. L. and C. B. as possible BD planters at your . . . um, place of residence."

"ID? D. L.? C. B.? BD? Are you babbling or just mad?"

Temple realized Molina must have dismissed all thought of that joint attempt to come up with a Barbie Doll Killer suspect now that the actual killer had convicted and executed himself, even that Dirty Larry and Crawford Buchanan had been hot candidates then for planting the Barbie doll in Mariah's bedroom.

And Molina had much more to worry about now, too.

"That guy . . . what's left of the guy in the burned-up room —" Temple choked up from smoke and trauma. "He's the Barbie Doll Killer. . . . It's a long and . . . winding story, but Dirty Larry . . . wanted you to smoke the BDK out, and here . . . I . . . finally did . . . accidentally, and —"

The more Temple talked, the more she coughed. She had so much more to say, but tears ran down her face and anything she tried to say was foiled by hiccups.

"So . . . Violet still alive? And Jayden?" Temple needed to be sure.

Molina gave an impatient nod. "What did Dirty Larry do? To who?"

"Enough," Matt told Molina. "You can get her statement in the morning."

"If you say so," Molina answered.

She suddenly crouched down, eye to eye with Temple. "You were ahead of me on all aspects of this case. I don't know who's who or what's what. When you feel better tomorrow, I'd much appreciate being brought up to date."

Molina stood and glared at Matt. "That okay?"

The glare kind of ruined it, but Temple just blinked, glad to hear the ambulances had so many customers. Her?

She eyed the woman who was efficiently tending her wounds.

"No burns, just scrapes." The EMT smiled to make such a mild diagnosis in this one case, on this terrible scene. "You can take her home and keep up the OTC treatments?" she asked Matt.

"Absolutely," he said.

"OTC, is that serious?" Temple asked. She still felt a little . . . muzzy.

"Over the counter," he translated. "Drugstore preparations for you, baby, that's all."

Temple sighed. She hurt way too much for Walgreens, but she just wanted to go home to the Circle Ritz and rest and sleep and . . . oh!

"Where's Midnight Louie?"

"Nowhere on the scene to be found, for

507

once," Molina declared from on high, now that she was standing again and looming over them.

Temple frowned. "And all the cats inside?"

"Also missing, every damn one. Highly suspicious," Molina said, "but that just clears up the crime scene."

"Wait? Violet's will?"

"No idea what you're talking about." Molina grinned evilly, like Cruella De Vil. Or maybe Temple was hallucinating.

"The elderly home owner —" Molina said, "apparently this Violet — was raving about 'Father Hell' when she was wheeled away. She couldn't have been referring to your fiancé. One hopes. You have a lot to nail down after you get your beauty rest and become coherent. Let me know. It might be interesting. Meanwhile, if you're well enough, the pair of you can join my little private postmortem at the flood-control channel up the street."

She left.

"Thanks for bailing me out of an interrogation right now," she told Matt. She sipped the water the EMT had handed her. "There's a lot more going on here than meets the eye," Temple whispered to Matt in a dramatic rasp. "Don't let them shuffle me off to Buffalo."

"You're pretty beat up, way more than I can live with."

"You have not seen 'beat up' until I'm left out of learning the real story."

"I don't have wheels. Molina hijacked me in the backseat of a squad car. No exit."

"Really? That was drastic of her."

"She somehow knew that things were going to turn bad at Violet's place."

"I gotta get to the end of the block and find out what's really happening."

"I doubt one of these emergency vehicles is going to give us a lift."

"Oh, no! My Miata keys were in the tote bag I dropped near Alexandra's shrine, which I'm sure is burned out, too."

The EMT dredged up a dripping-wet object from the ground. "The fire guys said you grabbed this as they were dragging you out."

Temple nodded. "I never go anywhere without my tote bag. Maybe the car keys stayed in it."

Matt felt inside it until he pulled out the keys.

Temple regarded him with pleading big baby-blue-grays.

"Okay. You stay here. I'll get the Miata." He picked up her tote bag and headed outside the claustrophobic circle of huge,

509

pulsing, squawking, flashing emergency vehicles.

"Here are three NSAIDs," the EMT said,
handing them over with a paper cup of
water. "It'll dull the pain." She looked over
her shoulder to where Matt had vanished.
"So will that."

Temple felt grateful to have no more
injuries than, say, a fall off a skateboard in a
flood channel. The kids were always sneaking off to them for practice. *Superficial
wounds* was the term.

The Miata's low red nose soon threaded
through the maze of heavy-duty trucks.

Matt got out to come around and lift her
into the passenger seat. Temple had to
remember to keep her gauze-covered palms
from contacting anything. And her knees
would burn like heck when she tried to
walk, but she just had to get in and out of
the car twice more.

"You're crazy to take Molina up on that
odd invitation. We should go straight home,"
Matt told her.

Temple leaned over to inspect his watch
face. "Oh. Ten thirty. You have to leave for
work soon."

Matt shut his eyes. Then he opened them
and got out his cell phone. "I'll alert Electra
to be there to help you out when we get

510

home. I can make the radio station in fifteen minutes from the Circle Ritz. You deserve to see Molina eat more crow. And I'm curious too."

An oddly unofficial group of vehicles formed a second circle at the small paved maintenance parking lot for flood-control workers at the end of Aloe Vera Drive, directly behind Violet Weiner's property.

The pale slash of empty concrete riverbed through the desert and the unlit empty acres that constituted one of Las Vegas's hundred or so retention basins made civilization seem far, far away.

Matt pulled the Miata to a stop next to Detective Alch's Crown Vic, obviously Molina's ride home, because she leaned against its side.

Dirty Larry's Impala looked low-down and dirty compared to the contemporary vehicles. He sat on the front hood, feet dangling and head down, like a juvenile delinquent.

Rafi Nadir's black SUV was parked opposite the white Crown Vic. *Interesting position and effect,* Temple thought.

It wasn't until Matt off-loaded her and sat her on the Miata's hood that Temple noticed Max standing on the fringe of the group, sans vehicle. They had converged on this site from all directions for an oddly unofficial, but appropriate, conference.

And it turned out that it all began and ended with . . . Dirty Larry.

"You planted that Barbie doll in my house," Molina told Dirty Larry. "Was whatever reason you did it worth your career in law enforcement?" Molina moved into close-confrontation distance.

"We burned the Barbie Doll Killer, didn't we?" Dirty Larry's words were a mumble, and his cynical, defiant eyes were downcast for once and stayed there.

Temple couldn't help thinking that Podesta was a latter-day Rebel with a Cause. But what cause, what point?

"You risked more lives," Molina said. "Miss Barr's tonight, for one. And you literally toyed with mine by making it look like my daughter was in danger."

"And *my* daughter," Rafi said, moving toward him, fists balled.

Molina put a hand on his arm. Rafi was off the force, too, and had been for a long time.

"You are through on this police force and any other," she told Larry.

He shrugged. "For what cause? Flirting with a homicide lieutenant with intent to

512

catch a killer?"

This time Molina took an infuriated step toward the guy, and Rafi put a cautioning hand on her arm.

Alch just pulled out his cuffs. "Lieutenant?"

"Obstruction," she said between set teeth. "Dereliction of duty. Endangerment of a minor. Public endangerment. Give me a minute. How can I count the ways?"

"Everybody might want to cool down," Max said, from his position aloof from the group. "You all could do each other a lot of career damage, and the loose canon is right: the main objective — identifying and stopping the Barbie Doll Killer — is a done deal."

"And you're an expert on not doing oneself a lot of damage," Molina argued bitterly.

"Yeah. I'm an expert." Max looked over at Matt, holding Temple protectively tight. "You're scaring the civilians, officers. Hell, you're scaring me. You better get your stories straight for the paperwork. Petty vengeance is not going to see any of you through."

They quieted as his words reminded them no one official had acted entirely "professionally" for the past few months.

Matt eyed him curiously. "You're not furious this guy got Temple going head-to-head and hand-to-hand with a serial killer?"

"You forget 'heart-to-heart.' " Max smiled at Temple. "Gandolph chided me for underestimating you. I didn't even remember you at the time. Sorry about that. Look, Devine. You're an advisor, a mediator. There's too much fear and fury bubbling under the surface here. Help us out."

Meanwhile, Temple couldn't keep her eyes off the case's odd man out.

It was rewarding to see all the crime-solving pros with their feathers ruffled over little her stumbling across the Barbie Doll Killer, but it was Dirty Larry who'd bullied the others into pressing forward on the case, no matter what.

"Did you know," Temple asked Larry, "that you messing with the lead detective's head and maternal instincts to get her personally involved risked making you a suspect yourself?"

"Sure." He quirked her a smile that could easily pass as a smirk. "Whatever it took." His glance ricocheted fast off of Molina's and Rafi's. "All I ever wanted was the guy who did that to my stepsister — strangled her almost to death and put her in a living nowhere — stopped. I don't care what happens to me now."

Another uneasy silence was turning into wakelike solemnity.

"Sure you do," a voice said.

Molina's. And she had more to say.

"And you have a lot more to enlighten us on, but Kinsella is right. We all went off the reservation, either on this case or . . . related issues. I don't know all the whys and wherefores of what you did, Larry, and we *will* go over every bit of it, but I still can't stomach letting you stay on the force."

Dirty Larry shrugged again.

Temple realized, hey, gosh, he'd probably grown up in the same nurture-starved environment as his stepsister and suffered from the same lack of — *ta-dah* — that psychobabble favorite: self-esteem. Actually, that terrible crime had motivated him to get into law enforcement and make sure the elusive killer was caught. So he was as obsessive in his way as the Barbie Doll Killer. . . .

Max was right. Temple was a bleeding heart. She looked over to find him winking at her.

Meanwhile, Matt was giving her an encouraging hug. *Ooh,* she was going to ache all over tomorrow from doing the Fireman Drag tonight.

"I'll mediate for you police persons," Matt said. "Someplace way more comfortable and conducive to compromise than this wilderness."

Rafi made a considering face and turned to D. L. "There's always private security work in Vegas."

"Not Vegas," Dirty Larry muttered.

Lieutenant C. R. Molina looked so relieved she actually quirked a smile at Rafi Nadir. He did a Dirty Larry and lowered his glance.

Temple smiled at Matt. He took that for an OK to kiss her hard back into the land of the living. . . . Danger was an aphrodisiac.

"Devine," Molina said, not commenting on the kiss. *But she could have been,* Temple thought. "I'll pick a neutral location and e-mail you. We'll . . . put all the pieces together before breakfast tomorrow."

Matt gave Temple a look. The last thing he needed tonight was an early-morning call, but it sure wasn't going to put a kink in anything. When he turned to lift her off the hood and into the Miata, she saw Max had vanished. Where had he parked, anyway? Had to be mysterious about everything.

Alch caught up with them before Matt could start the car to leave. "You kids. Get outta here. I'll calm Carmen and Rafi down," he told Matt, leaning in the driver's side open window. "You'll have sane people to deal with in the morning."

"I don't know if I'll be one of them," Matt answered.

Alch patted his shoulder. "Sure you will. Mister Midnight knows Elvis."

"You listen to my show?"

"Hey. I work late hours and live alone. There are worse things to do."

Alch moved back to the trio of boss and her two onetime suitors.

"I'd hate to be in Larry's shoes," Matt said, thinking the same thing Temple was. "For someone as buttoned-down as Molina is, she sure has stirred up a lot of sticky man trouble."

"And then there's Max," Temple said as they drove away.

"Max and Molina? Oil and water," he pronounced.

"Aren't those both 'holy' elements in your religion?"

"Yes, but holy hell in the romance department."

Chapter 47
Four-Posters and Postmortems

Temple had spent the night in her bedroom with piled feather pillows personally placed by Matt Devine under her knees, back, extended arms, and neck and head.

It was not the setup for a kinky sex scene she'd have preferred.

Electra was sleeping on the sofa bed in the living room, a cell phone call or a hoarse yell away. And Matt was doing his midnight–2:00 A.M. radio show.

She heard him come in about three, whisper with the landlady, and fade away.

She slept what they called "fitfully." She didn't know if that meant fit to be tied to a four-poster bed, which she certainly was, or fit to be consigned to a hospital bed, like Violet had been, which she almost was.

She lay there and felt the scabs on her hands and knees forming over the burning skinned portions. She would be her lively, fast-moving self sometime next week. First,

518

came the morning and the Big Reveal.

Temple understood her knowledge and theories were crucial to wrapping up the Barbie Doll Killer case since the murderer was dead. It was just that she had pictured herself, the triumphant but lowly PI, giving testimony in a killer noir-black, witness-stand suit and huge black picture hat. She hadn't expected to present her case while as scabby as one of her big brothers fresh from the football field with gauze and tapes swathing all joints.

Electra came in at about 6:00 A.M.

"Awake, are we?" She looked from Temple to Midnight Louie, who had commandeered half of her ankle pillow sometime in the night.

"I feel like Mister Bill, the Play-Doh patsy on *Saturday Night Live*," Temple said. "He was always being dropped from a skyscraper and cheerfully answering from the sidewalk in a pip-squeak voice. That was a sadistic routine."

"Of course you feel a bit down," Electra said, plumping the pillows. "I'll help you to the bathroom, and Louie and I will look through your wardrobe for something comfy and gentling to your joints."

"My most flattering clothes are neither of those," Temple snarled.

519

Yes, 'snarled,' as she limped to the adorably tiny and tiny-tiled fifties bathroom, which seemed bent today on knocking her hard in all her scraped places.

Matt picked her up at the front door in his smooth and creamy Jaguar, into which Electra helped her, as if they were about the same age. Actually, Electra was a lot sprier.

"Poor baby," Matt said, kissing her on the lips, which were probably her only unbruised portion. "Really."

By the time they got to Aloe Vera Drive, the swath of concrete at the side garage was occupied by a Crown Vic and that's all. Matt pulled the Jag beside it.

"I've got to say the ride is worthy of Saint Peter," Temple said, leaning her head against the fresh-smelling leather rest, "but the working cops in the Crown Vic are going to Tweet you on it when they leave."

"I can take it. Or leave it." Matt shook his head. "The note from the producers made it clear the car was mine whether I ever inked a deal with them or not. I thought consumer confidence was kaput."

"Not in the big-time media biz, apparently."

"Frankly," he said, "your crime-solving exploits are turning too rough for me. I might take that job just to get you and Louie out of Vegas and onto the genteel streets of Chicago."

She snorted at that characterization of Chi-Town, which she was meant to. "I blundered into this last mess," Temple said. "The temptation of one-upping Savannah was too sweet."

"Yeah, that's what I mean. There are too many temptations in Vegas to keep you safe, and maybe me, too."

"Nothing I can't handle," Temple said firmly. "I do think we need to make a quick trip to genteel Chicago, and maybe Minneapolis, before you make a decision on your career."

Matt frowned, but before he could say anything, Temple went on.

"Hey! Maybe we can drive. Road trip. Impress the elders with your new wheels."

He laughed. "I don't want to impress anyone besides you. Still, it wouldn't hurt to meet the future in-laws on either side. I'm just a part of the talk-show package. It'll take a while to put it together."

"Chicago, here I come. For a while. Now, let's get this not-genteel business over."

Matt came around the car to help her out.

"I'd rather have taken a bullet," Temple complained, walking gingerly up the walk

521

to the house with her knees bent to prevent scab-pulling.

"Don't joke about it," Matt warned her, "or I'll be booking the first flight to O'Hare so you can meet my family. They may be a little screwed up, but at least they're not deadly."

She shrugged, working on a basketball guard's shuffle that should see her through the next few days. "I'd love to meet them anyway, and dysfunction can be as deadly as dedicated criminals. Let's put Chicago to rest until this is tidied up."

"I'm amazed Molina called a meeting in Violet's house, after the fire." Matt opened the screen door and guided Temple through the ajar front door into a campfire aroma of embers and ashes.

She kept her eyes off the area leading to the rear of the house, then blinked after a few steps inside. The shutters on the main room had been folded open, admitting a flood of light. The empty hospital bed and its attachments still occupied the room's center, but now she could see sofas and chairs, mahogany ones with brocade upholstery under the various covers that had been turned back.

Molina and Alch were waiting on a camelback sofa like an old married couple. Matt saw Temple established on a Queen Anne chair and sat in its mate.

"This is it?" Temple asked. "Just us?"

"Consider it a visit to Headquarters West." Molina eyed her critically. "You look a mess, like Mariah after a nasty skateboard accident when she was ten. She really strutted those scabs in the school yard."

"Unfortunately, lieutenant," Temple said as stiffly as she walked, "I don't have a school yard to impress."

"Well, you impressed the hell out of me," Molina answered. "I don't know how you did it, but the firefighters said you saved Mister Jayden some nasty facial and hand burns by dragging him out of the most intense part of the blaze."

Alch was nodding soberly behind her.

"Where's poor Violet?" Temple wondered, eager to get their attention off of her.

"Nursing home," Molina said. "Her friend, Freddie LaCosta, arranged it. After the fire and Jayden's injury, Violet seemed to give up the ghost. And . . . all the cats are gone, spirited away, I guess."

"Freddie? I considered her a suspect, or at least a hopeful heir." Then Temple remembered. "Jayden said he witnessed the will yesterday, before the fire. I guess he wasn't a greedy would-be heir, after all."

"You seem to have thought everybody was a greedy would-be heir," Matt said.

"I was . . . investigating. I was supposed to be suspicious."

"Exactly right, Miss Barr." Alch nodded firmly as he came to her defense.

"So exactly where is Violet now?" Temple asked.

Alch gave a shrug. "St. Rose's Nursing Home. Once the fire forced her out of the house, she didn't want to cling to whatever was in it."

Temple inhaled too much secondary smoke as she sighed. "How ironic. Violet is under the same roof as a Barbie Doll Killer victim, Larry's stepsister, Teresa Paddock, and she doesn't even know it. Nor does poor Teresa. Lord! I'm tired of calling people 'poor.' "

"You can call me 'poor,' " Molina said, "because I haven't a clue to what you're talking about."

"Wait a minute," Alch said. "Now I remember. When Dirty Larry first showed up off the narc beat, he was using the last name of *Paddock*. Don't you remember, Carmen?"

"I go by 'lieutenant' in front of civilians. And Paddock is his stepsister's surname."

Alch grinned with gusto. "Exactly. He

524

either took on his stepfather's name or he'd been using Paddock as a tribute to his stepsister, in a way. He switched his narc pseudo to Podesta later when he got the idea of riling you up to get on the Barbie Doll Killer's trail, so the connection wasn't evident. Names were close enough we wouldn't notice. Those guys have identities all over the place."

Molina nodded, looking shell-shocked.

"We can trace that through later," she said. "Now I need to know who was the man who died in the fire? What was his connection and motive to Violet and her daughter? Who the flying sweet potato was named in the will that this Jayden witnessed, and where is it?

"And, by the way, why have two cats entered the house in the past two minutes?"

Temple looked down, expecting black and black. She got the white cat who was probably named Whisper and a yellow-striped one, both sniffing cautiously as they prowled the room's perimeter.

"Maybe they sense their enemies are gone." Temple thought for a moment and then asked Molina, "Is there anything left of the Chinese chest in the hall outside the bedroom wing?"

Molina passed the question on to Alch

with a quizzical look.

"The fire commander said the house's adobe walls made it into a little Alamo," he said. "The structure resisted burning, but not the contents, including the perp."

Temple winced at the memory of a burning man. She'd seen the first flames snatch at his heel and pants leg, and then . . . he'd run right into the flammable temple of Barbie dolls.

"Can someone check if there are any photo albums or a box in that Chinese cabinet?" she asked.

"I will." Matt jumped up, treading to avoid circling cats, now — four.

"I had a lot of time to think about this last night," Temple said.

"We're not interested in your nocturnal adventures, or the lack of them, Miss Barr." Molina gave a sardonic lift of one eyebrow.

"Yes, I can imagine pillow talk with a hard-muscled, black-haired, alpha male wouldn't hold much appeal for you."

Alch's chuckles made Molina shut up. "That Midnight Louie is an all-round lie-down guy, all right," he said. "Seriously, Miss Barr, superficial injuries usually hurt more than deeper ones."

"Over the short term," Molina added, inadvertently reminding them of her own knifing. She ought to know.

"Where's, uh, Larry?" Temple asked. Calling him "Dirty Larry" wouldn't help his case right now, and she sympathized with his misguided crusade after having seen his stepsister's condition at St. Rose's.

"He's not in on this," Molina said. "It's us and you. Your required chauffeur, Mister Devine, is here to be seen and not heard, like a good boy."

"An errand boy," Matt added just as sardonically, returning to the main room carrying the photo albums and box.

Temple gestured for him to give them to the couple on the sofa.

Her gauze-swathed hands still weren't good at keyboards or paging through ephemera, as papers and photographs were called, meaning they were dust in the wind of most lives, precious only to those they involved for only as long as they lived.

"Wasn't there a large portrait photo of a young woman above the chest?" Temple asked.

"It was fire-singed and water-soaked." Alch shook his head. "Pretty much just disintegrating cardboard with a fading image on it."

"The candle that started the fire was right in front of it," Temple told him. "It was big

527

and long-lasting, but it burned night and day and had no one to drain off the pooling melted wax since Violet became bedridden."

"Candle. Like a church shrine," Molina said. "Missus Weiner was asking about 'Alexandra's portrait,' and her cats, as she was transferred to a gurney."

"Those photo albums have lots more photos of her daughter. Violet will want them. And her diaries, in which she fretted about needing to arrange for her cats to live on in the house after Alexandra's death six years ago."

"Won't happen," Molina said. "No will was found in the house, just a business card from a downtown law firm. I reached the guy earlier this morning. Although he prepared the will and mailed it to Violet a couple weeks ago, unless it's signed and witnessed, his copy means nothing."

"Jayden told me last night the will *was* witnessed," Temple said. "He acted as one of the two needed witnesses, so Violet must have signed it just before this all blew up."

"Jayden isn't able to be interviewed in the hospital yet," Molina said. "That's why we're all here. Just what is 'this all,' and how did it 'blow up' into a stabbing, a fire, and a death? With you in the middle of it?"

Matt sat forward in his chair to accept the

photo albums Alch handed him. More people were looking at and thinking about Alexandra than since she had died.

Temple sat back in her chair. As a TV reporter, she'd been used to doing "stand-ups" for the camera. This would be a "sit-down," but she wanted to make the report as clear and factual as she could.

"Here's the story. The young woman in the photos is Violet's daughter, Alexandra. Something led to an estrangement, and Alex lived in Tucson, where she met a guy named Sylvan Smith."

"Sounds like another con man like Jayden," Molina commented. "They always have fancy names. Looks like, estranged or not, the daughter was into the same shaky New Age trends and hucksters her mother was."

"Maybe they both were susceptible to smooth talkers," Temple said, "but Sylvan Smith was a construction worker they nicknamed Rowdy on the job, an all-American blue-collar type, a hard worker but not overeducated. More beer than wine. Violet disapproved of him. Probably wanted Alexandra hooked up with a professional guy."

"This is our dead guy?" Alch wanted to establish that first.

"This is your Barbie Doll Killer."

"No way," Alch said. "Of course, roofers are itinerant workers. It might explain the geographical range."

Temple shrugged. "That's what I suspect. I also think that Alexandra was his first victim."

Molina had been shuffling through the Tucson newspaper clippings in the box and lifted them out. "These news stories make her the victim of a drugstore remedy tampering."

"Rowdy was smarter than he looked." Temple resumed her emphatic but deadpan on-camera delivery style, and it did seem to command attention from a difficult audience. "What a way to conceal a murder. Rowdy could slip potassium cyanide into an easy-to-open capsule, probably something herbal. Alexandra would be into that, like her mother. Over-the-counter remedies are all caplets nowadays to prevent tampering, after the first headache-remedy tampering murders back in the eighties."

"Aren't you a bundle of information?" Molina was not impressed. Probably found on the Internet and highly suspect. "Why would he kill his girlfriend?"

"For the same reasons he picked his victims and repeated the pattern. Alexandra was Violet's Barbie doll. You can see it in the hyper-girly way she was dressed all through childhood and in the three photos at the back of one of the two diaries."

Molina quickly checked both leather-bound volumes and found the adult Alexandra photos. "Definitely aspiring-model material. And this wigged-out Barbie doll model?" She held up the photo of the 1988 Happy Holiday Barbie.

"The first two photos of Alexandra playing with her cats came to Violet *from* Tucson. I think the Barbie doll photo was sent *to* Violet's daughter *in* Tucson and she reclaimed it on Alexandra's death, along with her daughter's cats. Alexandra was probably collecting Barbie dolls as an adult, but Rowdy took them before Violet arrived, and kept them to . . . experiment on, and leave at his death scenes later."

Matt couldn't contain himself any longer. "That guy would be sick beyond belief. He must have hated the mother and possibly tried to kill her through her daughter. And the dolls."

"Voodoo Barbie dolls," Molina said. "I like it. I'd most like to see you try to sell that theory to a prosecuting attorney, Miss Barr, but that's not possible now."

"It makes sense if you realize that one of

the three rooms beyond the hallway shrine to Alexandra was kept locked. That wrinkled satin-ribbon bookmark in diary number two is kinked because a key was tied to its bottom. I thought at first it was a weight or a commercial decorative touch, but it unlocked the door to Alexandra's bedroom."

"The fire room." Alch's seamed forehead grew more rumpled. "A bedroom is a psychological battleground in some murders."

"Enough already, Morrie." Molina was growing impatient. She was the one used to holding forth on sequences of events.

Temple decided she needed to present the heart of her case, what she had discovered here last night in Violet's house, besides heartbreak and delusion and missing cats.

"I opened the bedroom door and walked in. The walls were covered from floor to ceiling in stacked Barbie doll boxes, maybe two layers deep. I recognized some of the most collectible models from the Web."

"Obsessive," Matt said, "but a motive for murder or attempted murder?"

"They'd be worth plenty, the whole collection, maybe a couple hundred thousand dollars, but that's not the point. Nobody knew about them but Alexandra and Violet. Ironically, any greedy hangers-on would have had a jackpot, but the collection is only ashes now."

"Not even a shapely Barbie gam left to ID," Molina put in. "All the melted goo in the room puzzled the fire investigators."

"What are little girls made of nowadays?" Temple mused. "Not sugar and spice, but skin-soft vinyl bodies and synthetic hair. Not even the rare porcelain-bodied ones survived?"

Molina shook her head. "Must have shattered on impact from falling to the floor. All that cardboard and cellophane packaging was highly flammable tinder. Those hundreds of glamorous dolls melted like the Wicked Witch of the West. So why was the collection secret? What *is* the point, Barr?"

Things were getting tight when Molina dropped the "Miss" from Temple's surname.

"The point is that Violet never let Alexandra open a doll box. Can you imagine how frustrating that would be to a kid? No wonder she grew up into a Barbie kind of girl and woman and auditioned to become a star in her own right as a model. Alexandra probably began listening to her mother's put-downs of Rowdy Smith and dumped him.

"He found her shallow, and superior, so his infatuation turned into fury, such fury

that he needed more than the clever, unde-
tectable murder to end it. He needed to
destroy all the Barbie doll women out there
who in his mind would reject him again and
again if they lived to be able to do it. He
started to practice defacing the Barbie dolls
and then targeted Alexandra/Barbie look-
alikes auditioning for fame on the reality
shows. The first he attempted to strangle
was Teresa Paddock, Larry's stepsister."

Matt and Molina had both been nodding
agreement during Temple's recital.

"Meanwhile, he moved to Las Vegas on
the pretext of being near the bereaved
Violet, who still had no time for him. But
he clung on, playing the good guy and waiting for Violet to weaken so he could undo
her fondest hopes. He's the one who was
letting the cats out, leaving Violet bereft as
he had been and blaming her dislike of him
for Alexandra's death."

Molina stirred on the sofa. "What would
you call that, Mister Devine?"

"Turning the victim into the villain.
Someone else is always responsible for the
person's destructive actions."

"Rather like," Molina pointed out, "the
nut-job abuser who blamed you for convincing his wife to leave him through your radio
counseling show. Your job seems almost as

perilous as being a public-relations expert."

She pointedly returned her high-intensity blue gaze on Temple.

Golly, that laser-light stare would convince Temple to confess to something, even to acting as a private investigator for Savannah Ashleigh. She dearly hoped that little detail never had to become public knowledge beyond this small circle.

"Tell us," Alch urged, "how you ended up an action hero and saved Jayden's skin while the Barbie Doll Killer went up in smoke."

"I'll need an official statement taken at the office," Molina said. "Meanwhile, the jury of two is out on Larry Podesta, so we need to know all the facts you think you know."

"I think Rowdy Smith killed Pedro. He wasn't just letting cats out. He was trying to kill them so their bodies would be found and word would get back to further torment Violet. Pedro probably caught him attempting that by the flood channel."

"Speaking of cats," Molina interrupted, frowning at her khaki pants legs, against which a pair of tortoiseshell cats was rubbing . . . in between long, connoisseur sniffs of same, "where are all of these coming from?"

"They're all Violet's. They're coming back

from wherever they went when they were let out. They smell your own housecats on your clothes. It's nothing personal."

"It's damn annoying." Molina bent to brush the red and black hairs from her denim pants leg, but they clung like burrs.

"It's a great sign that some of Violet's cats survived Rowdy and the fire," Temple said. "To answer your question, Detective Alch, I was probably becoming too visible a snoop when I returned the box and albums I'd 'borrowed' to take home and study. Rowdy had probably arrived before me to find Jayden announcing the will had finally been signed, the last thing he wanted, a prospective heir-cum-executor taking over the care of Violet and the house.

"I'd, um, discreetly entered the locked bedroom and was standing there bedazzled by those walls of Barbie dolls, realizing the three cases were linked."

"Pardon, Miss Barr." Molina's voice was steel silk. "Just what 'three cases' are you referring to?"

"The Barbie Doll Killer case and death of Violet's handyman . . ."

Temple knew better than to say in front of Detective Alch "my case" investigating Pedro's death. It was bad enough that Molina knew she'd signed on as a PI for

536

Savannah Ashleigh. "And the attack on Larry's stepsister. I'm betting Teresa was found with that Barbie doll and it was taken for a talisman of hers personally, not a sign of a freshman killer's contempt, dropped before he could violate it, as well as before he'd actually strangled Teresa quite to death."

Matt's hand reached the unbandaged top of her left hand, ringless until she healed enough to ditch the dressings and the messy ointments. "And I think *I* handle some dark subject matter on my radio show," he said.

"The successful investigator," Molina answered him, "has to face the blackest depths of human nature and speculate from there."

Alch jumped up to dislodge a longhaired brown tabby cat that had come up on the sofa to settle in his lap and listen attentively to the proceedings.

"I heard that one called Maverick," Temple said. "All the cats are coming back. Isn't that interesting?"

Alch sneezed. "Not really. Tell me about the showdown at the shrine."

So she did, and had them all on the edges of their seats, even Lieutenant C. R. Molina.

Who, of course, had more questions.

"Why did Rowdy go off on Jayden? He

followed the man and stabbed him with a"
— Molina paused — "a kitchen knife."

"With the will signed, Jayden probably ordered Rowdy out of the house, and he snapped. Rowdy probably went for Jayden with a kitchen knife, and he fled. Then they both became mesmerized when they discovered Alexandra's bedroom door was finally open and glimpsed the Barbie doll–box walls.

"Jayden considered himself Violet's guru. But if he was a witness to the will, he couldn't be the executor-heir. I suppose he'll tell us who was when he can talk."

"It's bizarre," Matt said, "that Rowdy's homicidal pursuit of you after he'd knifed Jayden made Alexandra's candle tip over and catch his clothes on fire. Almost like . . . her revenge."

Molina snorted. "Don't go ghost-y on me. Many extremely rational people run when they discover their clothes are burning, even though they know they should drop and roll. It's not surprising that a delusional, vendetta-fueled killer would run from the flames climbing his body, and, of course, everything in that room but the walls and ceiling was highly flammable, and those Barbie tinderboxes surrounded the doorway. . . . The fire investigators will lay out the exact trail of the flames."

She bent to bat fruitlessly at the horizontal band of cat hairs on her pants legs, reminding Temple of how Rowdy had caught fire, and then stood.

"That's all for now, folks. I'll have more specific questions for Miss Barr when she comes in for her official statement. Larry had done some sharp figuring out about his stepsister's attack being connected to the Barbie doll killings later. He wanted to stir up a Vegas detective to pursue the case, and indeed he did when he planted that Barbie doll in Mariah's bedroom, but I doubt he's behind any other incidents on my home front."

Molina exchanged a long, simmering look with Temple.

"Resignation and relocation are in his immediate future. Also retraining for another line of work. He's burned out, anyway."

Molina absorbed her last sentence a second after it was delivered and firmly folded her lips. "I don't want to hear another word right now from anyone. Adios. Alch."

She started out of the room then paused. "The place is crawling with cats. Who's going to deal with this? I can call Animal Control."

Alch was staring at Violet's empty bed.

"There's a black one. It isn't — ?"

"No," Temple said as fast as she could. "Too small, longhaired, and delicate to be Louie. We'll get Violet's friend Freddie to deal with the cats."

Molina and Alch were moving on and out of the house as Temple and Matt looked at each other.

"But it could be Midnight Louise from the Crystal Phoenix," Temple told the vacant air.

Molina could never accuse her of less than full disclosure.

CHAPTER 48
A BLACK MOOD

Max ambled over elaborate inlaid marble floors in Renaissance patterns, under a lofty blue sky edged at the horizon with a lace of pinkish-gold clouds, either sunrise or sunset and perpetual.

It happened to be late morning after the night the serial killer had been revealed and struck by the lightning of justice. Max had played a minor role in that, but that act of that play was over. He was here because he had nowhere else to be.

The Forum Shops at Caesars Palace was among the most venerable of Las Vegas Strip high-end shopping arcades, lavished with marble statuary and fountains to echo the ancient Roman theme. Grandiose suited his mood, poised to see past and present but not future.

What was he to do here? Or anywhere?

He could count his blessings. He was alive to wander these commercial palace gardens.

At this leisurely pace, his gait was steady. No limp. He was far from becoming a trotter, though, or a racehorse. He could also count his recent sins. Using Temple to investigate Teresa's situation had been irresponsible, even though it had led to a resolution. Everyone who had known him in Vegas before his memory went AWOL was safe and satisfied, even the vengeful Dirty Larry, who hadn't known him.

Max listened to the many shoes echoing on the vast, marble-lined concourse. None paced him. If his mortal enemy was tracing him, she wasn't here now. She had no doubt she would reveal herself soon in her own sinister and psycho way. And he'd be ready.

Meanwhile, he supposed he would finish what Garry and he had begun: untangle the years-old schemes and crimes that created the magicians' club known as the Synth and left a stockpile of guns and money undiscovered and unclaimed by the authorities.

He paused to eye his reflection in a store window. Tall guy slouching in midnight-moss-colored European clothing. He eyed the faceless male mannequins behind the invisible shop-front window glass imprinted with the ghosts of the architectural glory that was Rome, whose gods now lodged in Las Vegas.

Without even looking up to the name above the display windows, he walked in. He didn't care if it was Burberry or Dior, or Fendi or Versace or Gucci.

He was intercepted in the suddenly quiet, carpeted store by a tall, slender charmer of maybe twenty-six wearing impossibly high platform heels and a magenta metallic short pencil skirt and strategically lacy top.

"Welcome," she said. "Before I ask about your needs, may I get you a Sock-It-to-Me-tini?"

"It isn't noon yet."

"Like the man sang, it's five o'clock somewhere. Bombay Sapphire and pomegranate? Quite healthful."

Max checked the Patek Philippe watch she had eyed on his wrist the moment he'd walked in. "You're correct. I must have been reading the second hand. Of course, you may get me anything you wish."

She smiled and vanished to the rear of the store, which was divided into women-and menswear. His old clothes, the shreds of which now inhabited trash bags in the house on Mojave Way, had been tailored to fit his lean six-four frame. This may be a fool's errand, but it was nice to talk to someone.

She was back almost instantly, offering a

martini glass with a Picassoesque wavy stem.

"Pardon me, but you look like you could use this," she said.

"I was up all night."

"Big winnings?" she asked.

"You could say so. It was certainly . . . exciting."

"And what can I help you with?"

"If you can fit me, I need a lightweight silk T. I wear the sleeves pushed up, so their length would be no problem."

"No, our fitting problem would be the shoulders. Luckily, the few things we have in your size range are slow to sell. What else, sir?" She led him among the sparsely populated built-in racks.

He really had to focus on how she balanced on those stilettos on the deeply cushy carpeting. That meant noticing her Gold's Gym–shaped rear. He was back in Vegas, no doubt.

Max sipped the drink. "I wear silk or silk blends."

"We also do some featherweight clothing in microfiber, and naturally any trousers will be fitted and hemmed to your length."

"A blazer?"

"More than an old Burberry blazer. Cutting-edge sharkskin fabric and cut," she promised. "Think subtly motorcycle jacket. You, of course, wear the sleeves pushed up. Retro–*Miami Vice* is so in now."

"That's so necessary for me with store-bought clothing."

"New in town, then."

"You could say so."

"There's only one hitch," she said.

"Which is?"

"Anything I've got in your size is only in . . . black. It does coordinate with your hair."

Max nodded. Maybe it was time to claim his territory back.

"Perfect," he said.

She gestured to the rear fitting rooms. "An expert sales associate will bring the options and the fitter to you, and he will total your purchases."

He nodded, glancing that way.

"My card," she added, holding out a slick, oversize business card embossed with the store name, her name, and various phone numbers in smaller print.

"Thank you . . . Vikki."

He felt something underneath, and his fingers traced the ring of an attached . . . condom.

"A token for guests of the store. Be safe while you're in Vegas," she said with a pleas-

545

ant smile.

"You bet."

Apparently he'd wandered into a den of high-end hipness. He lifted his glass in a farewell toast as he ambled back to try on his old self and see what adventures happened to it.

CHAPTER 49
ALL'S SWELL THAT ENDS SWELL

Now that the major excitement is over, I can recollect in tranquility.

Am I glad I avoided a close encounter with the local fuzz! I do not think that Miss Lieutenant C. R. Molina could bear to give due credit to yet another Vegas PI.

At least my Miss Temple has been recognized for her nimble mental gymnastics in a serial-murder case that involves years and multilocations, not to mention for her first-class physical exertions to save herself from said serial killer and to help save another human — and a big, heavy man, too, although flaky and somewhat light in the Earth shoes.

In fact, I was horrified to hear all the details of her ordeal while I concealed myself in the kitchen and made sure the returning feline nation broke their necessary desert fast with lots and lots of Free-to-Be-Feline.

I do not want any leftovers of that stuff coming home with Miss Temple.

I could see a climax coming in the harassment of Miss Violet Weiner and her indoor clowder of thirty-some descendents of Great Bast. So Miss Midnight Louise and I have been treading through the sand and dirt and young mesquite-tree thorns in dark of night as well as daylight to round up the "released" felines and herd them away from danger.

There was more trouble afoot than the secret avenger inside the house, now revealed. Face it. These were a bunch of domestic slaves with not a clue how to live outside on their own. They were in danger of falling into the flood channel, like their beloved caretaker, Mr. Pedro Gomez. They were in danger from coyotes because of the undeveloped land of the retention basin all around the house. They were in danger of people who take potshots at critters in the dark just for the fun of it.

So Miss Midnight Louise and I managed this what-they-call-a "Diaspora," where a whole gang of the same stripe is forced out into the wilderness. It sounds too much like "diapers" to me, but it is one tough assignment.

You may have heard of the difficulty of herding cats. I consider it a slam on my kind for being smart and independent, but some insensitive humans will have their little jokes about the feline kind, since most of those are one — a joke, that is.

Actually, since I have actually been in the herding business, I must admit that saying has a point.

I cannot claim I was anticipating the peril of a fire within Miss Violet's house, but it was indeed good to clear the premises of these endangered residents. Naturally, I am most unhappy with myself that I was not by Miss Temple's side when she had to scramble for her life.

I am searching diligently for a way to make it up to her, and, peeking in as she and Mr. Matt prepare to leave Miss Violet's house forever, I see Miss Midnight Louise on her hind feet, doing a claw-over-claw drag on the mattress side of the abandoned hospital bed, sniffing doggedly.

I am mortified! I do not doubt that a sickbed may have certain, shall I say "earthy" smells, but unlike we superior species, humans are fanatical about hiding, nay, denying that their noses are good for anything other than powdering or having changed to suit their face.

I rush over to stop Miss Louise's rude behavior, when Miss Temple cries, "Oh, Matt. Louie *is* here."

"Down," I instruct Louise in a low growl. "You are giving the firm a bad name. We use our brains and claws, not our noses. At least not

549

in front of impressionable humans."

"Your nose is always out to lunch," she says. "I am on a paper trail."

"Paper is for the use of young and uncontrollable dogs, Louise, not seasoned and sophisticated sorts like us."

"Not newspapers, Daddy Densest! The paper everyone is so concerned about around here: the will."

Oh. The will.

I must confess I have never heard of any sensible feline leaving a will, although I know some have been left things in a will, which sounds like it is a form of litter box. At this moment, though, I watch one of Miss Louise's foreclaws snag something white that is not a sheet. I jab out my own paw to help snag it and work it out and down. With the addition of my power and pizzazz, this long, thick sheaf sticks out like a triangular flag.

My Miss Temple and Mr. Matt are there before you can say "Captain Jack," showering our little ears with heavy praise.

"Louie, Louise," Miss Temple coos, like we are mourning doves, "you are so curious. You have found the missing will. Poor Violet must have heard the commotion and stuffed it down under the mattress with Father Hell's magnets."

"Temple, are you raving, too?" Mr. Matt asks.

"I will tell you later. Meanwhile, look at who the second witness to the will is."

"Sylvan Smith. Does it still count now that he is dead?"

"Probably. He was known to be here, even if they have to prove it with fingerprints or DNA on the ashes. And . . . that explains why he went so berserk. He was forced to play along and see someone else get everything Violet treasured, which was the one thing he could not stand."

"Who did get the estate?"

My Miss Temple uses her whole, bandaged right hand to flip awkwardly through the twenty-some pages. I watch with sympathy. Now she knows what it is to have no opposable thumbs, even if only for a few days.

"I cannot believe it," she says finally, looking up at Mr. Matt.

What! What can she not believe? I am down here. With Louise. Look at me!

"Matt," she says, with eyes only for him, the ingrate. "The whole shooting match, cat and caboodle, goes to Savannah Ashleigh."

I do not get it. There was not a gun involved.

And I would not give Savannah Ashleigh a used whisker.

CHAPTER 50
DONE AND GONE

Temple walked out of St. Rose's Nursing Home, knees and finger joints working, if still a little pink and scabby.

She stood under the portico and gave a final sigh. Her first case was officially over.

The machine-gun rat-a-tat behind her didn't make her jump. She knew the source.

"Wait up a minute," a light voice called.

Pretty soon the noisy gladiator-style ankle-high platform boots were teetering beside her kitten-heeled mules.

"That was pretty amazing," Savannah Ashleigh said, catching her breath from tottering along like a geisha girl.

"Violet seemed a lot better."

"She sure does get around on that scooter thing. Of course, she has to wear those awful scrubs and flannel slippers I wouldn't be caught dead, much less terminal, in."

Temple refused to be riled by Savannah-ese. "It's remarkable that Violet found

552

Teresa's room and sits and talks with her every day."

Savannah raised a painted, taloned, forefinger nail, not so different from one of Temple's albeit longer and falser, and made a rotating gesture in front of her chandelier-earring-accoutred right lobe.

"If she thinks that's Alexandra, I guess it's as good as a belief in Father Hell's magnets," Savannah chattered on. "I can't believe she named me the heir."

Neither could Temple.

"Once she was ensconced here, Violet told me the news and said she was much impressed by my maturity and faithful care of the cats. And she loves my 'little pet rat.'"

Captain Jack popped up from the status purse and seemed to wink at Temple over Savannah's shoulder. Then she realized that was because a tiny patch over one already masked eye gave him a bit of a leer.

"Naturally," Savannah said with an eye-roll of her own, "I'll have to keep up *all* that cat care and visiting Violet here. Still, a girl can use a financial cushion down the road."

A *girl?* Temple smiled and shook her head.

"By the way, Temp, I suppose you solved Pedro's murder along with a few others. We never did decide on a fee." Pause. "Now don't go getting stratospheric, because I

553

have that old house to keep up and only a couple hundred thousand that you only know about because you sneaked a peek at the will without my permission."

"Here's my fee, Savannah: give yourself a break and find good homes for all Violet's cats."

"Oh. Well, that's easy."

"It is? It's hard to find a home for one adult cat, even if it's fixed. What makes you think you can place thirty of them in good homes?"

"Easy. You just don't get it. I am a cel-eb-ri-tee. I will just do a charity event for some shelter, and since I'm in charge of the cats now, everyone will rush to get a pre-owned Savannah Ashleigh pussycat."

"What about Yvette and Solange?"

"Poor itty-bitty babies."

Savannah hoisted her huge designer bag on her shoulder.

"I have them back, safe and sound. They've both had 'lion cuts' to remove the knots," she said. "They look so ferrety and cute shaved, so I cut a cat- *and* ferret-food TV commercial deal for all three! 'Captain Jack and the Persian Pirates' for Fishy Feast Ahoy."

Savannah leaned down to whisper in Temple's ear. "I'll make out like a bandit.

You could have asked for real money, but I'll be sure to tell all my H-wood friends about your PI work. Ta-ta."

Temple watched Savannah and ferret clatter to the Sky convertible and glide away.

Temple's cell phone played "Hallelujah," and she got it out to read a text message.

"Howd ur 1st solo outing sans scabs go?"

"Supr. Home 4 suppr."

"Xpct gourmet."

"W/pillos?"

"W/everything."

Temple smiled at Matt's message and was about to close her cell when it hailed her again. *Hallelujah.*

"U kild that case. Gd t C U smlng n th sunshine. Mx."

She looked up and around. All she saw was a lot of Las Vegas sunshine.

Right.

CHAPTER 51

I stare through the window, hoping to spot a friendly face.

Heck, an unfriendly face would be welcome.

If I thought that clinging to a mesquite tree eight feet up was a risk to life and limb — my limbs, not the tree's — I have never been more wrong.

I am now on the twelfth floor of an ominously named high-rise, having inched along a ledge barely wide enough for a squirrel, much less a dude of size.

So it is with more than hope but sheer desperation that I tap my shivs on the double-paned glass, longing to see a familiar face, but willing to greet the Wicked Witch of the West if she will be let me in by the hairs of my chinny chin-chin.

I tap out an SOS. I even look skyward for a handy, lost California condor I could hitch a ride on.

At last! My window view fills with not one,

but two lovely faces.

They make sexy French moues at me, their green eyes as round as flying saucers as their spidery hair flattens against the glass that separates us.

With eye rolls and head nods the Persian sisters manage to indicate a balcony about twenty feet farther along the ledge.

Well, it is a toss-up if the balcony or retreat is nearer. I inch along, losing sight my motivation. When at last I squeeze my middle through the iron bars, I discover the balcony is only a foot wide. It has curtains over a sliding glass door, all right, but is not meant to be stepped on by human feet.

Luckily, mine are much daintier by those standards. Yet I do not confront the easy-opening French doors on my Miss Temple's condo, and on the second floor.

I hunch in a funk, safe behind prison bars, but with no way of entrance and my only egress requiring more pussyfooting than I can manage at this point.

The sound of the door sliding open has me pasted against the hot glass. I slither along it to the foot-wide crack, about to duck in when a sudden snowfall covers me in flakes the size of . . . dust bunnies. A mop is shaking them down on my head.

I sneak around the opening and hide behind

the inside curtains before you can say "sneezing spell."

Luckily, the maid is moving on to another room, and I am following in her footsteps.

"Louie!" a sweet mew greets me in double-time when I reach the main living area, which is full of overstuffed furniture in floral tones of pink and lavender.

I turn to meet the aforesaid green eyes, but my own grow wide with disbelief as I view lean torsos of yellow and gray.

"Yvette. Solange. You have turned . . . squirrelly since last we met."

"Are you saying we are lacking in the little gray cells, Louie?" Yvette huffs with attitude.

"I am saying you are all tail fluff with the skinny torsos of the breed know as Sphinx."

"Those cats have no fur at all," Yvette sniffs. "We have kept the best parts."

Well, I am always interested in best parts, and I see on longer inspection that only the torsos and the tops of their legs have been shaved to the skin, giving the girls a Puss-in-Boots look with fluffy lower legs and furry tail tufts on the end. And an Elizabethan ruff of hair around their faces.

"No wonder they call it the 'lion cut,' " I exclaim. "I am not sure it is flattering."

While Yvette hisses and spits at my last word, Solange smoothes her ruffled, golden-shaded feathers . . . er, fur.

"The style is light and comfortable in this Las Vegas heat, Louie," she says.

"You are under air-conditioning most of the time," I point out.

"It will be hot," snaps Yvette, putting on airs despite a ludicrous lack of hairs, "when we go before the cameras for our new cat-food commercial contract."

I have heard of this deal and well know I have been omitted in favor of a piece of vermin.

Speaking of which, I hear the maid scream in the other room, "A rat, a rat!"

I race to the scene of the crime, sensing the Persian girls hot on my tail. There is no breed better for the merciless pursuit called "bugging." I have seen the Divine Yvette take down a moth faster than the Jaws shark swallowed a fishing boat.

The maid has her eyes squeezed shut and stands atop a boudoir chair, embracing her mop like it was Ashton Kutcher.

I bound onto the foot-wide concrete ledge. Hanging from it between the bars is a pair of long-clawed feet. One swipe and my usurper would be a flying squirrel for twelve stories down. Then . . . history.

No one can see past my large muscled torso to see what I actually do.

The possibilities are tempting.

Then I sigh. I have been on rescue duty at Violet's house for too long. I stick my kisser through the bars and down, snag Captain Jack by the furry nape of his neck, and toss him over my shoulder to firm ground.

He is unsinkable. He scampers to his feet and heads straight for the maid's chair.

Meanwhile, the resident dames prepare to get grateful.

"Oh, Louie," Yvette and Solange simper, making me the meat in a purring, shaved Persian sandwich.

"You have saved our careers," the Sublime Solange says with a very effective ear lick.

"I am yours, body and soul," the Divine Yvette says, flipping down to curl up with her furry front boots under her dainty shaded-silver chin.

Then her gorgeous green eyes widen and stare above and beyond me.

I turn as she takes off like the Silver Streak train.

Yup. There is a moth on the ceiling at twelve o'clock high, as the fighter pilots used to say.

Solange has gone mothing, too.

I turn and make my way to the apartment's front door, hunkering down behind a gold-leafed wastepaper basket.

Either Miss Sue-Anna Weiner will walk in, or

the maid will get up the courage to go out and I will be on my way . . . to the bigger and better things that await a dude of swashbuckle and savoir faire.

Savvy?

TAILPIECE
MIDNIGHT LOUIE DEPLORES
THE STATE OF THINGS

I must say that this case has given me pause.

Previously, I thought I had a pretty good grip on the ways of the world, especially my special turf in Las Vegas and the art of crime solving.

It is no secret I was born on the streets and came up the hard way. I am a self-made dude. I may even have looked down my black nose leather at those of my kind who settled for being people-dependent "pets."

I know that I could lose access at any moment to Miss Temple's bed and, more important, that lumpy bed of Free-to-Be-Feline nuggets topped with shrimp, salmon, scallops, what have you — and she has plenty of those — and still eat.

Just the koi pond at the Crystal Phoenix could keep a large and lusty fellow like myself going indefinitely. What is the old saying? "Give a cat a fish and he is a happy cat. Give a cat a chance *to* fish and he is an independent contractor."

Midnight Louie's Koi Emporium would hold up nicely next to Chef Song's five-star restaurants at the Phoenix, and I would attract a better class of clientele.

But my entrepreneurial spirit is not the matter at hand. Or paw. Until this case, I had no idea that these willing domestic slaves could be so helpless and so abused if something happened to their loving masters.

Apparently, there are Cruella De Vils lusting to harm cat kind of all stripes as well as the spotted canine kind. (I still am not sure if Cruella De Vil is an actual person or a model of Cadillac.)

OK, *pet* is a politically incorrect word these days, and I quite concur. Call me a "pet" and I will staple your clothes to your epidermis for a couple feet.

"Animal companion" is more like it, putting us on equal footing with humans, even if "we," the animal part of that expression, can come as close to vermin as a, *ahem,* black-masked ferret of my acquaintance.

Anyway, I have become convinced that our human companions, if we so choose them, are obligated to plan for the dread day when they are no longer available to serve us.

Look at the sad case of Miss Violet Weiner's beloved cat clowder, at the mercy of whomsoever entered her home in her days of illness and weakness, none of whom could love her animal companions as much as she did, and some of whom harbored hatred of the helpless, whether human or animal.

Take nothing for granted, folks. We have cast our lots with you people since we became "domesticated" four thousand years ago. All we are asking is a little forethought of what dreadful fates might await us when the Grim Reaper starts tapping on your particular shoulder . . . say, when you are born! Do not get mad at me for saying so.

Remember, my kind's first so-called "masters," the ancient Egyptians, valued our vermin-catching ways and venerated us as gods. You can do no less, as you are four thousand years more evolved than those be-wigged pyramid-builders. So they tell me.

Therefore. I will let my sometimes useful collaborator give you all the dull particulars. My role is to mount the soap box and pontificate. To agitate. To play the gadfly and annoy. To bask in the roar of the crowd and the approving purrs of Miss Great Bast Herself, cat goddess of ancient Egypt. I do not know why Bast is a she.

Her only flaw, but even gods are not perfect these days.

Very Best Fishes,

Midnight Louie, Esq.

If you'd like information about getting Midnight Louie's free *Scratching Post-Intelligencer* newsletter and/or buying his custom T-shirt and other cool things, contact Carole Nelson Douglas at P.O. Box 331555, Fort Worth, TX 76163-1555 or the Web site at www.carolenelsondouglas.com. E-mail: cdouglas@catwriter.com. Facebook: Carole Nelson Douglas.

MISS CAROLE NELSON DOUGLAS SIGHS HEAVILY

Midnight Louie is such a seasoned diplomat . . . if you define *diplomat* as one who insults all sides equally.

He is right, though, that this note is going to be dull. Still, animal lovers need to think early and often about how to safeguard our surviving animals.

In most states, that will take a living trust, which sounds scarier than it is.

First, we as pet owners — and that's how the law regards us and our charges — need to designate relatives or neighbors to step in and take custody of any animals in the event of our sudden deaths.

The pet owners' dream is that some wonderful animal-loving soul would want to be an heir of their estate, move into their desirable house, and keep the environment stable until each of the surviving animals dies in turn. Say in, oh, fourteen years.

Good luck. Only the very wealthy have

estates worth enough that it pays other people to forsake their homes and life situations to babysit the estate owners' babies until they shuffle off this mortal coil. Many a comic mystery plot has been set around these circumstances.

The fact is, the situation is always more tragic than comic.

So, unless you want your animal companions to fall into the clutches of a Cruella De Vil, you will designate the veterinarian who will see the animals and be a temporary expert in their ultimate disposition and whose facility will be a temporary boarding place in case of your incapacitation or death.

Owners have choices, all hard. Realistically, relatives and friends cannot integrate all your pets into their homes and lives as one unit. If you're lucky, you have enough of both so that all your animals will get a chance to join another household. But most people, even your best-intentioned nearest and dearest, are not experts at integrating multiple households.

You can assign a shelter to evaluate the animals and place them in loving foster homes and ultimately new homes.

You can decide to employ the "kindest cut of all" — a visit to the vet, like any other, after all — that will put them "to sleep, perchance to dream."

Or, you can set up a living trust, designating a person who will inherit an appropriate amount of money to supervise all this, often a lawyer. And who trusts lawyers? Enter again the comic mystery plots, which are not really funny to the suddenly homeless but beloved animals involved.

One option is interesting. Leave your animals to a deserving established shelter, which will essentially pet-sit them in your house until their deaths, at which time the shelter will get the house as an asset to do good animal works. Well, you better have a really valuable house. Also, such shelters run on volunteer workers and they have turnover, and sometimes suddenly run out of funding, not a very stable situation for your pets.

Oh, Louie, you did leave me with the most ungrateful job . . . !

The bottom line is that we need to look into these options *NOW*. Meow. Me too.

I was first sent a book on this subject several years ago by Lisa Rogak, author of *PerPETual Care: Who Will Look After Your Pets If You're Not Around?* It's available on-line.

Here are some other books and online sites that can help get you started:

When Your Pet Outlives You: Protecting Animal Companions After You Die, by David Congalton and Charlotte Alexander.

All My Children Wear Fur Coats: How to Leave a Legacy for Your Pet, by Peggy R. Hoyt, JD, MBA

NOLO Legal Solutions: "Providing for Your Pet After You Die": http://www.nolo.com/legal-encyclopedia/article-29534.html

VeterinaryPartners: "Planning for Your Pets in Your Will": http://www.veterinary partner.com/Content.plx?P=A&A=1674 &S=4

ABOUT THE AUTHOR

Cat in a Vegas Gold Vendetta is the twenty-third title in **Carole Nelson Douglas**'s sassy Midnight Louie mystery series. Previous titles include *Cat in an Ultramarine Scheme, Cat in a Topaz Tango,* and *Cat in a Sapphire Slipper.* In addition to tales of her favorite feline, Douglas is also the author of the historical suspense series featuring Irene Adler, the only woman ever to have "outwitted" Sherlock Holmes. Douglas resides in Fort Worth, Texas.